PERSIAN GULF

GEO-POLITICS AND WARS

PERSIAN GULF
GEO-POLITICS AND WARS

by

Ashraf Ashrafpour

Foreword by

Prof. Shrikant Paranjpe
Department of Defence & Strategic Studies,
University of Pune, India

2012

Kaveri Books

New Delhi - 110 002

First Published in 2012

ISBN 978-81-7479-126-9

Published by

Kaveri Books

4832/24, Ansari Road, Darya Ganj
New Delhi-110002 (India)

Tel: 011-2328 8140, 2324 5799
Fax: 011-2328 8140,
E-mail : kaveribooks@vsnl.com,
kaveribooks@gmail.com
website: www.kaveribooks.com

Printed at
Salasar Imaging Systems, Delhi - 110 052

PRINTED IN INDIA

To

My Daughter Asal, For Her Love, Patience,
Encouragement and Support

Also

To My Late Father with Love and Respect

Foreword

The geopolitics of West Asia, or Middle East as those belonging to that region would prefer to consider themselves, revolves around several sets of contradictions. One is the contradiction that rests on the enmeshing of conflict between the Arab Islamic civilization and the Jewish Israeli civilization with the modern state system. The second is a product of the differing levels of political development that exist within the Arab world. The third is the divide between the Arab Islamic world and the Persian (Islamic) state system. Modern day Iran with its distinct religious ethnic identity has sought to influence the developments in the Middle East with increasing assertiveness. This book focuses on one of the critical geopolitical areas that has seen such long drawn conflicts like the Iran-Iraq war or the Kuwait war that was to begin the process of a more long drawn struggle over Iraq. It is a region that has witnessed hegemonic aspirations by both, the regional powers and extra regional powers. It is this complexity that makes any argument for the development of 'order' in the region a difficult task.

Regional order is a product of a continuous set of interactions that take place within the key participants of the region. These would include the regional hegemons or aspiring hegemons: the bargainer states who may not have a clout to replace the hegemon but, yet have enough power to bargain; the small actors of the region who have a 'nuisance value' and the extra regional powers who have vested interests in the region. In the Persian Gulf area Iran, Iraq and Saudi Arabia would be the aspiring hegemons while the smaller states like Kuwait, Bahrain, Qatar, UAE and Oman may be looked as the small, yet, significant powers of the region. Extra regional interests are mainly determined by the oil and natural gas resources of the region and the key players like United Kingdom, United States, Russia have had traditional stakes in the region.

The geopolitics of the Middle East began to alter radically after the Iranian revolution of 1979. The revolution created series of uncertainties in the region. It raised the threat of a shift to radical Islam that was looked as a threat to the Middle Eastern feudal regimes with the 'export of revolution' ideas that were propounded by the new regime. It threatened the semblance of the geo-economic order that the western states appeared to have in terms of access to the Middle Eastern oil resources. It also symbolized the beginning of an assertive Iran that now had aspirations that went beyond those dictated by the western powers. Iran was to eventually raise its stakes by intervening in the Arab Israel conflict through the Lebanon war by supporting the Hezboullah.

Two arguments seem to flow from the contents of this book : that the role of Iran and the United States would be crucial to develop an order, in the region and that in the development of such an order, the Persian Gulf would as a region be of seminal importance. The argument appears to be based on the geopolitical importance of the Persian Gulf to Iran in terms of global trade and also as the bridge to the Arab World that has failed to address the threat of Israel as they see it. The role of Iran can be understood in terms of the changes that have taken place in the post Kuwait crisis and the second Iraq war. The role that Iraq had once played as a 'front line' state of the Arab world vis-a-vis the onslaught of the Islamic Revolution of Iran is history. Iraq had been the only credible power that could have matched the Iranian power status in the Middle East. It is not an accident that Iran sought to play a crucial role in the Lebanon war through the Hezboullah and also has now raised the cry for going nuclear. The importance of the United States and the willingness to acknowledge this importance (by the Arab world) is seen more clearly after the Camp David accord between Israel and Egypt. The 'inevitability' of American role came to be accepted during the Kuwait war and also in the post Soviet world. The close American Israeli ties and the linkages that countries like Saudi Arabia have with the United States are indicators of the predominance of the American role.

Today, the geopolitical issues of the region have been further compounded by the threat of terrorism. The events of 9/11 altered the American perspective of its role in the region. This has been further complicated by the Iranian government's nuclear ambitions. As America seeks to exit from Iraq, from a war that appears to have come into a great deal of debate as to its objectives, it also seeks to ensure some concrete success on the Afghan front. The fear that the Middle Eastern states would not be willing to go along the American efforts to fight terrorism and that in some cases they may, in fact, create hurdles has complicated the scenario of the region.

This book represents a good effort to bring the geopolitical complexities of the region of the Persian Gulf in perspective. It also seeks to go beyond the narrow factual considerations and strives to provide a direction for the possible path for the development of order in the region.

Dr. Shrikant Paranjpe
Professor
Department of Defence and Strategic Studies
University of Pune, Pune.

Acknowledgments

An analysis of contemporary situation of the Persian Gulf region is an arduous task, given the various points of view and the problems inherent in the subject. It is all the more difficult when the case is as emotive as that of Geopolitical Importance of Persian Gulf region.

I would like to appreciate valuable contribution of Professor Shrikant Paranjpe, who at the first stage of this work, revived my faith in the honest pursuit of learning and persuaded me to take up the writing of this book. My heartfelt thanks go to him for his precious ideas, remarkable perspectives and invaluable support from the initial to the final stage of the work and his able supervision without which the accomplishment could not have been, perhaps, made.

Deepest gratitude is also due to Professor A.S. Dalvi for sharing the literature and valuable assistance in giving permission to use the NISDA (National Centre of International Security and Defense Analysis) facilities. Particular thanks go to Dr. Vijay Khare for his useful help and advices. I would also like to convey thanks to the staff of the Department of Defense and Strategic Studies for the necessary co-operation extended.

I am appreciative of Lt. Gen. D.B. Shekathar and Dr. Narawane who helped me in the editing stage of the contents and also for their valuable comments.

I am especially grateful to my dear brother, Hooshang, and his lovely wife, Zohreh, for supporting and encouraging me to undertake this work.

Last, but by no means least; I wish to express my love and gratitude to my beloved daughter, Asal, for her understanding, encouragement, support and endless love through out the effort made towards this piece of work.

Ashraf Ashrafpour

Department of Defence
and Strategic Studies
University of Pune
Pune-India

Contents

Foreword vii

Acknowledgments xi

List of Figures xv

1. Introduction 1
2. Geopolitics of the Persian Gulf Region 16
3. Geostrategic Importance of the Persian Gulf 117
4. Geostrategic Importance of the Strait of Hormuz and Persian Gulf Islands 176
5. Evolution of Regional Order of the Persian Gulf Region 230
6. Wars of the Persian Gulf Region Post 1979 278
7. Role of the USA in the Persian Gulf Region 343
8. Conclusion and Recommendations 381

Appendices

(A) The Disputed Islands' Chronology According to Iran 403

(B) The Disputed Islands' Chronology According to UAE

(C) Chronology of the Iran-Iraq war; 1980-1988

(D) Chronology of the Persian Gulf War; 1990-1991 317-321

(E) Chronology of the Iraq war; 2003 onwards

Bibliography 474

Index 489

List of Map and Figures

Chapter 1 : Introduction

Map 1.1 : The Persian Gulf Region

Map 1.2 : Areas of the Heartland and Rimland Theories

Chapter 2 : Geopolitics of the Persian Gulf Region

Map 2.1 : Shiite Population of the Region

Map 2.2 : Bahrain

Map 2.3 : The King Fahd Causeway between Bahrain and Saudi Arabia

Map 2.4 : Iran

Map 2.5 : Iraq

Map 2.6 : Iraq-Saudi Arabia Neutral Zone in 1990

Map 2.7 : Kuwait

Map 2.8 : Oman

Map 2.9 : Musandam Peninsula of Oman

Map 2.10 : Madha Exclave of Oman and Nahwa Exclave of UAE

Map 2.11 : Qatar

Map 2.12 : Saudi Arabia

Map 2.13 : United Arab Emirates

Chapter 3 : Geostrategic Importance of the Persian Gulf

Table 3.1 : Persian Gulf Countries' Petroleum Statistics
Table 3.2 : Persian Gulf Countries' Natural Gas Statistics
Map 3.1 : Saudi Arabia's Major Oil Fields
Map 3.2 : Saudi Arabia's Saudi Arabia's Rub Al Khali Desert
Map 3.3 : Iran's Major Oil Fields
Map 3.4 : Iran's Major Gas Fields
Table 3.3 : Iran's Rank in World Natural Gas Reserves
Map 3.5 : Iraq's Major Oil Fields and Pipelines
Map 3.6 : Kuwait's Major Oil Fields
Map 3.7 : Kuwait-Saudi Arabia's Neutral (Divided) Zone
Map 3.8 : United Arab Emirates' Major Oil Fields
Map 3.9 : Qatar's Major Oil and Gas Fields and Pipelines
Map 3.10 : Qatar's North Oil and Gas Fields
Map 3.11 : Oman's Major Oil Fields
Map 3.12 : Bahrain's Major Oil and Gas Fields

Chapter 4 : Geostrategic Importance of the Strait of Hormuz and Persian Gulf Islands

Map 4.1 : Strait of Hormuz
Map 4.2 : The Unsafe Areas for Tankers in the Strait
Map 4.3 : TSS of the Strait of Hormuz
Table 4.1 : Existing Key Pipelines in the Region
Map 4.4 : Location of the Iranian Islands near the Mouth of the Strait of Hormuz
Map 4.5 : Location of the Hormuz Island
Map 4.6 : Location of the Larak Island
Map 4.7 : Location of the Qeshm Island
Map 4.8 : Location of the Hengam Island

Map 4.9 : Location of the Tunb Islands

Map 4.10 : Location of the Abu Musa Island

Map 4.11 : Location of the Musandam Peninsula

Map 4.12 : Location of the Bubiyan Island

Map 4.13 : Location of the Hawar Archipelago

Chapter 5 : Evolution of Regional Order of the Persian Gulf Region

Table 5.1 : Ranking of the Regional Powers in 1990s

Chapter 6 : Wars of the Persian Gulf Region Post 1979

Map 6.1 : Map of Iran-Iraq War; 1980-1988

Image 6.1 : Iranian Soldier with Gas Mask in the Battlefield.

Map 6.2 : Map of Persian Gulf War; 1990-1991

Map 6.3 : Map of Persian Gulf War's Air Campaign

Map 6.4 : Map of Persian Gulf War's Ground Campaign

Map 6.5 : Map of Iraq War; 2003 Onwards

Map 6.6 : Occupation Zones in Iraq; September 2003

1

Introduction

As a part of Middle East, the Persian Gulf is a unique geographical region. Its role in human affairs began in remote antiquity and has continued to our own day. Traditionally, this role was due to the place it occupies as an avenue of cultures and trade; today, as the site of a resource vital not only for the inhabitants of the countries along its shores but for much of the modern world. It has long been a maritime trade route between the Middle East and South Asia. Its modern economy is dominated by petroleum production.

This book tries to analyze the Geopolitical Importance of the Persian Gulf Region. The Persian Gulf and its coastal areas are the world's largest single source of crude oil and related industries dominate the region. The Persian Gulf countries contain a significant percentage of the world's oil reserves, production, and capacity. The regional states consistently maintain most of the world's excess oil production capacity. According to the Oil and Gas Journal and EIA Short Term Energy Outlook, in 2006, the Persian Gulf countries (Bahrain, Iran, Iraq, Kuwait, Qatar, Saudi Arabia, and the United Arab Emirates) produced about 28 percent of the world's oil, while holding 55 percent (728 billion barrels) of the world's crude oil reserves. Due to their huge oil and gas resources, the regional states play a significant role in global economy and these natural wealth have made the region very important from the geostrategic and geopolitical points of view. To understand the contemporary geostrategic relevance of oil and gas resources of the region, the author has attempted to study and analyze the geopolitics of the regional states, regional order, and contemporary conflicts of the region, geostrategic importance of the Strait of Hormuz and the role of Iran and USA as two major powers of the region.

The following are the definition of the terms that are frequently used in the book along with their concomitant background and the role of two major players in the region viz. Iran and USA:

1.1. Persian Gulf Region

The Persian Gulf is a 251,000 square kilometer inland sea that is located between Iran and the Arabian Peninsula. The name derives from the fact that the great Achaemenid Empire in the sixth century B.C. had its centre of power in the province of Fars (Pars/ Persis) in the south-western region of the Iranian plateau.

The Persian Gulf lies in the Southwest Asian region. It is an extension of the Indian Ocean located between Iran and the Arabian Peninsula. Its length is 989 kilometres separating mainly Iran from Saudi Arabia with the shortest divide of about 56 kilometres in the Strait of Hormuz and rarely exceeds a depth of 300 feet (90 m).

This inland sea is connected to the Gulf of Oman in the east by the Strait of Hormuz, and its western end is marked by the major river delta of Arvand River (Shatt Al Arab), which carries the waters of the Euphrates and the Tigris.

The oil-rich countries with a coastline on the Persian Gulf, called the Persian Gulf States or the Gulf States, are (clockwise, from the north): Iran (Persia), Oman, United Arab Emirates, Saudi

Arabia, Qatar on a peninsula off the Saudi coast, Bahrain on an island, and Kuwait and Iraq in the northwest.

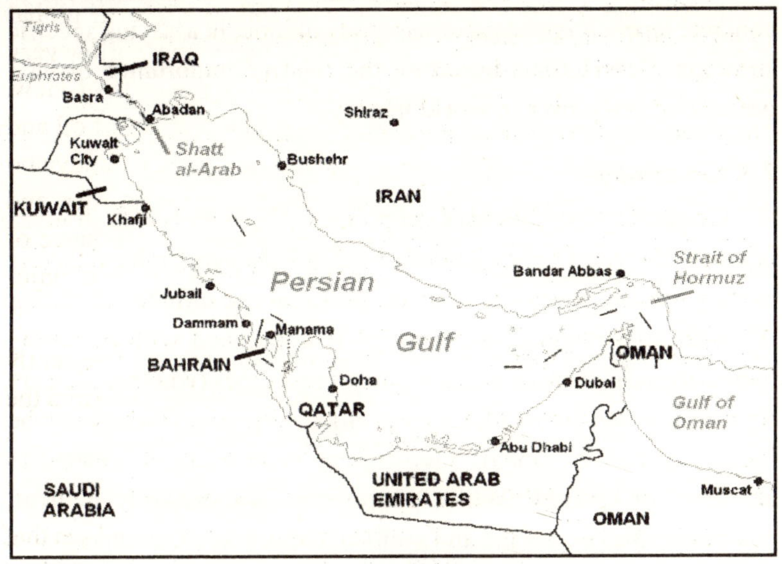

Map 1.1.: The Persian Gulf Region*

• *Source*: Wikimedia.org

1.2. Geopolitics

"Geopolitics is the art and practice of using political power over a given territory. Geopolitics is the study that analyzes geography, history and social science with reference to "spatial politics"[1] and patterns at various scales."[2] It examines the political, economic and strategic significance of geography, where geography is defined in terms of the location, size, function, and relationships of places and resources.

"Geopolitics, as a branch of political geography, is the study of reciprocal relations between geography, politics and power and also the interactions arising from combination of them with each other. According to this definition, geopolitics is a scientific discipline and has a basic science nature."[3]

Geopolitics, traditionally, indicates the links and casual relationship between political power and geographic space; in concrete terms, it is often seen as a body of thought assaying specific strategic prescriptions based on the relative importance of land power and sea power in world history.

1.3. Geostrategy

Geostrategy, a subfield of geopolitics, which deals with strategy, is a type of foreign policy guided principally by geographical factors as they inform, constrain, or affect political and military planning. As with all strategies, geostrategy is concerned with matching means to ends; in this case, a country's resources (whether they are limited or extensive) with its geopolitical objectives (which can be local, regional, or global). Geostrategy is most closely related to strategic geography. While geopolitics is ostensibly neutral, examining the geographic and political features of different regions, especially the impact of geography on politics, geostrategy involves comprehensive planning, assigning means for achieving national goals or securing assets of military or political significance.

"Geostrategy could be defined as applying strategy by governments based on geography, especially resources of states."[4]

Geostrategists advocate proactive strategies and approach geopolitics from a nationalist point of view. As with all political theories, geostrategies are relevant principally to the context in which they were devised: the nationality of the strategist, the strength of his or her country's resources, the scope of his or her country's goals, the political geography of the time period, and the technological factors that affect military, political, economic, and cultural engagement. Geostrategy can function normatively, advocating foreign policy based on geographic factors, analytically, describing how foreign policy is shaped by geography or predictively, by predicting a country's future foreign policy decisions on the basis of geographic factors.

Many geostrategists are also geographers, specializing in subfields of geography, such as human geography, political geography, economic geography, cultural geography, military geography, and strategic geography. Geostrategy is most closely related to strategic geography.

There are some distinguished scholars that have presented great geostrategic ideas. The most well-known are as follows:

1.3.1. Geostrategic Ideas of Mahan; Sea Power Theory

Alfred Mahan (1840-1914), an American geographer, played a leading role in persuading the United States to pursue a larger destiny overseas during the opening years of the twentieth century. He believed in sea power. He was a great advocate of the opening of the Panama Canal across the Panama Isthmus, connecting the Pacific and the Atlantic sea-boards of the United States. In his later years, Mahan was fully convinced that the United States would replace Britain as the leading sea power.

1.3.2. Geostrategic Ideas of Mackinder; Heartland Theory

Sir Halford Mackinder (1861-1947), a British geographer, has perhaps been the best known geographer in the non-geographic circles and his has been definitely been the best known global strategic scheme in modern times. He argued that landmarks such as mountains, canals, straits and sea basins are strategically very important. He named the huge united landmass of Europe, Asia and Africa as the World Island. This was his so-called Pivot Area that he later named as the Heartland. It stretched from the Volga River in the west to eastern Siberia in the east, and from the Himalayas and the associated mountains in the south to the Arctic in the north. Almost whole territory of Iran has been a part of the Heartland. He believed that to retain her supremacy, Britain must capture the Heartland.

1.3.3. Geostrategic Ideas of Spykman; Rimland Theory

Professor Nicholas Spykman (1893-1943), an American geographer, gave a very different interpretation of the relative importance of the Heartland vis-à-vis the surrounding tier, the Inner or Marginal Crescent, partly continental and partly oceanic, which he renamed as the Rimland.

To Spykman, the Heartland appeared less important than the rimland, and he was convinced that it is a combination of land and sea powers controlling the rimland that would in all probability control the essential power relations of the world; inevitably so, because this combination would emerge as the owner of far greater resources, man power and mobility, than the Heartland, or any other combination.

Writing at a time when the Second World War was still on, Spykman advocated that the Allied powers should base their future policy on preventing any consolidation of the Rimland by the enemy. His prescription became the basis, at least in part, of the American policy of containment.

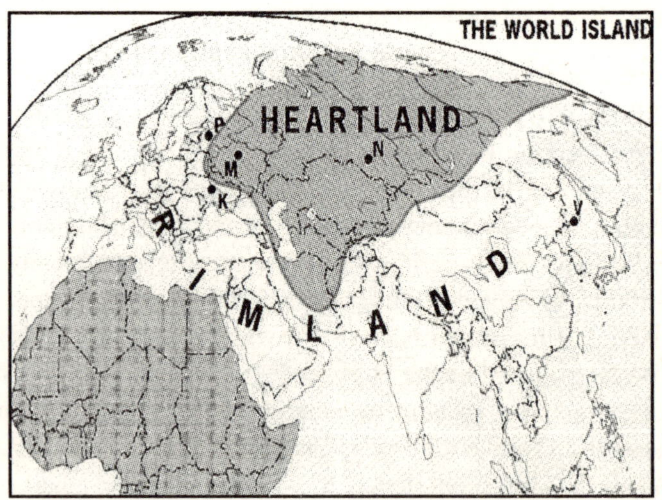

Map 1.2.: Areas of the Heartland and Rimland Theories*

• *Source*: Google Images

1.3.4. Geostrategic Ideas of Cohen; Geostrategic Regions

Saul B. Cohen, an American geographer, rejected the basic premise of the containment policy. He saw contemporary world politics functioning simultaneously at two levels of fragmentation, as follows:

1. First, was the fundamental division of the world into two-fold geostrategic regions, the Trade-Dependent Maritime World led by the United States on one side and the socialist bloc of continental States led by the USSR, on the other side. The Trade-Dependent Maritime World was visualized to contain five geopolitical regions. These are; Anglo-America and the Caribbean, South America, Maritime Europe and Maghreb, Offshore Asia and Oceania. The Eurasian Continental World consisted of; the Heartland together with Eastern Europe and East Asia. South Asia was described as a potential geopolitical region that might well arise from the ashes of the British Commonwealth.
2. Second, there was the lower order division of each of the two into geopolitical regions.

Between the two basic geostrategic regions were located two somewhat distinctive geopolitical regions, designed as shatter belts. These were; South-east Asia and the Middle East. Unlike the other geopolitical regions, the shatter belts lacked political unity and mutual sympathy owing to which they had remained fragmented. As a result, both the geostrategic regions had footholds in them. The chief geopolitical significance of the shatter belts laid in their strategic importance to both the superpowers. Accordingly, it was in these two areas that containment was required to be pursued.

Cohen defined shatter belts as regions that present an equal playing field to two or more competing powers operating from different geostrategic realms.

With the collapse of Soviet Union, Sub-Saharan Africa has now reverted back to the Maritime fold. South-east Asia has also lost its shatter belt character and its insular and southern peninsula portions have become economically and politically part of Offshore Asia and the Maritime World. Vietnam and Indochina; as a whole, are also likely to fall within the East Asian sphere. As regards the isolated and impoverished Myanmar (Burma), after the repressive military regime is eventually over-thrown, it may, in all probability, become reoriented to South Asia. Thus, the only remaining shatter belt is the Middle East, which is itself in transition, and is increasingly tilting towards the Maritime realm.

1.3.5. Geostrategic Ideas of Henry Kissinger; Polarity of the International System

Henry Kissinger implemented two geostrategic objectives when in office: the deliberate move to shift the polarity of the international system from bipolar to tripolar; and, the designation of regional stabilizing states in connection with the Nixon Doctrine. In Chapter 28 of his long work titled 'Diplomacy', Kissinger discusses the 'opening of China' as a deliberate strategy to change the balance of power in the international system, taking advantage of the split within the Sino-Soviet bloc. The regional stabilizers were pro-American states which would receive significant U.S. aid in exchange for assuming responsibility for regional stability. Among the regional stabilizers designated by Kissinger were Zaire, Iran, and Indonesia.

1.3.6. Geostrategic Ideas of Zbigniew Brzezinski; Eurasia as four Regions

Zbigniew Brzezinski laid out his most significant contribution to post-Cold War geostrategy in his 1997 book, The Grand Chessboard. He defined four regions of Eurasia, and in which ways the United States ought to design its policy toward each region in order to maintain its global primacy. The four regions (echoing Mackinder and Spykman) are:

1. Europe, the Democratic Bridgehead
2. Russia, the Black Hole

3. The Middle East, the Eurasian Balkans
4. Asia, the Far Eastern Anchor

In his subsequent book, The Choice, Brzezinski updates his geostrategy in light of globalization, 9/11 and the intervening six years between the two books.

1.4. Regional Order

Regional order can be defined as "a formal or informal arrangement that sustains rule-governed interactions among states in their pursuit of individual and collective goals in a specific region."[5]

The definition of regional order presupposes three following elements:

1.4.1. The first element is the idea of patterned regularity. Formal or informal arrangements of principles, rules, habits and institutions facilitate countries in the region to behave in patterned ways and anticipation of patterned behaviour in turn generates reciprocal reactions by other actors in the region. Such patterned regularity reduces chances for disorder and uncertainty.

1.4.2. Rule-governed behaviour is the second element. Reciprocal interactions and resulting patterned regularities are by and large a product of ruled-governed behaviour. Patterns of regularity would be inconceivable without corresponding rule-governed behaviour. Compliance with principles, norms and rules not only prevents any deviant behaviour but also creates and enhances purposive order.

1.4.3. The purposive regional order is in turn predicated on the satisfaction of normative conditions for coexistence of actors in the region. They involve, not only the reduction of the likelihood of regional violence, but also the creation of minimally acceptable conditions of economic well-being, social justice, ecological stability and participation in decision making in the region.

1.5. Strait of Hormuz

The role of Strait of Hormuz in the global economy and also the security and stability of the Middle East and Persian Gulf region is undeniable. Any halt of oil flowing from the strait will have not only serious impact on developed states' economy, but also on the economy, and most importantly, on the security of the whole region as well as the Middle East.

1.6. Iran

The significant role of Iran in the security and stability of the Middle East and the Persian Gulf region is very clear. Its effects on the regional fundamentalist groups, the influence on Iraq and connection with Iraqi Shiite parties, nuclear dilemma and current political unrest are the issues which have serious impacts on the regional stability and also regional as well as extra-regional states' policies.

1.7. United States of America

USA as an extra-regional power present in the region, is playing a very important role in regional strategies and policies.

2. Statement of the Problem

Since the Portuguese invasion of Persian Gulf in 1507, this small part of the world has become one of the most critical regions of the world. The importance of the region increased after the withdrawal of Britain in 1971 and expanded after Iran-Iraq War; 1980-1988. Gulf War in 1990, and Iraq War in 2003, have made the region more unstable.

2.1. Wars of the Region Since 1979

Since 1979, the region has been the battlefield of three devastating wars.

Iraq-Iran War: Iran and Iraq were engaged in a very long period war (1980-1988). Although external forces were not outwardly involved in this war, but both sides were supported by extra-regional countries. The Iran–Iraq War was extremely costly in terms of lives and material and was one of the deadliest wars since World War II.

Both countries were devastated by the effect of the war. The war left the borders unchanged. The end result of the prolonged war left both the countries enervated and economically exhausted.

Gulf War: Iraq invaded and occupied Kuwait on August 2, 1990. To liberate Kuwait and after Gulf States' request, the United States deployed over 500,000 US troops, joined by about 200,000 troops from 33 other countries. The result of war was liberation of Kuwait and withdrawal of Iraqi troops from Kuwait at the end of February 1991.

Iraq War: The war is an ongoing military campaign which began on March 20, 2003 with the invasion of Iraq by a multinational force led by troops from the United States and the United Kingdom. The outcome of war has been the removal of Saddam regime, seemingly the source of region's instability.

2.2. Historical Evolution of the Region

2.2.1. Cold War Era

Since 1971, when Great Britain formally pulled out of the Persian Gulf, the United States has played a very important role in this strategic part of the world. In spite of Britain's role as the Gulf's protector, the United States began to expand its role in the region from largely economic to political and military as well. In an attempt to gain some control of the oil of the region, Washington developed special relationships with the two foremost oil producers, Iran (under the Shah) and Saudi Arabia.

2.2.2. Post 1979 Era

In February 1979, Islamic revolutionaries overthrew the Shah of Iran, eliminating the main guarantor of stability in the Gulf. In December 1979, the Soviets invaded Afghanistan, establishing a regime in Kabul that was firmly in line with Moscow. Furthermore, the upheaval in Iran had led to a reduction in its oil exports, leading to rising prices and shortages in the developed nations.

2.2.3. Post-Cold War Era

Since 1991, the United States has become the pre-eminent global power. The collapse of the Communist regimes of Eastern Europe in 1989 and of the Soviet Union in 1991 had seen the main challenge to the United States in the international arena disappear. However, the threat of renewed Iraqi aggression in the Persian Gulf, as well as of Iran's rearmament program and aspiration to be the dominant power in the region, meant that the United States faced threats to its own and global security. The importance of Persian Gulf oil to stability and prosperity has demanded a continued American role in the region.

2.3. Present Problems in the Region

The long-standing Arab–Persian conflict, Shiite-Sunni rivalry to dominate the region, consequences of the wars waged since 1980, extra-regional states' presence in the region, disputed islands of the Persian Gulf; existing dilemma between Iran and Sharjah which could be the reason of the next conflict in the region, combined with the desire of neighboring states for control of large oil reserves seem the most important existing problems of the region.

The followings parts of this work which have been dealt in details in the later sections form its recurrent theme:

3.1. Geopolitics of the Region

The long-standing Arab–Persian conflict in the gulf, combined with the desire of neighbouring states for control of large oil reserves, has led to international boundary disputes. There have been, and continue to be, significant territorial disputes between Persian Gulf countries, such as an eight year war between Iraq and Iran. Although external forces were not outwardly involved in this war, but both sides were supported by extra-regional countries.

Another important dispute is between the UAE and Iran over ownership of three islands, Abu Musa, Greater Tunb Island, and Lesser Tunb Island, all strategically located in the Strait of Hormuz.

The Sunni-Shiite competition to dominate the region and other geopolitical aspects have also been extensively dealt.

3.2. Geostrategy of the Region

Today, the Persian Gulf is one of the most strategic places in the world due to its importance in world oil market. Reported by the Energy Information Administration (EIA) in 2006, it contains 728 billion barrels of proven oil reserves, representing over half (55%) of the world's oil reserves, and 2,462 trillion cubic feet of natural gas reserves (45% of the world total). Persian Gulf countries maintain about one-third of the world's productive oil capacity.

3.3. Geostrategy of the Strait of Hormuz

Two-thirds of the world's oil is transported by ocean; straits and canals are, therefore, vital in reducing the time and costs of transporting oil, as well as other goods, globally. Any political disturbances or upheavals can cause the "choking" of the few important straits for world oil transit and thus disrupt world oil prices. The abundance of oil and the world's dependence on imported oil from this region make the Strait of Hormuz one of the most important chokepoints to monitor. Located between Oman and Iran, the strait has a width of 54 km (34 miles) and is consequently a relatively easy passageway to obstruct. According to Energy Information Administration, roughly 17 million billion barrels per day or 40% of world's oil passes through this strait daily. Fortunately, the strait has never actually been shut down, yet the constant political, religious, ethnic, and territorial disputes between the Persian Gulf countries have made the world anxious in anticipation of obstruction.

3.4. Evolution of Regional Order of the Region

Since 1979, after Islamic Revolution in Iran, which changed the balance of power of the region, the region has been facing a kind of disorder. In this book, the problems arising from this disorder and remedies for solving the existing complicated situation have been presented.

3.5. Wars of the Region Since 1979

The Persian Gulf region was the centre of two conflicts involving Iraq and US-led coalitions in the late 20th and early 21st century.

The First Persian Gulf War (1991) was an armed conflict between Iraq and a coalition of 33 nations including the United States, Britain, Egypt, France, and Saudi Arabia. It was a result of Iraq's invasion of Kuwait on August 2, 1990; Iraq then annexed Kuwait, which it had long claimed. To liberate Kuwait from Iraq, the United States deployed over 500,000 U.S. troops, joined by about 200,000 troops from other countries. The Gulf war reduced Iraq's conventional military capabilities roughly by half.

Iraq's invasions of the oil regions of Iran (1980) and Kuwait (1990), if successful, would have gained for Iraq control of nearly half of known oil reserves and a fourth of total remaining resources. Success in these two invasions could have encouraged an Iraq influence, control, or occupation of the remainder of the Gulf countries. In this case, Iraq would have held three-fourths of known global reserves and one-half of the remaining oil.

The Second Persian Gulf War, also known as the Iraq War (2003 onwards) was a largely US-British invasion of Iraq.

Any kind of future hostilities or conflict in the region will affect other parts of the world. Instability of the region may spread to other regions, especially adjacent regions such as South-East Asia, Central Asia and significantly the Middle East. Insecurity of the region will have direct impact on global oil and gas markets, too.

3.6. Role of USA in the Region

Since 1991, USA and her allies have been present in the region and some of the region's ports have become their military bases and headquarters. For example, during the period of USA containment of Iraq, USA combat aircrafts based in Saudi Arabia flew patrols in the no fly zone over southern Iraq (Operation Southern Watch); in June 1995, the US Navy re-established its long dormant Fifth fleet, responsible for the Persian Gulf region, and headquartered in Bahrain; an April 21, 1980 facilities access agreement with Oman provided the United States access to Omani airbases at Seeb, Thumrait, and Masirah, and some pre-positioning of USA Air Force equipment; on September 19, 1991, Kuwait, which sees itself as the most vulnerable to Iraqi aggression, signed a 10-year pact with the United States (renewed in 2001 for another 10 years) allowing the United States to preposition enough equipment to outfit a US brigade and Qatar signed a defence pact with the United States on June 23, 1992 accepting the pre-positioning of enough armour to outfit one US brigade.

References

1. Spatial politics refers to the use of spatial terms to simplify and dramatize political differences and actions.
2. *Wikipedia,* Encyclopedia.
3. Hafeznia Mohammad Reza, "*Principles and Concepts of Geopolitics*", Popoli Publications, Iran, 2006, pp. 37-39.
4. Elahi Homayoun, "*The Persian Gulf and Its Problems*", 8th edition, Ghoomes, Tehran, 2005, p.17.
5. Ikenberry John and Moon Chung-in, "*The United States and Northeast Asia: Debates, Issues and New Order*", Rowman and Littlefield Publishers, USA, 2008, pp. 194-196.
6. In 1962, Admiral Burke co-founded the Center for Strategic and International Studies (CSIS) in Washington, D.C. with David Abshire. This chair in Strategy at the Center for Strategic and International Studies is for his memory and honoring his name.

2

Geopolitics of the Persian Gulf Region

1. Introduction

1.1. Definition of Geopolitics

Swedish political scientist Rudolf Kjellen first used the term geopolitics in 1899. He believed that the economic, political and military characteristics of nations derived from their physical features and environmental influences. He examined the political influence of natural resources, such as oil, and human resources, such as population.

"A simple definition of Geopolitics is to study the impact of geography on relations between nations."[1]

1.2. Geopolitics of the Persian Gulf Region

To understand the geopolitics of the region, the political impacts of geographical aspects, such as history, territory, religion, ethnic groups, military power, economy and natural resources should be studied. All of these aspects have a very strong impact on the geopolitics of the regional states.

From the geopolitical point of view, the sources of potential for internal conflict; which is present in the region, are mainly religion and ethnic diversity. Pressures for more representative forms of government are increasing and may become serious as monarchs' abilities to satisfy the needs and desires of their subjects are reduced. Other internal pressures created by population makeup and economic difficulties are posing interesting challenges.

Geopolitical consideration of the Persian Gulf region tends to revolve around petroleum. The complexity of the Persian Gulf region's landscape and life can, perhaps, best be summarized by a series of paradoxes. Above all, within the apparent unity of the region, there is great diversity. Culture, religion, language, climate, desert landscapes, the vital relationship with water and availability of oil money are all, to a greater or lesser degree, unifying factors. However, none is homogenous or monolithic.

1.2.1. History

The Persian Gulf is witness to thousands of years of civilisation, war, success and tragedy. The Persian Gulf is a waterway that stretches far back into history. It was from its shores that the mighty Persian Empire; the world's first and greatest civilisation, rose. By its shores, the ships of the ancient world traded, and paid homage to the mighty Empire for whom this Gulf was named. When the armies of the Macedonian King Alexander rampaged through the Orient, he stopped at the Persian Gulf, and believed it to be the end of the world.

For most of the history of human settlement in the Persian Gulf, the southern side was ruled by nomadic tribes. During the 7th century, the Sassanid Empire conquered the whole of the Persian Gulf. Between 625 BC and 226 AD, the northern side was dominated by the Median, Achaemenid and Parthian empires. After the fall of the Parthian Empire, the Sassanid Empire ruled the northern half and at times the southern half of the Persian Gulf.

In 16th century, Portuguese dominated the most part of the region. Since 1763 to 1971, some of the Gulf States were under the political control of Britain to varying degrees. Before the withdrawal of the Britain from the region in 1971, the Gulf of Aden was more important than Persian Gulf; that was being ruled by British Empire and was under its complete domination. But, since the Britain's withdrawal, and after the outbreak of Iran-Iraq War in 1980, the region has become more important and been the scene of the struggles of regional as well as extra-regional powers to form regional order. As another example, it could be stated that the Strait of Hormuz had no geopolitical or geostrategic importance before the presence of Portuguese sailors. These go to show that geopolitical importance of a region is being changed due to history.

1.2.2. Territory

Before the oil era, the Persian Gulf States made little effort to delineate their territories. Members of Arab tribes felt loyalty to their tribe or Sheikh and tended to roam across the Arabian Desert according to the needs of their flocks. Official boundaries meant little, and the concept of allegiance to a distinct political unit was absent. Organized authority was confined to ports and oases. The delineation of borders began with the signing of the first oil concessions in the 1930s. The national boundaries had been defined by the British, but many of these borders were never properly demarcated, leaving opportunities for contention, especially in areas of the most valuable oil deposits. Until 1971, British-led forces maintained peace and order in the gulf, and British officials arbitrated local quarrels. After the withdrawal of these forces and officials, old territorial claims and suppressed tribal animosities rose to the surface. The concept of the modern state, introduced into the Persian Gulf region by the European powers, and the sudden importance of boundaries to define ownership of oil deposits kindled acute territorial disputes.

The territorial disputes among the regional states have been the cause of skirmishes, conflicts and even wars in this strategic region. Somehow, the extra-regional states, such as USA, have been involved and played an important role. Some of the existing territorial disputes may be altered to another conflict in the future. Of these, the most important existing ones have been delved in detail later in the book.

1.2.3. Population

By studying the population of the region, one can easily find the diversity factors, such as religion and ethnic diversifications.

In the case of religion, there is a long-standing deep diversity between Sunni and Shiite faiths of Islam. Some of the Gulf monarchies face potential threats to political stability. Although, some, such as Bahrain and Saudi Arabia, have experienced open unrest since the 1991 Gulf war, virtually all of the governments appear to be firmly in power. Several are undergoing leadership transitions, and some are gradually opening up their political processes, in part, to help them cope with the challenges of modernization and globalization. The Gulf leaders undertaking these steps hope that political liberalization will ensure stability, although some fear that this process could backfire by empowering Islamic extremists and providing the Islamists a platform to challenge the incumbent regimes.

The region contains various kinds of ethnic groups such as Persian, Arab and Kurd. The diversification of interests among them, sometimes, causes conflict. The conflict between Gulf States, and between Arabs and Persians, is a product not so much of imperialist interference, or of long, millennial or atavistic, historical antagonisms, but of two interrelated; modern processes of state formation and the rise of nationalism. This is visible in the nature of the psychological gap that divides Arabs from Iranians: one of the most enduring features of the strategic situation in the Persian Gulf is the gap, as much psychological and cultural, as economic, military or political, between the Arab and Iranian perceptions of the region.

Map 2.1.: Shiite Population of the Region

Source: Muse Letter Energy Bulletin August 4, 2006

1.2.4. Military Power

The relationship between naval and terrestrial capabilities of a state, especially a state with long coastal areas and borders, is a part of its geopolitics.

The long and disputed borders of some of the regional states, apart from checking the hostile ones from threatening their security and stability are the reasons that most of the Gulf States strengthen their military forces. Many of them have signed defence pacts with the powerful states, such as USA.

1.2.5. Economy

The Persian Gulf, along with the Silk Road was very important for trading in the Persian Sassanid Empire era. The Persian Gulf region, since the ancient times, has been benefited economically from its strategically important ports. These ports have made the region one of the centers of the world's trade. Some of the regional states, such as Qatar and UAE, have the world's fastest growing GDP (Gross Domestic Product). At the same time, the Gulf States are coping with political change which has direct impact on their economies. All the regional states are economically depend on their oil and gas resources and have to plan for their future without oil. Some are taking steps to reform their economies and to shore up their key asset, energy resources; by inviting foreign investment in that sector. A sharp oil price decline in 1997-1998, prompted the Gulf monarchy states to re-evaluate their longstanding economic weaknesses, particularly, the generous system of social benefits they provide to their citizens.

1.2.6. Natural Resources

According to USA Energy Information Administration report in 2006, the eight countries around the Persian Gulf possess about two thirds of the world's proven reserves of oil, and produce about 28 percent of the world's oil supply. The Persian Gulf and its coastal areas are the world's single source of crude oil and related industries dominate the region. In the region, Saudi Arabia and Iran are first and second, respectively, in proven reserves. Iraq, which is relatively unexplored and in which new energy exploration was barred by UN sanctions, might ultimately be proven to hold more oil than Saudi Arabia does.

Gas is an increasingly important source of energy for Asian and European countries. Iran and Qatar, respectively, have the second and third largest reserves of natural gas in the world, after Russia. Large gas finds have also been made with Qatar and Iran sharing a giant field across the territorial waters "Median Line"[2] (North Field in the Qatari sector; South Pars Field in the Iranian sector). Using this gas, Qatar has built up a substantial liquefied natural gas (LNG) and petrochemical industry.

Difficulties in the discovery and transportation of oil and gas from the Central Asian/Caspian Sea countries ensure that the Gulf region will almost certainly be a major source of energy well into the 21st century, although many experts increasingly see the Central Asia/Caspian countries and Russia as energy sources likely to rival the Persian Gulf.

Within the complexity, there is cften an awe-inspiring simplicity. The complexities of an increasingly urban lifestyle remain dependent upon one simple resource, water. Some of the regional states face water scarcity and have to somehow solve the problem, by importing water purification technology or even importing drinking water from other countries. For example, in Qatar, water scarcity is identified as the main problem. In the absence of permanent surface water, agriculture is almost entirely dependent on irrigation from pumped groundwater. Further, with increasing urban and rural development, groundwater pollution is a clear probability. By and large, similar considerations apply to most countries in the region.

2. Geopolitics of the Regional States

2.1. Geopolitics of Bahrain

2.1.1. History

Bahrain entered recorded history about 5,000 years ago as a commercial trading centre.

Bahrain, known in ancient times as Dilmun, was an important centre of trade by the 3rd millennium BC. The islands were ruled by the Persians in the 4th century AD and were included in Persian Empire by Achaemenians, an Iranian dynasty. It was ruled by Arabs until 1541, when the Portuguese invaded them. Portuguese rule lasted for nearly 80 years, during which they depended mostly on Sunni Persian governors. In 1602, Persia again claimed Bahrain and the Portuguese were expelled from the islands by Shah Abbas, the First, of the Safavid dynasty of Iran, who instituted Shiite as the official religion in Bahrain.

The Iranian rulers retained sovereignty over the islands, with some interruptions, for nearly two centuries. For most of that period, they resorted to governing Bahrain indirectly, either through Hormuz or through local Sunni Arab clans, such as the Huwala. During this period, the islands suffered two serious invasions by the Ibadhis of Oman in 1717 and 1738.

In 1753, the Huwala clan of Al Madhkur invaded Bahrain on behalf of the Iranians, restoring direct Iranian rule. The Al Khalifa family gained control in 1783 and has ruled since that date. British assistance was sought to retain independence and from 1861 until 1971 Bahrain was in all but name a British protectorate.

In 1970, Iran laid claim to Bahrain and the other Persian Gulf islands. However, in an agreement with the United Kingdom, it agreed 'not to pursue' its claims on Bahrain if it's other claims were realized. The following plebiscite saw Bahrainis confirm their Arab identity and independence from Britain. Bahrain did not gain full independence until August 14, 1971.

A constitution was ratified in June 1973 providing for a National Assembly of 30 members, popularly elected for a four-year term, together with all members of the cabinet (appointed by Amir). However, in 1975, the National Assembly was dissolved and the Amir began ruling by decree. The Amir, Sheik Isa Ibn Sulman al-Khalifah, died in 1999 after four decades of ruling. He was succeeded by his son, Sheikh Hammed Ibn Isa Al-Khalifah, who gave himself the title of king but also began a sweeping democratization of the country; censorship has been relaxed and draconian laws repealed.

In a referendum in February 2001, which permitted women to vote for the first time, Bahrainis overwhelmingly supported the transformation of the traditional monarchy into a constitutional one. "Bahrain became a kingdom, with the Amir proclaiming himself king in February 2002."[3]

In October 2002, Bahrain had its first parliamentary election since 1973.

The government type is constitutional monarchy. It formerly was considered a State and officially called a 'Kingdom'.

2.1.2. Territory

Bahrain is the 193rd largest country in world, 3.5 times the size of Washington, DC and slightly greater than that of Singapore.

It measures 720 square kilometres, about 48 km from north to south and 16 km from east to west. The capital of Bahrain is Manama.

Bahrain does not share a land boundary with another country but has a 161 km coastline and claims a further 22 km of territorial sea and a 24 km contiguous zone. Seas around Bahrain are very shallow, heat up quickly in the summer, and produce high humidity.

The Kingdom of Bahrain forms a flat archipelago of 33 low-lying islands in the Persian Gulf, between the Qatar peninsula and the mainland of Saudi Arabia. The islands are mostly deserted, "only about 2.82 percent"[4] of these islands are arable, and most of the population lives in or near Manama, the capital. Desert constitutes 92 percent of Bahrain, and periodic droughts and dust storms are the main natural hazards for Bahrainis.

Desertification is one of the biggest environmental issues that Bahrain faces because of the small percentage of arable land; coastal degradation is also an issue resulting from oil spills, and industrial wastes.

It is important to mention that the main tanker routes from all of the four key oil states; Saudi Arabia, Iran, Iraq and Kuwait, pass near Bahrain. This is also another significant security concern which has arisen from its location in the Persian Gulf region. Any instability in oil transportation such as that happened during Iraq-Iran War; Tanker War, may threaten Bahrain's security.

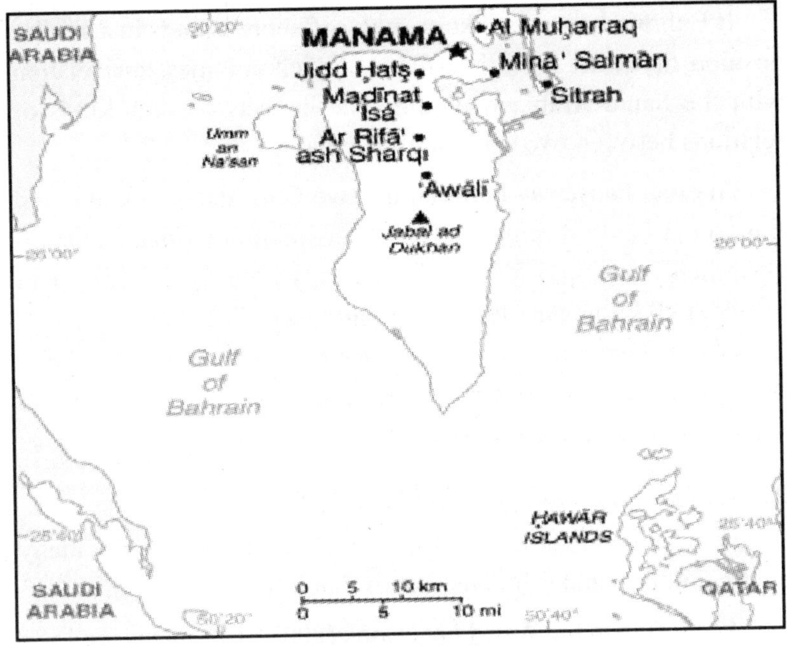

Map 2.2.: Bahrain

Source: World Fact Book (2007)

A causeway, King Fahd Causeway, links Bahrain with Saudi Arabia which is geopolitically significant. It is a four-lane road with 28 kilometres length. The King Fahd Causeway or Bahrain Causeway is a bridge connecting Khobar, the Eastern Province of the Kingdom of Saudi Arabia on the Persian Gulf and Bahrain.

An agreement signed in 1968 led to the beginning of construction the same year. The construction continued until 1986. The causeway officially opened for use in November 1982. The project, completely financed by Saudi Arabia, cost a total of US$ 1.2 billion.

The causeway means that Bahrain is no longer insulated from the Arabian Peninsula. The manner in which each country chooses to use the causeway, will dictate its long-term effect.

If Bahrain becomes, like so many offshore islands in a similar position, the centre for various forms of illicit activities, then relation with the Saudi Arabia will sour. The impacts of such kinds of relations between two states are imaginable.

Another causeway between the two Gulf States of Qatar and Bahrain is being discussed. The Qatar-Bahrain Bridge or Qatar-Bahrain Friendship Bridge is a long-discussed bridge. The link will be about 40 kilometers long. It was announced on December 13th, 2008 that construction would start in early 2009. In January 2009, discussions were entered into to lesser the gradient of the bridge to make it more suitable for rail traffic.

2.1.3. Population; Religious and Ethnic Groups

Bahrain has long been a location of settlement for the many ethnic, cultural and religious groups that inhabit the region.

According to the World Fact Book (2007), Bahrain is the 158th most populous country in the world with about 7,08,573 people, an increase of 2.87 percent over 2005. In 2007 population growth rate was estimated 1.392 percent. "The UN has given a projected population for 2010 of 791,000."[5] Arabic is the official language and English is widely used in business.

2.1.3.1. Religion

Islam is the state religion which the majority of the population practices. However, due to an influx of immigrants and guest workers from non-Muslim countries, such as India, Philippines and Sri Lanka, the overall percentage of Muslims in the country has declined in recent years.

Only three countries in the world have Shiite Muslim majorities: Iran, Iraq and Bahrain. Tiny Bahrain remains the only country in the world where a Shiite majority is led by a Sunni minority.

The unrest is naturally of great concern to the ruling Sunni elite in Bahrain, the Al Khalifa family, which has ruled the country since 1783, though not always autonomously. It's also of concern to Bahrain's neighbours: Kuwait to the north, Saudi Arabia to its west, and Qatar and the United Arab Emirates to its east and south. Each of these countries has restless Shiite minorities of its own. Sunni Arabs are relatively recent arrivals in Bahrain. Most came two hundred years ago with arrival of the ruling al-Khalifa family. Many of these Sunni Arabs, like the ruling family, came originally from Najd in the middle of the Arabian Peninsula.

Shia, which came to Bahrain in 1500, is the island's dominant religion. Between two thirds and three quarters of the Shiite population is native in origin, the remainder being of Iranian descent. This division is social as well as cultural. The Iranian Shiite, known as Ajam, is well represented in the middle class professions and is politically inactive. They see their relative privilege as contingent on the good will of the ruling Sunni al-Khalifas and are reluctant to jeopardize their position. Their native counterparts, known as Baharna, occupy the lowest strata of society and constitute ninety percent of the labour force. The two communities inhabit separate districts and rarely enter into matrimony.

The Baharna, defining themselves in opposition to the Ajam as well as ruling Sunnis, have retained a strong Arab identity. Despite the segregation of the two communities, antagonism arose in the 1950s and 60s as the schism between conservatives and Arab nationalists came to mark not only a division between Arab and Persian, but between rich and poor across the Arab world.

The huge influx of oil wealth after 1973 had widened the gap between rich and poor, while the revolution in Iran spread radical Shiite across the Arab world. When the Iranian revolution broke out in 1979, massive demonstrations in support of Iran broke out in Bahrain, with Shiite leaders demanding that Bahrain, like Iran, be proclaimed an Islamic Republic.

Generally, the Sunni-Shiite balance in the population provides grounds for continuing internal unrest.

2.1.3.2. Ethnic Groups

According to the World Fact Book (April 2009), 62.4 percent of population of the country are Bahrainis and 37.6 percent are non-Bahrainis. Bahrain has transformed into a cosmopolitan society with mixed communities which include immigrants and guest workers.

As much as one-third of the people are non-nationals, mainly foreign workers from Asia (19 percent) or other Arab countries (10 percent). Some 8 percent of the population is of Iranian descent. The growth of non-Bahraini population was around 3.76 percent in 2006. The non-Bahraini population is growing at a much faster rate than the Bahraini population in Bahrain. The Financial Times published on May 31, 1983 reported that "Bahrain is a polyglot state, both religiously and racially. Leaving aside the temporary immigrants of the past ten years, there are at least eight or nine communities on the island."[6]

Comprehensive health care is provided to all population. Wide range of preventive, curative and rehabilitative services are available to all population; free of charge to Bahrainis and heavily subsidized to non-Bahrainis. Primary health care is the cornerstone of the public health services.

"Bahrain has been criticised by human rights activists for its track record on combating racial discrimination."[7] Weak legislation, double standards within the system, a lack of public awareness campaigns and an absence of the standard from the national curriculum are just some of the reasons given. They also accused Bahrain of failing to implement all articles of the International Convention on the Elimination of All Forms of Racial Discrimination, which it signed back in March 1990.

The criticisms are spelled out in a shadow report submitted to the United Nations (UN) by members of the now-dissolved Bahrain

Centre for Human Rights (BCHR) and the International Federation for Human Rights. The members also criticised the process of obtaining Bahraini citizenship because of discrimination between Arab and non-Arab applicants; the fact that a Bahraini woman cannot pass on her nationality to her child if she marries a foreigner; and alleged discrepancies in awarding passports to foreigners depending on their gender.

Further, the report also criticises the treatment of foreign workers, whose lives may differ considerably depending on where they come from. This is especially true for domestic workers, such as housemaids, who are not even covered by the Labour Law.

2.1.4. Military Power

With an active military forces membership of 11,000, Bahrain has a small army supported by a very small navy and air force called the Bahrain Defense Force (BDF). Minimum 18 years of age is required for voluntary military service. The crown prince is Commander-in-Chief of the armed forces.

It is a small, but effective force. However, in any major emergency it would require support which is available from the USA and the EU. Originally, Britain provided the major military support for Bahrain; a series of treaties in the 19th century gave Britain control over Bahrain's defence and foreign affairs, but this role has been superseded by the USA. The BDF is primarily equipped with US equipment.

The Iran-Iraq War (1980-1988) brought further instability to the region. Concern over possible escalation of the war prompted fears about the weakness of Bahrain's military. Bahrain joined other Arab nations of the region, funding the Gulf Cooperation Council (GCC) in 1981, thereby receiving assistance with intelligence monitoring and gaining approval from the other member states to purchase weapons from the United States.

In 1987, Bahrain provided vital facilities for US naval forces escorting Kuwaiti vessels through the Persian Gulf to shield them from possible attack by Iran, which accused them of carrying Iraqi oil. It also played a key role in supporting naval vessels of the United States and other countries operating against Iraq during the Persian Gulf War (1991). In 1991 and 1994 Bahrain solidified its security arrangements with the United States, confirming its role as an American support base in the region.

Since October 1991, the Government of Bahrain has a cooperative agreement with the United States Military and has provided the United States a base in Juffair since the early 1990s. This is the home of the headquarters for Commander, United States Naval Forces Central Command (COMUSNAVCENT) / United States Fifth Fleet (COMFIFTHFLT), and about 1500 US and coalition military personnel.

Bahrain has been an important Western ally, serving as a Western air base during the Persian Gulf War in 1991 and the Iraq War in 2003. Tensions between the US and Iran are a concern for local and regional politics, but Bahrain's firm alliances with Saudi Arabia and the US mitigate the risks.

2.1.5. Economy

Situated along major Arabian and international trade routes between Asia and the West, the Kingdom has, for millennia, served as an important port and centre of business.

Geopolitically, Bahrain is a micro-state with certain indigenous problems, but a sound economy. It is chiefly of global significance for its location which is highly strategic and which ensures external support if problems arise. The major geopolitical issues result from this location which means that Bahrain is always likely to be embroiled with any Persian Gulf States over oil.

Bahrain has benefited from being an offshore island, developed early as a trading centre. This has allowed it to diversify its industry and commerce in the light of the decline in its oil resources. The economic strength of Bahrain was built upon oil resources which were exploited early and are now in sharp decline. Bahrain is actively pursuing the diversification and privatization of its economy to reduce the country's dependence on oil. This diversification has been successful, supplemented by services such as offshore banking and tourism. In the future, "Bahrain might develop a Singapore- or Hong Kong- type status."[8]

With its highly developed communication and transport facilities, Bahrain is home to numerous multinational firms with business in the Gulf. Bahrain and the USA implemented a Free Trade Agreement (FTA) in August 2006, the first FTA between the USA and a Gulf state.

The United Nations Economic and Social Commission for Western Asia found in January 2006, that in a region experiencing an oil boom, Bahrain has the fastest growing economy in the Arab world. Bahrain also has the freest economy in the Middle East according to the 2006 Index of Economic Freedom published by the Heritage Foundation/Wall Street Journal, and is twenty-fifth freest, overall, in the world.

In 2008, Bahrain was named the world's fastest growing financial center by the City of London's Global Financial Centers Index. Bahrain had been witnessing strong private/foreign participation over the past few years. The main reason that the foreign companies have looked Bahrain as the place to enter the region is primarily for its geographical environment, well-regulated authorities and low cost factor in setting up operations.

The global financial shakeup in the second half of 2008 jolted Gulf Cooperation Council (GCC) markets and Bahrain was no exception. Bahrain market declined by 33.5 percent in 2008 compared to a rise of 26.5 percent in 2007.

The major impact was felt in the second half of 2008 when commodity prices started to fall as recession fears loomed over the developed economies thereby forcing the high-growth GCC economies including Bahrain to slow down. The global financial crisis has brought an end to a prolonged oil boom in the Gulf including Bahrain and has reversed years of strong economic performance and massive fiscal surpluses.

2.1.6. Natural Resources

Facing declining oil reserves, Bahrain has turned to petroleum processing refining and has transformed itself to an international bank centre, thereby acquiring a greater commercial and strategic importance.

One major potential geopolitical weakness of Bahrain is its dependence on Saudi Arabia, not only for petroleum and oil refining, but also, more particularly for water.

Bahrain never had any difficulties concerning water scarcity, usage, distribution, etc. But, urbanization, change in climate and rapid increase of population contributed into creating difficulties for it. There were plenty of water springs that people used to rely on, but now with urbanization, the government was obliged to cut down trees and claim agricultural land. This coupled with climate change have contributed to the drying out of the springs.

"Bahrain and its neighbours could face a potential security crisis unless they take steps to protect their diminishing water resources. Also, there could be serious threat if the region does nothing to ensure there is enough water to go round."[9] Bahraini Works Minister Fahmi Al Jowder, who is also in charge of the Electricity and Water Authority, said in a conference held in Ritz-Carlton Bahrain Hotel on April 11, 2009. "The Middle East and the GCC countries in particular are considered to be amongst the worst areas that suffer from scarcity of water resources", he added.

It is worth mentioning that Bahrain is comparatively less dependent on oil compared to other GCC countries. So, in other words, Bahrain will be less vulnerable if the oil prices start dropping in the near future.

2.2. Geopolitics of Iran

2.2.1. History

With thousands of years of recorded history, and due to an unchanging geographic (and subsequently geopolitical) condition, Iran has had a long, varied, and chequered culture and history.

Iran is home to one of the world's oldest continuous major civilizations, with historical and urban settlements dating back to 4000 BC. The Medes unified Iran as a nation and empire in 625 BC.

Achaemenid Empire (550–330 BC) was the first of the Persian Empires to rule over Middle East, Greece and Central Asia. In 552 BCth, Cyrus led his armies against the Medes and captured Ecbatana in 549 BC, effectively conquering the Median Empire and also inheriting Assyria. Cyrus later conquered Lydia and Babylon. Cyrus the Great created the Cyrus Cylinder, considered to be the first declaration of human rights and was the first king whose name has the suffix 'Great'. Their greatest achievement was the empire itself. "The Persian Empire represented the world's first superpower."[10] It was based on a model of tolerance and respect for other cultures and religions.

They were succeeded by the Seleucid Empire, Parthian and Sassanid which governed Iran for more than 1000 years, during which the Zoroastrian religion took hold.

Arabian armies defeated the Sassanid in 641 AD and spread Islam in Persia. The Islamic conquest of Persia (633–656) and the end of the Sassanid Empire was a turning point in Iranian history.

Islamization in Iran took place during 8th to 10th century and led to the eventual decline of the Zoroastrian religion in Persia. The Islamization of Iran was to yield deep transformations within the cultural, scientific, and political structure of Iran's society: The blossoming of Persian literature, philosophy, medicine and art became major elements of the newly-forming Muslim civilization.

Inheriting a heritage of thousands of years of civilization, and being at the 'crossroads of the major cultural highways', contributed to Persia emerging as what culminated into the 'Islamic Golden Age'.

During this period, hundreds of scholars and scientists vastly contributed to technology, science and medicine, later influencing the rise of European science during the Renaissance. Sunnism was dominant form of Islam in most part of Iran from the beginning until rise of Safavi Empire. Sunni Islam was more than 90 percent of population of Persia before Safavi dynasty. Safavi dynasty (1502-1736) established the Shia sect of Islam as the state's region.

As summarized by Seyyed Hussein Nasr: "if the Achaemenian period is the golden age of Persia politically and the Sassanid period in administration, city planning and architecture, the first centuries of the Islamic period are without doubt the golden age of Iranian history in the domain of the sciences, particularly medicine and mathematics. To this period, belong those Persian scientists who stand among the foremost stars in the firmament of the history of science to this day."[11]

Qajar dynasty ruled Persia from 1779 to 1921. By the 17th century, European countries, including Great Britain, Imperial Russia, and France, had already started establishing colonial footholds in the region. Iran, as a result, lost sovereignty over many of its provinces to these countries via the Treaty of Turkmenchay, the Treaty of Gulistan, and others. A new era in the history of Persia dawned with the Constitutional Revolution of Iran against the Shah in the late 19th and early 20th century. The Shah managed to remain in power, granting a limited constitution in 1906 (making the country a constitutional monarchy). The first Majlis (parliament) was convened on October 7th, 1906. Following a bloodless coup in 1921, Reza Khan began his rise to power. He was crowned Reza Shah Pahlavi in 1925.

During World War II, Iran was a vital oil-supply source and link in the Allied supply line for lend-lease supplies to the Soviet

Union. British and Indian forces from Iraq and Soviet forces from the north occupied Iran in August 1941. In September, responding to Iran's support for Germany in the Second World War, the Allies forced Reza Shah to abdicate in favour of his son, Mohammad Reza Shah, who was sworn in on September 17th 1941. Soviet troops did not withdraw from Iran proper until May 1946 after receiving a promise of oil concessions. The Soviet republics in the north were soon overthrown and the oil concessions were revoked.

Known as Persia until 1935, Iran became an Islamic Republic in 1979 after the ruling monarchy was overthrown and Mohammad Reza Shah Pahlavi was forced into exile.

Foreign relations played as large a role as internal politics in shaping the new republic. The movement against the Shah had also been a movement against US involvement in Iran. In September 1980, Iraq launched a surprise invasion of Iran. Iraq wanted to prevent the new Iranian republic from inciting Iraqi Shiites to rise up against the Sunni Iraqi regime. The war, which continued until August 1988 when both states accepted the terms of an UN-mediated ceasefire agreement, took a toll on Iran.

According to the World Fact Book, 2007, Iran has certain international disputes Iran protests Afghanistan's limiting flow of dammed tributaries to the Helmand River in periods of drought. Iraq's lack of a maritime boundary with Iran prompts jurisdiction disputes beyond the mouth of the Shatt al Arab in the Persian Gulf. Iran and UAE dispute over Tunb Islands and Abu Musa Island which are occupied by Iran. Also, Iran stands alone among littoral states in insisting upon a division of the Caspian Sea into five sectors and last but not least, the Iran's disputed nuclear program.

2.2.2. Territory

Iran is the 18th largest country in the world. It measures (including inland waters) 1,684,195 square kilometres which means that its territory is larger than the combined territories of France,

Germany, the Netherlands, Belgium, Spain and Portugal. Iran is bounded in the north by Armenia, Azerbaijan, the Caspian Sea and Turkmenistan, east by Afghanistan and Pakistan, south by the Gulf of Oman and the Persian Gulf, and west by Turkey and Iraq. The capital is Tehran.

Iran's land boundaries are 5440 km; Afghanistan 936 km, Armenia 35 km, Azerbaijan-proper 432 km, Iraq 1458 km, Pakistan 909 km, Turkey 499 km and Turkmenistan 992 km.

Iran is defined by its mountains, which form its frontiers, enfold its cities and describe its historical heartland. Iran's most important mountains are the Zagros. They are a southern extension of the Caucasus, running about 900 miles from the north-western border of Iran, which adjoins Turkey and Armenia, southeast toward Bandar Abbas on the Strait of Hormuz.

The centre of Iran consists of two desert plateaus that are virtually uninhabited and uninhabitable. The eastern boundary of Iran marks the eastern edge of the Middle East, while its western boundary with Iraq defines the edge of the Arab World. Although it is in a sense peripheral, it is highly influential in that it provides the Middle Eastern links with the Trans-Caucasus, Central Asia and the Indian subcontinent. The boundary with Iraq, certainly at its southern extent along the Shat Al Arab, has been of major geopolitical significance.

Iran is a fortress. Surrounded on three sides by mountains and on the fourth by the sea together with a wasteland at its centre, Iran is extremely difficult to conquer. This, however, was achieved once by the Mongols, who entered the country from the northeast. The Ottomans penetrated the Zagros Mountains and went northeast as far as the Caspian but made no attempt to move into the Persian heartland.

Map 2.3.: Iran
Source: PBS Organization

For most countries, the first geographical imperative is to maintain internal cohesion. For Iran, it is to maintain secure borders, and then secure the country internally. Without secure borders, Iran would be vulnerable to foreign powers who would continually try to manipulate its internal dynamics, destabilize its ruling regime and then exploit the resulting openings. Iran must first define the container and then control what it contains.

Its coastline on the Persian Gulf and Gulf of Oman is 2440 km. Iran also borders the Caspian Sea with the coastline of 740 km.

Its most important port, Bandar Abbas, is located on the Strait of Hormuz. There are no equivalent ports along the Gulf of Oman. Iran is not a major maritime or naval power. It is and always has been a land power.

In the past, Iran benefited from the many trade routes that crossed its territory. Now it finds itself sitting astride the two great energy emporiums of the world: the Persian Gulf and the Caspian Sea. It is in many ways the linchpin of the region.

Even if Iran had not oil and gas of its own, this simple geopolitical reality would make it difficult to ignore.

2.2.3. Population; Religious and Ethnic Groups

Iran with 66,429,284 (July 2009 estimation) population is 18th populous country in the world. 58 percent of its inhabitants speak Persian and Persian dialects, 26 percent Turkish and Turkish dialects, 9 percent Kurdish, 2 percent Luri, 1 percent Baluchi, 1 percent Arabic and 3 percent other languages.

Iran is a nation of about 70 million dwellers. Even its biggest city, Tehran, is in the foothills of towering mountains. Its population is in a belt stretching through the Zagros and Elburz mountains on a line running from the eastern shore of the Caspian to the Strait of Hormuz. There is a secondary concentration of people to the northeast, centred on Mashhad. The rest of the country is lightly inhabited and almost impassable because of the salt-mud flats.

2.2.3.1. Religion

The official religion is the Shiite branch of Islam. Iranian population comprises 98 percent Muslims (Shiite 89 percent, Sunni 9 percent), while the rest 2 percent includes Zoroastrian, Jewish, Christian, and Baha'i.

Iran is divided between the vastly dominant Shiite and the minority Sunnis, who are clustered in three areas of the country; the northeast, the northwest and the southeast. Any foreign power interested in Iran will use these ethno religious groups to create allies in Iran to undermine the power of the central government.

Iranian Sunni Muslims are the largest religious minority. The majority of Kurds, virtually all Baluchis and Turkmen, and a minority of Arabs are Sunnis, as are small communities of Persians in southern Iran and the region of Khorasan. Generally speaking, Iranian Shias are inclined to recognize Sunnis as fellow Muslims, but as those whose religion is incomplete. The Constitution provides Sunni Muslims a large degree of religious freedom, although it forbids a Sunni Muslim from becoming President. Sunni Muslims claim that the government discriminates against them; however, it is difficult to distinguish whether the cause for discrimination is religious or ethnic, since most Sunnis are also ethnic minorities. "Sunnis cite the lack of a Sunni mosque in Tehran, despite the presence of over 1 million Sunnis there, as a prominent example of this discrimination."[12]

In towns with mixed populations in West Azerbaijan, the Persian Gulf region and Baluchistan-Sistan, tensions between Shiites and Sunnis existed both before and after the Islamic Revolution of Iran. Religious tensions have been highest during major Shiite observances, especially Moharram.

Thus, any Persian or Iranian government has, as its first and primary strategic interest, maintaining the internal integrity of the country against separatist groups. It is inevitable, therefore, for Iran to have a highly centralized government with an extremely strong security apparatus. For many countries, holding together its ethnic groups is important. For Iran, it is essential because it has no room to retreat from its current lines and instability could undermine its entire security structure. Therefore, the Iranian central government will always face the problem of internal cohesion and will use its army and security forces for that purpose before any other.

2.2.3.2. Ethnic Groups

Although with a population that is 55 to 60 percent ethnically Persian, Iran is divided into a large number of ethnic groups. By 2008, the main ethnic groups in Iran remained the Persians (65 percent). Other groups have been the Azerbaijani Turks (16 percent), Kurds (7 percent), Lurs (6 percent), Arabs (2 percent), Baluchis (2 percent), Turkmens (1 percent), Turkish tribal groups such as the Qashqai (1 percent), and non-Persian, non-Turkic groups such as Armenians, Assyrians and Georgians (less than 1 percent).

Roughly, one out of every four Iranians is Azeri, making it Iran's largest ethnic minority at over 18 million, some Azeris put the number higher. The Turkish-speaking Azeri community is predominantly Shiite and resides mainly in northwest Iran along the border with Azerbaijan (whose inhabitants are more secular than their Azeri cousins in Iran) and in Tehran. Although, they have grievances with the current regime in Tehran, most Azeris say they are not treated as second-class citizens and are more integrated into Iranian society, business, and politics (the Supreme Leader is an ethnic Azeri) than other minorities.

The Kurds, predominantly Sunni Muslim, reside mainly in the northwest part of the country (so-called Iranian Kurdistan) and comprise around 7 percent of Iran's population. There are roughly 4 million Kurds living in Iran.

Unlike Iran's other minorities, many of its Kurds harbour separatist tendencies. Those tendencies in the past have created tensions within the state and have occasionally turned violent (the largest separatist related violent incident in recent years occurred in response to Turkey's February 1999 arrest of Abdullah Ocalan, then-leader of the Kurdistan Workers' Party). The governments of Turkey and Iran fear that the creation of a semiautonomous state in northern Iraq might motivate their own Kurdish minorities to press for greater independence. But Kaveh L. Afrasiabi, a US-based expert on Iranian foreign policy, says "Iran's concern about Kurdish separatism does not approach the level of Turkey."[13]

Along the Iranian-Iraqi border in southwest, Iran has a population of some 3 million Arabs, predominantly Shiite. Arabs, whose presence in Iran stretches back 12 centuries, co-mingle freely with the local populations of Turks and Persians. During the 1980s, they fought on the side of the Iranians, not the Iraqi Arabs. However, as Sunni-Shiite tensions have worsened in the region, a minority of this group, emboldened by Iraqi Arabs across the border, have pressed for greater autonomy in recent years.

"In the southern oil-rich province of Khuzestan, clashes erupted in March 2006 between police and pro-independence ethnic Arab Iranians, resulting in three deaths and more than 250 arrests. The protests were reportedly organized by a London-based group called The Popular Democratic Front of Ahwazi Arabs."[14]

Iran has roughly 1.4 million Baluchis, comprising 2 percent of its population. Predominantly Sunni, they reside in the Iranian section of an area known as Baluchistan, a region divided between Pakistan and Iran. The south-eastern province where Baluchis reside remains the least developed part of Iran and boasts high unemployment rates. That, plus the porous border between the two countries and perhaps the close cross-border cultural or tribal affinities of the Baluchis, has encouraged widespread smuggling of various goods, including drugs.

Iranian Baluchistan, despite holding few resources, remains a militarily important region because of its border with Pakistan.

In early 2007, the Iranian government built a military base there. Tehran has also kept a watchful eye on Baluchi militants in the region.

2.2.4. Military Power

From purely military perspective, Iran is strong compared to other countries in the region. Iran's military doctrine is based on deterrence.

The Islamic Republic of Iran has two types of armed forces: the regular forces consisting Islamic Republic of Iran Army, Islamic Republic of Iran Air Force and Islamic Republic of Iran Navy, and the Islamic Revolutionary Guards Corps (IRGC), totaling about 545,000 active troops. Iran also has around 350,000 Reserve Force totaling around 900,000 trained troops. It is worthy to mention that, despite a strong army, Iran has not invaded any country over the past two centuries.

Iran has a paramilitary, volunteer militia force within the IRGC, called the Basij, which includes about 90,000 full-time, active-duty uniformed members. Up to 11 million men and women are members of the Basij who could potentially be called up for service. Iran could mobilize "up to one million men."[15] This would be among the largest troop mobilizations in the world. In 2005, Iran's military spending represented 3.3 percent of the GDP or US$ 91 per capita, the lowest figure of the Persian Gulf nations.

Minimum 18 years of age is required for compulsory military service; 16 years of age for volunteers; soldiers as young as 9 were recruited extensively during the Iran-Iraq war.

2.2.5. Economy

Iran has the 28th largest economy in the world but ranks only 71st in per capita GDP (as expressed in purchasing power). It ranks with countries like Belarus or Panama. The reason is geographic problem. Iran has a huge population mostly located in rugged mountains. Mountainous regions are rarely prosperous. The cost of transportation makes the development of industry difficult.

Economy of Iran is dominated by oil and gas exports which "constituted 70 percent of government revenue and 80 percent of export earnings as of 2008."[16] It has a large public sector, with an estimated 60 percent of the economy directly controlled and centrally planned by the state. "A unique feature of Iran's economy is the large size of the religious foundations, or Bonyads, whose combined budgets are said to make up as much as half that of the central government."[17]

Combination of price controls and subsidies, particularly on food and energy, continue to weigh down the economy, and administrative controls, widespread corruption, and other rigidities undermine the potential for private-sector-led growth.

Iran has an observer status at the World Trade Organization (WTO) since 2005. The United States has consistently blocked Iran's bid to join the WTO since Tehran first asked for membership several years ago.

Iran is hoping to attract billions of dollars worth of foreign investment while creating a more favorable investment climate, such as reduced restrictions and duties on imports and the creation of free trade zones like in Qeshm, Chabahar and Kish Island.

Iran's geography and large population make substantial improvements in its economic life difficult. Unlike under-populated and less geographically challenged countries such as Saudi Arabia and Kuwait, Iran cannot enjoy any shift in the underlying weakness of its economy brought on by higher oil prices and more production. The absence of inhabitable plains means that any industrial plant must develop in regions where the cost of infrastructure tends to undermine the benefits.

"High oil prices in recent years have enabled Iran to amass nearly US$ 80 billion in foreign exchange reserves."[18] Yet this increased revenue has not eased economic hardships, which include double-digit unemployment and inflation, "inflation climbed to 26 percent as of December 2008."[19] The economy has seen only moderate growth. Oil keeps Iran from sinking even deeper, but it alone cannot catapult Iran out of its condition.

2.2.6. Natural Resources

From the geopolitical point of view, the location of Iran's oil fields is critical, since oil remains its most important and most strategic export.

Oil is to be found in three locations of the country. The southwest is the major region, with lesser deposits along the Iraqi border in the north and one near Qom.

The south-western oil fields are an extension of the geological formation that created the oil fields in the Kurdish region of northern Iraq. Hence, the region east of the Shatt al-Arab is of critical importance to Iran. As Iran ranks fourth in terms of crude oil reserves after Saudi Arabia, Iraq and Kuwait, as well as fourth in terms of oil production after Saudi Arabia, the USA and Russia, one would expect it to be one of the wealthiest countries in the world. But unfortunately it isn't.

Since the first known human empire was established thousands of years ago in the south-western part of Iran, water has played a key role in any social changes that have taken place in this country. For many people viewing Iran from outside of the country, water scarcity in this country may not appear to be as serious as in other countries of the Middle East. Nevertheless, with a population of more than 70 million people, Iran is actually one of the driest countries of the world.

Today, the consequence of rapid population increase and the immigration of millions of Afghans is increased pressure for rapid water and land development. In addition, the processes of urbanization and industrialization and the development of irrigated agriculture to support population growth have raised the demand for water, but at the same time have reduced the supply. Iran is an oil rich country, but water, unlike petroleum, has no substitutes and cannot be purchased in a world market that has many alternative suppliers. If the problem of water scarcity, not only in Iran, but also in other countries of the Middle East, is not solved, its most obvious consequence will be that millions of the people of these countries will seek refuge in other nations.

2.3. Geopolitics of Iraq

2.3.1. History

Iraq, officially the Republic of Iraq, is a country in south-western Asia. Some of the world's greatest ancient civilizations; Assyria, Babylonia and Sumer, developed in the area that now makes up Iraq. Mesopotamia, a Greek word that means the land between the rivers, the Tigris and Euphrates, meeting at the cradle of Western civilization, known today as Iraq, was and is, inhabited predominantly by these Arab tribes.

Iraq is an Arabic word that appears in the Koran and has been a geographical term for the Mesopotamia area throughout the Muslim era.

Iraq became a target of rivalry between the Persian and Ottoman empires, both Islamic, for almost five centuries beginning around 1500. Shah Ismail, the Safavi ruler of Persia, put Iraq under Persian occupation in 1508. The Ottoman Sultan Selim, the First, regained control of Iraq in 1514, after the battle of Jaldiran. In 1529, Iraq was reoccupied by Persia, but was retaken by the Ottoman Sultan Suleiman the Magnificent in 1543.

By the 19th century, British imperialist expansion in the region had transformed the Ottoman/Persian power balance and changed the geopolitical nature of the conflict. By 1917, British occupation of Iraq began.

Arabs in southern Iraq, who helped the British against the Ottoman Turks in the First World War, began resistance in 1920 against the British, who failed to honour their promise to end British occupation after the defeat of the Ottoman Empire. Notwithstanding the British response to Iraqi nationalist resistance with overwhelming military force, Britain soon was forced to face the inescapable fact that it would be impossible to effectively control the Arab country by military means. To avoid heavy casualties to the occupation force, the British were forced to restrict their control to only critical neighbourhoods in key urban centres. This in turn allowed more attacks on British occupation forces. Britain then decided to form a pro-British Iraqi government as a proxy to protect British interests, just as the US is doing now in Iraq.

The modern state of Iraq was created in 1920 by the British government. With the ending of the British mandate in 1929, economic domination and control from London continued through Faisal's pro-British monarchy and the institution of private property imposed on a tribal culture. Iraq was declared an 'independent' kingdom on October 3, 1932, with Faisal as king and admitted to the League of Nations.

Iraq, after all, was the artificial product of Western geopolitical manoeuvres in the cradle of civilization during the age of European imperialism, and Iraq's full geopolitical spectrum has always included Pan-Arabism beyond narrow state interests.

The king of Iraq, Qasim, was assassinated in February 1963 and the Baath Party took power under the leadership of General Ahmed Hassan Al-Bakr (prime minister) and Colonel Abdul Salam Arif (president). Nine months later Abdul Salam Muhammad Arif led a successful coup against the Baath government. On April 13, 1966, President Abdul Salam Arif died in a helicopter crash and was succeeded by his brother, General Abdul Rahman Arif. Then the Baath Party felt strong enough to retake power in July 17, 1968. Ahmad Hasan Al-Bakr became president and chairman of the Revolutionary Command Council (RCC).

Iraq under its Baath leader, Saddam Hussein, started an eight years war with Iran in 1980. The war with Iran, the most costly and bloody conflict not involving a Western power directly since World War II, and the Iraqi invasion of Kuwait, were not mere conflicts over borders, or access to the Shatt al-Arab waterway. The Iran-Iraq war was a clash between extremist Islamic fundamentalism espoused by Ayatollah Ruhollah Khomeini of Iran and the pan-Arab nationalism of the Baathists, both in and out of Iraq.

Iraq invaded Kuwait in 1990, and was invaded in 2003 by the US-led coalition. The details of these three wars have been studied in sixth chapter.

After the US invasion, violence has spread across Iraq. On June 28, 2004, the occupation was formally ended by the US-led coalition, which transferred power to an interim Iraqi government led by Prime Minister Iyad Allawi. On January 30, 2005 the legally disputed transitional parliamentary elections took place.

Developments in post-Saddam Iraq will not only affect its foreign relations, they will also significantly affect the foreign policy framework and even the fractious political system of its most geopolitically significant neighbour, Iran. Although Tehran and Baghdad have dominated the security picture of the Persian Gulf for more than 20 years, Iran and Iraq are not somehow destined to be rivals. Iraq to rebuild the country and end the existing violence needs Iran's cooperation more than any other states. On the other hand, a stable and safe neighbour helps to keep Iranian borders safer.

Despite severe tensions through the years, since the end of the Iran-Iraq War in 1988, these two countries have demonstrated the capacity to cooperate with one another. Nevertheless, several fundamental problems must be resolved before Tehran will view Iraq as a reliable neighbour.

With the spotlight now very much on the political contours and emerging structures of a post-Saddam regime in Iraq, the situation is opportune to explore Tehran's concerns and the methods available for addressing them, as well as the effects of the demise of the Baath regime on Iran's regional policy and the prospects for US-Iranian relations.

2.3.2. Territory

Spanning 434,128 sq. km, Iraq is the 58th largest country in the world.

Iraq is bounded in the north by Turkey, east by Iran, southeast by the Persian Gulf, south by Kuwait and Saudi Arabia, and west by Jordan and Syria. Iraq's land boundaries are 3,650 km; Iran 1,458 km, Jordan 181 km, Kuwait 240 km, Saudi Arabia 814 km, Syria 605 km, Turkey 352 km, and its coastline is 58 km. The capital is Baghdad. Baghdad, located in the centre of the country, lies in the transitional zone between north and south where the Tigris becomes navigable and large-scale irrigation possible. The capital city is a historical centre of trade and communication.

"Iraq is close to primary Middle Eastern petroleum sources and it has strategic location in Persian Gulf, through which much of the Western World's petroleum must transit to reach open seas."[20]

Map 2.4.: Iraq

Source: Greenwich Meantime

The present boundaries of Iraq, undefined until 1926, were drawn in the 20th century by European political and economic interests with little regard for indigenous demographic patterns. There is a tension between the Iraqi state, representing the central authority within its borders, and the Iraqi nation, a tribal society divided by religious schism. As Faisal, the first Hashemite king of Iraq lamented in the early 1930s: "I say in my heart full of sadness that there is not yet in Iraq, an Iraqi people."[21] This is the root argument of pan-Arabism in Iraqi politics.

The border with Iran has been a continuing source of conflict and was partially responsible for the outbreak of the war in 1980. In 1988, the boundary with Kuwait was another outstanding problem. It was fixed in a 1913 treaty between the Ottoman Empire and British officials acting on behalf of Kuwait's ruling family, which in 1899 had ceded control over foreign affairs to Britain. The boundary was accepted by Iraq when it became independent in 1932, but in the 1960s and again in the mid-1970s, the Iraqi government advanced a claim to parts of Kuwait.

Most geographers, including those of the Iraqi government, discuss the country's geography in terms of four main zones or regions:

1. The desert in the west and southwest; the desert zone, an area lying west and southwest of the Euphrates River, is a part of the Syrian Desert, which covers sections of Syria, Jordan and Saudi Arabia.
2. The rolling upland between the upper Tigris and Euphrates rivers (in Arabic the Dijlis and Furat, respectively); the uplands region, between the Tigris north of Samarra and the Euphrates north of Hit, is known as Al Jazirah (the island) and is part of a larger area that extends westward into Syria between the two rivers and into Turkey.
3. The highlands in the north and northeast; the north-eastern highlands begin just south of a line drawn from Mosul to Kirkuk and extend to the borders with Turkey and Iran. High ground, separated by broad, undulating steppes, gives way to mountains ranging from 1,000 to nearly 4,000 meters in height near the Iranian and Turkish borders.
4. The alluvial plain through which the Tigris and Euphrates flow.

2.3.2.1. Neutral Zone

To solve the border dispute between Iraq and Saudi Arabia, in 1922, British officials concluded the Treaty of Mohammara with Abdul Aziz Ibn Abdul Rahman Al Saud, who in 1932 formed the Kingdom of Saudi Arabia.

The treaty provided the basic agreement for the boundary between the eventually independent nations. No military or permanent buildings were to be built in or near the neutral zone and the nomads of both countries were to have unimpeded access to its pastures and wells.

In April 1975, an agreement signed in Baghdad fixed the borders of the countries. Despite a rumoured agreement providing for the formal division of the Iraq-Saudi Arabia Neutral Zone, as of early 1988 such a document had not been published. For unknown reasons the treaty was not filed with the United Nations and nobody outside Iraq and Saudi Arabia was notified of the change or shown maps with details of the new boundary.

Map 2.5.: Iraq-Saudi Arabia Neutral Zone in 1990

Source: Wikipedia

As the Gulf War approached in early 1991, Iraq cancelled all international agreements with Saudi Arabia since 1968. Saudi Arabia responded by registering all previous boundary agreements negotiated with Iraq at the United Nations in June 1991. Thus Saudi Arabia ended the legal existence of the Saudi-Iraqi neutral zone.

2.3.3. Population; Religious and Ethnic Groups

Iraqi population is 28,221,181 (April 2008 estimate). It ranks 39th populous country in the world. Arabic is the most spoken language. Kurdish, Iraqi Turkish and Syrian are spoken in the north, and English is the most spoken Western language.

2.3.3.1. Religion

Islam is the state religion; Iraq's Muslims follow two distinct traditions, Shiite and Sunni Islam. According to the CIA World Fact Book, Iraq comprises 97 percent Muslim population (Shiite 60 percent-65 percent, Sunni 32 percent-37 percent), but the constitution provides for freedom of religious belief and expression. The other 3 percent are Jews, Christians and of other religions. The question of religious demographics is controversial and some Iraqis who follow Sunni Islam dispute these figures, claiming that many reports only include Arab Sunnis as 'Sunni', missing out the Kurdish and Turkmen Sunnis.

Reported acts of violence conducted by independence activists and opponents of foreign domination steadily increased by the end of 2006. These attacks become predominately aimed at Iraqi collaborators rather than foreign occupation forces.

Violence was conducted by Sunni groups, nationalists and others who sought an Iraq freed from foreign rule that include the Iraq insurgency, which has been fighting since the initial US invasion of 2003. Also, criminal elements within Iraq's society seemed to perpetuate violence for their own means and ambitions.

Iraqi nationalist and Baathist elements who were part of the insurgency remained committed to expelling US forces and also seemed to attack Shia populations, presumably, due to the Shia parties' collaboration with Iran and the United States in making war against their own nation. In response to attacks like the one against the "Askari Mosque"[22], violent reprisals escalated. Shiite organizations associated with the American occupation forces within Iraq gained increasing power and influence in the collaborationist Iraqi government. Additionally, the militias, it appeared in late 2006, had the capability to act outside the scope of government. As a result, these powerful militias, it seemed as of late 2006, were leading reprisal acts of violence against the Sunni minority.

A cycle of violence, thus, ensued whereby Sunni insurgent or nationalist attacks followed with government and American backed reprisals, often in the form of Shiite death squads that sought out and killed Sunnis. Conflict between Shiite and Sunni Muslims in Iraq has turned into riots, tit-for-tat bombings, and violence throughout Iraq. Many commentators on the Iraq War began, by the end of 2006, to refer to this violent escalation as a civil war.

Due to US invasion and violence in Iraq, many Iraqi people have left their country. In November 2006, the United Nation High Commissioner for Refugees (UNHCR) estimated that 1.8 million Iraqis had been displaced to neighboring countries, with nearly 100,000 Iraqis fleeing to Syria and Jordan each month, while another 1.6 million were displaced internally.

In both 2006 and 2007, the average monthly death toll for civilians alone was over 2,000. "Iraq's government says that 355 Iraqis were killed in April 2009, making it the bloodiest month so far in 2009. The bulk of the deaths came from a number of big explosions, and the death count did not include at least 80 Iranian pilgrims killed in Iraq.

April 2009 was also the deadliest month for US troops since September 2008, with 18 soldiers killed. The casualties are nowhere near the 2006-07 levels when the insurgency and sectarian strife were at their peak."[23]

2.3.3.2. Ethnic Groups

Iraq is home to several ethnic groups, the most numerous being Arabs, followed by Kurds, Iraqi Turkmen and Assyrians. Other distinct groups are Armenians, Persians, Shabaks and Lurs. Arabs constitute about 75–80 percent of the total population of Iraq.

The Kurds, an Islamic non-Arab people, are the largest and most important minority group, constituting about 15–20 percent. A semi-nomadic pastoral people, the Kurds live in the north-eastern Zagros Mountains, mostly in isolated villages in the mountain valleys near Turkey and Iran. Kurdish opposition to Iraqi political dominance has occasioned violent clashes with government forces.

Most Kurds are Sunnis, although the Feyli Kurds (about 10 percent of Iraqi Kurds) are largely Shiite. Feyli Kurds live in Baghdad and the Diyala Province of Iraq around Khanaqin and Mandali. The roots of the Feyli go back to the Aryan immigrants of the first millennium BC, and more specifically, the Parthian Pahlavi/ Pahlavanid settlements of the 2nd century BC. They embraced Islam in the early stages of the Islamic conquest and colonization of Mesopotamia (Iraq) and Iran, though archaeological evidence from the Ilam Province in Iran indicates that a significant proportion of Feyli were Nestorian Christians until the 18th Century. When the Safavid dynasty (1507-1721) held sway over Persia, Feyli Kurds switched to the Shiite Gafarean doctrine under Persian influence. In modern times, the Feylis have been subject to state persecutions. They are considered as a stateless people, with both Iran and Iraq claiming they are citizens of the other country. In the mid 1970s, Iraq expelled around 40,000 Shiite Feyli Kurds who had lived for generations near Baghdad and Khanaqin, alleging that they were Iranian nationals.

2.3.4. Military Power

Iraqi security forces (ISF) are composed of forces serving under the Ministry of Interior (MOI) and the Ministry of Defence (MOD). MOD forces are the army, the air force and the navy. MOI forces are the police, the paramilitary national police and the border enforcement forces.

Geographically, the ISF are responsible for more than 70 percent of Iraq, including most populated areas. First, ISF will assume responsibility for counter-insurgency operations, with Coalition help in medical evacuations and logistics. In the next step, ISF will develop capacity to sustain themselves.

The Iran–Iraq War ended with Iraq fielding the world's 4th largest military, with more than 70 "army divisions."[24] Losses during the Gulf War from the United Nations coalition resulted in the reduction of Iraq's ground forces to 23 divisions. Military and economic sanctions prevented Iraq from rebuilding its military power. As of November 2007, all of the original ten Iraqi Army divisions have been transferred to an all-Iraqi chain of command.

The Iraqi military was disbanded and the Iraqi Ministry of Defence was dissolved shortly after the toppling of the Saddam Hussein regime in 2003 by Coalition Provisional Authority's (CPA) order in May 23rd, 2003.

On June 28th, 2004, the CPA transferred power to a sovereign Iraqi interim government, the CPA officially dissolved, and Iraq's transitional period began. Under Iraq's transitional law, the transitional period covers the interim government phase and the transitional government period, which was scheduled to end by December 31st, 2005. After the dissolution of the Coalition Provisional Authority, the Coalition stayed in country at the request of the Iraqi government and under a UN Mandate to help the fledgling government develop its security forces and fight insurgency.

Developing host-nation security forces is a cornerstone of the United States Counter-Insurgency (COIN) doctrine. In the end of 2004, the insurgency was mainly directed against the occupation and it was believed that if the Coalition would reduce its presence then the insurgency would diminish. Military planners had hoped that national elections would change the perception of being under occupation, stabilize the situation and allow the Coalition to reduce its presence. After national elections in December 2005, however, the insurgency shifted focus from a resistance against the occupation towards sectarian conflict. Accelerated by the Golden (Al Askari) mosque bombing in February 2006, the levels of sectarian violence rose dramatically and the security situation deteriorated.

The Iraqi army is described as the most important element of the counter-insurgency fight. The force generation plan as of March 2008 includes 13 divisions. The tactic is to provide security and other services on a local level by using infantrymen on dismounted patrols. As insurgents lose the passive or active support from the local population, they will easily be defeated, it is believed.

2.3.4.1. The Multi-National Force - Iraq (MNF-I)

The Multi-National Force- Iraq is a military command, led by the United States that is fighting the Iraq War against Iraqi insurgents or resistance forces. The MNF objectives, as at June 2004 and as expressed in an annex to United Nations Security Council Resolution (UNSCR) 1546, a letter from US Secretary of State Powell to the UN Security Council, appear to be:

"The MNF under unified command is prepared to continue to contribute to the maintenance of security in Iraq, including by preventing and deterring terrorism and protecting the territory of Iraq. The goal of the MNF will be to help the Iraqi people to complete the political transition and will permit the United Nations and the international community to work to facilitate Iraq's reconstruction."[25]

Briefly, one mission objective for the MNF-I is an 'Iraq that has a security force that can maintain domestic order and deny Iraq as a safe haven for terrorists'. The strategy to achieve this is basically to train and equip Iraqi Security Forces and gradually transition security responsibilities to the ISF.

"On February 27th, 2009, the President of the United States announced a plan to commence a phased pullback of US Forces from Iraq with a change of mission to occur by August 31, 2010. Additionally, the Multi-National Forces- Iraq (MNF-I) Commander has judged that the Iraqi Security Forces (ISF) are ready to accept responsibility for the security of Iraq's cities by June 30, 2009."[26]

2.3.5. Economy

According to the CIA World Fact Book, June 2009, Iraq's economy is dominated by the petroleum sector, which has traditionally provided about 95 percent of foreign exchange earnings.

In the 1980s, financial problems caused by massive expenditures in the eight-year war with Iran and damage to oil export facilities by Iran led the government to implement austerity measures, borrow heavily, and later reschedule foreign debt payments; "Iraq suffered economic losses of at least US$ 80 billion from the war."[27] After the end of hostilities in 1988, oil exports gradually increased with the construction of new pipelines and restoration of damaged facilities.

Iraq's seizure of Kuwait in August 1990, subsequent international economic sanctions, and damage from military action by an international coalition beginning in January 1991 drastically reduced economic activity. The government's policies of supporting large military and internal security forces and of allocating resources to key supporters of the regime have exacerbated shortages. The implementation of the UN's Oil for Food program in December 1996 has helped improve economic conditions. For the first six six-month phases of the program, Iraq was allowed to export limited amounts of oil in exchange for food, medicine, and other humanitarian goods. In December 1999, the UN Security Council authorized Iraq to export as much oil as required to meet humanitarian needs.

Iraqi economy was adversely affected by four major factors: the war with Iran during the 1980s, an international oil glut in the 1980s and 1990s, the economic sanctions imposed by the United Nations (UN) after the invasion of Kuwait in 1990, and the Persian Gulf War in 1991. The combined effect of all these factors was the destruction of Iraq's basic infrastructure (roads, bridges, power grids, and the like) and the country's financial bankruptcy. It is difficult to imagine any regime surviving intact through turmoil such as that experienced by Iraq over the past three decades.

In 1980, Iraq was a net creditor and considered home to one of the region's most advanced economies. By early March 2003, as US and British forces amassed on its southern border, it had become one of the world's poorest and most underdeveloped countries. "Average annual income had fallen from between US$ 3,600 and US$ 4,000 in 1980 to between US$ 500 and US$ 600 by the end of 2003."[28]

Inevitably, as the ability and willingness of state officials to govern economic life through formal channels dissipated, new configurations of regulatory power arose to take their place. These configurations were not necessarily congruent with, or contained within, Iraq's borders. Transnational tribal allegiances were mobilized to facilitate and regulate trade across international borders. Businessmen-politicians in neighbouring countries cultivated links with members of Iraq's Republican Guard (among others) in order to facilitate and protect networks of transport and distribution. And small-time trade networks emerged to profit from differentials between Iraq and its neighbours in prices for petroleum and other products. Major multinational corporations also took advantage of the multiple jurisdictions. A case in point is that of RJ Reynolds, whose involvement in cigarette smuggling to Iraq was the subject of European Union legal action in 2002; RJR knowingly sold billions of cigarettes to Iraq in violation of US and United Nations sanctions, by setting up a special operation in Cyprus. Part of the plan included creating false paperwork that would misstate the destination of the cigarettes, usually listing Russia instead.

Decreasing insurgent attacks and an improving security environment in many parts of the country are helping to spur economic activity. Total government revenues have benefited from high oil prices in recent years; however, revenues have declined significantly since the oil price drop in fall 2008.

According to the CIA World Fact Book, June 2009, the International Compact with Iraq, chaired by the Government of the Republic of Iraq and the United Nations with the support of the World Bank, was established in May 2007 to integrate Iraq into the regional and global economy, and the Iraqi government is seeking to pass laws to strengthen its economy. This legislation includes a hydrocarbon law to establish a modern legal framework to allow Iraq to develop its resources and a revenue sharing law to equitably divide oil revenues within the nation, although both are still under contentious political negotiation. Some foreign entities have expressed interest in reinvigorating Iraq's industrial sector.

The government of Iraq is pursuing a strategy to gain foreign participation in joint ventures with State-owned enterprises.

2.3.6. Natural Resources

Iraq's oil fields are located in two main regions; 65 percent or more Iraq's proven reserves are concentrated largely in southern Iraq, particularly in the southernmost province of Basra, and significant proven oil resources are also located in the northern governorate of Al Tamim near the disputed city of Kirkuk.

The atmosphere of violence and unresolved political tension prevailing in Iraq threatens the produce and export of oil, which forms a huge amount of the government's revenues.

The sovereign control of Iraq's oil resources and revenues remains a subject of intense scrutiny, debate, and sensitivity in Iraq.

Iraq started the nationalization of its oil resources and completed that, in 1975, and oil exploration, production, and exports were managed subsequently by state-run entities that employed thousands of Iraqis. Given the effects of war, sanctions, and mismanagement of the country's oil infrastructure since 1980, many energy experts believe Iraq will need significant infusions of investment, technology, and expertise in order to rehabilitate and eventually expand its oil production capacity in line with the current government's plans. Iraq's own oil revenues may provide a significant resource base for such investment and for attracting technology and expertise.

Political differences continue between the Shiite-led central government and the Kurdistan Regional Government (KRG) over federal and regional oil-related decision-making powers.

On October 2, 2007, "the KRG announced it had signed four additional production sharing agreement contracts with subsidiaries of French and Canadian companies."[29]

Some analysts believe that the Kurdish moves signal the KRG's intention to begin large scale oil development activities regardless of progress on federal legislation. The KRG opposes proposals to require federal approval of its existing or future contracts.

Al Basrah governorate holds most of Iraq's proven oil resources and, as such, local political actors exert influence over the hydrocarbon sector.

Press reports suggest that "competition between local politicians, militia groups, union members, and federal ministry representatives is fuelling conflict that has intensified since mid-2007."[30]

Iraqi attitudes on the future of the country's oil industry are shaped by a number of factors, including geography, ethnicity, political ideology, and party affiliation.

Sectarian identity politics undoubtedly is one important factor, particularly with regard to the concerns of some members of the minority Sunni Arab community who fear exclusion from decision-making bodies and inadequate revenue sharing.

Besides history, Iraqi politics is influenced by its location and geography, climate and the availability of water, which in many ways is more critical than oil. It is endowed with large quantities of water, supplied by its two main rivers; the Tigris and the Euphrates, and their tributaries. The scarcity of water in the Middle East, heightened by rapid urbanization and industrialization, has placed more importance on Iraq's two rivers, the Tigris and the Euphrates. Even with the ascendance of oil as a source of wealth, agriculture relying on renewable water remains the main source of employment. These factors have influenced settlement patterns, tribalism, resource utilization and the development of diverse regional economics.

2.4. Geopolitics of Kuwait

2.4.1. History

Kuwait is a tiny but incredibly wealthy Arab Kingdom that has been ruled for almost 250 years by a single family, the Al Sabah.

The area around Kuwait has been settled for thousands of years. Military and commercial activities by various Mesopotamian empires passed through Kuwait. Kuwait is part of the civilization created on Dilmun, in present-day Bahrain. In 1650, drought forced Bedouin families, later known Bani Utab, to migrate from Najd in Central Arabia. The ruling family, Al Sabah was among the immigrants.

Al Sabah family settled in Kuwait in 1710. Sabah Bin Jaber elected Sheikh of Kuwait in 1756 and founded the Al Sabah dynasty. During that time Kuwait was a vassal state to the Ottoman Empire. The Ottoman Empire recognized Mubarak the Great, sheikh and ruler of Kuwait, as the provincial sub-governor of Kuwait in 1897. Mubarak al-Sabah signed an agreement with Britain, making Kuwait a protectorate of the British Empire in 1899. Britain gained control over Kuwait's foreign and defence affairs and in return protected Kuwait and allowed the Sabah to rule over internal affairs.

Arguably, Kuwait, the most independent of the Persian Gulf nations, spent most of the 20th century as a protectorate of Great Britain before turning to the USA in recent decades for additional defence security. Kuwait became an independent Emirate in June 19, 1961.

Iraq, which had long claimed that Kuwait was part of southern Iraq, argued that Kuwait had been separated from it illegitimately. The first Iraqi claim to Kuwait surfaced in 1938; the year oil was discovered in the emirate. After being pressurised by Arab countries and Britain, Iraq eventually retracted from its claim. In 1990, relations with Iraq worsened. Iraq accused Kuwait of exceeding OPEC production quotas for oil and "stealing" more than $2 billion in oil from a contested reserve that lay beneath both countries. Iraq also demanded Kuwait cancel the debt Iraq owed from the Iran-Iraq War.

On August 2, 1990, Iraq invaded Kuwait and quickly overwhelmed Kuwaiti forces. An international force assembled in neighbouring Saudi Arabia and evicted Iraq from Kuwait after six weeks of fighting in early 1991. The survival of the Baath regime of Hussein in Iraq spawned an ambient fear among Kuwaitis of a repeat of the events of 1990–91.

A tense standoff atmosphere prevailed, exacerbated by Iraqi troop movements along the border, until 2003, when USA and British forces launched an invasion of Iraq, largely from bases inside Kuwait. The fall of the Baath regime in the Iraq War was greeted with great relief in Kuwait, which offered critical logistic support to the United States and its allies. However, the subsequent occupation of Iraq (and the attraction of some Kuwaitis to the guerrilla insurgency that it produced) led to new political tensions.

2.4.2. Territory

Occupying 17,818 square kilometres, Kuwait is 157th largest country in the world. Kuwait is one of the world's smallest countries. Kuwait city, the political capital and economic heart of the nation, is also the only major metropolitan area of the country. In size, Kuwait is often compared to the state of New Jersey of the United States. Pure size is hardly an adequate measure of modern Kuwait's geostrategic importance, either regionally or throughout the world, but the importance is that what is laid beneath this small state, which is huge amount of oil.

Kuwait's physical location is the first key to its importance in today's volatile world. Located in the heart of the Middle East, Kuwait is strategically positioned at the head, or north-west corner, of the Persian Gulf. Kuwait is bounded in the east by the Persian Gulf, north and west by Iraq and southwest by Saudi Arabia. "In 1992-93 the UN Boundary Commission redefined Kuwait's border with Iraq, moving it slightly northwards in conformity with an agreement of 1932."[31]

Kuwait's land boundaries are 462 km; Iraq 240 km, Saudi Arabia 222 km and its coastline is 499 km. Kuwait's land and ocean boundaries have always been a matter of contention. In the aftermath of the two recent Gulf Wars, those borders have begun to become finalized. One of these disputes was between Kuwait, Saudi Arabia and Iran on the Dorra gas field, of which largest part is located on the Saudi-Kuwaiti common maritime border, while a part of it is disputed by neighbouring Iran.

"Kuwait and Saudi Arabia discussed joint oil operations in their shared border areas, including the Dorra gas field"[32], Kuwait's Energy Ministry Under Secretary, Issa al-Oun said on January 4, 2004. "We will outline future operations in the areas and discuss potential operators, in addition to legal matters; the border issue of

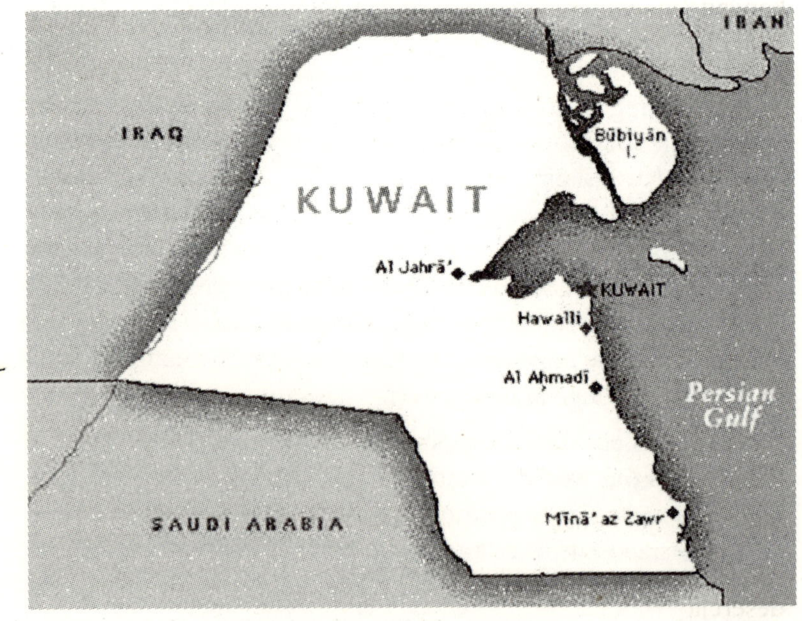

Map 2.6.: Kuwait

Source: Greenwich Meantime

the field (with Saudis) was discussed in the past. Now, we will talk about the issue of operations. We will be talking about the distant future," he added.

A part of Dorra gas field is also disputed by neighbouring Iran and has been an area of contention between Tehran and Kuwait since the 1960s. "I hope we can find a solution to this issue as soon as possible,"[33] Kuwait's Foreign Minister Sheikh Mohammad al-Salem al-Sabah said on January 15, 2008. State-owned Kuwait Petroleum Corporation called for the rapid development of the Dorra field, as the Gulf Arab state struggles to meet demand from power stations for gas, in July 2007.

Offshore, nine islands add to the nation's limited land area, though most of these islands are either uninhabitable- with the exception of Failaka Island which is located near the entrance of Kuwait Bay and has been populated since prehistoric times - or insignificant in size. The ownership of several of these islands is disputed, as Iraq, Iran and Saudi Arabia also contend for the potential prize of oil that might be existing under these islands. Even today, the Kuwaiti Coast Guard and Naval Force must aggressively patrol these waters to prevent squatters from other nations, sometimes state sponsored, from staking their claims to a Kuwaiti islet.

Bubiyan Island with an area of 860 square kilometres, the largest of Kuwait's nine islands, now is connected to the mainland by a wide bridge 2380 metres long. Since the Gulf War, this large island, that was once home to thousands of Kuwaitis, has been reserved exclusively for military purposes.

2.4.3. Population; Religious and Ethnic Groups

In not-too-distant past, the people of Kuwait were primarily desert nomads. Less than a century ago, the people of Kuwait were among this planet's poorest by almost any standards. Nowadays, the citizens of Kuwait collectively probably hold more economic power per capita than almost any other society in existence.

According to the Kuwait's Central Statistical Office, the population of Kuwait was estimated at 33,28,136 persons, in June 30, 2008. It is 136th most populous country in the world.

The native and official language is Arabic, fluency in which is a requirement for naturalization. Kuwaitis speak a dialect of Gulf Arabic, and Modern Standard Arabic is taught in schools. English is the second language taught in public schools. Hindi, Urdu, Persian (Farsi), and other languages also are widely spoken among the foreign population.

2.4.3.1. Religion

Kuwaiti citizens are almost entirely Muslim, and a law passed in 1981 limits citizenship to Muslims. The majority are Sunni, but about one-third are Shiite. Both the Islamic revolution of Iran in 1979 and the Kuwaiti government's subsequent discrimination against Shiites fostered a heightened sense of community among the country's Shiite population in the 1980s and 1990s, and this led to political tension between the two groups. The Shias have not possessed a fair share in neither the parliament nor the government cabinet. Presently, only one Shia minister sits on the 16-member cabinet, and only five Shia are among the parliament's 50 members.

Despite the veneer of Western practices, since the Gulf War Kuwait has become a more conservative Islamic society. Islamists constitute a third of the parliament, pushing the government to impose gender segregation and education reforms. Though the US saved Kuwait from Saddam Hussein's grip in 1991, anti-Americanism has been on the rise in recent years. Some of the country's leading charities have been linked to terrorism; a small group of Kuwaitis travelled to Afghanistan to join the Taliban and small minority of the anti-American conservatives have even turned to violence.

It is worthy to mention that thousands of foreigners, primarily Shiites, were expelled from Kuwait in 1985 to quell internal unrest. Airplane hijackings, explosions, car bombings, and an assassination attempt against the Amir ensued. Kuwait steadfastly rejected demands for release of terrorists in its custody, most of who were still in jail at the time of the Iraqi invasion and subsequently disappeared. A number of Kuwaiti Shiites were sentenced for setting fires at oil installations in 1986 and 1987. The attacks declined in 1988, and no attack was recorded in 1989 or 1990. Kuwait's support for Iraq in the Iran-Iraq War accounted for much of the violence that disturbed internal stability during the 1980s. A series of terrorist bombings in 1983 aimed at Kuwaiti installations and the United States and French embassies were ascribed to Iranian retaliation. A network of Hezbollah terrorists was uncovered, and, in the spring of 1984, seventeen Shiites were sentenced to long prison terms, and three were condemned to death.

2.4.3.2. Ethnic Groups

Kuwait's population includes ethnic groups as follows: Kuwaiti 45 percent, other Arab 35 percent, South Asian 9 percent, Iranian 4 percent and others 7 percent. Arabs; either Bedouin, sedentary or descendants of immigrants from elsewhere in the region, constitute the largest ethnic group, and a small number of ethnic Persians have resided in the country for centuries.

Kuwait is a destination country for men and women who migrate legally formerly from other Arab states but now largely from South and Southeast Asia for domestic or low-skill labour, but are subject to conditions of involuntary servitude by employers in Kuwait including conditions of physical and sexual abuse, non-payment of wages and withholding of passports to restrict their freedom of movement. These migrants may threaten Kuwait's internal security.

Palestinian workers presented problems for the Al Sabah rulers for several decades, but during the 1980s, militants and terrorists advancing the new brand of Islamism overshadowed the Palestinians as troublemakers.

Many of the domestic strains in Kuwait arise from the disparities between the living standards of Kuwaiti nationals and the majority of Kuwait's foreign population. The non-nationals do not enjoy citizenship rights, economic or political, which are reserved for Kuwaiti citizens, defined as those able to prove Kuwaiti ancestry prior to 1920.

Despite a government policy to reduce the number of foreign workers following the Iraqi invasion in 1990, Kuwaitis remain a minority in their own country. The government rarely grants citizenship to foreigners to maintain status quo.

"In October 2002, two Kuwaiti gunmen suspected of having ties to Osama bin Laden's al-Qaeda terrorist network carried out an attack against US troops on Failaka Island, killing one Marine and injuring another."[34]

2.4.4. Military Power

Kuwait's Military branches are Land Forces, Kuwaiti Navy, Kuwaiti Air Force and National Guard. Under the constitution, the Emir of Kuwait is the supreme commander of the armed forces with a Minister of Defence who directs the Military of Kuwait through the Chief of the General Staff. The National Guard has its own commander, who reports directly to the minister of defence. Minimum 18 years of age is required for compulsory and voluntary military service; reserve obligation is up to age 40 with 1 month annual training. Kuwaiti males are required to serve two years in the armed forces.

Kuwait's military expenditure per capita is among the highest in the world. Such spending is largely a result of the hostile relationship with Iraq; after the Persian Gulf War, Kuwait undertook significant measures to modernize and increase its armed forces. US troops have been stationed there since the early 1990s. Before the Persian Gulf War, Kuwait maintained a small military force whose equipment was supplied by the United Kingdom and the United States. Apart from the few units that were able to escape to Saudi Arabia, including a majority of the air force, all of this equipment was either destroyed or taken by the Iraqis. Much of the property that was returned by Iraq after the Persian Gulf War was damaged beyond repair.

Since the war, Kuwait, with the help of the United States and other allies, has made significant efforts to increase the size and modernity of its armed forces. These efforts are succeeding. In September 1991, the USA signed a ten-year agreement with Kuwait to store equipment, use ports and carry out joint training exercises, which has been renewed for ten more years in 2001. The agreement did not officially provide for the stationing of United States service personnel in Kuwait as the 1,500 US personnel remaining after the Gulf War were scheduled to leave within a few months. The government also continues to improve defence arrangements with other Arab states, as well as UN Security Council members, including Russia, the United Kingdom, and France.

2.4.5. Economy

Kuwait has a small, rich and relatively open economy. Kuwait is one of the world's richest countries per capita, making it "the third richest country in the world."[35]

"In December 2007, the Kuwaiti Dinar was the highest valued currency unit in the world."[36]

Virtually all of Kuwait's wealth is derived directly or indirectly, by way of overseas investments, from petroleum extraction and processing. The most dramatic element of Kuwait's economic development has been the steady and rapid expansion of its oil industry since the 1970s. However, both the Iraqi invasion which nearly exhausted Kuwait's overseas investment revenues; the expenses of the Iraqi invasion and post-war reconstruction placed a heavy economic burden on the country, and the increasing volatility of the global oil market in the 1980s reduced this income substantially, but income levels rebounded when oil prices rose dramatically in the early 21st century.

Kuwait experienced rapid economic growth over the last several years on the back of high oil prices and in 2008 posted its tenth consecutive budget surplus. High oil prices in recent years have resulted in large budget surpluses in 2005-2008. As a result of this positive fiscal situation, the need for economic reforms was less urgent and the government did not push through new initiatives. Non-oil sectors such as banking, financial services, logistics, telecommunications and construction have enjoyed strong growth in the past three to four years. The drop in oil prices in late 2008 reduced Kuwait's fiscal surplus in 2009.

The global financial crisis affected Kuwait in late 2008, with the Kuwait Stock Exchange; the region's second-largest bourse, losing almost 40 percent of its market capitalization during 2008. The global financial crisis may slow the pace of investment and development projects, but Kuwait has vowed to use its considerable financial resources to stabilize the economy if necessary.

"Falling oil prices and production and the global financial crisis would cause the Kuwait economy to shrink."[37] Sami Alanbaee, manager of the Central Bank of Kuwait's economic research department said. Alanbaee predicted inflation levels of 5-6 percent in 2009-2010, down from 11.6 percent in 2008-2009. "I expect the economy to shrink by 3.4-4 percent over the coming year". Alanbaee added. He attributed the fall in these key economic indicators to the global financial crisis and its impact on prices and demand for oil alongside Kuwait's commitment to cut its oil production by about 10 percent from 2008 levels in line with OPEC production quotas. "The negative growth is in the oil sector but the non-oil sector in real terms will see very modest growth of around 2.5 percent.", he added.

2.4.6. Natural Resources

Kuwait is synonymous with oil and has been named; Oil Well. Certainly one can not understand modern-day Kuwait without first recognizing Kuwait's key niche in the oil industry, which drives the world's economies.

Beginning with the 20th century, Kuwait's vast petroleum reserves brought equally vast economic clout to this small desert country. Unfortunately, that same oil wealth also made Kuwait the financial envy of much of the world, especially of its large neighbour, Iraq.

Kuwait also has considerable natural gas reserves, almost all in the form of associated gas; the gas that is produced together with crude oil.

Although Kuwait is sometimes noted as "the only nation in the world without a lake"[38], fresh water has been discovered underground to the west side of the country. A smaller aquifer was located deep underground to the south, as well, but the water it provides is extremely brackish and requires expensive distillation processing. These two aquifers, although insufficient for wide-spread agricultural irrigation, are nonetheless vital to adequately addressing Kuwait's drinking water needs and other commercial requirements. Prior to the discovery, much of Kuwait's water had to be imported.

For fresh water in earlier days, people depended on a few artesian wells and on rainwater collected from the roofs of houses or from cisterns at ground level. Dhows piloted by Kuwaiti seamen also brought fresh water from the Shatt al-Arab near Al Basra, Iraq. With the rapid growth of population, however, the government of Kuwait built desalination plants at Kuwait city, Al Shuaybah, and several other locations. Important sources of fresh water have been discovered at Al Rawthatayn and Al Shiqaya, but desalination still provides the great bulk of Kuwait's daily consumption of potable water.

2.5. Geopolitics of Oman

2.5.1. History

The history of Oman goes back a very long way. Oman's history begins in the early 3rd or late 4th millennium BC, with the rise of a society that had cultural and trade ties to ancient Mesopotamia. Between the 4th century BC and the 7th century AD the area was dominated by successive Persian empires.

"In the first century AD, Arab tribes began to migrate into Oman and, when it accepted Islam just before the Prophet Muhammad died in 632 AD, Persian rule ended and Oman's Arab character was firmly established."[39]

In the 9th century, maritime trade flourished Sohar became the greatest sea port in the Islamic world. In the early 16th century the Portuguese occupied Muscat. Portuguese ousted by Sultan bin Saif, a powerful Yaaruba leader in 1650.

The Yaaruba dynasty introduced a period of renaissance in Omani fortunes both at home and abroad, uniting the country and bringing prosperity; but, on the death of Sultan bin Saif ll, civil war broke out over the election of his successor. Persian troops occupied Muttrah and Muscat but failed to take Sohar which was defended by Ahmad bin Said, who expelled the Persians from Oman after the civil war had ended.

In 1744, independent Sultanate of Muscat and Oman was established by Ahmad bin Said, founder of the Al Bu Said dynasty that still rules Oman.

In first half of 19th century Muscat and Oman was the most powerful state in Arabian Peninsula; ruling Zanzibar until 1861.

Not being a formal colony or protectorate, Britain's involvement with Oman was a very subtle one, but nonetheless powerful for all that. A combination of a political consul at the Omani court in Muscat and the presence of the Royal Navy based in Bushire and ships constantly traversing between Europe and India, meant that effective political control was never seriously doubted. British help was crucial in suppressing repeated revolts by Muslim fundamentalists in the interior.

Oman remained largely isolated from the rest of the world until 1970 when Said bin Taimur was deposed by his son, Qabus in a bloodless coup. The sultanate of Oman has been the nation's name since the beginning of Sultan Qabus' reign (he changed it from Muscat and Oman into the Sultanate of Oman in 1970).

During the early 1970s relations between Oman and the neighbouring People's Democratic Republic of Yemen (PDRY)[40] deteriorated, following a separatist revolt and conflict in Dhofar Province with a guerrilla organization, known from 1974 as the People's Front for the Liberation of Oman (PFLO), which the PDRY supported.

With the help of British, Jordanian and Iranian troops, Qabus crushed the PFLO by 1975. Although, a ceasefire was mediated by Saudi Arabia in March 1976, the situation remained tense. Oman's acceptance of US assistance in defence aroused protests from the PDRY in 1981, but mediation by other Gulf States led to a 'normalization' agreement in 1982 and diplomatic relations between Oman and the PDRY were resumed in 1983.

In October 1988, Oman and the PDRY signed an agreement to increase co-operation in the areas of trade and communication, and in February 1990, the two countries reached an agreement to delineate their common border. Since 1975, Oman has been politically stable and has grown significantly economically and Sultan Qabus has ruled in unashamedly royal style. He uses the modern trappings of a cabinet of ministers, but reserves for himself the portfolios of prime minister, foreign minister, finance minister and minister of defence.

The Iranian revolution of 1979 and the Iran-Iraq War (1980-88) led to increased international awareness of Oman's strategic importance, particularly regarding the Strait of Hormuz, a narrow waterway at the mouth of the Persian Gulf, between Oman and Iran. Ironically, while itself being free of the constraints of the Strait of Hormuz, the tip of the Musandam Peninsula is within Omani territory and thus Oman with Iran exercises control over the chokepoint.

Briefly, in the recent past, there have been three key disputes. The first two, over Buraimi oasis (1952) and over the possible independent state claimed by the Imam in Nizwa (1957-59), occurred before the coup which began the reign of Sultan Qabus. Until that time, the state was effectively medieval, but Sultan Qabus immediately began modernization. Oman was admitted in United

Nations in 1971. However, until 1976, a third dispute, with the People's Democratic Republic of Yemen (former South Yemen), dominated events.

Oman's independence has been demonstrated by a lack of involvement in many Arabian issues, continuing close links with Iran and its willingness to host the US Rapid Deployment Force. As a result of its partial detachment from Arabian affairs, Oman has enjoyed support from most important sources, regionally and globally. There have been traditional close links with the UK, which was responsible for training the military and relations with the USA are close.

Oman played key role in establishment of six-member Gulf Cooperation Council in 1981. A Memorandum of Understanding with UK was signed in 1982, providing for regular consultation on international issues. In 1991, Oman joined US-led coalition opposing Iraq's occupation of Kuwait. Sultan Qabus formally defined Oman as a hereditary and absolute monarchy in 1996.

The United States has maintained relations with the Sultanate since the early years of American independence. A treaty of friendship and navigation, one of the first agreements of its kind with an Arab state, was concluded between the United States and Muscat in 1833. According to Professor Kechichian, a renowned historian and political scientist specializing on the Persian Gulf region, Oman has a unique foreign policy. "Today's Oman is internally stable, economically prosperous, and established as a nation integral to foreign relations in the Middle East and the world."[41]

2.5.2. Territory

The area of Oman is 3,09,500 square kilometres, "2.6 percent of the Middle East."[42] It is a medium-sized state and ranks 84th largest country in the world and the second-largest country after

Saudi Arabia on the Arabian Peninsula. Comparatively, the area occupied by Oman is slightly smaller than the state of Kansas of the United State.

Situated at the southeast corner of the Arabian Peninsula, Oman is bounded in the northeast by the Gulf of Oman and southeast by the Arabian Sea, southwest by Yemen and northwest by Saudi Arabia and the United Arab Emirates. Oman's land boundaries are 1,374 km; Saudi Arabia 676 km, UAE 410 km, Yemen 288 km. An agreement of 1992 completed the demarcation of the border with Yemen, and an agreement of March 1990 finalized the border with Saudi Arabia. The capital is Muscat.

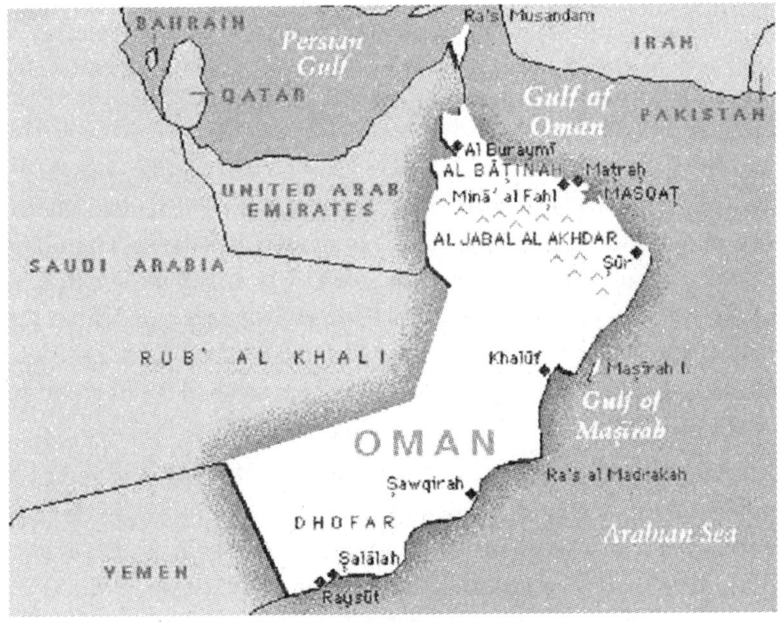

Map 2.7.: Oman

Source: Greenwich Meantime

With a coastline of 1,700 km from the Strait of Hormuz in the north to the borders of the Republic of Yemen, the Sultanate occupies a highly strategic position in the region. Like Yemen to the southwest, the territory of Oman has always benefited from its fine trading position at the southern extremity of the Arabian Peninsula. From here, merchants, without needing to sail far from land, can make easy contact with Persia to the north, India to the east and Africa to the south. This stretch of coast, together with that of Muscat just round the corner, is valuable territory. It comprises coastal plains in the north and south, separated from the interior desert by high mountain ranges.

Internally, the country is effectively split into two or even three units by the terrain. The coastal strip and Muscat are divided from Nizwa by a high mountain range and Nizwa is separated from Salalah and the Dhofar in the south by desert.

Oman's territory includes an enclave and an exclave; Musandam and Madha. As these two parts are geopolitically important, they have been described separately, as follows:

2.5.2.1. Musandam

The Musandam Peninsula has an area of 1,800 square kilometers and a population of 28,727 people. It is the northernmost part of Oman jutting out into the Strait of Hormuz at the entrance to the Persian Gulf. Musandam Peninsula is separated from the rest of the country by the territory of the United Arab Emirates (UAE). Governorate of Musandant is distinguished for its strategic location, with part of it known as Ras Musandam.

It is worth noting that not the whole of the Strait is good for navigation and the part which is suitable for sea navigation falls within the territorial waters of the Sultanate, which made Omanis shoulder a huge responsibility in organizing navigation in this Strait since the old ages. At its nearest point, Musandam is just 55 km from Iran across the strait.

Musandam more or less begins where the mountains rise from the plains of Ras al Khaimah. The mountains have isolated communities for centuries.

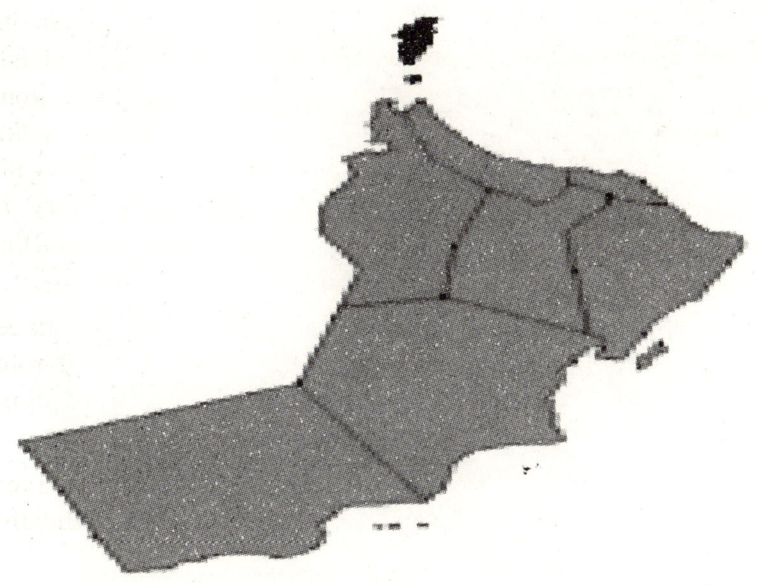

Map 2.8.: Musandam Peninsula of Oman

Source: Wikipedia

Musandam Peninsula is shown by red colour.

Connectivity has traditionally been a problem for the region; it could earlier be accessed only by a weekly flight or by a ten hour drive that also involved passing through four immigration posts. But this has greatly improved since August 2008 "with the world's fastest passenger ferry service between Muscat and the peninsula."[43]

2.5.2.2. Madha

The Omani territory of Wadi-e-Madhah (Madha Valley) is a wholly Omani exclave within UAE, surrounded by the United Arab Emirates, halfway between the Musandem Peninsula and the rest of Oman.

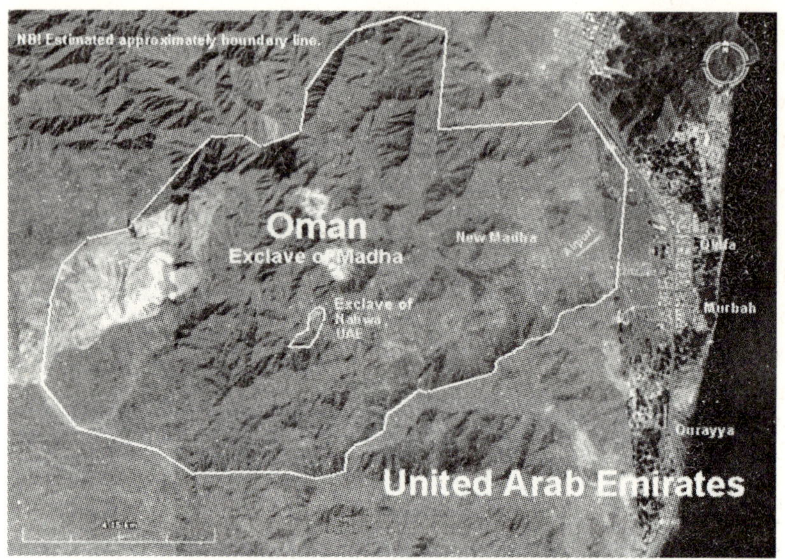

Map 2.9.: Madha Exclave of Oman and Nahwa Exclave of UAE

Source: Jan Krogh's Geosite/ Oman

The north-east corner of Madha is closest to the Fujairah- Khor-Fakkan road in the Emirate of Sharjah. It covers approximately 75 square km. The boundary was settled in 1969. There is also a Royal Oman Police patrol.

The Omani exclave of Madha is quite big but mostly empty, belonging to the Musandam territory of Oman further north. The only big development, the city of New Madha, is a very calm and quiet place. There are several villages outside New Madha if one continues the roads further into the exclave. There is no border control entering Madha. There are two roads leading to Madha, both from the United Arab Emirate of Fujairah. One reaches New Madha from the north, and the other from the east.

Interestingly, mobile phone switches from UAE-providers to Oman Mobile; clearly stating that it is a different country.

There is an exclave of UAE wholly within Madha called Nahwa. It legally belongs to Emirate of Sharjah.According to the

World Fact Book, 2007, Oman has signed a boundary agreement and ratified with UAE in 2003 for entire border, including Oman's Musandam Peninsula and Al Madha exclave, but details of the alignment have not been made public.

2.5.3. Population; Religious and Ethnic Groups

According to US Department of State's Background Note of July 2007, estimated Oman population was 32,04,897 including 5,77,293 non-nationals, and ranks 137th populous country in the world. Arabic is the official language; English, Baluchi, and Urdu are also spoken.

2.5.3.1. Religion

Islam is the official religion of the country. According to the CIA World Fact Book (2004), 75 percent of the Omani population is Ibadi while the remaining 25 percent is Sunni, Shiite, or Hindu. This suggests that while Oman is not a democracy, Sultan Qabus, the King of Oman, hails from the majority community within Oman. Further, Oman is the only Muslim country where the rulers have traditionally been Ibadis.

As is well known, Islam has two main branches: Sunni and Shiite. Oman, though, is one of the few Muslim countries where adherents of a third branch, Ibadism, are prevalent.

Ibadism is the only extant branch of Kharijsm, Islam's earliest schism. Ibadism is conservative, but tolerant of other forms of Islam. A traditional belief of the Ibadis is that their Imam should be the most worthy person of the Ibadi community, that he was to be chosen by the community's notables, and that he could be removed from office if he proved himself unworthy of it. The Ibadi branch of Islam, a moderate Kharijite group, claims the most adherents. In belief and ritual, Ibadism is close to Sunni Islam (the major branch of Islam), differing in its emphasis on an elected, rather than a hereditary imam as spiritual and temporal leader of the Ibadi community.

Sunnis elsewhere, especially in Saudi Arabia, have an extremely negative view of Ibadism. It is not clear whether the Sunnis of Oman share this view. It is highly probable, though, that the majority Sunnis resent being ruled by the Ibadi minority. One account of the arrest in 1994 of hundreds of regime's opponents said that most of them were Sunni Muslim, suggesting the presence of just such resentment in this community.

2.5.3.2. Ethnic Groups

More than half of Oman's population is Arab. However, large numbers of ethnic Baluch, who migrated to Oman from Iran and Pakistan over the past several centuries, live near the coast in Al-Bathina. There are also minorities of South Asians, East Africans and migrant workers of varied ethnicities.

The Muscat-Mataran urban area has long been home to significant numbers of ethnic Persians and to merchants of South Asian ancestry, some of whom also live along Al-Baminah. Notable among the latter are the Liwatiyyah, who originally came from Sind (now in Pakistan) but have lived in Oman for centuries. Several large Arab groups predominate along Dhofar's coastal plain.

The inhabitants of the Dhofar's mountains are known as jibalis, or 'people of the mountains'. They are ethnically distinct from the coastal Arabs and are thought to be descendants of people from the Yemen highlands.

Oman was a hub for the slave trade in the 18th and 19th century and although this practice was abolished in the 20th century, many continue to work for the families that previously owned their ancestors. The foreign labour force is large—estimated at 58 percent of the working population. Since 1970, increasing numbers of foreigners have come to reside in the country, particularly in the capital. These include Western businessmen, as well as government advisers, army officers, and labourers from the Indian subcontinent, the Philippines, and other Asian countries. Since the 1980s, the government has followed a policy termed "Omanization"[44], to reduce the country's dependence on foreign labour and increase employment opportunities for Omani citizens.

Oman has not been exposed to a significant internal threat since the defeat of the Dhofari insurgents in 1975. The security services are described as large and efficient but not overly intrusive. Tribal dissension, a factor in the past, is considered unlikely to recur because most tribal chiefs and leading families share the advantages of rising oil income. While the political opposition in Oman is not strong now, this could change if Oman faces economic and political crises simultaneously. While Oman is arguably better off than most states in the Middle East, it also appears to have a much more limited political capacity for dealing with a severe economic crisis than many of these other countries where a state of crisis is the norm.

The sultanate has not been the target of terrorist acts; it faces few problems from the narcotics trade and considers the level of general crime to be remarkably low.

2.5.4. Military Power

Oman's Military branches are Royal Omani Armed Forces: Royal Navy of Oman, Royal Air Force of Oman, and Royal Army of Oman. The Navy is one of the most modern in the region, and the Air Force is respected.

With a personnel total of only "46,500"[45] in 2005, the armed forces are relatively small, but they are well balanced and extremely well trained, with high-quality equipment. Minimum 18 years of age is required for voluntary military service.

Since their formal establishment in the early 1950s, with British assistance, Oman Military has twice overcome insurgencies which have threatened the integrity or social structure of the state, and more recently has contributed contingents or facilities to coalitions formed to protect the Persian Gulf states.

"Many British military personnel are part of the Omani armed forces, and Oman maintains close military cooperation with

Britain."[46] During October 2001, the Sultan's Armed Forces and British troops staged the joint exercise, Saif Sareea "Swift Sword"[47], in Oman which coincided with first strikes launched against Taliban in Afghanistan in 2001. Preparation and planning began in 1998. Omani officers worked alongside British officers.

The training exercises like Operation Swift Sword are often conducted in the Gulf by NATO countries to ensure a state of readiness in a volatile region.

United States influence in Oman widened with the signing of a facilities access agreement in June 1980 (renewed in 1990) providing United States military access to Omani bases under specified conditions.

2.5.5. Economy

Oman is a middle-income economy in the Middle East with notable oil and gas resources, a substantial trade surplus, and low inflation. Oman joined the World Trade Organization in November 2000 and continues to liberalize its markets.

When Oman declined as an entre-pot for arms and slaves in the mid-19th century, much of its former prosperity was lost, and the economy turned almost exclusively to agriculture, camel and goat herding, fishing, and traditional handicrafts. Today, oil and gas fuel the economy, and revenues from petroleum products have enabled Oman's dramatic development over the past decades.

In anticipation of the eventual depletion of oil reserves, the government initiated a plan for the post-oil era that focused on developing the country's natural gas resources to fuel domestic industry and for export in the form of liquefied natural gas (LNG) in 1996. The country's development has been aided in part by the Gulf Cooperation Council (GCC).

The Omani Government embarked on its seventh 5-year plan in 2006. In its efforts to reduce its dependence on oil and expatriate labor, the government projects significant increases in spending on industrial and tourism-related projects to foster income diversification, job creation for Omanis in the private sector, and development of Oman's interior. Government programs offer soft loans and propose the building of new industrial estates in population centers outside the capital area. The government is giving greater emphasis to 'Omanization' of the labor force, particularly in banking, hotels, and municipally sponsored shops benefiting from government subsidies. Currently, efforts are underway to liberalize investment opportunities in order to attract foreign capital.

Oman ratified a Free Trade agreement with the US in September 2006 and, through the Gulf Cooperation Council (GCC), seeks similar agreements with the EU, China and Japan.

2.5.6. Natural Resources

In contrast to several Gulf States, Oman possesses relatively modest oil reserves. The obvious implication of this is that Oman is going to have to adjust to life without oil long before its more richly endowed neighbours. Oman lagged behind such neighbouring gulf emirates as Kuwait and the UAE as a result of the late discovery of oil, financial constraints, and political instability in the first half of the 1970s.

Although Oman's oil reserves will be exhausted in the near future, natural gas reserves are being increasingly tapped as a domestic energy source and are likely to become the second major source of income for the country.

Given that Oman's population is growing rapidly, its petroleum reserves are much lower than previously thought, and its non-oil economy is limited, it appears that the Sultanate will face a serious economic crisis in the next 10 to 15 years, or even sooner if oil prices continue to plummet.

2.6. Geopolitics of Qatar

2.6.1. History

Qatar has been settled since the Stone Age, the first known inhabitants being Canaanite tribes. The country was later subject to various rulers, including Sargon of Akkad, who reigned about

2335 to 2279 BC, and it was most likely connected with the federation of Dilmun in the 1st millennium BC.

Islam swept the peninsula in the 7th century AD, and Qatar then became a part, of the Arab Caliphate and the Ottoman Empire. At the beginning of the 16th century, the Peninsula of Qatar along with the rest of the Western part of Persian Gulf came under the hegemony of the Portuguese. Establishing their hold over the Strait of Hormuz, the most important strategic point in the Gulf, the Portuguese conquered Qatar in 1515.

Iranians long held sway in the country, but in the late 18th century Wahhabis, from what is now Saudi Arabia took control. They were replaced in the early 19th century by the Thani dynasty, although its rule after the middle of the century was at the sufferance of the Ottoman government.

In 1916, Qatar became a British protectorate but continued to be ruled as an absolute monarchy by the Thanis. Under the treaties of 1916 and 1934 Qatar ceded Britain control over its external affairs in return for British military protection.

In 1968, British troops left Qatar and Qatar adopted a constitution confirming the emirate as an absolute monarchy in 1970. It led negotiation to establish a union of Arab emirates but terms could not be agreed. Qatar, the mainly barren country and a British protectorate until 1971, "assumed full independence under the rule of Sheikh Ahmad and joined the Arab League and the United Nations in September 3rd, 1971."[48] Most Arab states, the UK, and the US were among the first countries to recognize Qatar.

On February 22nd, 1972, Khalifa Ibn Hamad deposed Ahmad Ibn Ali. Khalifa Ibn Hamad had the tacit support of the Al Thani and of Britain, and he had the political, financial, and military support of Saudi Arabia.

In 1981 it was a founder member of the Gulf Cooperation Council and in 1988 established diplomatic relations with the USSR and the People's Republic of China. Qatar allied itself with Saudi Arabia on many regional and international issues.

Since the Amir, Sheikh Hamad Bin Khalifa Al Thani assumed power in 1995, the State of Qatar with its limited financial and human resources took a turning point on the political, media, economic, social and information levels.

During the Persian Gulf War (1991), international coalition forces were deployed on Qatari soil. Palestinians were expelled from Qatar in retaliation for the pro-Iraqi stance of the Palestine Liberation Organization (PLO), but since then, the war relations with the Palestinians have returned to normal. After the Persian Gulf War, Iraq was still regarded as a threat to Qatar's oil interests; Qatar signed a defence pact with the United States but also restored relations with Iraq.

The State of Qatar, since its independence and out of its historical, political and national commitment, is following a policy that is based on the unification of destiny and goal of the Gulf, Arab and Islamic states. This consolidates cooperation with all neighbouring, friendly peace loving countries in a context of mutual respect and common interests, promotes and serves international peace and security thus achieving prosperity for all countries and people. Now Qatar is a stable country and faces no immediate threats to its security.

2.6.2. Territory

Qatar has strategic location in central Persian Gulf near major petroleum deposits. The capital is Doha. As the 164th largest country in the world, Qatar is slightly smaller than the state of Massachusetts of USA.

Qatar occupies 11,437 square kilometres on a peninsula that extends approximately 160 kilometres north into the Persian Gulf from the Arabian Peninsula.

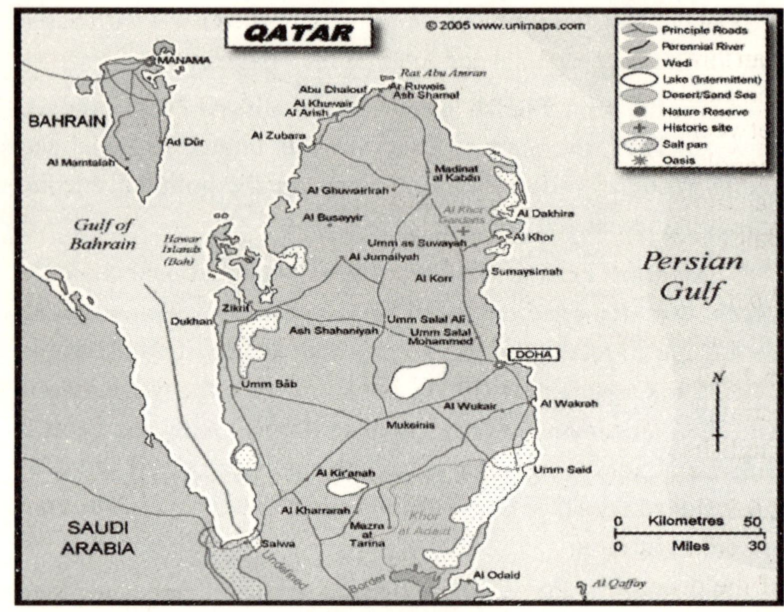

Map 2.10.: Qatar

Source: unimaps com

Varying in width between fifty-five and ninety kilometres, the land is mainly flat and rocky. Notable features include coastal salt pans, elevated limestone formations (the Dukhan anticline) along the west coast under which lies the Dukhan oil field, and massive sand dunes surrounding Khawr al Udayd, an inlet of the gulf in the southeast known to local English speakers as the Inland Sea.

Of the islands belonging to Qatar, Halul is the most important. Lying about ninety kilometres east of Doha, it serves as a storage area and loading terminal for oil from the surrounding offshore fields.

Its land boundary is 60 km with Saudi Arabia as it is contiguous only with Saudi Arabia. The boundary with Saudi Arabia was settled in 1965 and its longstanding border disputes with Saudi Arabia resolved in 2001.

Qatar's coastline is 563 km. Qatar's northwest coast is fewer than thirty kilometres from Bahrain. Hawar and the adjacent islands immediately off the west coast was the subject of a territorial dispute between Qatar and Bahrain, which was the only significant geopolitical issue. In 2001, Qatar agreed to give the islands to Bahrain in exchange for territorial concessions relating to previous Bahrain claims on mainland Qatar.

2.6.3. Population; Religious and Ethnic Groups

According to the World Fact Book 2007, population estimated in July 2007 was 9,07,229. In 2007, population growth rate was estimated 2.386 percent. The official language is Arabic, although English is widely used in government and commerce.

2.6.3.1. Religion

Islam is the predominant religion and makes up 77.5 percent of the population of Qatar, 8.5 percent Christian and 14 percent other religions. Most native Qataris belong to the Islamic Wahhabi sect, an orthodox branch of Sunni Muslims, which constitute 90 percent percent of Muslim population and Shiite Muslims account for approximately 10 percent.

Religion is not a criterion for citizenship, according to the Qatar Nationality Law. However, nearly all Qatari citizens are either Sunni or Shiite Muslims.

There were no reports of societal abuses or discrimination based on religious belief or practice, and prominent societal leaders took positive steps to promote religious freedom.

2.6.3.2. Ethnic Groups

Of the total population, Qataris and other Arabs formed nearly 40 percent in mid-2006 while Indians and Pakistanis amounted to roughly 18 percent each. About 10 percent were Iranians. And other ethnic groups amount 14 percent of the population.

The Qataris are the descendants of the different Omani tribes and others of populations in areas neighbouring Qatar. Qataris are a minority in their own country, accounting for less than a quarter of the total population.

For security reasons, official statistics or censuses do not include breakdowns for nationals and non-nationals but independent estimates show that the indigenous population is estimated at around 150,000.

Although the country has experienced little internal unrest, the large number of foreigners, forming 80 percent of the work force, is regarded as possible sources of instability. Qatar is determined to maintain control over their activities and limit their influence.

A significant number of resident Palestinians, some of whom included prominent businessmen and civil servants, were expelled after the Iraqi invasion of Kuwait.

Qatar and the other Gulf States have been a target of international drug gangs because of their wealth, openness, the presence of a large foreign community; including emigrants from Asian drug producing countries, lack of deterrent laws and their location midway between Asia and the Western markets. In the past, drug gangs had used Iran to reach Western markets but intensified security and the execution of hundreds of narcotics smugglers in Iran forced those gangs to switch routes and use Arab States of the Persian Gulf region as a transit route. Large quantities of narcotics were also seized in 2004 and 2005 but no official data has been provided on the exact volume and number of offenders. Qatari officials have acknowledged the drugs problem, but say, it remains under control through the introduction of tough security measures including long jail terms and the use of capital punishment, deportation of foreign criminals and the installation of advanced detection and surveillance systems at the country's ports and along the coastline.

"According to Independent Newspaper, a suicide-bombing killed a British teacher at the Doha Players Theatre in March 2005, shocking for a country that had not previously experienced acts of terrorism. The bombing was carried out by Omar Ahmed Abdullah

Ali, an Egyptian residing in Qatar, who had suspected ties to Al-Qaeda in the Arabian Peninsula."[49]

The potential geopolitical issues concern the proportion of expatriate labor in the population and the limited water supply.

2.6.4. Military Power

According to the World Fact Book 2007, Qatar's Military branches are Qatari Amiri Land Force, Qatari Amiri Navy and Qatari Amiri Air Force. Minimum 18 years of age is required for voluntary military service. Land forces enlisted personnel are largely unprofessional foreign nationals. Qatar maintains a modest military force of approximately 11,800 men.

The military of Qatar is small, only marginally larger than the military of Bahrain. Despite its limited size, the military cannot be totally discounted as it possesses modern equipment.

At the time of independence on September 3, 1971, the armed forces consisted of little more than the Royal Guard Regiment and some scattered units equipped with a few armoured cars and four aircrafts.

Initially outfitted with British weaponry, Qatar shifted much of its procurement to France during the 1980s in response to French efforts to develop closer relations. By 1992, it had grown to a force of 7,500, including an army of 6,000, a navy of 700, and an air force of 800. The lack of sufficient indigenous manpower to staff the armed forces is a continuing problem. By one estimate, Qatari citizens constitute only 30 percent of the army, in which, more than twenty nationalities are represented. Many of the officers are of the royal family or members of leading tribes. Enlisted personnel are recruited from Bedouin tribes that move between Qatar and Saudi Arabia and from other Arab groups. Many Pakistanis serve in combat units. In 1992, there were still a number of British officers, as well as French, Jordanians, and Pakistanis in advisory or technical positions. More young Qataris are being recruited, and the number of trained and competent Qatari officers is steadily increasing.

Qatari forces played an important role in the First Gulf War. Qatar served as the headquarters and one of the main launching sites of the US invasion of Iraq in 2003 and hosts CENTCOM; The United States Central Command, Forward Headquarters.

After Bahrain, Qatar is believed to have the second smallest army in the Arab world, but, it enjoys USA protection as it is home to a major American military presence in the Gulf. Furthermore, Qatar is one of the biggest defence spenders in the world in terms of budget allocations, with such spending accounting for nearly a third of its total current expenditure.

2.6.5. Economy

Before the discovery of oil, the economy of the Qatar focused on fishing and pearling. After the introduction of the Japanese cultured pearl onto the world market in the 1920s and 1930s, Qatar's pearling industry faltered. However, the discovery of oil; beginning in the 1940s, completely transformed the state's economy.

Now the country, a former pearl-fishing centre and once one of the poorest Gulf States, is one of the richest countries in the region and has a high standard of living, with many social services offered to its citizens and all the amenities of any modern state.

Qatari standards of living are double those of the United Arab Emirates, over five times those of the rest of the oil producing countries of the region and only slightly lower than those of the world's advanced industrialized countries.

Qatar is considered to be one of the most competitive economies in the world and is highly rated by credit agencies. The country's economy is open, barriers to trade are low and no income taxes are levied.

The economy of Qatar is one of the active economies in the Middle East and is mainly dependent upon the ebb and flow of revenues generated by Qatar's hydrocarbon wealth and its related industries. Qatar has experienced rapid economic growth over the last several years on the back of high oil prices, and in 2008, posted its eighth consecutive budget surplus. With only about 20 years left as a major oil exporter, Qatar has made a priority of diversifying and attracting foreign investment. The country has become a regional banking centre.

Economic policy is focused on developing Qatar's non-associated natural gas reserves and increasing private and foreign investment in non-energy sectors, but oil and gas still account for more than 50 percent of GDP, roughly 85 percent of export earnings, and 70 percent of government revenues.

"Oil and gas have made Qatar the second highest per-capita income country- following Liechtenstein - and one of the world's fastest growing."[50]

2.6.6. Natural Resources

Although, oil was discovered in 1939, the discovery in 1971 of a large offshore oil field gave further impetus to the economy and Qatar rapidly developed a modern infrastructure, building up its health and education services.

What oil was to the 20th century, natural gas will be to the 21st century. The rising worldwide demand for gas is also influencing relations between the major consuming nations and their principal suppliers. A key factor in the geopolitics of natural gas is the heavy concentration of reserves in a relatively small number of producing countries. "The top five, Russia, Iran, Qatar, Saudi Arabia and the United Arab Emirates, hold nearly 67 percent of the world gas resources."[51] This means, of course, that these countries are in a very strong position to control the global flow of gas and to influence market forces.

A vast gas reserve which is divided between Iran and Qatar; Iran's part is called South Pars and Qatar's part is called North Field, is one of the huge gas reserves of the world. Its location, like many other huge hydrocarbon proven reserves, is distant from today's major consuming areas. Country risk will become an important factor in decision making for export pipelines, LNG and other mega projects and even domestic downstream projects. Political and economic instability means higher project risk, which in turn translates into the requirement of much higher return on investment. Geopolitical factors are especially important for cross-border pipelines that transit third countries.

2.7. Geopolitics of Saudi Arabia

2.7.1. History

Saudi Arabia, geographically a sparsely populated largely desert wasteland, is so important from a geopolitical point of view; for some states because of its oil, and for others, as the heartland of Islam.

Nomadic tribes have existed across the Arabian Peninsula for thousands of years. Persian influence was prevalent along Saudi Arabia's eastern coast, centred on Dilmun which covered parts of the mainland and the island of Bahrain.

By the 6th century AD, the Hejaz region in north-western Saudi Arabia was becoming increasingly powerful and an important link in the overland trade route from Egypt and the Byzantine Empire to the wider east. Prophet of Islam, Mohammad, and his followers took control of Mecca, one of the principal cities of Hejaz, in 630. The leaders who succeeded Mohammad, known as caliphs, spread the Islamic faith throughout and beyond the Arab world. Saudi Arabia's origin as a political entity, lay in the rise of the puritanical Wahhabi movement of the 18th century, which called for a return to the original principles of Islam and gained the allegiance of the powerful Al Saud dynasty in the Nejd region of central Arabia. By 1811, the Al Saud/Wahhabi armies controlled most of the peninsula and were seen as a threat to the Ottoman Turkish overlord.

In 1891, after a long period of tribal warfare, the rival Al Rashid family, with Ottoman support, seized control of the city of Riyadh. The Al Saud family was exiled to Kuwait, but Abdul Aziz Ibn Abdul Rahman (known to Europeans as Ibn Saud) restored Wahhabi fortunes, recapturing Riyadh in 1902 and reasserting Al Saud control over Nejd in 1906. In 1914, he gained the Al Hasa; the east region of Nejd on the Gulf from the Ottoman Turks. In 1920, he captured the Asir region and in 1921, Jebel Shammar territory. In 1926, he became both Sultan of Nejd and King of the Hejaz. Britain recognized him as an independent ruler by the Treaty of Jeddah on May 1927, and in 1932, Nejd and Hejaz were unified as the Kingdom of Saudi Arabia, ruled as an absolute monarchy under Islamic law.

King Abdul Aziz died in 1953 and was succeeded by his eldest son, Saud, who reigned for 11 years. In 1964, Saud was forced to abdicate in favor of his half-brother, Faisal, who had served as Foreign Minister. Proclaimed King in 1964 by senior royal family members and religious leaders, Faisal also continued to serve as Prime Minister. This practice has been followed by subsequent kings.

In 1975, King Faisal was assassinated by a nephew, who was executed after an extensive investigation concluded that he acted alone. Faisal was succeeded by his half-brother Khalid as King and Prime Minister; their half-brother Prince Fahd was named Crown Prince and First Deputy Prime Minister. King Khalid empowered Crown Prince Fahd to oversee many aspects of the government's international and domestic affairs. Economic development continued rapidly under King Khalid, and the kingdom assumed a more influential role in regional politics and international economic and financial matters.

King Khalid died in June 1982. Fahd became King and Prime Minister in a smooth transition. Under King Fahd, the Saudi economy adjusted to sharply lower oil revenues resulting from declining global oil prices. Saudi Arabia supported neutral shipping in the Persian Gulf during periods of the Iran-Iraq war and aided Iraq's war-strained economy.

King Fahd played a major part in bringing about the August 1988 cease-fire between Iraq and Iran and in organizing and strengthening the Gulf Cooperation Council (GCC).

In August 1990, Saddam Hussein's forces invaded Kuwait. Iraqi troops began massing on the border of Kuwait and some feared that they were about to invade Saudi Arabia. King Fahd allowed American and Coalition soldiers to be stationed in Saudi Arabia to counter the Iraqi threat. King Fahd played a key role before and during the 1991 Persian Gulf War. Saudi Arabia accepted the Kuwaiti royal family and 4,00,000 refugees while allowing deployment of Western and Arab troops on its soil for the liberation of Kuwait the following year. King Fahd's action also consolidated the coalition of forces against Iraq and helped define the tone of the operation as a multilateral effort to re-establish the sovereignty and territorial integrity of Kuwait. Many Muslims were angered by this move, because, it allowed foreign armies to be stationed in their holiest land.

After the attacks of September 11, 2001, it became known that 15 of the 19 suspected hijackers were Saudi. Saudi Arabia became the focus of worldwide attention once again, as it was questioned whether the government was indeed cracking down on radicals. The Saudi government pledged their support to the War on Terror, and vowed to try to eliminate militant elements. However, in May 2003, an insurgency in Saudi Arabia began, believed to be conducted by Al Qaeda affiliates. This consisted mainly of attacks on foreigners in an attempt to expel them from the country and hurt the Saudi government. While the number of attacks dropped significantly in 2005, they exposed the vulnerability of the country. King Fahd died in July 2005. He was succeeded by his brother Crown Prince Abdullah Bin Abdul Aziz, who is now ruling the country.

Since ascending to the throne, King Abdullah has followed a more activist foreign policy, offering Saudi assistance and support in efforts to resolve regional crises in Lebanon, Sudan, and Somalia, fostering Israeli-Palestinian peace efforts, and increasing Saudi diplomatic engagement around the world. "In particular, he has pursued an Interfaith Dialogue Initiative to encourage religious tolerance on a global level, which was endorsed in a session of the UN General Assembly in November 2008."[52]

The Kingdom has been involved in the geopolitics of conflicts. More importantly, Saudi Arabia is always likely to be implicated in resource geopolitics and any use of oil weapon.

2.7.2. Territory

Saudi Arabia, with an area of about 2,149,690 square km, occupies the bulk of the Arabian Peninsula, nearly 80 percent of it and about 19.2 percent of the Middle East.

It ranks 15th largest country in the world. It is roughly one-third the size of the continental United States, and the same size as all of Western Europe. The capital is Riyadh.

Saudi Arabia is bounded in the west by the Red Sea, east by the Persian Gulf, Qatar and the United Arab Emirates, north by Jordan, Iraq and Kuwait and south by Yemen and Oman. Saudi Arabia's land boundaries are 4,431 km; Iraq 814 km, Jordan 744 km, Kuwait 222 km, Oman 676 km, Qatar 60 km, UAE 457 km and Yemen 1458 km. Saudi Arabia's coastline is 2,640 km.

Its extensive coastlines on Persian Gulf and Red Sea provide great leverage on shipping (especially crude oil) through Persian Gulf and Suez Canal.

In the southwest, the mountain ranges of Asir Province rise to over 9,000 feet.

As a result of its position, geographically and within Islam, and particularly its possession of the world's major oilfields, Saudi Arabia has been assured of external support, both regionally and globally.

The major geopolitical issues to concern Saudi Arabia have been international boundaries, both land and maritime. In boundary

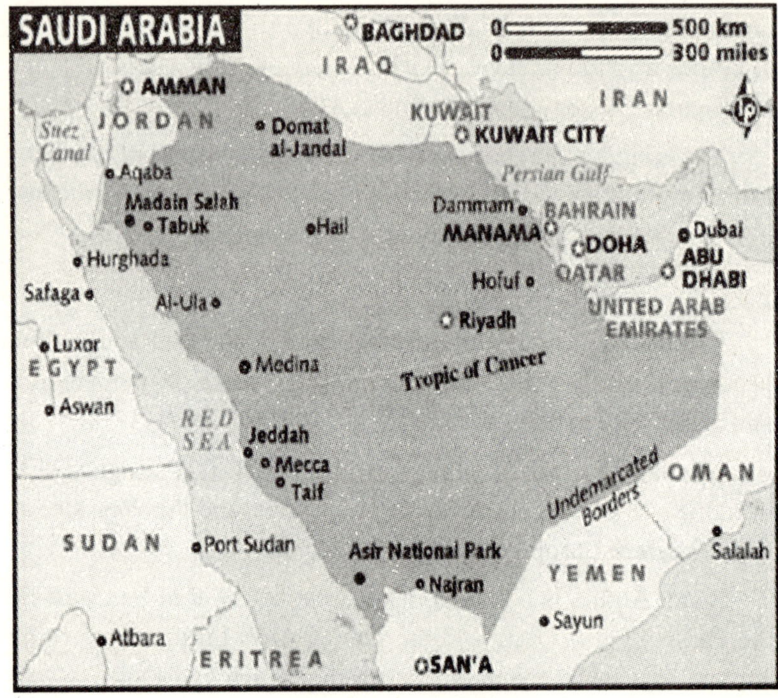

Map 2.11.: Saudi Arabia

Source: Lonely Planet site

settlement, Saudi Arabia has consistently shown flexibility in agreeing to shared areas or porous boundaries.

The major issue was marine and most of the land boundary with Yemen. For more than 60 years, Yemen and Saudi Arabia quarrelled over their largely undefined border. The dispute was eventually settled by the Treaty of Jeddah in June 2000. The one sector of the boundary which is agreed, is the demarcated sector from the Red Sea coast across the mountain chain to the western edge of the interior.

The location and status of Saudi Arabia's boundary with the United Arab Emirates is not final; a de facto boundary reflects in the 1974 agreement.

"In June 2005, the Saudi Minister of the Interior; Prince Nayef Bin Abdul Aziz, said that he had discussed in Abu Dhabi the issue of the border between Saudi Arabia and the UAE, denying the existence of any differences between the two states."[53]

The border between Saudi Arabia and Qatar was resolved in March 2001. Tentative agreement on the partition of the Saudi-Iraqi Neutral Zone was reached in 1981, and partition was finalized by 1983, which has been described in details in Iraq's section in this chapter.

The border dispute between Saudi Arabia and Kuwait is also described in Kuwait section of this chapter. According to USA Department of State, January 2009, the border with Oman is not demarcated.

2.7.3. Population; Religious and Ethnic Groups

Until the 1960s, most of the population of Saudi Arabia was nomadic or semi-nomadic; due to rapid economic and urban growth, more than 95 percent of the population now is settled. According to USA Department of State's Background Notebook on Saudi Arabia (January 2009), Saudi Arabia's 2008 population was estimated to be about 28 million, including, about 5.6 million foreigner residents. The country ranks the world's 46th most populous country. "Its population increased at least 300 percent between 1973 and 2000."[54]

Official language of the country is Arabic and is used by most of the native population. English is an important second language, used in government, commerce, the media, and among the non-Arab expatriate community.

2.7.3.1. Religion

Islam is the official religion. The law requires that all Saudi citizens be Muslims. Saudi Arabia is known as the birthplace of Islam. A majority of Saudi citizens are Sunni Muslims (Wahhabi). The Government does not provide legal recognition or protection for freedom of religion, and it is severely restricted in practice. As a matter of policy, the government guarantees and protects the right to private worship for all, including non-Muslims who gather in homes for religious practice.

The cultural environment in Saudi Arabia is highly conservative; the country officially adheres to the strict Wahhabi interpretation of Islamic religious law (Sharia). Cultural presentations must conform to narrowly defined standards of ethics. Men and women are not permitted to attend public events together and are segregated in the work place.

"Shiite people are a minority in Saudi Arabia, about 15 percent."[55] They live mostly in the eastern districts on the Persian Gulf (Qatif, Al-Ahsa, Dammam), where they constitute, approximately, three-quarters of the native population, and in western highlands of Saudi Arabia. In Saudi Arabia, the Shiites are a special case, constituting 75 percent of the population in the Eastern Province, the Kingdom's main oil-producing region, and identifying far more strongly with Shiites across the border in Iraq than with the Saudi state.

Indeed, the empowerment of Iraq's long-suppressed Shiite has raised expectations among Saudi Arabia's Shiite that they, too, can gain first-class status. Some Saudi authorities are extremely concerned about any possible connection between the Shiite in Saudi Arabia and Iraq. Therefore, failing to pay attention to their Shiite citizens, some Saudi authorities frequently express concern that the Shiite are conspiring to form a Shiite bloc comprising Iran, Iraq, Syria and Lebanon. At the same time, regional authorities have embarked on certain moves in order to improve the present conditions, like holding broader elections.

From a theological perspective, relations between the Shiite and the Wahhabi Sunnis are inherently strained because the Wahhabis consider the rituals of the Shiite to be the epitome of Sherk (polytheism; literally association), especially the Ashura mourning celebrations, the passion play re-enacting Husain's death at Karbala, and popular votive rituals carried out at shrines and graves.

"The worst bout of confrontations in years between Shiites and authorities in the overwhelmingly Sunni country began with an argument in the vicinity of Al Baqee Cemetery in Medina in February 20, 2009."[56] A group of Shiites pilgrims visiting the cemetery complained that officers from the religious police were filming women among the group. A Saudi official blamed the Shiite pilgrims for the trouble, accusing them of performing religious rituals offensive to other worshippers and authorities at the cemetery. On February 24, 2009, the dispute erupted into two protests involving several hundred people in an eastern town, and Shiite leaders differed over whether demonstrations and shouting slogans would resolve the issue better than quiet dialogue with the government.

2.7.3.2. Ethnic Groups

About 90 percent of Saudis are ethnically Arab while Afro-Asian people constitute 10 percent of Saudi Arabia's population. Some are of mixed ethnic origin and are descended from Turks, Iranians, Indonesians, Indians, Africans, and others, most of who immigrated as pilgrims and reside in the Hijaz region along the Red Sea coast.

Although the country's tribes are often considered 'pure Arabs'; certainly they are the descendants of the peninsula's original ethnic stock, a certain degree of ethnic heterogeneity is evident among both the sedentary and nomadic populations of Saudi Arabia. Variations have developed because of a long history of regionalism and tribal autonomy and because some localities have been subjected to important outside influences. Thus, the proximity of sub-Saharan Africa along the Red Sea littoral and the constant historical influx of peoples from Iran, Pakistan, and India along the Persian Gulf coast have left traces of the physical types characteristic of those people among the native population.

Likewise, the Hajj to Mecca has long brought hundreds of thousands of people annually from various ethnic groups to the country. About half of all pilgrims travel from Arab countries and half from African and Asian countries. A small number of such visitors have settled in and around the holy cities throughout the years, either out of religious devotion or because penury prevented their returning home.

By the early 21st century, the estimated number of foreign workers was between one-fourth and one-fifth of the country's total population, despite efforts by the Saudi authorities to encourage citizens to occupy positions typically held by foreigners. At first, most expatriated workers were Arab, such as Yemenis, Egyptians, Palestinians, Syrians, and Iraqis. Increasing numbers of non-Arab Muslims such as Pakistanis have been employed, as have large numbers of non-Muslim Koreans and Filipinos, who have been hired under group contracts for specified periods. Many Arabs from nearby countries are employed in the kingdom. Most specialized technical workers are Europeans and Americans.

2.7.4. Military Power

Saudi Arabia's Military branches are; Land Force, Navy, Air Force, Air Defence Force, National Guard and Ministry of Interior Forces (paramilitary). Minimum 18 years of age is required for voluntary military service and there is no conscription.

"The armed forces comprise 1,05,500 active personnel and there is a strong army and air force and a developing navy. All are equipped with the latest technology. There is also a Peninsula Shield Force of 7000, supplied by the USA, France and UK."[57] This raises the question of when, with its powerful military, Saudi Arabia will act independently and when it will require western assistance. Despite the relatively small population for its area, by Middle Eastern standards, Saudi Arabia is militarily powerful.

5000 US troops were stationed in Saudi Arabia after the 1991 Gulf War and were joined by a further 20,000 during the 2003 conflict. However, virtually all US troops have now been withdrawn.

The politically vulnerable oil-rich Gulf States had been subject to outside intervention in the past. For this reason, Saudi Arabia and the smaller states planned to form a system for collective security.

In 1984 the Defence Ministers of the Gulf Cooperation Council (GCC) agreed on the creation of a two-brigade Peninsula Shield Force consisting of 10,000 personnel. This joint intervention force was based in Saudi Arabia near King Khalid Military City at Hafar Al Batin under the command of a Saudi officer. In addition to a headquarters' staff, the force consisted of one infantry brigade of about 5,000 men with elements from all GCC states. Its mission, however, had not been publicly defined. It was not clear, for example, whether the joint force would have authority to intervene in a domestic emergency. The force could be enlarged at a time of threat; it was apparently reinforced prior to the Persian Gulf War in 1991 but did not take part in the war as a distinct unit.

In 1990-91, Saudi Arabia played an important role in the Gulf War, developing new allies and improving existing relationships between Saudi Arabia and some other countries, but also suffering diplomatic and financial costs. During the war, Iraq fired Scud missiles into Saudi Arabia and even penetrated its northern border. Iraqi forces were expelled from Kuwait. American forces as well as some multinational contingents continued to occupy bases in the kingdom. However, American or foreign forces no longer occupy bases in Saudi Arabia.

The foreign military presence caused militants to orchestrate attacks inside Saudi Arabia. In November 1995, a Saudi National Guard base was bombed, killing seven people. In June 1996, a truck bomb killed 19 American servicemen at the Khobar towers in Al-Khobar. These bombings caused the monarchy to focus on militancy inside their own kingdom, yet they denied there was much of a problem.

"Saudi Arabia has become the only Southern Persian Gulf power able to develop military forces strong enough to play a major role in defending itself against any aggressive state and capable of playing a significant role in military action in the Red Sea area."[58]

During the Gulf war, Saudi Arabia was the only Southern Gulf power with enough air power and armour to play a major war fighting role in a US-led coalition; its development of advanced air bases, ports and facilities made it critical to any western effort to project military power in the Persian Gulf.

Concern was voiced over the large number of Saudis fighting American soldiers in Iraq following the 2003 invasion.

2.7.5. Economy

When the Kingdom of Saudi Arabia was established in 1932, its economy was fragmented and small. People in the Al (ijaz cities of Mecca, Medina, and Jeddah, derived most of their income from the annual influx of thousands of Hajj pilgrims.

Some of the world's largest oil and natural gas fields lie beneath Saudi Arabia and its offshore waters, representing the country's most economically important natural resource. Before the discovery and exploitation of these reserves in the mid-20th century, Saudi Arabia was one of the poorest countries in the world. Oil revenue transformed the Saudi economy in the mid-20th century.

The weakness of the US dollar in much of the first half of the 2000s caused the Saudi Rial to depreciate, enhancing the competitiveness of non-oil exports. Further structural reforms, less corruption, more privatization and vigilant macroeconomic management will be necessary in order for the Saudi economy to remain buoyant.

In April 2000, the government established the Saudi Arabian General Investment Authority to encourage foreign direct investment in the country. Saudi Arabia signed a Trade Investment Framework Agreement with the US in July 2003, and joined the WTO in December 2005. In 2005, the country's financial sector continued to perform well and the Saudi stock market was among the world's best performing.

According to the Oxford Business Group (OBG), the economy of Saudi Arabia is beginning to feel the effects of the global financial turmoil.

Arbah Capital is an investment company that is established by a group of strategic investors who are leading businessmen in the Persian Gulf region. CEO of the company, Saad Al Hassosah, was reported as saying that "It is important to assess the effects that the current global crisis will have on the local market. Project finance will be mostly affected and liquidity as well."[59]

"As most projects in the kingdom are being partially financed by international banking institutions, the current financial crisis will affect reserve requirements, therefore reducing the amount of credit that will be available for the market." he added.

The impact of the recent recession on Saudi Arabia, as elsewhere, depends ultimately on how long the slowdown is likely to last. As with many other oil states in the Gulf, Saudi Arabia started the current slowdown from a strong position given that it comes against a background of many years of high oil prices, which have left the Saudi's public finances in good shape after years of chronic deficit. The impact of the financial crisis is more muted in Saudi Arabia compared to elsewhere, as government spending has not only been sustained, but, in fact, increased in the budget for 2009.

According to Hassan Hakimian, Senior lecturer in Economics at the London's Cass Business School, in an interview with the Director of Middle East Youth Initiative on February 25, 2009, the Saudi Arabia's Finance Minister, Ibrahim Abdulaziz Al-Assaf has stated that, "despite the combined effects of the collapse in oil prices and the envisaged increase in budgeted spending for 2009, which yields a projected budget deficit of 65 billion riyals ($ 17.3 billion), the Saudi's vast financial reserves would be its first line of defence to meet any deficits for this and next year, hence averting the need to resort to external borrowing."[60]

2.7.6. Natural Resources

With more than one-fourth of the world's total proven oil reserves and up to 1 trillion barrels of ultimate recoverable oil, Saudi Arabia is the world's leading oil producer and exporter.

Production comes from 14 major oilfields, mostly in the eastern provinces and offshore and including production from the Saudi-Kuwait Neutral Zone.

Scarcity of water is a perennial problem in the kingdom. Saudi Arabia has the largest single desalination program in the world, which meets most domestic and industrial needs. Underwater aquifers provide a limited amount of potable water, and a great deal of energy has been committed to constructing dams for water storage and to developing water-recycling plants.

2.8. Geopolitics of United Arab Emirates

2.8.1. History

Recent archaeological research indicates the presence of an advanced trading culture in the early 3rd millennium BC in what is now the UAE. The small trading states that emerged along the Persian Gulf coast were later overwhelmed by Persian empires; the Achaemenid Empire from the 6th to the 4th centuries BC and the Sassanid Empire from the 3rd to the 7th centuries AD. These empires took over and controlled the extensive maritime trade that the small states had already carried as far as China.

In the early AD centuries, Arab tribes flocked to the region; first, along the southern coast of the Arabian Peninsula, then from the north, helping to make it receptive to the religion of Islam before the death of the prophet Muhammad in 632. In the Middle Ages, much of the region was part of the Persian Kingdom of Hormuz (from 1300).

European intervention in the Gulf began in the early 16th century, first by Portuguese, then Dutch and then by the British. The Trucial States of the Persian Gulf coast granted the UK control of their defence and foreign affairs in 19th century treaties. In January 1968, Britain announced the withdrawal of its military forces from the area by 1971.

In 1971, six of these states; Abu Dhabi, Ajman, Al Fujairah, Al Sharjah, Dubai and Umm al Qaiwan, merged to form a federation, the United Arab Emirates (UAE). They were joined in 1972 by Ras Al Khaimah. Each Sheikh runs the internal affairs of his own emirate, while at the federal level, authority lies with the Supreme Council of Rulers, with the membership comprising all seven Sheiks.

The Presidency and Premiership of the United Arab Emirates is de facto hereditary to the Al Nahyan clan of Abu Dhabi and the Al Maktoum clan of Dubai. The President of the United Arab Emirates and the head of state is the ruler of Abu Dhabi and the Prime Minister and Vice President of the United Arab Emirates, is the ruler of Dubai and the head of government. The political influences and financial obligations of the Emirates are reflected by respective positions in the Federal government.

On November 2nd, 2004, Sheikh Zayed Bin Sultan Al Nahyan, died. He was the UAE's first and only president. His eldest son, Caliph Bin Zayed Al Nahyan, succeeded him as Ruler of Abu Dhabi. In accordance with the constitution, the UAE's Supreme Council of Rulers elected Caliph Bin Zayed Al Nahyan as UAE Federal President. Mohammed Bin Zayed Al Nahyan succeeded Caliph as Crown Prince of Abu Dhabi.

During the 1980s, the UAE suffered, partly as a result of the Iran-Iraq War and partly through the drop in oil prices and, like Kuwait, sold more than its OPEC quota. This drew the condemnation of Iraq in 1990 and the UAE joined the coalition which won the Gulf War.

2.8.2. Territory

The area of UAE is approximately 83,600 square km, excluding over 100 offshore islands. However, its exact size is indeterminable as much of the border area with Saudi Arabia lies on the Rub al Khali (Empty Quarter) desert and remains undemarcated. It ranks 116th largest country in the world.

The largest emirate, Abu Dhabi, accounts for 87 percent of the UAE's total area; approximately three times the size of the other six combined, is the capital of UAE. The desert area of Abu Dhabi includes two important oases with adequate underground water for permanent settlements and cultivation.

It is located on the Southeast of the Arabian Peninsula and is bounded in the north by the Persian Gulf, northeast by Oman, east by the Gulf of Oman and Oman, south and west by Saudi Arabia.

The country's north-easternmost tip is an enclave belonging to Oman and forms the strategically located Strait of Hormuz. The other significant factor of its location is that it coincides with the end of the major oilfield zone which extends from Iraq and the neighboring parts of Iran through Kuwait and Al Hasa Province of Saudi Arabia.

UAE land boundaries are 867 km; Oman 410 km, Saudi Arabia 457 km and its coastline is 1,318 km.

Prior to withdrawing from the area in 1971, Britain delineated the internal borders among the seven emirates in order to preempt territorial disputes that might hamper formation of the federation. In general, the rulers of the Emirates accepted the British intervention, but in the case of boundary disputes between Abu Dhabi and Dubai, and also between Dubai and Sharjah, conflicting claims were not resolved until after the UAE became independent. The most complicated borders were in the Al Hajar Al Gharbi (West Mountain), where five of the emirates contested jurisdiction over more than a dozen enclaves. There are two areas under joint control. One is jointly controlled by Oman and Ajman, the other by Fujairah and Sharjah.

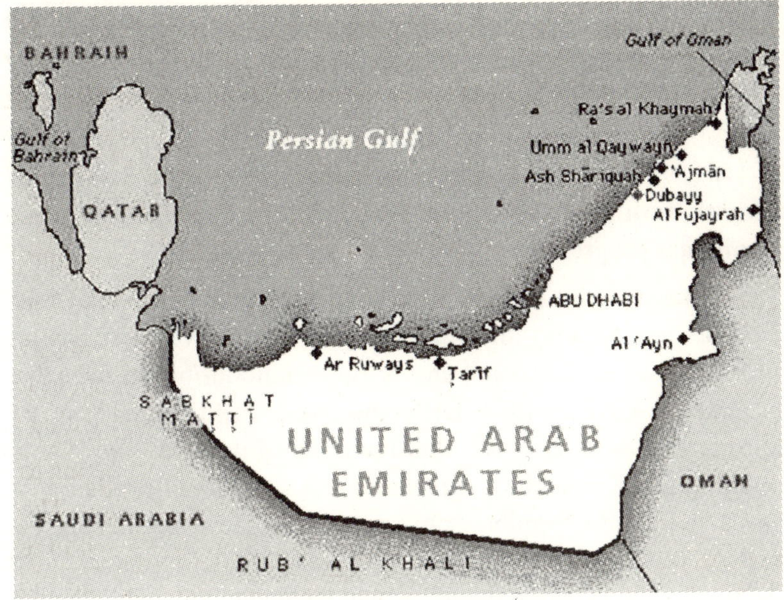

Map 2.12.: United Arab Emirates

Source: Greenwich Meantime

At its birth on December 2, 1971, the UAE faced challenges that caused many to predict that the new federation would fail. There were border disputes with Saudi Arabia and Oman, rivalries among the Emirates were strong and threats to regional stability since then have included the 1979 Iranian Islamic Revolution, the Iran-Iraq War (1980-1988), and Iraq's invasion of Kuwait in 1990. The UAE has survived these dangers and prospered largely because its president, Sheikh Zayed, has used the oil wealth of his emirate, Abu Dhabi, to the benefit of all emirates as well as to promote the UAE's security in the international arena.

UAE lies on the Persian Gulf with a number of ports available for shipping crude oil and natural gas exports.

Proximity to Iran has resulted in close relations with that State, although there are three disputed islands. In April 1992, the dispute resurfaced with Iran over three islands in the approaches to the

Strait of Hormuz; Abu Musa, Greater Tunb and Lesser Tunb, which is still going on. The conflict had flared up when Iran refused to allow several hundred expatriates to return to the island, which is jointly administered by the two nations under a 1971 agreement.

In 1993, a dispute between the UAE[61] and Iran over administration of the island of Abu Musa continued without significant progress.

Earlier, the physical separation of the southern portion of Oman from its territory on the Musandam Peninsula was a source of friction between Oman and the various neighbouring emirates that became the UAE in 1971. Differences over the disputed territory appeared to have subsided after the onset of the Iran–Iraq War in 1980. In 2003, boundary agreement was signed and ratified with Oman in for entire border, including Oman's Musandam Peninsula and Al Madhah enclaves, "but contents of the agreement and detailed maps showing the alignment have not been published."[62]

2.8.3. Population; Religious and Ethnic Groups

Population estimated in July, 2007 was 44,44,011; based on the results of the 2005 census that includes a significantly higher estimate of net immigration of non-citizens than previous estimate. About 88 percent of the population of the United Arab Emirates is urban. The remaining inhabitants live in tiny towns scattered throughout the country or in one of the many desert oilfield camps in the state.

A harsh environment and marginal economic conditions kept the population of the region low and economically depressed until the exploitation of oil. According to estimates, between 1900 and 1960 there were 80,000 to 95,000 inhabitants in the Emirates, mostly in small coastal settlements. Whereas Sharjah was dominant in the 19th century, by 1939, Dubai was the most populous Emirate, with an estimated population of 20,000, one-quarter of whom, were foreigners.

The largest minorities were Iranians and Indians in Dubai and in other Emirates. Abu Dhabi's onshore oil exports began in 1963, bringing wealth and a demand for foreign labour. Population growth has slowed since 1985. The population in 1995 was 15 times larger than it was in 1965; largely due to the immigration of oil workers. Official language is Arabic, and English also is widely spoken. Persian, Urdu and Hindi too are spoken.

2.8.3.1. Religion

According to the World Fact Book 2007, 96 percent of UAE's population are Muslims (84 percent of Muslim population are Sunni and 16 percent Shiite) and other 4 percent are Christians and Hindus. Many foreigners are Muslims, although Hindus and Christians make up a portion of the UAE's foreign population.

Though, Islam is the UAE's state religion, the government follows a policy of tolerance towards other religions and rarely interferes in the activities of non-Muslims. However, it is illegal in the UAE to spread the ideas of any religion apart from Islam through any form of media, as it is a form of proselytizing.

However, varying from emirate to emirate, the degree of religious freedom afforded to non-Muslims is greater in the UAE than in Saudi Arabia and Qatar. Most of the Christians in the country are from Philippines, Lebanon and India, while, almost all Hindus in the country are of Indian origin.

In the past, internal dynastic rivalries within individual emirates were often sources of tension and even bloodshed. In part, this resulted from the absence of clearly established rules of succession. More recently, however, heirs apparent have usually been designated, most often the eldest son of the Amir.

Intra-UAE rivalries no longer take a violent form, but the continued existence of independent military forces and competition in acquiring arms bring with them a costly proliferation of weapons that complicates training and logistics. The threat of subversion from resident Iranians and native Shites seems to be less acute in the UAE than in other Gulf States in spite of the large Shiite population in Dubai.

2.8.3.2. Ethnic Groups

UAE has one of the most diverse populations in the Middle East. About 87 percent of the total population consists of ethnic Arabs. 19 percent of the country's population is Emirati. Several aspects of the UAE's population are unusual.

The largest non-Arab group consists of Asians from India and Pakistan, about 9.5 percent of the population. Some 2 percent are Iranians.

Other groups, including Africans and Europeans, make up less than two percent of the population.

The number of foreign workers has increased dramatically since 1968, when they constituted 36 percent of the total population. Approximately, "78 percent of the population are foreigners; foreign workers in all level of jobs, the highest percentage of any country,"[63] including significant numbers of other Arabs; Palestinians, Egyptians, Jordanians, Yemenis, Omanis, as well as many Indians, Pakistanis, Bangladeshis, Iranians, Afghans, Filipinos, and West Europeans. As a consequence, UAE nationals form a minority of those who reside in the country.

In 2007, there were approximately 1.4 million Indian nationals residing in the UAE, making them the single largest expatriate community in the oil-rich nation. Thousands of Palestinians, who came as either political refugees or migrant workers, also live in the United Arab Emirates. There is also a sizable population of people from Egypt, Somalia and Sudan who migrated to the UAE before its formation. The UAE has also attracted a small number of expatriates from developed countries.

2.8.4. Military Power

The Trucial Oman Scouts, for long the symbol of public order on the coast and commanded by British officers, were turned over to the UAE as its defence forces in 1971. The UAE armed forces, consisting of 48,800 troops, are headquartered in Abu Dhabi and are, primarily, responsible for the defence of the seven Emirates.

UAE Military branches are; Army, Navy (includes Marines and Coast Guard), Air and Air Defence Force, paramilitary forces (includes Federal Police Force). Minimum 18 years of age is required for voluntary military service and there is no conscription.

Although small in number, the UAE armed forces are equipped with some of the most modern weapon systems, purchased from a variety of other countries. The military has been reducing the number of foreign nationals in its ranks, and its officer corps is composed almost entirely of UAE nationals. The Air Defence Force is linked into a joint air defence system with the other six Gulf Cooperation Council (GCC) nations aimed at protecting the airspace of the allied states. The UAE Special Operations Command (SOC) is a small but effective force centered on the counter-terrorism mission within the country. SOC is well-financed, trained, and equipped and is capable of executing its mission with a level of expertise equal to, or above, the rest of the GCC.

Following the 1990 Iraq invasion of Kuwait, the UAE has maintained extensive relations with its Western allies for security and cooperation towards increasing interoperability of its defence forces and for liberating Kuwait. Since then, the UAE has sought to rely on the GCC, the United States, and other Western allies for its security. The UAE believes that the Arab League needs to be restructured to become a viable institution and would like to increase strength and interoperability of the GCC defence forces.

The UAE contributes to the continued security and stability of the Gulf and the Strait of Hormuz. It is a leading partner in the campaign against global terrorism, providing assistance in the military, diplomatic, and financial arenas since September 11, 2001.

France and the USA have played the most strategically significant roles with defence cooperation agreements and military material provision in UAE.

"The UAE government supported the US-led war against the Iraqi occupation of Kuwait in 1991 and has provided major logistical support for the US armed forces since then, though, as with the vast majority of Arab governments, the UAE opposed the US invasion of Iraq in 2003."[64]

Most recently, its relations with Western countries culminated in a joint nuclear deal for the US to supply the UAE with nuclear technology, expertise and fuel. According to CNN News Agency's report on April 29, 2009, the civil nuclear agreement was signed in January 2009, between the United Arab Emirates and the Bush administration, but after the new administration took office, the deal had to be recertified.

US Secretary of State, Hillary Clinton, recently signed the document and sent it to US President Obama for his signature, but President Obama has not yet signed it, as of March, 2010.

2.8.5. Economy

Prior to the first exports of oil in 1962, the separate Emirates that now constitute the UAE had similar economies which were dominated by pearl production, fishing, agriculture, and herding. Since the discovery of oil in the UAE, the UAE has undergone a profound transformation from an impoverished region of small desert principalities to a modern state with a high standard of living. The UAE, rich in oil and natural gas, has become highly prosperous after gaining foreign direct investment funding in the 1970s.

Since the rise of oil prices in 1973, however, petroleum has dominated the economy, accounting for most of its export earnings and providing significant opportunities for investment. Dependence on a large expatriate workforce and oil are significant long-term challenges to the UAE's economy.

Although the United Arab Emirates is becoming less dependent on natural resources as a source of revenue, petroleum and natural gas exports still play an important role in the economy, especially in Abu Dhabi.

A massive construction boom, an expanding manufacturing base, and a thriving services sector are helping the UAE diversify its economy.

The UAE's liberal climate towards foreign cooperation, investment and modernization has prompted extensive diplomatic and commercial relations with other countries. It plays a significant role in OPEC, the UN and is one of the founding members of the Gulf Cooperation Council.

More than 6,000 companies from more than 120 countries operate at the Jebel Ali complex in Dubai, which includes a deep-water port and a Free Trade Zone for manufacturing and distribution in which all goods for re-export or transshipment enjoy a 100 percent duty exemption. "A Trade and Investment Framework Agreement (TIFA) was signed with the USA in 2004 and a Free Trade Agreement (FTA) is under negotiation."[65]

Abu Dhabi remains the UAE's dominant economy but Dubai's growth makes it an increasingly important economic region.

As a member of the Gulf Cooperation Council (GCC), the UAE participates in a wide range of GCC activities that focus on economic issues. These include regular consultations and development of common policies covering trade, investment, banking and finance, transportation, telecommunications and other technical areas; including protection of intellectual property rights.

Recent global recession has shown its signs in the UAE's economy. Falling oil prices, cooling real estate and construction markets, together with a slowdown in the tourism sector, especially in Dubai, means the UAE is expected to post low or possibly negative GDP growth.

But some of the professionals do not believe that recession is going to be as hard as it is in Western countries. Hamad Bu Amim, Director General of the Dubai Chamber of Commerce and Industry, in an interview with Saifur Rahman, the Business Editor of Gulf News Agency stated that: "Unlike the US and other Western economies, about 95 percent of UAE enterprises are small and medium-sized family companies, employing mostly family equity with much less dependence on international capital markets. Therefore, the impact of the financial crisis on family enterprises is assumed to be mild and might be limited to indirect impact through reduced global demand for re-export. However, there is the need to protect minority shareholders to regulate bankruptcy and to regulate further development of the financial market etc. These policies should be governed by transparent laws and regulations with the required institutions to maintain and internalise them."[66]

On the other hand, some other professionals like Marios Maratheftis, the head of research at Standard Chartered bank in Dubai, stated that: "There is a possibility. In an environment when you have the US economy in a recession, the Euro zone in a recession, the UK and Japan in a recession, you cannot say there is no chance or risk of seeing a recession here, especially when there are job losses in different sectors of the economy, when we see that real estate and construction are suffering, when we see that tourism has been hit because of international factors. You cannot dismiss the risk."[67]

2.8.6. Natural Resources

The UAE's proven oil reserves make up almost one-tenth of the world's total, with about 90 percent in the emirate of Abu Dhabi and significant amounts in Dubai and Sharjah.

Although Abu Dhabi officials represented the other Emirs, the officials exercised no power over the Emirs because each maintained control of his Emirate's underground wealth. Each ruler oversaw arrangements for concessions, exploration, and oil field development in his own territory and published limited information about such arrangements.

UAE has reserves of natural gas, nationalized in 1976. The Emirates have a network of domestic pipelines linking fields with processing plants and exit ports for trade. There are also inter-emirate pipelines primarily for natural gas injection to increase oil recovery levels in existing Dubai oil fields.

The Dolphin natural gas project linking Qatar and the UAE is the most important recent development in the area. The Dolphin project was launched in March 1999 following an announcement by the UAE and Qatar of plans for a joint venture aimed at transporting gas from Qatar's huge reserves to industrial consumers in the UAE, Oman and other countries. Dolphin, which is being developed under the auspices of the UAE Offset Group (UOG), is intended to provide a framework to stimulate investment in a variety of related industries throughout the value-added gas chain.

References

1. Encarta, Encyclopedia
2. The line which divides the surface of water is called Territorial Median Line or Median Line.
3. Statesman's Year Book (2008) p.171
4. CIA World Fact Book 2005/ Bahrain
5. Statesman Year Book (2008) P.171
6. "*Bahrain Country Profile*", All'o Expat Bahrain, January 2nd, 2006
7. Smith Robert, "*New Laws Urged to Deter Racism*", Gulf Daily News, January 26th, 2005
8. Anderson Ewan W. and Bayne Fisher William, "*The Middle East: Geography and Geopolitics*", Rutledge, USA, 2000, p. 207
9. Gulf Daily News, the Voice of Bahrain, April 11th, 2009
10. www.encyclopedia.com
11. Bayne Fisher William, "*The Cambridge History of Iran*", Cambridge University Press, Volume 4, 1975, p. 398
12. US Department of State/ Human Rights, and Labor/ Report on Iran
13. Congressional Research Service's Report to USA Congress, November 25th, 2008, p. 8
14. globalsecurity.org/ military/world/ Iran/ Arabs
15. globalsecurity.org/ military/world/ Iran/ Basij

16. "*Crude price pegged at $39.6 a barrel under next year's budget*", IRNA, December 5th, 2008
17. Abrahamian Ervand, "*History of Modern Iran*", Cambridge University Press, New York, 2008, p. 178
18. "*Foreign exchange Reserves Reach $80 billion*", Iran Daily, December 4th , 2008
19. www.presstv.com, November 30th , 2008
20. The World Fact Book 2007 (CIA; Central Intelligence Agency)
21. Liu Henry C K; Independent Critical Analysis and Commentary, "*The Burden of Being Superpower*"; part 5, Asia Times Online, August 14th, 2004
22. Al Qaeda in Iraq attacked Al Askari Mosque in Samarra, one of Shiite Islam's holiest sites in February 23, 2006.
23. "*Big rise in Iraq deaths in April*", BBC News Agency, May 1st, 2009
24. One division has, in most cases, come to be units of 10,000 to 30,000 troops with enough support organic to the unit to be capable of independent operations
25. Official Documents System of the United Nations
26. USA Department of Defence, Report to Congress, June 2009
27. Parker Christopher, Moore Pete W., "*The War Economy of Iraq*", Middle East Report Online
28. Alnasrawi Abbas, "*Iraq: Economic Sanctions and Consequences, 1990–2000*", Carfax Publishing Ltd., London, 2001, p.215
29. *www.krg.org*, October 2nd, 2007
30. Dagher Sam, "*Basra Oil Fuels Fight to Control Iraq's Economic Might*," Christian Science Monitor, September 19th, 2007
31. Statesman Year Book (2008), p.759
32. "*Kuwait, Saudi Arabia to discuss joint oil projects in border areas*", Kuwait Times, January 5th, 2004
33. Reuters News Agency, January 15th, 2008
34. Institute for the Analysis of Global Security; Report on Kuwait, 2004
35. The World Fact Book 2007 (CIA; Central Intelligence Agency)
36. Floating exchange rate data taken from www.xe.com, on December 22nd, 2007

37. "*Kuwaiti economy set to contract*", Middle East Business Intelligence, March 30th, 2009
38. Casey Michael S., "*The History of Kuwait*", Greenwood Publishing Group, USA, 2007, p. 5
39. Encarta, Encyclopedia
40. PDRY united with the Yemen Arab Republic in May 1990.
41. Kechichian Joseph A., "*Oman and the World; The Emergence of An Independent Foreign Policy*", RAND, USA, 1995, p.124
42. Anderson Ewan W. and Bayne Fisher William, "*The Middle East: Geography and Geopolitics*", Rutledge, USA, 2000, p. 240
43. "*Muscat to Musandam by Sea*", BBC News Agency, July 30th, 2008
44. Omanization is a policy enacted by the government of Oman in 1988 aimed at replacing expatriate workers with trained Omani personnel.
45. www.NationMaster.com/ Military Statistics/ Personnel/ Oman
46. GulfSecurityReport.com/Oman/2003
47. Ministry of Information/ Sultanate of Oman, 2002-2003
48. Statesman Year Book (2008), p.1019
49. Coman Julian, "*Egyptian Suicide Bomber Blamed for Attack in Qatar*", The Independent, March 21st, 2005
50. CIA World Fact Book/ Qatar, April 2009
51. Klare Michael T., "*The Geopolitics of Natural Gas*", The Nation Magazine, January 30th, 2006
52. USA Department of State/ Background Note/ Saudi Arabia, January 2009
53. "*Saudi Arabia Confirms Discussing Border Disputes With UAE*", www.arabicnews.com, June 16th, 2005
54. Cordesman Anthony H., " *Saudi Arabia Enters the Twenty-first Century*", Greenwood Publishing Group, USA, 2003, p.6
55. Beehner, Lionel "*Shiite Muslims in the Mideast*", Council on Foreign Relations, USA, June 16th, 2006
56. "*Rare Shiite protests in eastern Saudi Arabia*", DAWN, A Leading Daily English Newspaper of Pakistan, February 25th, 2009, www.dawn.com
57. Anderson Ewan W. and Bayne Fisher William, "*The Middle East: Geography and Geopolitics*", Routledge, USA, 2000, p. 247

58. Cordesman Anthony H., " *Saudi Arabia Enters the Twenty-first Century*", Greenwood Publishing Group, USA, 2003, p. 13
59. Khaleej times, October 23rd, 2008
60. "*Global Economic Crisis: A Catalyst for Change in Saudi Arabia*?", The Brookings Institution, May 3rd, 2009, www.brookings.edu
61. Gray Colin S. and Sloan Geoffrey, " *Geopolitics, Geography and Strategy*", Routledge, USA, 1999, p. 127
62. The World Fact Book 2007 (CIA; Central Intelligence Agency)
63. Statesman Year Book (2008) , p.1258
64. "*US Democrats in dry dock over ports*", Asia Times, March 15th, 2006
65. Statesman Year Book (2008), pp.1259-1260
66. "*Impact of Crisis on UAE Economy is Mild*", Gulf News Agency, November 7th, 2008
67. "*Recession in UAE cannot be Ruled Out*", Arabian News Agency, May 6th, 2009

3

Geostrategic Importance of the Persian Gulf

1. Introduction

1.1. Definition of Geostrategy

Academics, theorists, and practitioners of geopolitics have agreed upon no standard definition for 'Geostrategy'. Most all definitions emphasize the merger of strategic considerations with geopolitical factors.

"The term geostrategy was first used by Frederick L. Schuman in his 1942 article "Let Us Learn Our Geopolitics."[1] It was a translation of the German term 'Wehrgeopolitik' as used by German geostrategist Karl Haushofer. Previous translations had been attempted, such as 'defense-geopolitics'. Robert Strausz Hupe had coined and popularized 'war geopolitics' as another alternate translation.

There are some distinguished scholars that have presented great geostrategic ideas. The most well-known are as follows:

1. Geostrategic Ideas of Mahan; Sea Power Theory
2. Geostrategic Ideas of Mackinder; Heartland Theory

3. Geostrategic Ideas of Spykman; Rimland Theory
4. Geostrategic Ideas of Cohen; Geostrategic Regions
5. Geostrategic Ideas of Henry Kissinger; Polarity of the International System
6. Geostrategic Ideas of Zbigniew Brzezinski; Eurasia as four Regions

The geostrategic ideas of the above mentioned scholars, have been described in Introduction, in details. In this book, OCI Geostrategy or petroleum politics of the Persian Gulf Region alongwith the role played by huge gas resources of the region in regional states policies has been delved into.

1.2. Importance of Oil and Gas Resources

1.2.1. Importance of Oil Resources

The need for oil is one of the most vital one in all countries. Its importance is such that even the most solid political alliances are subordinate to it.

All the Great Powers have 'oil policy'. Oil Geostrategy or Petroleum politics have been an increasingly important aspect of international diplomacy since the discovery of oil in the Middle East in the early 1900s. As the world population increases rapidly, energy required to fulfil their needs is also increasing. To provide required energy for transportation system; such as ships, trains, aircrafts or any other individual or public transport means, producing electricity, or any other human needs, we need energy resources. Previously, man provided the required energy mostly by the use of basic energy resources; like wood, charcoal, fertilizer, or renewal energy resources such as; solar energy, wind or water energies. With Industrial Revolution, need of a stronger energy resource like coal was felt. In the beginning of twentieth century, oil gradually came to the forefront and its particular specialities caused ever-increasing demand; especially after Second World War.

The strategic importance of oil was first realized at the beginning of the 19th century by the British, and later underscored during First World War where oil was used not only to power naval fleets, but also new instruments of warfare like planes, tanks and lorries. Winston Churchill acknowledged the importance of oil mainly because Britain had none, but also because it was well understood that relying on other countries to supply crucial resources during wartime created dependence that could pose enormous threats to security. Lack of oil during the Second World War proved to be exactly the type of strategic necessity Churchill noted in 1919. For the Third Reich, the need for oil was matter of critical importance since Germany only produced about a half million tons when she needed nearly four times that during wartime.

The world's demand for oil will continue to rise as developing nations, such as China, and industrialized ones increase their use of oil.

Dr. Mohammad Reza Hafeznia, professor of political geography in Tehran's Tarbiat Modares University, in his book, 'Persian Gulf and Strategic Role of Strait of Hormuz', has stated that "the factors of oil superseding coal are as follows:

1. Oil is cheaper than other fuels.

   Demand is controlled by a few very large multinational conglomerates, each with its own production and distribution systems that include refineries, storage facilities and distribution centres and, at the end of the supply chain, gas stations. Supply is controlled by a few countries where the oil industry is often nationalized or under a uniform price-fixing policy of OPEC which controls approximately 37% of world oil production.

2. Oil is easy to transport, especially crude oil which could be carried by ships, pipelines and super-tankers.

Since the first oil tanker began shipping oil in the Caspian Sea in 1878, the capacity of the world's maritime tanker fleet has grown substantially, to become a specialized segment of the maritime industry.

3. Oil has special chemical compounds. Many kinds of derivatives are obtained after refining that could be used in petrochemical industries.
4. Oil creates lesser environmental pollution than coal.
5. Oil's exploitation is much easier than coal's, but its exploration needs a huge amount of funds."[2]

The whole issue of oil dependency among nations that lack political stability or reliability opens the door to occasional disruptions, price changes and a transfer of wealth, such as oil crisis in 1990, which was the result of Iraq invasion of Kuwait. According to the US Department of Energy, the cost of political instability has been over US$ 3.4 trillion in the last 30 years, and the transfer of wealth to oil exporters has accounted for US$ 1.16 trillion over the same period.

According to OPEC Annual Statistical Bulletin 2008, demand for energy is set to grow and fossil fuels will continue to provide more than 90% of the world's total commercial energy needs, accounting for 93% of the demand growth to 2030. Oil has been the leading supplier of the world's energy needs for the past four decades.

On the report of the International Energy Outlook 2008, published by USA's Energy Information Administration; reference case, which reflects a scenario where current laws and policies remain unchanged throughout the projection period, world marketed energy consumption is projected to grow by 50 percent over the 2005 to 2030 projection period. Over the next 20 years, world demand for liquid fuels and those from other petroleum derivatives is expected to increase more rapidly in the transportation sector than in any other end-use sector.

Gas consumption is also expected to grow at fast rates, steadily approaching coal in its importance in the energy mix, although coal has recently seen impressive growth. The total contribution of hydropower, nuclear and new renewable energies is presumed to flatten out, despite the extreme high growth rates for some renewable sources. The low initial renewable base makes the growth in absolute terms rather limited. "Some growth in nuclear power in developing countries is assumed to be accompanied by mixed trends in industrialized regions. The scope for increases in hydropower is likely to be limited to developing countries."[3]

Studies show that in spite of expanding the use of other energy resources, especially, nuclear energy, fossil energy has still remained as the most important consumption energy and "will keep its superior role at least for the next 25 years; up to 2030."[4]

1.2.2. Importance of Gas Resources

The formation of gas takes thousands and possibly millions of years. Therefore, understanding the availability of the supply of natural gas is important as the use of this fossil fuel increase rapidly.

As natural gas is essentially irreplaceable (at least with current technology), it is important to have an idea of how much natural gas is left in the ground for us to use. However, this becomes complicated by the fact that no one really knows exactly how much natural gas exists until it is extracted.

The oil reserves are declining very fast, and gas resources seem to be the best substitute energy resource, due to which their importance is undeniable.

1.3. Oil Crisis Since 1973

1.3.1. Definition of Oil Crisis

An oil crisis is any severe bottleneck or price rise in the supply of oil to an economy. It usually refers to the shortage of oil. Market failure is possible when monopoly manipulation of markets occurs. A crisis can develop due to industrial actions like union organized strikes and government embargoes. The cause may be over-consumption, ageing infrastructure, choke point disruption or impediments at oil refineries and port facilities that restrict fuel supply. An emergency may emerge during unusually cold winters. Pipeline failures and other accidents may cause minor interruptions to energy supplies. A crisis could possibly emerge after infrastructure damage from severe weather. Attacks by terrorists or militia on important infrastructure are also a possible problem for energy consumers. Political events such as; when governments change due to regime change, monarchy collapse, military occupation, and coup may disrupt oil and gas production and create shortages.

Followings are the oil crises which have occurred since 1973:

1.3.1.1. 1973 Oil Crisis

The 1973 oil crisis began on October 17, 1973, when the members of Organization of Arab Petroleum Exporting Countries (OAPEC) consisting of the Arab members of OPEC and Egypt and Syria announced, as a result of the ongoing "Yom Kippur War"[5] Ramadan War or October War; Fourth Arab-Israeli War, from October 6 to October 26, 1973-, that they would no longer ship oil to countries like the United States, its allies in Western Europe, and Japan, that had supported Israel in its conflict with Syria, Egypt, and Iraq. At the same time, OPEC members agreed to use their leverage over the world price-setting mechanism for oil in order to raise world oil prices, after the failure of negotiations with the Seven Sisters, refers to seven oil companies that dominated mid 20th century oil production, refining and distribution, earlier in October, 1973.

Because of the dependence of the industrialized world on crude oil and the predominant role of OPEC as a global supplier, these price increases were dramatically inflationary to the economies of the targeted countries, while at the same time, suppressive of economic activity. The targeted countries responded with a wide variety of new, and mostly permanent, initiatives to contain their further dependency such as economizing energy consumption in their countries. "The market price for oil immediately rose substantially, from US$ 3 per barrel in 1973, to US$ 12 in 1974."[6]

The West could not continue to increase its energy use 5% annually, pay low oil prices, and yet sell inflation-priced goods to the petroleum producers in the Third World. This was stressed by the Shah of Iran, whose country was the world's second-largest exporter of oil and the closest ally of the United States in the Middle East at the time. "Of course [the world price of oil] is going to rise," [7] the Shah told the New York Times in 1973. "Certainly and how...; You [Western nations] increased the price of wheat you sell us by 300%, and the same for sugar and cement...; You buy our crude oil and sell it back to us, refined as petrochemicals, at a hundred times the price you've paid to us...; It's only fair that, from now on, you should pay more for oil. Let's say ten times more." He added.

On October 16, 1973, OPEC cut production of oil and placed an embargo on shipments of crude oil to the West, with the United States and the Netherlands specifically targeted. The price rises had a much greater impact in Europe than the embargo, particularly in the UK "where they combined with strike by coal miners to cause an energy crisis over the winter of 1973-74, a major factor in the change of UK government."[8]

1.3.1.2. 1979 Oil Crisis

The second oil crisis occurred in 1979 in the United States in the wake of the Iranian Revolution. Amid massive protests, the Shah of Iran; Mohammad Reza Pahlavi, fled his country in early 1979, and Ayatollah Khomeini gained control of the country. The protests shattered the Iranian oil sector. While the new regime resumed oil exports, it was inconsistent with a lesser hold forcing prices to go up.

Saudi Arabia and other OPEC nations, under the presidency of Dr. Mana Alotaiba increased production to offset the decline, and "the overall loss in production was about 4 percent."[9] A widespread panic resulted, driving the price far higher than expected under normal circumstances.

During 1980s, several events, such as, global economy stagnation and using unusual mechanisms on oil production, consumption and exportation markets, caused unusual decrease in oil prices. Amongst those unusual events, using full production capacity by Saudi Arabia, using oil reserved resources, dumping policy, artificially keeping oil prices low and creating unreal competition in the global markets are noteworthy. But those strategies did not last for a long time. After recovery of global economy in 1982, economic use diminished and energy consumption increased and as a result main pressure remained on oil consumption.

1.3.1.3. 1980s Oil Glut

The 1980s oil glut was a surplus of crude oil caused by falling demand following the 1973 and 1979 energy crises.

"In the United States, Europe and Japan, oil consumption had fallen 13% from 1979 to 1981, due to in part, in reaction to the very large increases in oil prices by the Organization of Petroleum Exporting Countries and other oil exporters, continuing a trend which began during the 1973 price increases."[10] After 1980, reduced demand and overproduction produced a glut in the world market, causing a six-year-long decline in oil prices culminating with a 46 percent price drop in 1986. "The world price of oil, which had peaked in 1979 at over US$ 35 per barrel, collapsed in 1986 from US$ 27 to below US$ 10."[11]

1.3.1.4. 1990 Oil Price Shock

The third energy crisis which occurred in 1990 was milder and more brief than the two previous oil crises of 1973 and 1979. It lasted only six months and occurred as a result of the First Gulf

War. As Saddam Hussein retreated, the oil fields of Kuwait were set on fire, causing damage that reduced the oil output until repairs could be performed. Organization of Arab Petroleum Exporting Countries (OAPEC) decided that since the oil production in the Kuwait was falling, they would increase their oil supply and stabilize the oil market. "Oil hit a then-record of US$ 50.50 per barrel during this crisis."[12]

1.3.1.5. 2000s Oil Crisis

The sharp spikes in oil prices associated with the 1973-74 oil embargoes, the 1979 Iranian Revolution, the Iran-Iraq War in 1980s, and the First Persian Gulf War in 1990 were each followed by an economic recession.

However, when oil prices started to rise again since 2003, many experts suggested that things would be different this time, in part, because the price was rising much more gradually and so should be less disruptive of consumer spending patterns. Others emphasized that, despite the price increases, oil was still cheaper than it had been historically if inflation was taken into account.

For a time, certain international events and natural disasters not directly related to the global oil market had strong short term effects on oil prices, such as North Korean missile tests, the 2006 conflict between Israel and Lebanon, worries over Iranian nuclear plans in 2006, Hurricane Katrina in USA and various other factors. If Iranian revolution sent oil shock waves worldwide almost three decades ago, it was speculators ruling the markets in 2008, driving prices to a record high of US$ 147 a barrel on July 11, 2008. By 2008, such pressures did not appear to have as much of a significant impact on oil prices given the onset of the global recession. The recession caused demand for energy to shrink in late 2008 and early 2009 and the price plunged as well. However, it surged back in May 2009, bringing it back to November 2008 levels. On June 10, 2009, the price reached US$ 71 per barrel on hopes of an economic recovery, as reported by the BBC News Agency on that date.

1.4. Strategic Petroleum Reserves (SPR)

To provide economic and national security during an energy crisis, many countries maintain government-controlled oil reserves.

According to the United States Energy Information Administration 2007 Report, approximately, 4.1 billion barrels of oil are held in strategic reserves, of which, 1.4 billion barrel is government-controlled. The remainder is held by private industry. At present, the US Strategic Petroleum Reserve is one of the largest strategic reserves, 700 million barrels on August 17, 2005, with much of the remainder held by the other 26 members of the International Energy Agency. Recently, other non-International Energy Agency countries have began creating their own strategic petroleum reserves, with China being the largest of these new reserves. Since current consumption levels are neighboring 0.1 billion barrels per day, in the case of a dramatic worldwide drop in oil field output as suggested by some "peak oil"[13] analysts, the strategic petroleum reserves are unlikely to last for more than a few months. For example at current US consumption rates of over 7 billion barrels per year, the SPR would supply all normal US demand for approximately 37 days while Japan's SPR will supply the state's demand for about 169 days. To avoid facing any shortage of energy, the countries have to use alternate kind of energies or try to use the existed reserves more economically until situation becomes back to normal.

2. Persian Gulf Region's Oil and Gas Resources

2.1. Persian Gulf Oil Resources

The strategic importance of its large oil resources has turned the Persian Gulf region into one of the most internationalized regions in the world. The Persian Gulf and its coastal areas are the world's largest single source of crude oil and related industries dominate the region. The Persian Gulf countries contain a significant percentage of the world's oil reserves, production, and capacity. The Persian Gulf countries consistently maintain most of the world's excess oil production capacity.

The raw data of reserves estimates is considered a state secret in some countries, so independent assessments of their reserves cannot be made, but "it has been predicted that Persian Gulf region will remain the biggest oil holder and producer of the world at least for next two and half decades more."[14] Estimates in developed countries are generally much more accurate than those for undeveloped countries. For instance, reserves estimates in the United States are considered highly accurate, while those in Iraq are highly uncertain. In many countries, particularly OPEC producers, the estimates may involve a great deal of political influence.

In 2006, the Persian Gulf countries namely Bahrain, Iran, Iraq, Kuwait, Qatar, Saudi Arabia, and the United Arab Emirates, produced about "28 percent of the world's oil"[15], while holding 55 percent which constituted 728 billion barrels of the world's crude oil reserves. Major offshore Persian Gulf oil fields include Khafji and Hout, both of which are connected to Saudi Arabia's Safaniyah, the world's largest offshore oilfield, with estimated reserves of 19 billion barrels.

The following key oil data extracted from Energy Information Administration; (EIA) Report in 2007, depicts the importance of the Persian Gulf region:

1. Proven oil reserves of 728 billion barrels, representing over half (55 percent) of the world's oil reserves at the end of 2006,
2. Oil production capacity of 25.4 million barrels per day; 33 percent of the world total at the end of 2006,
3. Total oil production of 23.6 million barrels per day; 28% of the world total at the end of 2006,
4. About 2.4 - 2.9 million barrels per day of excess world oil production capacity as of March 2007, of which, 1.9 to 2.4 million barrels per day was located in Saudi Arabia and most of the remainder, about 0.5 million barrel per day, located in other Persian Gulf countries such as Kuwait and the United Arab Emirates.

According to the reference case estimate in the Energy Information Administration's International Energy Outlook (2006), Gulf oil production is expected to reach about 28.3 million barrels per day by 2010, 31.1 million barrels per day by 2020, and 36.8 million barrels per day by 2030.

Oil holder countries of the region are respectively Saudi Arabia, Iran, Iraq, Kuwait, UAE, Qatar, Oman and Bahrain.

Table 3.1.: Persian Gulf Countries Petroleum Statistics*

Country	*Reserves (2006) (Billion barrel)*	*Capacity of Production (2006) (Million barrel per day)*	*Production (2006) (Million barrel per day)*	*Consumption (2006) (Million barrel per day)*
Saudi Arabia	262.3	12.1	10.7	2.1
Iran	136.3	4.3	4.1	1.6
Iraq	115.0	2.0	2.0	0.6
Kuwait	101.5	2.8	2.7	0.5
UAE	97.8	3.1	2.9	0.4
Qatar	15.2	1.2	1.1	0.1
Oman	6.1	0.8	0.76	0.08
Bahrain	0.125	0.125	0.05	0.03

*Source: Extracted from EIA Short Term Energy Outlook, 2006

With regard to the petroleum industry, there remain three basic problems for Gulf States which are as follows:

1. To ensure that the benefits of the resulting GDP, for Saudi Arabia, the UAE and Kuwait, among the highest per head of population in the world, reach as widely as possible among their own people.
2. To make provision by development of their activities, for the time when oil wealth will decline.
3. To devise a means whereby the economic power of the oil states is used globally and particularly for the Arab and Islamic Worlds in a positive and constructive way.

All this can only be achieved by ensuring stability within the Persian Gulf region.

2.1.1. Discovery of Oil in the Persian Gulf Region

At the end of First World War, the Arab states of the gulf were weak, with faltering economies and with local rulers who maintained their autonomy only with British assistance. The rulers controlled mainly the small port cities and some of the hinterland.

The discovery of oil in the region changed all this. Oil was first discovered in Iran in 1908, and by 1911, a British concern, the Anglo-Persian Oil Company (APOC), was producing oil in Iran. One reason for the increased activity was that, in 1932, the new Iranian government of Reza Shah Pahlavi revoked APOC's concession. Although the Shah and the British later agreed on new terms, the threat of losing Iranian oil convinced the British, in particular, that they must find other sources.

The small states of the Persian Gulf were a natural place to look. Geological conditions were similar to those in Iran, and, because of treaties signed between 1820 and 1920, the British had substantial influence and could restrict foreign access.

The British found oil in Iraq after First World War in 1922. In 1932, Standard Oil Company of California (SOCAL) discovered oil in commercial quantities in Bahrain.

SOCAL then obtained a concession in Saudi Arabia in 1933 and discovered oil in commercial quantities in 1938. A flurry of oil exploration activity occurred in the gulf in the 1930s with the United States and Britain competing with one another for oil concessions. Oil exploration did not mean immediate wealth for Arab rulers of the area. Although, the oil companies struck large deposits of oil in Bahrain almost immediately, it took longer in other countries to locate finds of commercial size.

Second World War delayed development of whatever fields that had been discovered in the 1930s; so it was not until the 1950s, that countries still technically dependent on Britain for their security began to earn large incomes. Moreover, "in 1930 no one knew the size of gulf oil reserves."[16]

The oil fields in Kuwait were developed the fastest, and by 1953, that country had become the largest oil producer in the gulf.

Considerably smaller fields in Qatar came on stream in commercial quantities in the 1950s, and Abu Dhabi began to export offshore oil in 1962. Dubai began to profit from offshore oil deposits in the late 1960s. Until the 1970s, foreign companies owned and managed the gulf oil industry.

In most cases, European and United States-based concerns formed subsidiaries to work in specific countries, and these subsidiaries paid fees to the local rulers, first for the right to explore for oil and later for the right to export the oil. When the first arrangements were made, local rulers had a weak bargaining position because they had few other sources of income and were eager to get revenues from the oil companies as fast as possible.

As production increased and the extent of oil deposits became known, indigenous rulers improved their terms. In the 1950s, rulers routinely demanded an equal share of oil company profits in addition to a royalty fee.

By the 1970s, most of the gulf countries, which by then were independent of British control, bought major shares in the subsidiary companies that worked within their borders. By the early 1990s, many of these subsidiaries had become completely state-owned concerns. They continued to employ Western experts at the highest decision-making levels, but the local government had ultimate responsibility and profits.

In 1971, Mr. William Rogers, former American Foreign Minister, said that; "Saudi Arabian Peninsula, Iraq and Iran possess two thirds of the world's proven oil reserves and using this oil; in suitable political and economical conditions, is vital for USA's allied countries".[17]

2.1.2. Persian Gulf Region's Exporting Oil

Oil production in the Persian Gulf region began in 1908 and "European countries took possession of revenue of oil exporting for almost five decades."[18]

In the most of the regional states, exploitation and exportation were conducted simultaneously, but some of them stopped exporting during Second World War. "For example, Saudi Arabia started to export oil in 1946, Qatar in 1950, Dubai in 1969, Sharjeh in 1974 and Ras Al Khaimeh in 1984."[19]

According to the Energy Information Administration; (EIA), in 2006, the Persian Gulf countries had estimated net oil exports of 18.2 million barrels per day of oil, including, about 17 million barrels per day via the Straight of Hormuz, representing roughly one-fifth of world's oil supply. Saudi Arabia exported the most oil than any other Persian Gulf country in 2006, with an estimated 8.7 million barrels per day, and 6.25 million barrels per day in 2007. Iran had estimated net exports of about 2.5 million barrels per day, while the figures for United Arab Emirates are 2.5 million barrels per day, for Kuwait as 2.2 million barrels per day, Iraq as 2 million barrels per day, for Qatar as 1.0 million barrels per day and for Bahrain as 0.02 million barrels per day.

According to the EIA, gross oil imports of the Organization for Economic Cooperation and Development (OECD)[20] from Persian Gulf countries averaged about 10.4 million barrels per day during 2006, accounting for 31 percent of the OECD's total net oil imports. Because the world's lowest-cost oil reserves are currently concentrated in the Middle East, especially in the Persian Gulf, the United States and other oil -importing countries will rely more on this historically unstable region to supply a rising share of their oil imports. "The extent of the economy's vulnerability depends on the likelihood or probability of a disruption, the economy's dependence on oil, and the nation's ability to respond to a disruption."[21]

2.1.2.1. Exports to USA

USA gross oil imports (mostly crude) from the Persian Gulf averaged as 2.2 million barrels per day during 2006. The majority of Persian Gulf oil and petroleum products imported by the United States came from Saudi Arabia (66 percent), with significant amounts also coming from Iraq (25 percent), Kuwait (8 percent), and small amounts (less than 1 percent total) from Qatar and the United Arab Emirates. Iraqi total liquids exports to the United States reached 5,53,000 barrels per day in 2006. Saudi exports fell from 1.54 million barrels per day in 2005 to 1.46 million barrels per day in 2006. "Overall, the Persian Gulf accounted for about 18 percent of US net oil imports and approximately 11 percent of US oil demand in 2006."[22]

2.1.2.2. Exports to Europe

Europe has extensive strategic, political, economic, and historical/cultural interests in the Persian Gulf. Europe depends heavily on oil imports from the Gulf, notwithstanding its efforts to diversify sources of energy supplies from North Africa, Russia, and the Atlantic Basin.

Western Europe, defined as European countries belonging to the Organization for Economic Cooperation and Development - OECD in the context, averaged 2.8 million barrels per day of oil imports from the Persian Gulf during 2006, a decrease of less than 0.1 million barrels per day from 2005. The largest share of Persian Gulf oil exports to Western Europe came from Saudi Arabia (44 percent), with significant amounts also coming from Iran (33 percent), Iraq (13 percent), and Kuwait (7 percent).

2.1.2.3. Exports to Japan

Japan averaged 4.4 million barrels per day of net oil imports from the Persian Gulf during 2006. Japan's dependence on the Persian Gulf for its oil supplies increased sharply since the low point of 57 percent in 1988 to a high of 83 percent in 2006. About 35 percent of Japan's Persian Gulf imports in 2006 came from Saudi

Arabia, 29 percent from the United Arab Emirates, 12 percent from Iran, 12 percent from Qatar, 10 percent from Kuwait, and over 1 percent from Bahrain and Iraq combined.

2.2. Persian Gulf Gas Resources

The Persian Gulf countries continue to expand their roles in the natural gas market and its global market share continues to grow. Natural gas exports from the Persian Gulf travel through the Strait of Hormuz in LNG tankers.

According to the Energy Information Administration in its Region's Analysis Brief of June 2007, the Persian Gulf region contains huge reserves; 2528 Trillion Cubic Feet of natural gas "amounting to over 40 percent of the world's total. The reserves of gas are more giant fielded by far than any of the other 27 regions of giant gas fields in the world."[23]

Iran, Qatar, Saudi Arabia and the United Arab Emirates hold the world's second, third, fourth, and fifth-largest reserves, after those of Russia, respectively.

Table 3.2.: Persian Gulf Countries Natural Gas Statistics*

Country	*Reserves per day (TCF)** 2008*	*Production per day (TCF) 2006*	*Consumption per day (TCF) 2007*
Iran	948	5.5 (2009)	5
Qatar	910	0.104	0.1
Saudi Arabia	253	2.59	2.59
UAE	214	1.7	1.5
Iraq	112	0.1	0.1
Kuwait	63 (2009)	0.5	0.5
Oman	18	0.8	0.38
Bahrain	3.25	0.4	0.4

* Source: EIA (2008) and Oil and Gas Journal (January 2009)

** Trillion Cubic Feet

In late 2000, Saudi Arabia resolved a long-standing offshore Persian Gulf border dispute with Kuwait, opening the door to development of the huge (13 Tcf) Dorra gas field, which lies in waters straddling Iranian, Saudi, and Kuwaiti territories. Large gas finds have been made with Qatar and Iran sharing a giant field across the territorial median line (North Field in the Qatari sector; South Pars Field in the Iranian sector). Most of Qatar's gas is located in the North Dome Field, which contains 380 Tcf of in-place and 239 Tcf of recoverable reserves, making it the largest known non-associated gas field in the world.

"In the high price case, the higher world crude oil price is expected to result in increased natural gas consumption in overseas energy markets, exerting upward pressure on LNG prices."[24] This likely will become increasingly important in coming years, as both domestic gas consumption and gas exports [by pipeline and also by liquefied natural gas (LNG) tankers] increase.

3. Regional States' Oil and Gas Resources

In this section, the regional states' oil resources have been examined separately in decreasing order of their reserves.

3.1. Saudi Arabia

3.1.1. Oil Resources

According to the OPEC Annual Report of 2007, Saudi Arabia had 262 billion barrels of estimated oil reserves, which, at the rate of production in 2004 as 9 million barrel per day, its reserves would last about 75 years. "Above the proven reserves, Saudi Arabia has an estimated 100 billion barrel 'possible and probable' reserves, and 'contingent reserves' of 240 billion barrel."[25]

Saudi Arabia is perhaps the best example of a contemporary energy superpower, in terms of having power and influence on the global stage on account of its energy reserves and production of not only oil, but natural gas as well. Saudi Arabia is often referred to as the world's only "oil superpower."[26] Saudi Arabia has been described as the world 'mother lode' of oil and gas reserves. It possesses both the world's largest known oil reserves, which are 25% of the world's proven reserves, and produces the largest amount of the world's oil.

Saudi Arabia ranks as the "largest exporter of petroleum"[27], and plays a leading role in Organization of Petroleum Exporting Countries (OPEC); its decisions to raise or cut production almost immediately impact world oil prices.

In Saudi Arabia, oil was discovered in 1937. Commercial quantities of oil were discovered in the country in 1938, but Second World War (1939-1945) delayed large-scale exports until the 1950s. The bulk of Saudi Arabia's crude oil production is exported. In 1980, for example, crude oil exports totaled about 9.2 million barrel per day which was 93 percent of oil production.

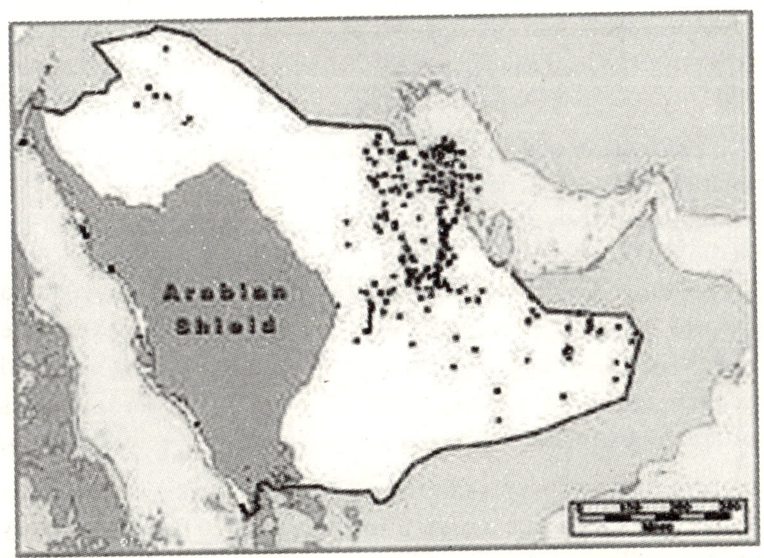

Map 3.1.: Major Saudi Arabia's Oil Fields• #

• Source: oilempire.us/saudi

Black dots indicate oil fields

Initial exploration and drilling were carried out by the Arabian American Oil Company (ARAMCO) (which is now 100% state-owned and accounts for about 99% of total crude oil production), the operating company of Standard Oil of California (SOCAL). Several other US oil companies acquired shares in Aramco in 1948. The Saudi government bought 25 percent share of the company in 1973, took its complete control in 1980, after which the company was called Saudi Aramco.

Oil production in Saudi Arabia is cheap relative to elsewhere, increasing its attraction to the global market. Whereas the finding and development costs of oil production in Saudi Arabia come to "US$ 0.50 per barrel, the global average is US$ 4-5 per barrel."[28]

Lower oil prices and more aggressive pricing structures enabled Saudi Arabia to place greater quantities of oil in North America by the early 1990s when this market constituted almost one-third of Saudi crude oil sales overseas. By contrast, Western Europe's importance to Saudi Arabia as an importer of crude fell during the 1980s from 41 percent in 1981 to about 18 percent by 1990.

Production comes from 14 major oilfields, mostly in the Eastern Province and offshore and including production from the Neutral Zone. Although Saudi Arabia has around 300 oil and gas reservoirs, 90 percent of its oil production comes from only five fields, and according to the British Petroleum's Statistical Review of World Energy in June 2008, up to 60 percent of its production comes from one field, the Ghawar field. The Ghawar oilfield, located between Riyadh and the Persian Gulf, is the largest in the world, with estimated reserves of 70 billion barrels.

Production rose steadily from about 1.3 million barrels per day in 1960, to 3.8 million barrels per day in 1970. As a member of the Organization of Petroleum Exporting Countries (OPEC), Saudi Arabia had joined other member countries in moderate oil price increases beginning in 1971.The increased production coupled with rising oil prices, especially in 1973 and 1974, brought huge revenues to the Saudi government. Another rapid increase in revenues followed the Islamic Revolution of Iran (1978-1979), when Saudi Arabia increased production to compensate for the drop in Iranian production, and prices rose due to the uncertain market. Oil prices declined along with world demand for oil during the worldwide economic recession of the early 1980s.

Saudi Arabia is an oil-based economy with strong government controls over major economic activities.

Saudi Arabia's short-term oil policy in the early 1990s has been shaped by two major sequences of events, as follows:

1. The first was Saudi Arabia's refusal to play the role of 'swing producer' in the mid-1980s, its subsequent bid to maintain its market share, and abandonment of the fixed oil price system after the 1986 price crash.
2. The second was Iraq's invasion of Kuwait, the kingdom's replacement of most of the oil lost from these two OPEC members, and its ascendance as unchallenged leader within OPEC after August 1990. Both periods have shaped an oil policy that called for OPEC decisions to promote moderate and stable oil prices but not compromise the kingdom's demand for its market share. Before the Persian Gulf War, Saudi Arabia demanded about 25 percent of the OPEC production ceiling; after the Iraqi invasion of Kuwait the share rose to 35 percent.

Saudi Arabia produced 10.3 million barrels of oil in 1980, 10.6 million barrels in 2006 and "8.8 million barrels per day in 2007."[29]

The country produced 8.358 million barrels in March 2009, compared with around 8.056 million barrels in February 2009. According to the Energy Business Review, published in May 2009, Saudi Arabia raised its oil production by nearly 3,00,000 barrels per day in March 2009 in spite of a collective agreement by the Organization of Petroleum Exporting Countries (OPEC) to cut crude supplies to support prices, official figures revealed.

Under the cartel's (OPEC) latest accord, Saudi Arabia was allocated a quota of 8.051 million barrels per day. Saudi Arabia gave no explanation for the output increase in its report to the Riyadh-based Joint Oil Data Initiative (Jodi).

But its March 2009 production was way below its output of 9.463 million barrels per day in September 2008, when the oil cartel group decided to begin a series of output reductions after crude prices began crumbling under the pressure of slackening demand due to the global financial turmoil. After hitting a record high level of US$ 147 in July 2008, prices tumbled below US$ 40 in late 2008 before they rebounded above US$ 60 in the middle of May 2009.

The kingdom recently announced its intention to increase production capacity to 12.5 million barrels per day by mid 2009, however, there are experts who believe Saudi oil production has already peaked or will do so soon. In a study discussed in Matthew Simmons[30] book, "Twilight in the Desert", 200 technical papers on Saudi reserves by the Society of Petroleum Engineers were analyzed to reach the conclusion that Saudi Arabia's oil production faces near term decline, and that it will not be able to consistently produce more than current levels. Simmons also argues that the Saudis may have irretrievably damaged their large oil fields by over-pumping salt water into the fields in an effort to maintain the fields' pressure and boost short term oil extraction amounts.

Saudi Arabia is a key oil supplier to the US, Europe and Japan. In recent years, however, Western Hemisphere producers viz. Canada, Venezuela and Mexico have challenged Saudi Arabia's dominance in the US market. For the last several years, Asia has imported more Saudi oil than the US. Still, Riyadh is eager to maintain and even expand its market share in the US for a variety of economic and strategic reasons. Indeed, for more than seven decades, Riyadh and Washington have established and maintained a very special relationship to ensure their mutual oil interests.

3.1.2. Gas Resources

According to the January 2009 issue of Oil and Gas Journals Saudi Arabia has the fourth largest proven natural gas reserves in the world, estimated at 253 trillion cubic feet, in 2008. According to Saudi Aramco, only 15 percent of Saudi Arabia has been adequately explored for gas.

Saudi Arabia began producing natural gas liquids in 1962. In 1982, the first phase of the so-called Master Gas System was put in place. This system was built to capture the natural gas that was released as a by-product of oil production and distribute it to power petrochemical plants, steel factories, and other manufacturing enterprises. By the late 1990s, plans were put forward to exploit the kingdom's other gas fields.

According to OPEC and other sources, an estimated 13 to 14 percent of total production is lost to venting, flaring, reinjection and natural processes. Saudi Arabia has no net imports or exports of natural gas.

Up until recently, the production of natural gas has been heavily controlled as it is so closely linked to oil production. However, the government of Saudi Arabia and Saudi Aramco were criticized for providing heavily subsidized natural gas to its consumers by the World Trade Organization.

The gas sector has been opened up to foreign investment. In June 2001, Saudi Arabia awarded concessions for the projects to several foreign companies, marking the return of foreign companies for the first time since 1975.

In 2001, Saudi Arabia produced 1.9 trillion cubic feet (Tef) of natural gas. In 2005, natural gas reserves were 242.7 trillion cubic feet; output in 2005 was 2.4 trillion cubic feet and 2.59 trillion cubic feet in 2006.

Over the last decade and a half, Saudi Aramco has added around 75 Tcf of non-associated reserves, including the fields: Mazalij, Manjura, Shaden, Niban, Tinat, Al-Waar, and Fazran in the deep Khuff, Unaizah and Jauf reservoirs.

According to Energy Information Agency's Country Analysis Briefs 2007, around one third of Saudi Arabia's proven natural gas reserves consist of associated gas at the giant onshore Ghawar field and the offshore Safaniya and Zuluf fields.

Saudi Arabia has prioritized gas development outside the Empty Quarter (Rub al Khali) and recent non-associated gas finds are promising. The Karan gas field, discovered in April 2006, is the largest gas deposit yet discovered in the offshore Khuff formation, some 100 miles north of Dhahran. Initial data shows at least eight gas-bearing structures in the Khuff region around the Karan reservoir containing an estimated 9 Tcf of reserves. Of those, Karan alone is expected to produce some 1.5 billion cubic feet per day when it comes online in 2012.

Both associated and non-associated natural gas has also been discovered in the country's extreme northwest, at Midyan, and in the Empty Quarter in the country's south-eastern desert.

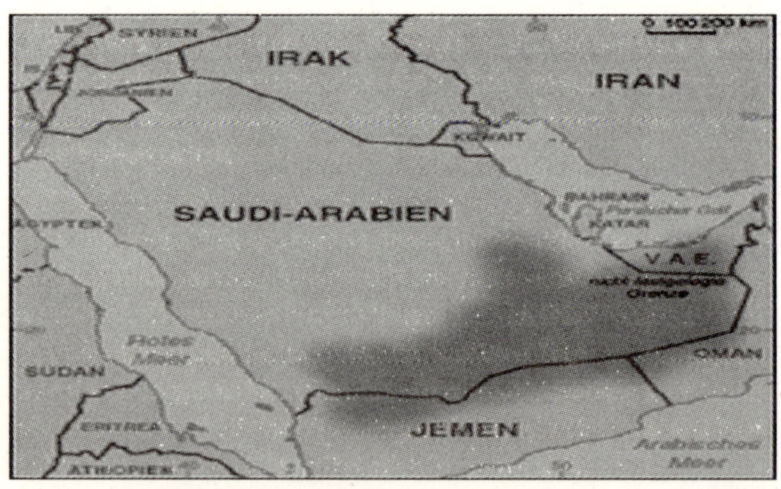

Map 3.2.: Saudi Arabia's Rub Al Khali Desert• #

• Source: Wikipedia

Red colour shows Rub al Khali desert.

The Rub al Khali is believed to contain natural gas reserves potentially as high as 300 Tcf, although these are not proven. The area remains under exploration.

Another large non-associated offshore natural gas field, Dorra (Durra), is located offshore near Khafji oil field in the Saudi-Kuwaiti Neutral Zone. The Dorra field has been claimed by Saudi Arabia, Kuwait, and Iran, and may contain up to 11 Trillion cubic feet of recoverable natural gas reserves. It is not currently in production. Dorra development has been controversial since the late 1960s, however, because 70 percent is also claimed by Iran. In addition, the maritime border between Kuwait and Iran remains un-demarcated.

Saudi Arabia reached an agreement with Kuwait in July 2000 to share Dorra output equally, although, the Kuwaitis are reportedly trying to purchase the Saudi share.

As with oil, negotiations continue between Kuwait and Iran regarding the disputed Dorra offshore natural gas field and any development requires resolution of demarcation issues.

In January 2004, Russia's Lukoil won a tender to explore for and produce non-associated natural gas and natural gas liquids in the Saudi Empty Quarter in Block A extending 11,000 sq miles, near Ghawar, as part of an 80/20 joint venture with Saudi Aramco, known as Luksar.

3.2. Iran

3.2.1. Oil Resources

According to Oil and Gas Journal; January 2009, Iran has an estimated 136.3 billion barrels of proven oil reserves, or roughly 10 percent of the world's total proven petroleum. Iran has 40 producing fields, 27 onshore and 13 offshore, with the majority of crude oil reserves located in the giant offshore fields in south-western Khuzestan region near the Iraqi border. According to the same source, Iran's oil reserves would last 98 years if no new oil was found. A 2007 National Academy of Sciences study reports that if decline rates are allowed to continue, Iran's exports, which in 2007 averaged 2.4 million barrels per day could decrease to zero by 2015. To offset natural decline rates, Iran's oil fields require structural upgrades including Enhanced Oil Recovery (EOR) efforts such as natural gas injection.

Iran is an energy giant and claims to have the world's second largest reserves of oil; it will be the third holder of oil reserves if we consider Canada's oil sands.

Iran as a rich and ancient history, and both its energy resources and its geostrategic position, make it the main actor in the present political and energy confrontations. Oil is both Iran's strategic strong point and its strategic weak point. It has given the state an unrivaled ability for maneuvering in both the domestic and the global spheres and Iran can use its large oil reserves as a geostrategic weapon. But because of the same reasons, if the present structural distortions, such as petrol smuggling via Iran's border with Iraq, Pakistan and Turkey, are not corrected, it can pose major security problems for the government. Given the growing importance of the Persian Gulf in the world oil market, Iran's position will strengthen with time.

In Iran, oil was discovered in 1908 in the Zagros Mountains; west of the country, and the main oilfields are in this area. Anglo-Iranian Oil Company was founded in 1909.

Oil has been the main industry in Iran since 1920s. Nationalization of the oil industry in 1951 resulted in temporary political and financial chaos. Production did not resume until late 1954. As part of the nationalization process, the government formed the National Iranian Oil Company (NIOC). A's owner, the government directed NIOC policy.

As a result of the Consortium Agreement reached in 1954 between the government and a consortium of foreign oil companies, industry control of the oil companies was left virtually intact, but the agreement greatly increased the government's share of income from each barrel of oil produced and also led to a policy of increased economic and political cooperation between Iran and states outside the Soviet sphere of influence.

The combination of the larger share of income and rising oil production provided the government with increased revenues with which to finance industrial development. In addition, slow but steady progress was made in re-establishing Iran's relations with Western powers in the aftermath of nationalization.

Iran is a founding member of the Organization of the Petroleum Exporting Countries (OPEC). In 1961, Iran joined with other major oil-exporting countries to form OPEC and participates in the cartel's restrictive output practices to drive up the price of oil on the world market. It is OPEC's second largest oil exporter, after Saudi Arabia. Iran's rate of oil production and its share of OPEC's oil output are much lower than they were prior to the Iranian revolution and the subsequent war with Iraq. Oil production did increase after the war but is only now approaching the level of 35 years ago; in 1975. Iran's share of OPEC production was 12.5 percent in 2005 compared to 19.8 percent in 1974.

The global recession of the early 1980s depressed the demand for oil. Iranian exports were also affected by the increased production by countries that were not members of the Organization of Petroleum Exporting Countries (OPEC). The resulting glut in the market caused a decline in Iranian oil revenues.

In 1999, the most important discovery in more than 30 years was made, with the Azadegan oilfield in the southwest of the country being found to have reserves of approximately 26 billion barrels and Iran hopes to increase production to 50,000 barrels per day by 2009 as part of the first phase of Azadegan oil field. Achieving the production goal of 1,40,000 barrels per day by 2014-2015 (Azadegan Phase II) will likely require significant further investment, as well as an international partner to provide the technical expertise.

Iran's oil production has been declining steadily from its pre-revolution peak of 6 million barrels per day to its present 4 million barrels per day - below its OPEC quota - due to war, sanctions, low investment and depletion. Despite its enormous oil reserves, Iran imports 43 percent of its petrol needs from other countries, primarily due to huge domestic demands as well as lack of sufficient refining capacity.

According to the Energy Information Administration's 2008 report, at 2006 Iran was producing an estimated 3.8 million barrels per day of crude oil, equal to 5% of global production, and "4 million barrels per day in 2007."[31]

Iran plans to increase oil production capacity to over 4.5 million barrels per day by 2010 and 5 million barrels per day after 2015, but foreign assistance will, likely, be necessary. Foreign investment in Iran's energy sector has been tempered by international unease related to US economic sanctions. According to the IEA 2008 Medium-Term Oil Market Report, Iran will not be able to expand oil production capacity through 2013.

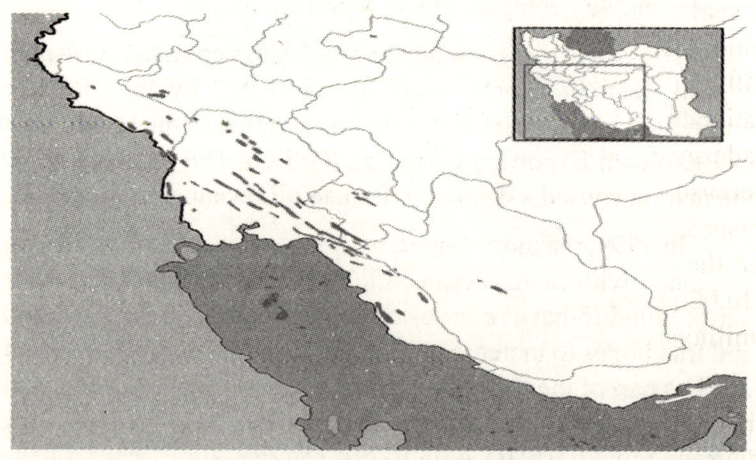

Map 3.3.: Iran's Major Oil Fields
Source: Wikipedia

In June 2008, Director of Iranian National Oil Company, Mr. Seifallah Jashnsaz, declared Iran's oil reserves as 136 billion barrels and emphasized that oil production will be increased. "Iran as second largest oil producer of OPEC has focused on expanding small oil fields and enlargement of exploiting current active fields."[32] He added. As an example, he stated that "a new oil field with the capacity of 750 million barrel has been discovered in Jofeir oil field; consequently, its capacity which was 25,000 barrel per day will be increased to 33,000 barrel per day. The mentioned field's development will be done with the participation of two companies; Petro Iran Company and Belarus Oil Company with each of them having 50% of shares."[33]

In August 2008, Gholam-Hossein Nozari, former Iran's oil minister, said in an interview with Islamic Republic News Agency (IRNA) that "the Iranian oil industries' greatest challenge in recent years the provision of parts, reiterating that we turned it to an opportunity, manufacturing what we needed in Iran."[34] He further reiterated, "During the past three years the most important goods and spare parts required by our oil industries were manufactured inside our country." He referred to the manufacturing of facilities to seal the oil wells and drilling oil derricks as spectacular achievements of the Iranian oil industries, adding, "The number of drilling oil derricks in the year 2005 was about 56, but today the National Drilling Company, which is the private sector, too, has made investments, owns over 75 derricks, which shows a 50% increase." Nozari reiterated, "These are the opportunities we grasped during the course of the past three years." He announced that the highest daily production of Iran has been 4 million and 2,30,000 barrels per day, while Iran is today capable of producing 4 million and 2,35,000 barrels per day.

Though, Iran is one of the major owners and producers of oil, it has very limited refinery facilities. Due to its nuclear dispute, Iran is under very prohibitive sanctions, especially, with regard to importing petrol. The government of President Mahmud Ahmadinejad began rationing petrol in 2008, to 'vaccinate' the country against possible sanctions. Due to current situation in Iran, which has begun since June 13, 2009 after declaration of the result of the presidential election, there is possibility of stopping petrol export to Iran by the states which oppose the Iranian government's reaction against protesters.

The geostrategy of the 21st century requires a mode of perception of the organization and representation of power, its contents and the space in which it emerges. Iran is now a unique case in the emergence of a regional power and can be understood only in a geopolitical and geostrategic approach.

3.2.2. Gas Resources

More important than oil, however, is Iran's position as the country with the second largest natural gas reserves in the world, after Russia. Although Iran's oil reserves are being rigorously exploited, her gas reserves remain largely untouched.

According to Oil and Gas Journal; January 2009, Iran's 2008 estimated proven natural gas reserves stand at 948 trillion cubic feet. Roughly two-thirds of Iranian natural gas reserves are located in non-associated fields, and have not been developed.

Major natural gas fields include: South and North Pars, Tabnak, and Kangan-Nar, all located near the Persian Gulf coastal area in south-west of Iran.

The National Iranian Gas Company (NIGC) is responsible for natural gas infrastructure, transportation, and distribution. Due to the poor investment climate, some international oil companies including Repsol, Shell, and Total have divested from Iran's natural gas sector. In response, Iran has looked toward eastern firms, like state-owned Indian Oil Corporation.

Currently, China's Petroleum and Chemical Corporation and Russia's Gazprom have taken an increased role in Iranian natural gas upstream development.

The most significant energy development project in Iran is the offshore South Pars field (called the North Field in Qatar), which is estimated to have 450 trillion cubic feet of natural gas reserves, or around 47 percent of Iran's total natural gas reserves.

Map 3.4.: Iran's Major Gas Fields
Source: Wikipedia

Discovered in 1990, and located 62 miles offshore in the Persian Gulf, South Pars has a 25 phase development scheme spanning 20 years. The entire project is managed by Pars Oil & Gas Company, a subsidiary of the National Iranian Oil Company. Each phase has a combination of natural gas with condensate and/or natural gas liquids production associated with it. Phases 1-6 are online, and Phases 7-10 are at varying levels of completion.

The majority of South Pars natural gas development will be allocated to the domestic market for consumption and gas re-injection. The remainder will either be exported to South Asia or Europe, used for LNG production, and/or used for gas to liquids (GTL) projects.

In 2009, Iran was producing only a small share of its gas reserves, about 5.5 trillion cubic feet per year. This means that Iran is one of the few countries capable of supplying much larger amounts of natural gas in the future. Iran still has huge potential for new significant gas discoveries. The areas like Caspian Sea, North East, Central Kavir and, especially, areas starting from Aghar and Dalan gas fields in Fars province up to the Strait of Hormuz and Central Persian Gulf have considerable amount of undiscovered gas resources. "According to Exploration Directorate of National Iranian Oil Company (NIOC), there are about 150 unexplored anticlines in Iran."[35]

Table 3.3.: Iran's Rank in World Natural Gas Reserves

World Natural Gas Reserves by Country, January 1, 2009

Country	Trillion Cubic Feet
Russia	1,680.0
Iran	991.6
Qatar	891.9
Saudi Arabia	258.0
USA	237.7
UAE	214.4
Nigeria	184.2
Venezuela	170.9
Algeria	159.0

Trillion Cubic Feet

Source : Oil & Gas Journal, Jan. 1, 2009

In January 2008, former Iranian Minister of Petroleum, Gholam Hussein Nozari, said that "NIOC has a target of producing one billion cubic meters of gas per day."[36]

In April 2008, Oman and Iran signed an agreement to develop Iran's offshore Kish field. With estimated reserves of 50 Trillion Cubic Feet, Oman will invest US$ 7 billion in developing Kish in the hope of producing 3 Billion Cubic Feet per day of natural gas. Phase one of the project, tentatively scheduled for first delivery to Oman by 2013, will produce approximately 2 Billion cubic feet per day; 65% of production will remain in Iran, the remaining 35% goes to Oman. Second Phase of the project will produce 1 Billion cubic feet per day to be used for Iranian purposes.

According to Wall Street Journal; October 2009, as stated by Iran's official Press TV, on September 14, 2009, the National Iranian Gas Export Company (NIGEC), has signed a contract with a foreign company to export gas to the United Arab Emirates for 25 years. Iranian media quoted the Managing Director of the National Iranian Gas Export Company, Reza Kasaeizadeh, as saying the unnamed foreign company is to develop an Iranian gas field in the Persian Gulf. It will export an annual 3 billion cubic meters of gas a year to the UAE for 25 years. The deal comes as UAE-based Crescent Petroleum, said it would take Iran's state oil company to arbitration over a gas supply deal after Iran refused to deliver the gas following a pricing dispute. Separately, the Oil Ministry's news agency Shana quoted the head of the Liquid Gas Production Company, Ali Kheirandish, as saying liquefied natural gas capacity will reach 45 million metric tons a year by 2016 if the Persian and Pars LNG projects are completed. He also said if negotiations related to the two projects aren't successful with the foreign partners, the work may go ahead with domestic companies. Iranian semi-official Mehr news agency also said on September 14, 2009, that with 19,000 tons a day capacity, Zarand tar refinery will come into operation by September 23, 2009, in south-eastern Iran. The announcements come as Iran seeks to develop its oil and gas production capacity, despite the threats of new sanctions over its nuclear program.

3.3. Iraq

3.3.1. Oil Resources

Iraq is potentially one of the richest countries in the world. It contains enormous deposits of petroleum and natural gas. Petroleum is the most important natural resource of Iraq.

The oil fields are located in two main regions:

1. In the southeast, just inland from the Persian Gulf, near Ar Rumaylah, and
2. In the north-central part of the country, near Mosul and Kirkuk.

For more than a hundred years, major powers have battled to control this enormous source of wealth and strategic power. The major international oil companies, headquartered in the United States and the United Kingdom, have been keen to regain control over Iraq's oil, lost with the nationalization in 1972.

Oil was discovered in Mosul situated in northern part of Iraq in 1918. In 1920, under the aegis of the League of Nations, Britain cobbled together the Kingdom of Iraq from the Ottoman provinces of Basra, Baghdad, and Mosul in order to better exploit the holdings of the Turkish Petroleum Company, forerunner of the Iraq Petroleum Company (IPC).

Later, Iraqi nationalists and the Baath Party of Saddam Hussein nationalized the IPC, provoking unrelenting British and American hostility. Hussein rewarded his Sunni allies in the Baath Party by giving them lucrative positions in the state company, part of a process that produced a deep rift with the country's Shiite majority. And these are but a few of the ways in which modern Iraqi history has been governed by oil.

Iraq is one of the world's great hydrocarbon preserves. According to oil giant British Petroleum (BP), it harbors proven oil reserves of 115 billion barrels, more than any country except Saudi Arabia and Iran.

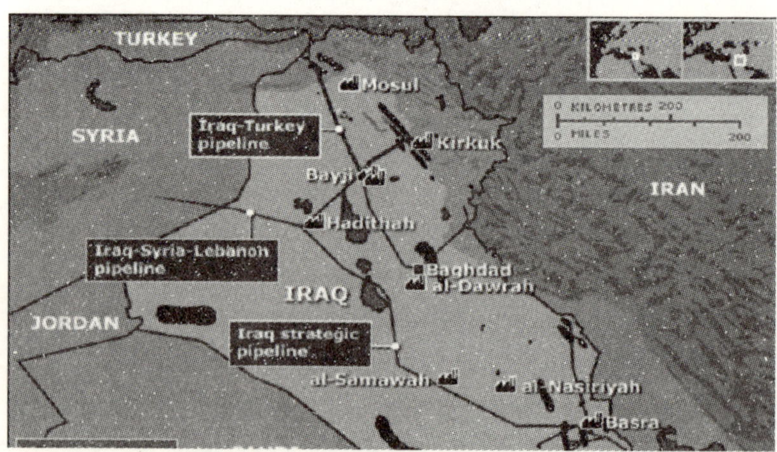

Map 3.5.: Iraq's Major Oil Fields and Pipelines•

•Source: BBC News/ Iraq/ Key Maps

A measure of the uncertainty about Iraq's oil reserves is indicated by the fact that the US Department of Energy estimated that Iraq had 112 billion barrels, whereas, the United States Geological Survey (USGS) estimated it was closer to 78 billion barrels and according to the US Department of Energy's Report of 2007, Iraq's prewar deputy oil minister claimed it might have 300 billion barrels. The source of the uncertainty is that due to decades of war and unrest, Iraq's western desert (which possibly contain almost all of the undiscovered oil), remains almost completely unexplored. After more than a decade of sanctions and two Gulf Wars,.Iraq's oil infrastructure needs modernization and investment.

Despite a large reconstruction effort, the Iraqi oil industry has not been able to meet hydrocarbon production and export targets.

However, there are some facts that are undisputed:

1. First, Iraq has considerable oil reserves and low production costs. Finding cost is a fraction of a dollar per barrel and estimated finding and development costs are between US$ 1.50 and US$ 2.25 per barrel, among the lowest in the world.
2. Second, because of Iraq's isolation over the last decade, during which exploration technology has greatly improved, there has been almost no use of the most sophisticated exploration techniques. Furthermore, most of the fields have not been explored down to the deepest layers of the ground, where plenty of oil can be found.

International geologists and consultants have estimated that unexplored territory may contain an estimated additional "45 to 100 billion barrels of recoverable oil"[37]. However, in the absence of exploration data these estimates are highly speculative and do not meet the industry definitions of proven, probable, or possible oil reserves. If all its reserves, known and suspected, were developed to their full potential, Iraq could add as much as six to eight million barrels per day to international output, postponing the inevitable arrival of peak oil and a contraction in global energy supplies.

In addition, since Iraq is the least explored of the oil-rich countries, there have been numerous claims of huge undiscovered reserves there as well, oil thought to exist, and expected to become economically recoverable, to the tune of hundreds of billions of barrels. The credible Petroleum Economist Magazine estimates that there may be as many as 200 billion barrels of oil in Iraq; the Federation of American Scientists estimates 215 billion barrels; a study by the Council on Foreign Relations and the James A. Baker III Institute at Rice University claimed that Iraq has 220 billion barrels of undiscovered oil; and another study by the Center for Global Energy Studies and Petrolog and Associates offered an even more optimistic estimate of 300 billion barrels—a number that would give Iraq reserves greater even than those of Saudi Arabia.

If true, this would mean that Iraq has roughly a quarter of all of the world's oil. These assessments have been repeatedly cited in news articles, conferences, think tank briefings, congressional testimonies and academic works because they raise the prospect that America's energy security could significantly improve if Iraq were able to challenge Saudi Arabia's position as the world's preeminent oil producer.

There is no doubt that Iraq has a huge oil potential that still needs to be developed, and once opened for exploration, it could again be one of the world's most attractive oil domains for investors.

An Oil & Gas Journal article dated January 19, 2009 titled, "Iraq's Oil Prospects Face Political Impediments", notes that Iraq's proved reserves are 115 billion barrels, of 80 fields only 15 have been partially developed, the 7 largest fields contain 66% of total reserves proven to date, and it's potential reserves are 215 billion barrels, possibly the largest of any country in the world. The Iraqi Deputy Prime Minister, Barham Salih, told "The Times" that new exploration showed that his country has the world's largest proven oil reserves, with as much as 350 billion barrels. The figure is triple the country's present proven reserves and exceeds that of Saudi Arabia's estimated 264 billion barrels of oil. Barham Salih said that "the new estimate had been based on recent geological surveys and seismic data compiled by reputable international oil companies. This is a reliable figure from credible sources."[38]

In sum, oil reserves in Iraq, according to its government, rank fourth largest in the world, at approximately 115 billion barrels.

Organizations such as the Global Policy Forum (GPF) have asserted that "Iraq's oil is the central feature of the political landscape there, and that as a result of the invasion, friendly companies expect to gain most of the lucrative oil deals that will be worth hundreds of billions of dollars in profits in the coming decades."[39] According to GPF, US influence over the 2005 Constitution of Iraq has made sure it contains language that guarantees a major role for foreign companies.

In 2007, Iraq's oil production averaged "2.1 million barrels per day"[40], down from around 2.6 million barrels per day of production prior to the coalition invasion in 2003.

It would seem that to boost Iraq oil production, three conditions must be met:

1. First, Iraq must settle on a model for obtaining the required technology and skills from foreign operators. Iraqis see the state oil company model all around them and thus may be reluctant to allow private exploitation. On the other hand, Iraq may not have the funds to pay contracting firms to do all the work without giving them an incentive. So a viable business model must be determined and negotiated.
2. Secondly, Iraq is a founding member of OPEC, which is currently restricting production. It seems clear that Iraq would be constrained from increasing their exports for some time to come. Such a constraint might not prevent them from starting exploitation activities, but it could depress the value of equity incentives they might need to provide to contractors,

as discussed above. It may be necessary for the global economy to show signs of recovery before OPEC will lift export quotas, which could be a year or two from now.

3. Thirdly, Iraq must secure its territory from any substantial risk of terrorist interference with oil production. Such security seems to be emerging, but complete assurance may require a working agreement with Iran which might take some time to negotiate. It seems likely that the start of expanded oil production in Iraq may be 2-4 years into the future. Iraq claims to aim for production of 6 million barrel per day by 2013.

Currently, the world's largest publicly traded company, Exxon Mobil Corp, is in the race for contracts to work on Iraq's biggest oilfields.

"Exxon Mobil Corp, which is a brand of fuel sold by ExxonMobil, and from 1972 to 1999 was the corporate name of the company previously known as Standard Oil of New Jersey or Jersey Standard, is in constant dialogue with Baghdad to create the investment climate that would allow it to become a significant player in Iraq's energy sector"[41], Exxon's chief executive said on March 9, 2009.

3.3.2. Gas Resources

According to the Oil and Gas Journal; January 2009, Iraq's gas reserves are 112 trillion cubic feet and gas production was one billion cubic feet per day in 2007. Large gas reserves have been discovered in fields in northern Iraq and other gas fields may be found elsewhere in the country. Though Iraq's gas may not prove to be as lucrative as its oil, this resource is also coveted by the companies and could be a source of additional multi-billion dollar profits. In December, 1996, Gaz de France and ENI of Italy formed a consortium to build a pipeline from the Iraqi fields to Turkey, a project that could eventually link up with the European gas grid. But because of the UN sanctions against Iraq, this project could not proceed. In post-war Iraq, the big US and UK companies will seek gas production and transport deals along with oil deals in hope of snatching these lucrative prospects away from continental European competitors. Other pipeline projects, to bring gas from Qatar and other Gulf states through Iraq to the European market, are also under study and offer huge profits to whichever companies that get permission to build them.

3.4. Kuwait

3.4.1. Oil Resources

Oil was discovered in Kuwait in the late 1930s, but not until after Second World War did Kuwait begin to export large quantities of oil.

Kuwait is OPEC's third largest oil producer and claims to hold approximately 101.5 billion barrels, at the end of 2008, 8% of the world's world oil reserves, according to the OPEC Annual Statistical Bulletin 2008. This includes half of the 5 billion barrels in the Neutral Zone, or Divided Zone, which Kuwait shares with Saudi Arabia.

Most of Kuwait's oil reserves are located in the Burgan field containing 70 billion barrels and is the second largest conventional oil field in the world producing oil since 1938. The greater Burgan field has a capacity, estimated at 1.4 million to 1.5 million barrels a day of oil and "that was forecast to be sustained for more than 10 years with the help of international oil companies,"[42] said Imad Al Atiqi of the Supreme Petroleum Council, the body in charge of the country's oil policy, in a recent interview with Zawya Dow Jones. Production from the world's second-largest oil field in Kuwait may decline without the help of international oil companies to boost crude output, he added. "Kuwait's Al Burqan oil field the world's second largest oil field, will be depleted within 40 years."[43]

Since most of Kuwait's major oil fields are over 60 years old, maintaining production rates is becoming a problem. The size of Kuwait's reserves came into question in 2006 when a leaked memo from the Kuwait Oil Company (KOC) indicated reserves were only half the size claimed.

The relatively low cost of oil production in Kuwait stems from certain unique advantages. Most important, there are a number of highly productive wells, the output of which can be varied at short notice, which thus eliminates the need for large numbers of storage tanks.

While retreating from Kuwait at the end of the Persian Gulf War, Iraqi forces set fire to more than 700 of the country's 950 wells. By the fall of 1991, the fires, which had consumed about six million barrels of oil per day, had been extinguished, and production soon returned to pre-invasion levels.

Beginning the twentieth century, Kuwait's vast petroleum reserves brought equally vast economic clout to this small desert country. Unfortunately, that same oil wealth also made Kuwait the financial envy of much of the world, especially of its large neighbour, Iraq.

In 1911, the Anglo-Persian Oil Company (APOC), which was developing oil fields in Iran, requested permission to negotiate a concession from Kuwait. The British government refused the request (as it was entitled to do so under an 1899 treaty that granted Britain substantial control of Kuwait's foreign policy), but two years later the British government commissioned a geological survey of the area. In 1913, the British government signed an agreement with Kuwait's Sheikh Mubarak the Great in which he promised to grant concessions only to companies approved by the British government clarifying and reaffirming the agreement of 1899. First World War interrupted another effort to negotiate a concession. By this time, the British government had purchased 51 percent ownership in APOC as part of an effort to ensure oil supplies for the Royal Navy.

In the 1920s, Gulf Oil of the United States began to seek concessions in the gulf to overcome its lack of crude oil sources. British treaties with most rulers in the gulf, including Kuwait, made it difficult for non-British companies to gain access, although the United States government pressured the British to provide equal treatment to United States' oil firms.

By the 1980s, Kuwait controlled its hydrocarbon resources and had created an international oil company, Kuwait Petroleum Corporation; (KPC), which was among the world's largest corporations. "Through its subsidiaries, KPC was involved in all aspects of the oil industry and in many countries of the world. This was a remarkable achievement in view of the fact that only twenty-five years had passed since Kuwait entered the oil industry."[44]

According to OPEC Annual Statistical Bulletin (2008), Kuwait's current oil production capacity is estimated to be 2.67 million barrels per day, exporting 1.739 million barrels per day. Kuwait plans to increase its capacity to 3.5 million barrels per day by 2015 and 4.0 million barrels per day by 2020. Many analysts question whether these goals are feasible. Oil revenues comprise about 95% of exports and 95% of total government revenues.

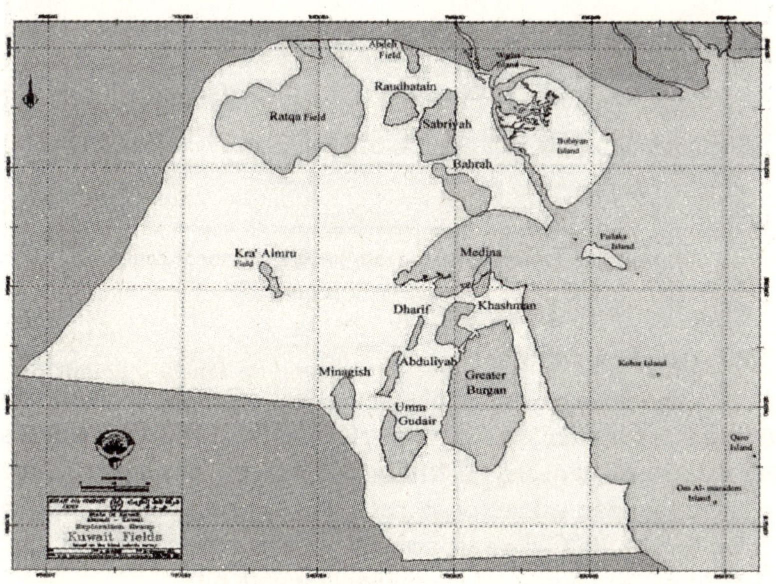

Map 3.6.: Kuwait's Major Oil Fields•

•Source: Kuwait' s Ministry of Oil

Divided Zone: The Divided Zone covers an area of some 6,200 square miles divided equally between Kuwait and Saudi

Arabia in accordance with agreements dating as far back as the 1920s. It is split into four sections, two offshore and two onshore, with Kuwait and Saudi Arabia each administrating their half of the zone. The Divided Zone's total production capacity of about 580,000 barrels a day is split evenly between the two. The partitioned area contains an estimated 5,000 million barrels of oil reserves and 1 trillion cubic feet of gas.

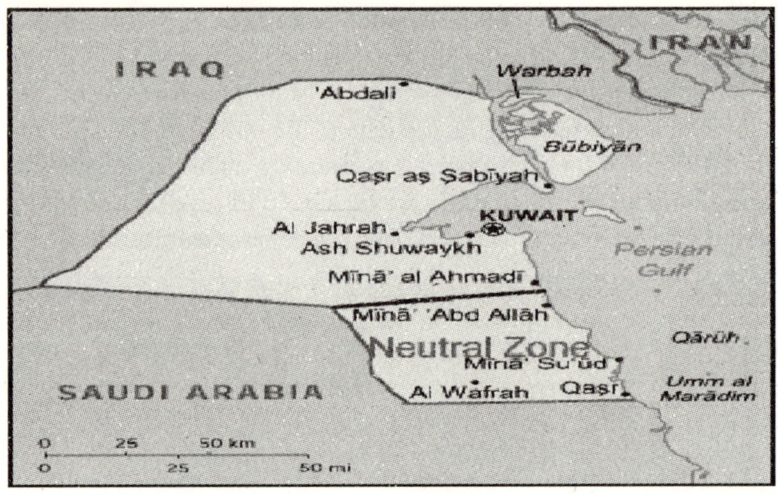

Map 3.7.: Kuwait-Saudi Arabia Neutral (Divided) Zone•

•Source: Wikipedia

3.4.2. Gas Resources

Kuwait has considerable natural gas reserves According to Oil and Gas Journal, January 2009, Kuwait's estimated natural gas reserves stood at nearly 63 trillion cubic feet. Kuwait produced a relatively modest volume of dry natural gas, an estimated 441 billion cubic feet in 2006, the vast majority of which is 'associated gas' (i.e., found and produced in conjunction with oil).

Kuwait seeks to significantly increase its use of natural gas in electricity generation, water desalination, and petrochemicals to free up as much as 1,00,000 barrels per day of oil for export. Kuwait hopes to accomplish this through increased drilling for natural gas and tying together gathering centres to create the infrastructure necessary to reduce associated gas flaring.

In 2005, an estimated 35 trillion cubic feet of non-associated gas was discovered in several fields near Sabriya and Umm Niga in northern Kuwait. In the summer of 2008, Kuwait began production of approximately 175 million cubic feet per day and planned it to raise to nearly 1 billion cubic feet per day by 2015. The new production is not expected to offset Kuwait's rising demand.

In March 2009, Kuwait and Qatar signed an agreement whereby Kuwait would import nearly 67 billion cubic feet of liquefied natural gas each summer for 5 years, beginning in June 2009. Besides Qatar, Kuwait seeks to import natural gas from Iran, most likely from its huge South Pars gas field.

Iran and Kuwait signed a preliminary memorandum of understanding for natural gas sales in March 2005 but commerce requires the resolution of maritime border issues in the region, specifically with regards to Dorra.

3.5. United Arab Emirates

3.5.1. Oil Resources

Before the discovery of oil in the 1950s, the UAE was a group of largely undeveloped emirates under the protection of the British. Oil brought rapid growth and modernization to the area. UAE lies on the Persian Gulf with a number of ports available for shipping crude oil and natural gas exports.

The UAE holds the fifth largest proven oil reserves in the region. "UAE Proven recoverable oil reserves are currently put at 97.8 billion barrels or 10 percent of the global crude oil proven reserves"[45] and as big as Kuwait's claimed reserves. Oil and gas production has been the mainstay of the economy in the UAE and will remain a major revenue earner long into the future, due to the vast hydrocarbon reserves at the country's disposal.

Most of the oil is in the Zakum field which is the third largest in the Middle East with an estimated reserves of 66 billion barrels.

According to OPEC Annual Report, 2008, the UAE produces about 2.9 million barrels per day of total oil liquids, but has stated its intention to increase this to 5 million barrels per day by 2014. "At current rates of production, the UAE has about 93 years of remaining oil reserves."[46]

3.5.1.1. Abu Dhabi Oil Resources

Oil was discovered in 1960, production and export commenced in 1962 offshore and in 1963 onshore. Abu Dhabi National Oil Company (ADNOC) is one of the ten largest oil companies in the world.

Abu Dhabi leads the other Emirates with 92.2 billion barrels oil reserves. Abu Dhabi is by far the biggest oil producer in the UAE, controlling more than 85 percent of the UAE's total oil output capacity and over 90 percent of its crude reserves. Principal offshore oil fields are Umm Shaif, Lower Zakum, Upper Zakum, Al Bunduq and Abu Al-Bukhoosh. The main onshore fields are Asab, Bab, Bu Hasa, Sahil and Shah.

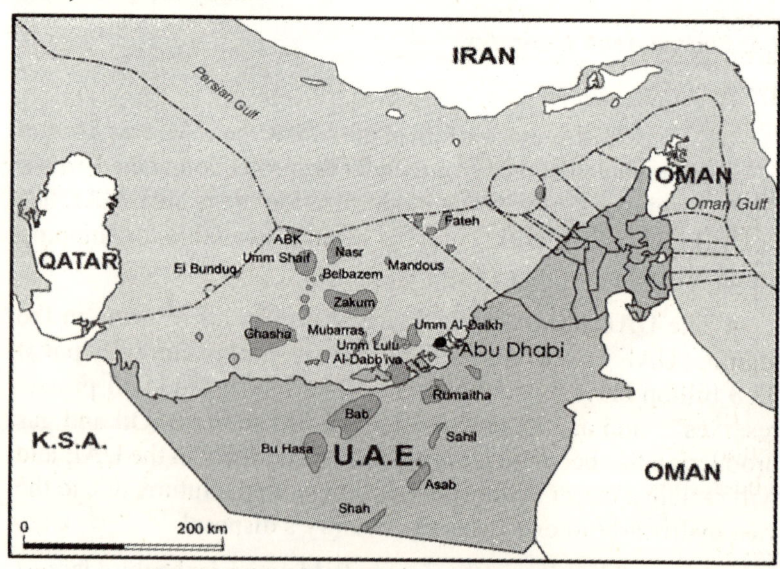

Map 3.8.: United Arab Emirates' Major Oil Fields•

•Source: Paleopolis

3.5.1.2. Dubai Oil Resources

Dubai is believed to have 4 billion barrel oil reserves.

According to the UAE official website's oil and gas report of September 29, 2009, Dubai's oil reserves have reduced over the past decade and are now expected to be exhausted within 20 years. The main fields are offshore including Fateh, Southwest Fateh and two smaller fields; Falah and Rashid. The only onshore deposit is the Margham field. Dubai Petroleum Company (DPC) is the main operator.

3.5.1.3. Sharjah Oil Resources

Sharjah oil reserves have been estimated as 1.5 billion barrels.

In 1969, the Amir of Sharjah granted a forty-year concession for offshore exploration and production to a consortium of small United States oil companies known as Crescent Oil Company.

Oil was discovered in 1973 in the Mubarak field off the island of Abu Musa, and production began in 1974. Because of conflicting territorial claims, Sharjah has production and drilling rights but shares production and revenue with Iran (50 percent), Umm al Qaywayn (20 percent), and Ajman (10 percent). By about 1984, Iran reportedly ceased transferring to Sharjah its half-share of oil revenues, presumably because of the financial drain of the war with Iraq, as well as Arab support of Iraq. In 1988, Iran attacked the facilities at Mubarak, causing their closure for two months.

3.5.1.4. Other Emirates Oil Resources

Ras al Khaymah has limited oil and gas reserves, which were initially exploited in the early 1980s.

Exploration and drilling in Ajman, Umm al Qaywayn, and Al Fujayrah have not yielded significant finds. Some of this activity has been funded by the federal government.

3.5.2. Gas Resources

UAE has reserves of natural gas which were nationalized in 1976. According to Oil and Gas Journal as of 2008, the UAE's proven natural gas reserves were 214 trillion cubic feet as of January 1, 2007. UAE holds the fourth largest proven natural gas reserves in the Middle East after Iran, Qatar and Saudi Arabia.

The United Arab Emirates is one of the world's leading owners of gas reserves, which Abu Dhabi National Oil Companies (ADNOC) is developing both onshore and offshore for export as LNG and for supply to local electricity and water utilities, to other industries including petrochemical plants and for re-injection into reservoirs to improve oil and condensate production. "Eight new LNG tankers have been purchased to transport LNG exports."[47]

According to Statesman Book 2008, the current rate of utilization of 1.7 trillion cubic feet per day and excluding any new discoveries, these reserves will last for over 200 years.

3.5.2.1. Abu Dhabi Gas Resources

The UAE's largest gas reserves are located in Abu Dhabi.

Almost 92 per cent comprising 198.5 trillion cubic feet of the country's gas reserves are located in Abu Dhabi and the non-associated Khuff reservoir beneath the oil fields of Umm Shaif and Abu al-Bukhoosh ranks among the largest single gas reservoirs in the world.

3.5.2.2. Dubai Gas Resources

Dubai has a 2 per cent share of the UAE's gas reserves with 4 trillion cubic feet reserves. The Dubai government established the Dubai Natural Gas Company (Dugas) in 1975 to process gas from offshore oil fields. The state-owned company is responsible for processing natural gas produced in Dubai's offshore oil fields as well as the gas piped from Sharjah.

By the early 1990s, the company also planned to process associated gas from the onshore Margham field. Dubai's Margham gas-condensate field can deliver up to 140 million cubic feet per day for domestic use and offshore fields can provide another 100 million cubic feet per day. Sharjah also supplies Dubai with 430 million cubic feet per day through a pipeline installed in 1992.

3.5.2.3. Sharjah Gas Resources

Emirate of Sharjah contains 10.7 trillion cubic feet gas reserves consisting 5 percent of the UAE's gas reserves, mostly non-associated gas which is being utilised domestically. The Emirate's most important gas deposits are at the offshore Mubarak field and the onshore Sajaa, Moveyeid and Kahaif fields.

In 1980, the American Oil Company (Amoco—later Amoco Sharjah) announced a major discovery of onshore oil and gas in the Saghyah field. By late 1983, output reached 35,000 barrel per day of condensate, which was exported. In 1984, total production reached 62,000 barrel per day. In the same year, the Emirates General Petroleum Corporation completed a 224 kilometer pipeline to supply dry gas to power plants in the northern Emirates. The pipeline had a capacity of 60,000 barrels per day of condensate and 1.1 million cubic meters per day of gas. After Dubai and Sharjah settled their border dispute in 1985, a pipeline was built to supply gas from the Saghyah field to the power and desalination plant of the Dubai Electrical Company at Mina Jabal Ali.

An LPG (Liquefied Petroleum Gas) processing plant that came online in 1986 was producing 11.3 million cubic meters of wet gas per day in 1987. The Emirate's outlook was optimistic in 1992, with Amoco Sharjah announcing a new onshore gas and condensate field and increased reserves at existing fields.

3.5.2.4. Other Emirates Gas Resources

Emirate of Ras al-Khaimah contains small reserves of 1.2 trillion cubic feet.

According to WAM, News Agency of Emirates, the United Arab Emirates has started producing gas from the offshore field located 20 km off Umm Al Qaiwain (UAQ) Emirate. "According to UAQ Crown Prince Sheikh Saud Bin Rashid Al Mulla, up to 92 million standard cubic feet per day of "wet gas"[48] has been produced from the well from May 2 to May 5, 2008."[49]

The gas would be transported through an undersea pipeline for processing to the Rakgas plant in the Emirate of Ras Al Khaimah (RAK). The UAQ field's unmanned gas exploration facility has been set 110 feet under water.

3.6. Qatar

3.6.1. Oil Resources

In Qatar, oil was discovered in 1939 and, after a delay caused by the Second World War, exports began in 1949. The first offshore oil well, Idd El Sharqi, was discovered in 1960.

The first shipment of Qatar marine/offshore crude oil was exported on February 1, 1964. In 1952, a concession covering the entire offshore continental shelf was granted to Shell Company of Netherlands, and later transferred to the Shell Company of Qatar Limited (SCQ), which ran offshore operations until 1977. By 1977, onshore and offshore operations were fully nationalized and service contracts were given to former concessionaires. To gain some leverage over the oil company with regard to revenues, pricing and production, Qatar joined the Organization of the Petroleum Exporting Countries (OPEC) in 1961, one year after it was formed.

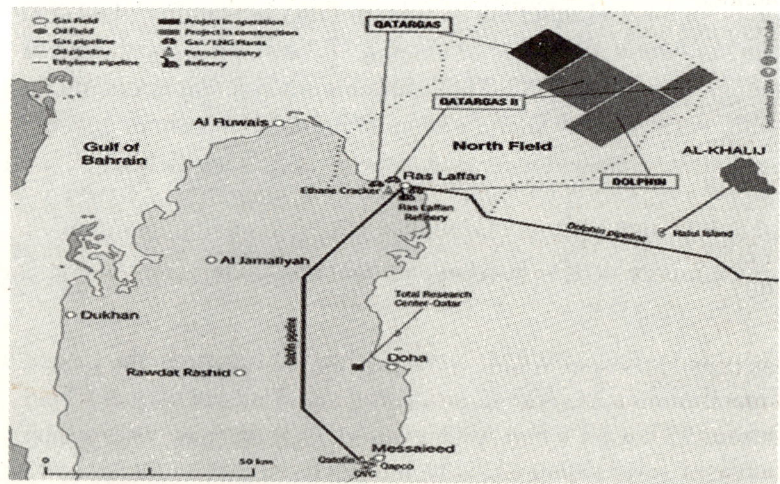

Map 3.9.: Qatar's Major Oil and Gas Fields and Pipelines•

•Source: Website of Total Oil Company

According to BP (British Petroleum) report in 2008, "Qatar's proven oil reserves have been about 27.4 billion barrels at the end of 2007."[50]

Qatar's hydrocarbon products are produced from the onshore Dukhan Field, two offshore oil fields of Bul Hanine and Maydan Mahzam and the North Gas Field. All fields are located within Qatar's territorial waters.

Qatar retrieves crude oil, associated gas, condensate and non-associated gas from the Dukhan Field, which produces from four major hydrocarbon reservoirs, three of which produce oil and the fourth produces non-associated gas. The field is approximately 60 km long and 25 km wide. Oil production from the Dukhan Field started in 1949.

Halul Island is part of the state of Qatar located around 80 km north east of the city of Doha, with an area of 1.5 square kilometres. It has all the facilities of a major international oil terminal. The island is home to 11 large crude oil storage tanks with a total capacity of 5 million barrels, crude oil pumping facilities, power generation and water desalination plants. Oil is blended and exported from Halul to customers' oil tankers moored offshore. In 2003, 108 commercial tankers were loaded at Halul.

Halul Island expansion plans include the Phase II upgrade of the harbour to accommodate larger vessels, a new control room building, a new marine building and the upgrade of power and water utilities.

According to the Energy Information Administration report in 2008, "Qatar produced 1.1 million barrels crude oil per day in 2007."[51]

Qatar has rapidly growing liquids production. For years, it has been producing at near full capacity despite the country being a member of OPEC but had reduced output a little in 2008/2009. Onshore production is declining slowly but offshore production is increasing as a result of new investment in existing fields and, more especially, due to increasing liquids production from the giant North gas field.

3.6.2. Gas Resources

Although total oil reserves are somewhat modest in comparison to other Persian Gulf countries, Qatar is one of the largest natural gas producers in the world.

Qatar's proven reserves of natural gas are nearly "26 trillion cubic meters or 910 trillion cubic feet",[52] about 14% of the world total and third largest gas reserves, after Russia and Iran. Its gas production in 2006 was about hundred billion cubic feet per day according to the Oil and Gas Journal, January 2009.

In addition to the crude oil development, the emphasis of Qatar government is on the development of the large non-associated gas reserves of North Field. The North field, discovered in 1979, came on-stream in 1991 and output rises as each new LNG train is brought into operation. The Dolphin project, that sends piped gas to the United Arab Emirates, began producing in 2006 and a large GTL (Gas to Liquid) plant is also being built. Qatar's gas production is surging ahead.

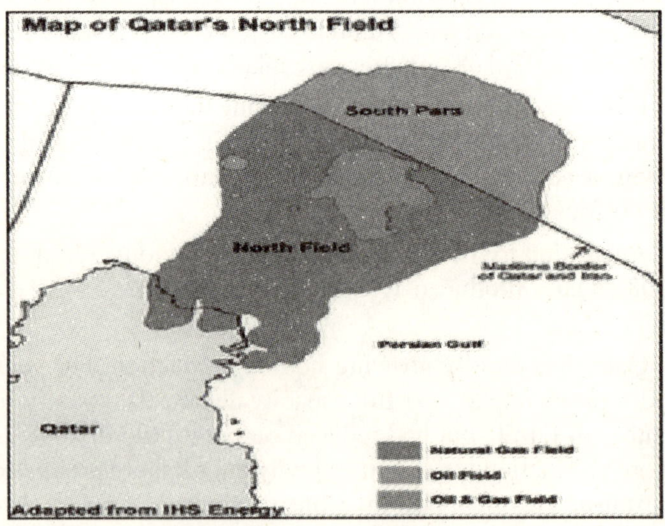

Map 3.10.: Qatar's North Oil and Gas Field •

•Source: Worldpoliticswatch.com

Three projects; North Field Alpha, Qatargas and RasGas are already tapping the North Field; while several other major projects are in the various stages of finalization for implementation. The vast North Field gas reserve, an underwater field northeast of the Qatar peninsula, began production in the 1990s. Qatar's North field with over 900 trillion cubic feet of proven natural gas reserves, is a giant by any standard.

Qatar has welcomed foreign investment in the development of its gas fields over the last decade and is soon likely to become the world's leading liquefied natural gas exporter.

3.7. Oman

3.7.1. Oil Resources

Oil was first discovered in the interior, near Fahud, in the western desert of Oman in 1964. Petroleum Development Oman (PDO) began production in August 1967. Oman is not a member of OPEC.

Oman's most important mineral resource is oil, although its reserves are modest compared to those of neighbouring Saudi Arabia and the UAE.

According to British Petroleum's Statistical Review of World Energy, June 2008, total proven reserves were estimated at the end of 2007 to be 6.1 billion barrels.

The Omani Government owns 60% of PDO, and foreign interests own 40% (Royal Dutch Shell owns 34%; the remaining 6% is owned by Compagnie Francaise des Petroles [Total] and Partex).

In 1976, Oman's oil production rose to 3,66,000 barrels per day but declined gradually to about 2,85,000 barrels per day in late 1980 due to the depletion of recoverable reserves. From 1981 to 1986, Oman compensated for declining oil prices, by increasing production levels to 6,00,000 barrels per day. With the collapse of oil prices in 1986, however, revenues dropped dramatically.

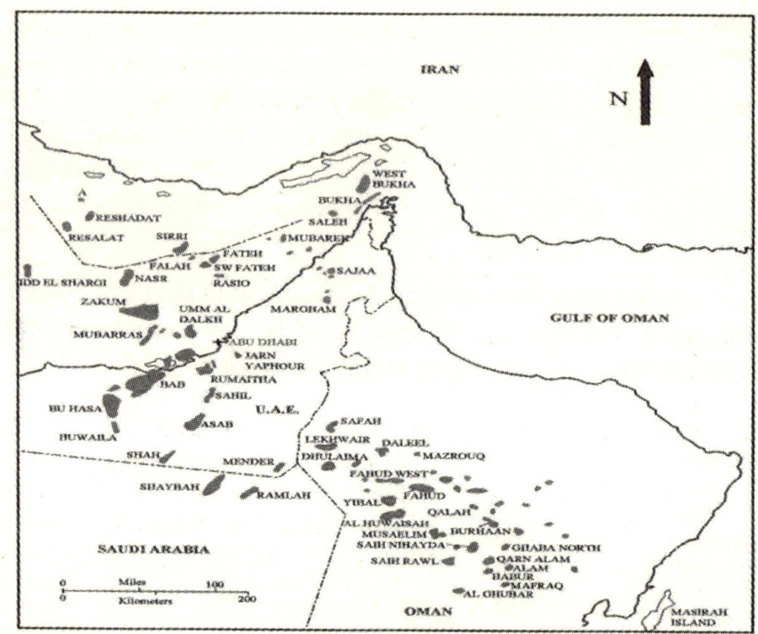

Map 3.11.: Oman's Major Oil Fields •

•Source: Greg Croft Inc.

Production was cut back temporarily in coordination with the OPEC, and production levels again reached 6,00,000 barrels per day by mid-1987, which helped increase revenues. Oman's oil production increased slightly in 2008, after a fairly constant state of decline from the total oil liquids peak of 9,70,000 barrels per day in 2000.

According to the 2008 EIA; Energy Information Administration's report, Oman has produced "714 thousands barrel crude oil per day in 2007."[53]

"According to data released by the National Economy Ministry of Oman, in March 2009, the Sultanate boosted oil and gas output and exports in the first two months of 2009."[54] According to the same source, Oman had produced 46 million barrels of oil by end-February 2009, a rise of almost 2 million barrels from the same two months in 2008, representing a 4.3% rise in output in the year.

3.7.2. Gas Resources

Oman does not have the immense oil resources as some of its neighbors. Oman seeks to increase natural gas production to meet rising domestic demand, provide stock for its enhanced oil recovery projects, as well as increase exports of liquefied natural gas (LNG). The recent economic downturn, combined with improved efficiencies in production, have provided more time for Oman to come up with new supplies to meet these goals.

Expanding natural gas production has become a chief focus of Oman's strategy to diversify its economy away from the oil sector.

Rising natural gas production over the last several years has resulted in the expansion of natural gas-based industries, such as petrochemicals, power generation, and the use of natural gas as a feedstock for enhanced oil recovery projects. However, despite the recent rise in production, additional natural gas reserves have not been located as quickly as the government had hoped.

Oman's natural gas reserves, which will increasingly provide the fuel for power generation and desalination, stand at 18 trillion cubic feet as of January 2009, according to Oil & Gas Journal, January 2009 issue.

According to EIA report, August 2009, Oman's natural gas production in 2008 is estimated at nearly 848 billion cubic feet, exported approximately 385 billion cubic feet of LNG, nearly two-thirds of which went to South Korea, while the remainder went to Japan, India, Taiwan, and Spain. Oman contracts with foreign companies to produce gas from technically challenging fields, such as the "tight gas"[55] believed to be in the Khazzan and Makarem fields in Oman's central interior.

The Khazzan and Makarem fields are estimated to contain significant volumes of natural gas; some estimates indicate that the two fields could nearly double Omani reserves. British Petroleum (BP) is currently developing Oman gas fields. BP signed two gas-processing deals in April 2009, as part of its work programme on the Khazzan and Makarem gas field, intended to reduce natural gas flaring. Gas production of these fields is due to start in mid-2010.

3.8. Bahrain

3.8.1. Oil Resources

Bahrain's proven oil reserves are limited in comparison with the extensive oil fields of Kuwait and Saudi Arabia.

In 1929, the San Francisco-based Standard Oil Company of California (Socal), now known as Chevron, set up a subsidiary to acquire an oil exploration and production concession on the island of Bahrain. Socal drilling crews discovered oil in 1931, the first such discovery on the Arabian coast of the Persian Gulf, and brought rapid modernization to Bahrain and two years later the first shipment of crude oil was exported from Sitrah. This discovery made relations with the United Kingdom closer, as evidenced by the British establishing more bases there.

In 1936, Socal sold half of its oil interest to Texas Oil Company (Texaco) and, with its new corporate partner, formed the Bahrain Petroleum Company (Bapco).

In the years up to independence in 1971, Bapco oil revenues annually averaged 60 percent of government income and helped to finance major development, education, and health programs.

The government of Bahrain acquired a 60 percent interest in Bapco in 1975 and assumed control of the remaining 40 percent in 1980.

According to the EIA Short Term Energy Outlook's 2006 report, Bahrain's oil reserves in 2006 were 1.25 million barrels. All of Bahrain's onshore proven oil reserves are located in the Awali field, the first oil field to be developed in the Persian Gulf.

According to the Energy Information Administration's report, 2008, Bahrain has produced "48.6 thousands barrel crude oil per day in 2007",[56] and reserves are expected to last 10 to 15 years.

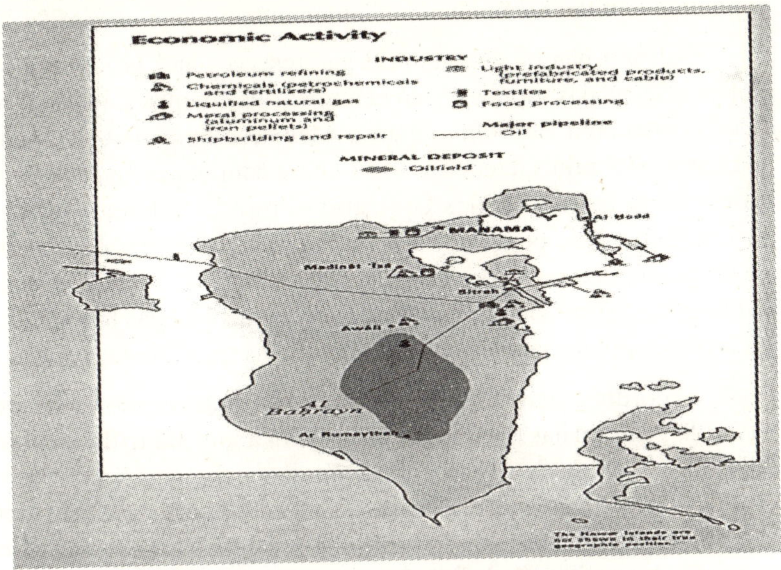

Map 3.12.: Bahrain's Major Oil and Gas Fields

Source: University of Texas/ Libraries

In addition to what is produced in its territory, the country's main source of petroleum comes from its shared production with Saudi Arabia's Abu Saafa oilfield which provides Bahrain with a further 1,50,000 barrels per day. This oil is exported through the Saudi terminal at Ras Tannurah, but sales are handled by the Bahrain Petroleum Company (Bapco), and Bahrain receives the revenue. Bahrain exports much of its oil in the form of refined petroleum products rather than crude oil.

3.8.2. Gas Resources

For a long time, gas from the wells was allowed to escape into the air. Before 1979, when the government established the Bahrain National Gas Company (Banagas), an estimated 3 million cubic meters per day of this gas were being vented to the atmosphere. Banagas opened a gas liquefaction plant that collected this gas and processed it into propane, butane and naphtha. There are also large deposits of natural gas in the Khuff field, which is separate from the oil fields.

Bahrain has modest natural gas reserves and is looking to import natural gas supplies from neighbouring countries. In January 2002, Qatar and Bahrain signed a Memorandum of Agreement indicating Bahrain's intentions to purchase natural gas from Qatar's North Field Enhanced Gas Utilization Project. Although further negotiations were pending for sometimes, but the first deliveries of Qatari natural gas were made by the end of 2002. Qatar, which is planning to build a pipeline for exporting natural gas to Kuwait, has considered the possibility of connecting a spur line to Bahrain.

According to the Energy Information Administration's report of 2008, Bahrain has natural gas reserves of about 3.2 trillion cubic feet, most of which is associated gas from the Awali oil field. Further, as per the report Bahrain produced 400 billion cubic feet of natural gas in 2006, all of which was consumed locally, but also exports some liquefied petroleum gas (LPG) and gas-derived petrochemicals.

References

1. Gyorgy, Andrew, "*The Geopolitics of War: Total War and Geostrategy*", the Journal of Politics, Volume 5, November 1943, pp. 347–362
2. Hafeznia Mohammad Reza, "*Persian Gulf and Strategic Role of Strait of Hormuz*", 4th edition, Samt, Tehran, 2005, p299
3. OPEC Annual Statistical Bulletin 2008, Chapter 1, p.21
4. "*Directory of Persian Gulf Region and Countries*", Abrar Moaser, Iran, 2005, p.21
5. Ramadan War or October War; Fourth Arab-Israeli War, from October 6th to October 26th, 1973, is also called Yom Kippur War.
6. Frum, David, "*How We Got Here: The '70s*", Basic Books, New York, 2000, p. 318

7. Smith William D., *"Price Quadruples for Iranian Crude Oil at Auction"*, The New York Times, December 12th, 1973
8. "*The World; British Miners Settle for Less"*, New York Times, January 24th, 1982
9. "*Oil Squeeze"*, Time Magazine, February 5th, 1979
10. Garvin Jr. C.C., "*The Oil Glut In Perspective"*, Annual American Petroleum Institute Issue; Oil and Gas Journal, November 9th, 1981, p. 151
11. Hershay D. Robert, "*Worrying Anew Over Oil Imports"*, The New York Times, December 30th, 1989
12. "*Oil Price Increase of 1990"*, Wikipedia/ Second Oil Crisis
13. Peak oil is the point in time when the maximum rate of global petroleum extraction is reached, after which the rate of production enters terminal decline.
14. *Directory of Persian Gulf region and countries*, Abrar Moaser Iran, 2005, p.21
15. Oil and Gas Journal and EIA Short Term Energy Outlook
16. www.country-studies.com;
17. Ebrahimi-far Tahereh, "*The Patterns of Confidence Building Measures in The Persian Gulf*", The Institute for Political and International Studies, Iran, 2006, p.61
18. Elahi Homayoun, *The Persian Gulf and Its Problems*; 8th edition, Ghoomes, Tehran, 2005, p.389
19. Ibid.
20. OECD includes 23 European states and USA, Mexico, Canada, Australia, South Korea, New Zealand and Japan.
21. United States General Accounting Office (GAO), Chapter 1, p.16
22. Energy Information Administration; Region's Analysis Briefs June 2007, www.eia.gov
23. Halbouty Michel Thomas, " *Giant Oil and Gas Fields of the Decade; 1990-1999*", AAPG, USA, 2003, p. 40
24. EIA; Annual Energy Outlook, June 2008, p. 79
25. N.17
26. "*Saudi vows to keep oil flowing*", CNN, May 31st, 2004

27. CIA, World Fact Book; 2007
28. Niblock Tim, "*Saudi Arabia; Power, Legitimacy and Survival*", Routledge, USA, 2006, p. 2
29. OPEC Annual Report; Statistical Bulletin, 2007, p.21
30. He is a prominent oil-industry insider and also was the Energy Adviser to former US President George W. Bush.
31. EIA Report, 21st April, 2007
32. Mashaal; National Iranian Oil Company's Employees' Gazette, June 1st, 2008, volume 396, p.5
33. Ibid. June 16th, 2008, volume 397, p.1
34. Islamic Republic of Iran News Agency, IRNA, August 31st, 2008
35. Fars News, April 17th, 2008
36. No. 30
37. Klare Michael , "*Will Iraq be a Global Gas Pump?*", Huffington Post, August 27th, 2009
38. www.timesonline.co.uk, May 20th, 2008
39. Global Policy Forum, July 26th, 2007
40. OPEC Annual Report; Statistical Bulletin, 2007, p.21
41. "*Exxon Aims for Big Role in Iraq's Oil Sector*", Reuters News Agency, March 9th, 2009
42. "*Kuwait Oil Field, World's 2nd Largest Needs IOC; International Oil Companies*", Dow Jones Newswires, September 22nd, 2009
43. Ame Information; www.ameinfo.com, November 12th, 2005
44. www.country-studies.com;
45. OPEC Annual Statistical Bulletin, 2008
46. "*United Arab Emirates Oil*"/USA Energy Information Administration; Country Analysis Briefs (2007)
47. UAE Official Website
48. Wet gas is a mixture of hydrocarbons that contain a significant amount of liquid, usually water.
49. WAM, Emirates News Agency, May 5th, 2008
50. British Petroleum's Statistical Review of World Energy, June 2008, p.6
51. EIA; Energy Information Administration's April 21, 2008, Sheet 1

52. Statesman Year Book (2008), pp.1019-1021
53. EIA; Energy Information Administration's April 21, 2008, Sheet 1
54. Petroleum Economist Magazine, May 2009
55. This is gas that is stuck in a very tight formation underground, trapped in unusually impermeable, hard rock, or in a sandstone or limestone formation that is unusually impermeable and non-porous (tight sand).
56. EIA; Energy Information Administration's April 21st, 2008, Sheet 1

4

Geostrategic Importance of the Strait of Hormuz and Persian Gulf Islands

1. Strait of Hormuz

1.1. Introduction

According to the Rimland theory of "Spykman"[1], any country which captures Rimland, will control the whole World, and "in this theory, the Strait of Hormuz has been considered as Rimland's centre."[2]

Albuquerque, the Portuguese navigator (1453-1515), believed that any country which dominates three straits; Bab-el Mandeb, Hormuz and Malaka, would dominate the whole world. "In this theory the Strait of Hormuz is the dominant key over the other two straits. He occupied Hormuz Island in the mouth of the Strait of Hormuz to ease capturing India."[3]

Admiral Mahan (1840-1914), who has been known as the 'Father of Maritime Strategy', regarding the important role of the Indian Ocean stated that "Any power which controls Indian Ocean will predominate the World .This ocean is the key of Seven Oceans and in 21st century the World's future will be determined in Indian

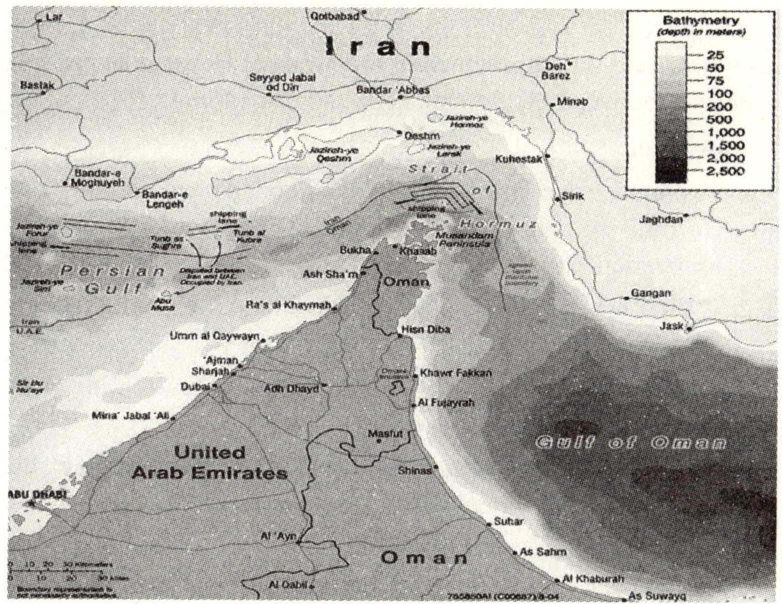

Map 4.1.: Strait of Hormuz

Source: Pars times

Ocean."[4] The Strait of Hormuz is the connecting point of the most of the Middle East countries to the Indian Ocean.

Regarding the critical role of strategic straits of the world, in 1804, Napoleon Bonaparte said: "If we could be the master of world's straits for six hours, we will become the master of the world."[5]

As these theories are still acceptable by majority of the theorists, the importance of the Strait of Hormuz seems undeniable.

The Strait of Hormuz has been well known since ancient times, when the first seafarers in modern civilization departed the Babylonian Empire to the Arabian Sea to conduct trade with tribes to the east and west.

After Second World War, some reasons, which have been mentioned below, caused the region becoming the centre of conflicts and competition, the centrality of this region in the global politics also increased the importance of the Strait of Hormuz as the sole waterway between the Persian Gulf and open seas.

Following are some of these reasons:

1. Increasing the importance of the Persian Gulf's States; due to their oil; its quantity as well as the world economy's dependence on that,
2. "Vital role of the Persian Gulf in The Allies victory in the Second World War"[6],
3. Military, Economic and Political weakness of European States, due to the Second World War,
4. Emergence of two superpowers; USA and USSR in the international political scene as two leaders of the rival pillars, and starting the Cold War era,
5. Expansion and success of the anti-colonial movements in colonial regions.

Persian Gulf was under the complete dominance of Britain for more than one century and for most of the 20th century, the strait was controlled by the Royal Navy of England. In 1968, when Britain declared that it will withdraw from the East part of Suez Canal (including the Persian Gulf) in 1971, regional and global motions to obtain and keep the dominance over the Persian Gulf and the Strait of Hormuz increased rapidly, and power in the Persian Gulf shifted to the United States and its allies. At the time, Iran was a pro-western country ruled by the Shah.

Britain's withdrawal had two different impacts on region's political-military circumstances:

1. Some of the regional States which had recently become independent; Kuwait, Qatar, Bahrain, Abu Dhabi, Dubai, Ajman, Sharjeh, Ras-al-Khaima, Om-al-Quain and Fujairah, were anxious about their future security.
2. Iran, Iraq and Saudi Arabia as the powerful regional states, considered Britain's withdraw as their more effective presence

> in the region. For Iran, the strait was (and still is) vital passageway for oil exporting and moreover, dominating it would strength Iran's international position. Therefore, Iran and Saudi Arabia's role in protecting the region's security gradually increased.

Today, the Strait of Hormuz gets attention as one of the most volatile and politically edgy stretches of water in the world. The narrow Strait of Hormuz is considered one of the most, if not the most, strategic straits of water on the planet and world's most critical oil traffic chokepoint. According to the U.S. Energy Information Administration report in July 2008, more than 15 million barrels of crude oil onboard enormous ships, called 'super tankers', each of which carries more than 2 million barrels of crude, pass through the strait, every day. This represents 40% of the world's seaborne oil shipments, and 20% of all world shipments. It is necessary to mention that the role of Strait of Hormuz is proportional and depends on the safety and security of it, such as what happened in 1980s, when the oil export of Saudi Arabia from Strait of Hormuz decreased from 100% in 1980 to 75% in 1990, due to Iran-Iraq and First Gulf Wars, which threatened the security of this hub. As Strait of Hormuz connects Gulf countries with Indian Ocean, it has become an operational centre in military strategies.

1.2. Geographical Specifications of the Strait

The Strait of Hormuz is a narrow waterway that forms the entrance to the Persian Gulf. It is a channel linking the Persian Gulf (west) with the Gulf of Oman and the Arabian Sea (southeast).

The northern shore is formed by the coastline of Iran. The southern shore is formed by the Musandam Peninsula which belongs to Oman.

The strait is 55 to 95 kilometres wide and separates Iran (north) from the Arabian Peninsula (south).

The Strait is deep and relatively free of maritime hazards. Its depth is greatest near the Musandam Peninsula and tapers as one moves north toward the Iranian shore and is, therefore, difficult for large ships to navigate.

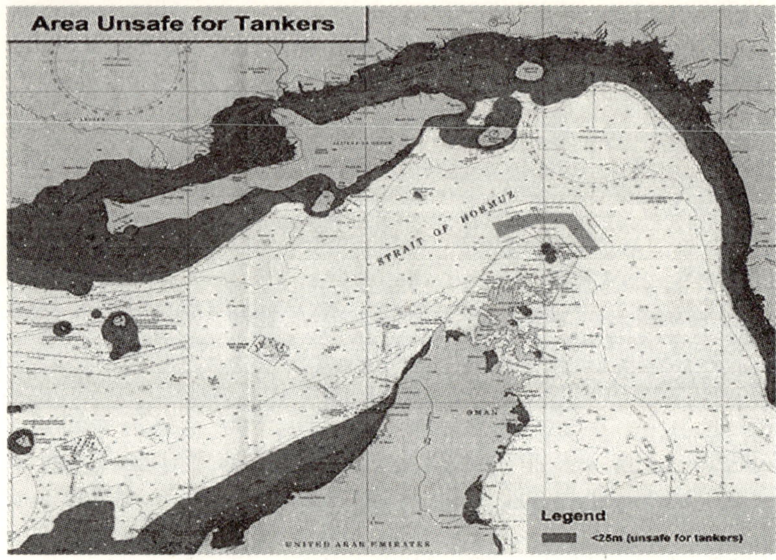

Map 4.2.: The Unsafe Areas for Tankers in the Strait

Source: Strauss Centre for International Security and Law, the University of Texas

However, 50 nautical miles to the west of the strait, inside the Persian Gulf, the situation is reversed and the deeper water lies within Iranian territorial waters. At its narrowest point, it is made up of Omani and Iranian territorial waters and is only 54 kilometers wide and is consequently, a relatively easy passageway to obstruct.

The Strait contains eight major islands, seven of which are controlled by Iran. Iran and the United Arab Emirates disagree as to the ownership of the strategically located Abu Musa, Greater Tunb, and Lesser Tunb islands. Nonetheless, Iran has maintained a military presence on these islands since the 1970s. Additionally, Iran's navy has good access to open sea from bases at Bandar Abbas, Bushehr and Chah Bahar. The de facto Iranian control of these islands certainly strengthens Iranian influence in the waters of the Strait.

From the strategic point of view, in the Middle East, Strait of Hormuz is the most important connecting centre which connects Mediterranean Sea and Red Sea with Indian, Pacific and Atlantic Oceans.

1.3. Law of the Sea on the Strait of Hormuz

Historically, a nation's territorial waters were said to extend for 3 miles from shore. After the Second World War, this was reviewed and the current distance accepted by most countries is 12 nautical miles. Under the 1982 United Nation's Law of Sea (LOS) Convention, a coastal state may claim a territorial sea up to 12 nautical miles from the coastline. Each nautical mile is equal to 1852 meters.

The waters inside this 12 mile limit are broadly considered to be an extension of the nation that forms its coastline. In addition to their right to enforce any law within their territorial seas, coastal states are also empowered to implement certain rights in an area beyond the territorial sea, extending for 24 nautical miles from their shores, for the purpose of preventing certain violations within the territorial sea. "This area, known as the 'contiguous zone', may be used by a coast guard or its naval equivalent to pursue and, if necessary, arrest and detain suspected drug smugglers, illegal immigrants and customs or tax evaders violating the laws of the coastal state within its territory or the territorial sea."[7] However, foreign ships can pass through these waters as long as they don't linger unnecessarily or cause aggravation while there. This is termed the right of 'innocent passage'.

While passing through straits, such as the Strait of Hormuz, that run through territorial waters, ships in transit have more rights. In particular, warships can maintain an appropriate degree of combat-readiness. Foreign warships are usually required to minimise their military profile in order to reduce their potential threat to the coastal state.

Warships which do not comply with the laws and regulations of the coastal state concerning passage through the territorial sea can be ordered to leave the territorial sea immediately.

In the Strait of Hormuz and the waters to the west of it, shipping lanes run close to and in some areas through Iranian territorial waters. Under international maritime law, the Iranians are entitled to monitor this traffic but the traffic, including warships, is entitled to unimpeded transit. As the US and Iran view each other with great mistrust, the potential for conflict is high. Two things, as follows, complicate the matter further:

1. The USA has not ratified the relevant legislation on international maritime law i.e. the United Nations Convention on the Law of the Sea (UNCLOS).
2. According to UNCLOS, if there are islands lying off a nation's coast, then the 12 miles extend from the outermost island. The area of sea around the Strait of Hormuz contains several islands, for many of which, the ownership is claimed by both Iran and the United Arab Emirates (a pro-western country). Whoever owns the islands will own the territorial waters around them according to international maritime law as it is usually interpreted.

1.3.1. Traffic Separation Scheme

Ships moving through the Strait follow a Traffic Separation Scheme (TSS), which separates inbound traffic from that of outbound to reduce the risk of collision.

Northern route has been determined for inbound traffic from Gulf of Oman to the Persian Gulf and Southern route for outbound traffic from Persian Gulf. To traverse the Strait, ships pass through the territorial waters of Iran and Oman under the transit passage provisions of the United Nations Convention on the Law of the Sea. The strait consists of 2-mile wide channels for inbound and outbound tanker traffics, as well as a 2-mile wide buffer zone.

Iran and Oman, as the countries in northern and southern shores of the strait, were controlling this waterway in 1971. In 1973, as Oman was engaged with internal problem in Dhufar and also because of lacking capable naval force, Iran achieved its goal of bringing the strait under her complete control. Following the 1979 revolution in Iran, Iran's control of the strait was initially dropped and Oman reinforced its military, especially, naval power and became sole controller of the strait.

By the outbreak of Iraq-Iran war in 1980, Iranian government realized the importance of this vital waterway and again started to cooperate with Oman to control the Strait of Hormuz. After 1980-1988 war, Iranian armed units again were deployed at the strategic ports and islands.

At present, the strait is being controlled by two regional and extra-regional powers. Iran as a regional power controls Northern shore and USA and Britain with the help of Oman control Southern shore of the strait.

Map 4.3.: TSS of the Strait of Hormuz (The arrows mark the location of the Traffic Separation Scheme)

(Source: Pars times)

Huge oil tankers enter the Persian Gulf via northern part of the Strait of Hormuz; empty, and after loading; when more depth is required (due to the increased weight), exit via southern part.

1.4. Geostrategic Role of the Strait of Hormuz

Nowadays, petroleum is the most important strategic commodity. The dependence on this resource can be felt in the way society reacts to even minor shifts in oil markets. With demand and consumption increasing, mankind's dependence on oil continues to grow. The dependence is such that any minor interference in the production or distribution of oil has profound economic and political consequences.

The world's oil dependence is facilitated by a complex delivery system, which, if disrupted, could dramatically impair global economy. Oil supplies are particularly vulnerable at specific geographic chokepoints en route to their final destinations. Chokepoints are waterways or overland pipelines that transport large quantities of oil across narrow channels or vulnerable regions.

The consequences of natural disaster, accident, or terrorist attacks at any of these points would affect our way of life, from the financial markets and international trade to airline travel and gas prices, for months. The Strait of Hormuz is by far the world's most important chokepoint; over 17 million barrels of oil per day, "roughly one fourth of the world's total oil consumption, which by 2020 this flow is expected to more than double"[8], travel out of the Persian Gulf through this strait.

As oil which is being exported through the Strait of Hormuz is projected to increase, ensuring the flow of oil through this hostile region will continue to be a crucial issue in the years to come. The abundance of oil and the world's dependence on imported oil from the Persian Gulf region make the Strait of Hormuz one of the most critical places to watch.

Closure of the Strait of Hormuz would dramatically affect the world oil market, sending oil prices well over $100 per barrel and restricting access to oil products to only the wealthiest buyers.

According to the Energy Information Administration (EIA), June 2007, the regional states own proven oil reserves of 728 billion barrels, representing 55 percent of the world's oil reserves, oil production capacity of 25.4 million barrels per day (33 percent of the world total) and total oil production of 23.6 million barrels per day in 2006.

Much of this oil is transported to Japan, Western Europe, and the United States, who have a vital interest in securing free passage through this strait. The potential for conflict over the strait and the resources that traverse them are great. If wars were to break out in this region, oil would certainly be used as a weapon.

Moreover, European dependence on Gulf energy supplies is likely to grow substantially over the "next 10 to 15 years" [9], particularly as North Sea oil and gas resources are depleted.

Many countries, including the United States and European countries, are trying to develop alternative sources of oil and to conserve energy, but, thus far, with modest success. The enduring reality is that, an adequate worldwide supply at fair-market prices, will remain reliant on unfettered access to Gulf oil.

Consumers of Persian Gulf's oil in order to reduce their dependency on the region's oil have chosen some strategies. "Some of them are as follows:" [10]

1. Economizing energy consumption
2. Producing substituting energies; such as atomic energy
3. Increasing other oil basins' productions.

1.4.1. Impacts of the Closure of the Strait

The vital role of the Strait of Hormuz; especially in peace time, is undeniable. About 80% of the region's oil is being exported through this strait and only 20% by using pipelines which have not any economic justification. There is no doubt that by its obstruction under any circumstances, the oil exportation will face very serious problems.

It should be noted that any action to stop the oil flow from the Persian Gulf region; such as blocking the Strait of Hormuz, attacking the shipping lines and trying to blow up the pipelines or the production and refinery facilities of the regional countries, will be considered as a serious violation of the international laws and regulations for the concerned states. It would be in practice like giving a declaration of war to them.

At the same time, it would be a serious challenge to the interests of the major oil importing states; especially to the USA's interests, as Persian Gulf has been considered as an area of vital interests. US governments are intent to stop any serious challenge to its vital interest, by all means; including the military actions.

Any blockade of this strategic strait would restrict supplies to consumers in Asia, Europe and US. Japan, which gets more than 70% of its oil from the Persian Gulf and the USA would be most sensitive to a blockade.

Closures of the strait, even in short term will create political and economic consequences, some of which are as follows:

1. The region's oil supply to the international market will be diminished,
2. Political and military presence of regional and global powers to reopen the strait will be certain. By the failure of political efforts, the disputes will be changed to war and as a result, the war will spread to the Indian Ocean and the littoral countries involvement ultimately will increase the possibility of another world war,
3. As the Gulf countries depend on oil and its income and they have to import food and other commodities, mostly via the Strait of Hormuz, the closure of the strait will cause decreasing their incomes, and economic pressure on the people. These circumstances most probably will cause social and political riots or even regime change in some of the states,
4. Closure of the strait will also affect Western World in some ways such as; decreasing the imported oil from the Persian

Gulf region and decreasing the exported industrial products to the region's huge markets which will subsequently decrease their national revenue.

1.4.2. Events Which Threaten the Strait's Oil Transit

Obstruction of the strait seems very difficult, but not impossible. Amongst the regional states, Iran will suffer more than others by closure of the strait. Saudi Arabia, Iraq, UAE and Oman have substantial possibility for their oil exporting or commercial activities and Bahrain, Kuwait and Qatar could use the territory of Saudi Arabia or UAE.

The Strait of Hormuz has been a matter of serious concern for the world for some time due to the mounting tension and bellicose rhetoric between the US, Israel and Iran.

A serious threat to the Strait of Hormuz involves the ongoing dispute between the UAE and Iran over three islands – Abu Musa, Greater Tunb and Lesser Tunb Islands – all located near the Strait of Hormuz. Abu Musa Island is of particular interest because it is thought to contain large deposits of oil. By 1992, Iran managed to informally secure the islands even though no official agreement had been made with the UAE.

"The Iranian forces have done several manoeuvres aimed at closing the Strait of Hormuz at the time of crisis and the Western forces in the region (in cooperation with the some of the littoral countries or independently) have conducted several manoeuvres aimed at deterring such plans."[11]

Any attempt by Iran to close the Strait of Hormuz would involve tragic costs, but most of them would be paid by Iran. As long as the United States and its allies in the region remain alert to the threat and maintain adequate precautions, there is little reason to fear catastrophic consequences. The first thing to bear in mind about closing the Strait is how much damage it would do to Iran and its interests even to try. A threat against the oil traffic is a threat against every oil user which would gain Iran all but universal enmity. In such a situation Iran's enemies, and particularly the United States, would enjoy largely a free hand to act as they see fit to break the blockade, and do what injury they chose to Iran in the process. Iran could find itself entirely stripped of air and naval defences in the wake of US strikes. The United States would probably find it necessary to seize many of the Iranian and Iranian-occupied islands in the Persian Gulf, and would scarcely be in any hurry to return them. The military bases and commercial facilities around Bandar Abbas would no doubt be extensively damaged and perhaps even occupied. Moreover, the one state whose oil traffic would most assuredly be seriously affected is Iran. American naval forces effectively control the seas throughout the region and could block all ships carrying oil or oil products to or from Iran. Not only would this cut off most of the revenues of the Iranian government and most of the nation's foreign exchange, but Iran actually depends on imports for many critical petroleum products, due to its mismanagement of its own resources. Even the limited flow of oil through pipelines would not necessarily be safe from US precision-weapons attacks.

"The closure of the Strait of Hormuz will have grave consequences for Iran"[12], Riad Kahwaji, founder and director of Institute for Near East & Gulf Military Analysis (INEGMA) told Al Arabia News Agency in March 2009. "Iran will be bringing a disaster upon itself," he said. "This could place Iran in a military confrontation with the entire world since all countries have an interest in the Gulf region." He added.

Kahwaji stated that the US could possibly engage in a war against Iran and would destroy anything that blocks the marine traffic in this region. "The US could occupy the Iranian islands that might be in the way and could eventually occupy the entire Strait of Hormuz." He added.

1.4.2.1. Possible Events

There are some events which could threaten the strait's transit and even cause the closure of the strait:

1. Closure by Sinking Vessels

   This situation due to its depth is impossible or at least very difficult because the depth of the strait is between 70-100 meters while any sinking ship will cover only 30 meters.

2. Closure by Mining

   Although this is possible, but mine clearance system could make the straits secure very rapidly. It is highly likely that surveillance would discover the mining before it had gone far. Surveillance would reveal the locations of fields, greatly improving the effectiveness of mine clearance.

   It is not necessary to clear the entire width to permit resumption of traffic – a comparatively narrow channel is all that is needed. It is most likely that the US Navy, assisted by Arab state forces in the Gulf, could accomplish this in a few days. Merchant mariners and ship-owners have always been ready to sail in harm's way as long as there was adequate compensation for doing so.

3. Closure by Making Ships' Transiting Insecure

   By the use of missiles, bombardment, guerrilla operations or other threats, the strait could be insecure, but on the other hand the operation's headquarters, in form of islands or the coastal ports or cities, also could be targeted or destroyed by enemy. Tanker War during the Iraq-Iran War (1980-1988) is a manifest example of this bilateral vulnerability.

   The anti-ship missile problem must be seen in an end-to-end perspective. The weak points in such systems have always been in their methods for finding targets in the first place and guiding the missile to a hit. Destroying or neutralizing these capabilities will quickly make anti-ship missiles ineffective, even if it proves difficult to destroy the missiles themselves. The only feasible way to detect and locate targets is with radars. Since these must identify the position, they can fairly quickly be located and destroyed, even if they are mobile and move frequently. Jamming could reduce the radars' effectiveness. Even without attacks and jamming, the environment in the region of the Strait of Hormuz is generally unfavourable for radar due to massive clutter as well as frequently difficult propagation conditions, resulting in many missed detections and false tracks. A missile with a radar seeker will also be affected by clutter, and this will serve to make relatively simple countermeasures more effective in diverting the missile from its intended target. The propagation environment in this area also is poor for infrared missile seekers, again increasing the effectiveness of countermeasures. US and allied warships armed with anti-air missiles would provide an added layer of protection by shooting down many incoming anti-ship missiles.

4. Submarines

   Due to its suitable depth, submarines also could make it insecure, though this will become a maritime war.

   Although, the strait has never actually been shut down yet, the constant political, religious, ethnic and territorial disputes between the Persian Gulf countries have made the world anxious in anticipation of obstruction.

1.5. Significant Events in the Strait Since 1980

1.5.1. Iran Threatened to Close the Strait in 1984

In 1984, Iran threatened to close the Strait of Hormuz after repeated attacks by Iraq disrupted Iranian shipping. However, in order to continue exporting oil and maintain its economy's stability, Iran needed to keep the strait open and ultimately backed down from this threat.

1.5.2. Praying Mantis

On April 18th, 1988, the US Navy waged a one-day battle against Iranian forces in and around the strait. The battle, dubbed Operation Praying Mantis by the US side, was launched in retaliation for the April 14, 1988 mining of the "USS Samuel B. Roberts"[13]. The US forces sank two Iranian warships and as many as six armed speedboats in the engagement.

1.5.3. The Downing of Iran Air Airbus 655

On July 3, 1988, 290 people were killed when an Iran Air Airbus A300 passenger jet was shot down over the strait by the United States Navy guided missile cruiser USS Vincennes. There is still lingering controversy about the event, considered among the most controversial tragedies in aviation history.

1.5.4. Iran Threatened to Close the Strait in 1997

In 1997, Iran once again threatened to close the strait if the United States attempted to interfere in its relation with other Gulf countries.

1.5.5. Collision between USS Newport News and Japanese Tanker Mogamigawa

On January 10, 2007, the nuclear submarine USS Newport News, traveling submerged, struck Mogamigawa; a 3,00,000-ton Japanese-flagged very large crude tanker, south of the Strait.

1.5.6. US- Iranian Naval Dispute in 2008

A series of naval stand-offs between Iranian speedboats and US warships in the Strait of Hormuz occurred in December 2007 and January 2008. US officials accused Iran of harassing and provoking their naval vessels; Iranian officials denied these allegations. On January 14, 2008, US naval officials appeared to contradict the Pentagon version of the January 16 event in which US officials said US vessels were near to firing on approaching Iranian boats. The Navy's regional commander, Vice Admiral Kevin Cosgriff, said "the Iranians had neither anti-ship missiles nor torpedoes, and I wouldn't characterize the posture of the US 5th Fleet as afraid of these small boats."[14]

1.5.7. Iran Threatened to Close the Strait in 2008

"Naturally every country under attack by an enemy uses all its capacity and opportunities to confront the enemy. Given the main route for energy to exit from the region, one of Iran's steps will definitely be to exercise control on the Persian Gulf and the Strait of Hormuz. Should a confrontation erupt between us and the enemy, the scope will definitely reach the oil issue. Oil prices will dramatically increase. This is one of the factors deterring the enemy from taking military action against Iran,"[15] the commander of Iran's Revolutionary Guard Corps (RGC), Major General Mohammad Ali Jafari, said in his interview with the Iran's local Jam-e Jam newspaper in June 1, 2008.

"In response to these threats, Vice Admiral Kevin J. Cosgriff, commander of the US 5th Fleet stationed in Bahrain across the Persian Gulf from Iran, with a carrier strike force led by the aircraft carrier USS Abraham Lincoln, warned that such an action by Iran would be considered an act of war and that the US would not allow Iran to effectively hold hostage nearly a third of the world's oil supply."[16] So with Iranian threats and counter-threats by the US Navy, the Strait of Hormuz is again at the forefront of a possible military confrontation between the parties.

Chief of Staff of Iran's Armed Forces said on July 5, 2008 that Iran's strategy is to keep the Strait of Hormuz in southern Iran open, the official IRNA news agency reported. "But if the country's interests are jeopardized in the region, we will not let any ship pass through the Strait of Hormuz"[17], Major General Hasan Firouzabadi was quoted as saying. The army chief underlined the role of the strait, saying that the Hormuz Strait is a strategic canal with vital importance to Tehran.

1.5.8. Collision between USS Hartford and USS New Orleans in 2009

CNN News Agency reported on March 21, 2009, that the USS Hartford collided with the USS New Orleans in the strait, on March 20, 2009. There was no damage to the submarine's nuclear propulsion system and no disruption to shipping in the strategic

Strait of Hormuz. The collision mildly injured 15 sailors aboard the Hartford and ruptured a fuel tank aboard the New Orleans, spilling 25,000 gallons of marine diesel fuel.

1.6. Substitute Routes for the Strait

1.6.1. Pipelines

Constructing oil pipeline networks is one of the available methods which could diminish the involved regional and extra-regional countries' dependency on the Strait of Hormuz. Although, for the purpose of accessing to the markets, some oil pipelines have been constructed from the region to the eastern shore of Mediterranean Sea, but economic concerns, especially using tankers and super tankers to transit oil, are the reasons which exporters and importers still prefer to use marine transporting.

1.6.1.1. Existing Pipelines

In 1980s, due to Iran-Iraq War; especially Tanker War in the Persian Gulf which caused numerous problems for oil transiting by ships, Gulf States and the consumer countries had to react very seriously. They coordinated by establishing pipeline networks from the Persian Gulf to Mediterranean and Red sea to transit the region's oil. This, decreased dependence of regional and industrial states on the Strait of Hormuz.

"Iraq, the commencer of the war, and responsible for spreading insecurity and crisis in the region, was the first regional state which completely cut its dependence on the Strait of Hormuz, by transiting oil via Turkey, Jordan and Saudi Arabia".[18] Oil flows through the Strait of Hormuz account for roughly two-fifths of all world traded oil, and closure of the Strait of Hormuz would require use of longer alternate routes, if available, at increased transportation costs. The most viable alternative to the Strait of Hormuz for oil exports is the East-West Pipeline (Petroline), which traverses Saudi Arabia. Oil from the Persian Gulf can travel through this pipeline to the port of Yanbu for export via the Red Sea. "As of 2006, the East-

West Pipeline operated at only 50% capacity, leaving slack capacity of about 2.5 million barrels per day."[19]

Other pipelines in the region have minimal capacity relative to the amount of oil passing through the Strait of Hormuz. It is possible to inject chemical Drag Reduction Agents (DRA); any material that reduces frictional pressure during fluid flow in a conduit or pipeline, into existing pipelines to increase throughput without new construction.

However, most pipelines, including the Petroline, need additional pumps and other equipment upgrades to use DRAs. In general, increasing pipeline capacity is costly and time consuming.

Table 4.1.: Existing Key Pipelines in the Region *

Pipelines	*Capacity (barrels per day)*
East-West Pipeline (Petro-line)	*5 million*
Abqaiq-Yanbu Natural Gas Liquids Pipeline	*290,000*
Trans-Arabian Pipeline (Tap-line)	*50,000*
Iraqi Pipeline through Saudi Arabia (IPSA)	*1.65 million*
Strategic Pipeline	*1.4 million#*
Iraq-Turkey Pipeline	*300,000#*
Iraq-Syria-Lebanon Pipeline (ISLP)	*700,000*

* The pipeline needs repair and/or significant upgradation before operating at this capacity.

* Source: Data has been taken from Energy Information Administration, Country Analysis Briefs/Persian Gulf

In 1997, the "Baker Institute"[20] published a study proposing different options for increasing pipeline capacity in Saudi Arabia. The most ambitious option would increase Petroline capacity to 11 million barrels per day at a cost of $600 million.

1.6.1.2. Planning Pipelines

The Gulf Cooperation Council (GCC) seems to have agreed to construct a new strategic pipeline through Oman to a port on the Gulf of Oman. Gulf governments are planning oil pipelines that would bypass the world's most vulnerable energy choke point, the Strait of Hormuz.

If built, two pipelines; which have been described below, could ferry as much as 6.5 million barrels of oil a day around the strait, an amount equal to nearly 40 percent of the daily exports currently shipped through the narrow channel at the entrance of the Gulf.

1. The first, 224-mile pipeline would carry oil only from the United Arab Emirates, extending from the country's Habshan oil field, across a mountain range, to the Emirate of Fujairah, located outside the strait on the Gulf of Oman. But this pipeline would only carry UAE oil, leaving producers such as Qatar, Kuwait, Saudi Arabia and Iraq still without an alternative shipping route to Hormuz.

   Abu Dhabi's International Petroleum Investment Co. is planning to build the line, which would carry 1.5 million barrels per day of crude oil, about 55 percent of the Emirates' production. A third of the crude would be used for a refinery planned in Fujairah.

2. The second line, dubbed the Trans-Gulf Strategic Pipeline, would bring as much as 5 million barrels a day from various Persian Gulf terminals to a newly built export terminal outside the straits, perhaps in Oman.

   "A forthcoming Gulf Research Centre study suggests six possible routes for the trans-Gulf pipeline, which could bring oil from as far north as Iraq, passing through Kuwait, Saudi Arabia and the UAE to the Omani capital of Muscat on the Arabian Sea",[21] Mustafa Alani, a security analyst for the Dubai-based Gulf Research Centre, said.

Other possible routes could be the pipeline terminating in Yemen or Fujairah. The idea of the new pipelines among traders is so popular, "they think it's a dream," Alani said, "Crisis after crisis is threatening stability. We need a permanent solution. Any threat, real or imaginary, will increase the price a dollar or two. This project will give a new boost to the stability of oil," he added.

1.6.1.3. Advantages of the Oil Pipeline Networks

1. As the Strait of Hormuz might be closed in any conflict, using multi-routes, pipeline and marine transporting, to and from the Persian Gulf will reduce the possibility of harming commercial activities. In any situation of insecurity, if one of the routes is being threatened, another one will be used.
2. Some of the oil pipelines will reduce the distance to reach to the destinations. For example to get the European and American oil markets, "Saudi Arabia's Guar-Yanbu oil pipeline, compared with the Persian Gulf route, reduces the distance by about 3000 km."[22]

1.6.1.4. Disadvantages of the Oil Pipeline Networks

1. Geographical conditions such as cold weather, mountains, marshes and water basins, could make the construction of pipelines very difficult or even impossible.
2. In most areas, the pipelines must pass through the cities, which will make the construction very difficult.
3. Transport system via pipelines needs huge investments in construction, observation and maintenance. In fact, using pipelines for transportation is "7.7 times more expensive than marine transportation".[23]
4. As from starting point to the destinations (consumption points), there are large water basins like Red Sea and Mediterranean Sea. Therefore, to reach to final destinations, double-transport system; pipelines and marine transportation, should be used. This, however, will increase the transportation costs.

5. Oil, which is transported by pipelines to Red Sea shores, must be carried by tankers and passed through Suez Canal or Strait of Bab-el Mandeb to reach open seas:
   5.1. To reach open seas via Suez Canal, oil must be transited by the tankers with the capacity of less than 1,50,000 tonnes, because the draught of Suez Canal is not suitable for higher capacity. Therefore, super-tankers which transit oil to America and Europe ought to pass through Strait of Bab-el Mandeb and go round the south of Africa (Cape of Good Hope). This increases the path and consequently the cost of transportation. But, a significant problem is that any instability in Yemen, Eritrea, Djibouti and Somalia will affect the Strait's traffic.
   5.2. The other route that can be used to carry oil, which reaches to the Red Sea' shores by pipelines, is Red Sea-Suez Canal- Mediterranean Sea- Strait of Gibraltar. To reach USA and European markets, this route is much more suitable than Strait of Hormuz, but not for East Asian, Japan and Australia's markets due to the distance factor. Any crisis in Israel or Lebanon which are located in the east mouth of Mediterranean Sea seems the worst possibility of disrupting oil transiting.
6. To reach Eastern Asia, Australia and Japan markets, the Strait of Hormuz is the shorter way and also capable for super-tankers' transiting.
7. The possibility of sabotaging or exploding oil pipelines is a very serious threat which makes the pipelines vulnerable. Explosion of the Hams (in Syria) - Tripoli (in Lebanon) oil pipeline in 1981 and 1982, and subsequently destroying the Tripoli refinery, and explosion of the Kirkuk (in Iraq) - Dortiul (in Turkey) oil pipeline by Iraqi Kurd rebels in 1980 are examples which confirm the vulnerability of oil pipelines in insecure areas.

8. Any conflict in countries where the oil pipelines are passing through their territories could cause the pipelines' closure; such as happened in Lebanon and obstructed Iraq and Saudi Arabia's oil pipelines in 2006.
9. The most suitable route for Western consumers would be a pipeline through Saudi Arabia, a nation friendly to the US. Any new pipelines, like the two already in existence, would traverse Saudi Arabia and exit at the Red Sea where it could be loaded onto tankers. While this would reduce insecurity, it is unpopular with many of the Gulf States. If a pipeline is built, it will benefit Saudi Arabia and forcing other nations to pay transit fees for their oil transporting via pipelines.

1.6.2. Substituting Canal

Constructing a substituting canal is another way to reduce the vital role of the Strait of Hormuz. The idea of constructing a canal in Musandam Peninsula in Oman after the threat of obstruction of the Strait of Hormuz in early 1980s took shape. But there are some serious problems, such as follows:

1. The unsuitable geographical conditions of the area,
2. Such canal could be controlled or even threatened or attacked by short-range and medium-range missiles from Tunb, Geshm, Hengam and Abu Musa Islands.

Due to these problems, it has remained just as an idea.

According to The Times correspondent, David Robertson, in a September 9, 2008 report, Dubai is studying plans to build a US$ 200 billion (£114 billion) mega-canal that would allow oil tankers to bypass the Strait of Hormuz. The Gulf Emirate is understood to be considering the idea as a means of reducing Iran's influence on the flow of oil from the region. Engineers are understood to have presented the plans for a 112-mile canal to the Dubai Government.

It would link the Gulf coast with the port of Fujairah on the Indian Ocean coast, crossing the Hajar Mountains with a network of enormous locks. However, the proposed canal project would be fraught with difficulty. Oil tankers weighing more than 3,00,000 tonnes would need a route through the mountainous region between Dubai and its Indian Ocean coast. The massive cost and complexity of the project is thought to have stalled a decision on the canal, but it could be a popular initiative with other Gulf States.

"Many studies on this have been presented, but nothing is solid,"[24] a senior official of the Dubai Government, Mustafa Alani, of the Dubai-based think-tank, Gulf Research Center, told Dow Jones on September 8, 2008. "Iran has clearly stipulated its intention to close the Strait of Hormuz in case of a military conflict in the region", he added.

2. Persian Gulf's Islands

2.1. Introduction

There are about 130 explored islands in the region with different areas. According to their location, they can be classified as follows:

1. Iranian Islands;

   Iranian Islands are located in the northern part of the Persian Gulf. Most of the Iranian islands are inhabited. Amongst them, seven islands by the reason of their strategic importance are considered as the gulf's key which are; Hormuz, Larak, Qeshm, Hengam, Tunbs (both Lesser and Greater) and Abu Musa.

2. Arabian Islands;

   The Islands, which are mostly located in the centre or south part of the gulf, belong to the Arab regional states. Most of them are uninhabited and stony or coral islands.

Map 4.4.: Location of the Iranian Islands near the Mouth of the Strait of Hormuz

Source: Space Image Taken by NASA

2.2. Iranian Strategic Islands

2.2.1. Hormuz Island

Albuquerque, Portuguese navigator, in a letter to Portugal king wrote that:

"Your Majesty, if we consider the World as a ring, Hormuz (Hormuz Island) is its stone. To occupy India and its sea routes, domination of following strategic points is necessary:

1. Hormuz Island in the entrance of Persian Gulf
2. Aden to keep Bab el-Mandab under control
3. Malaya Strait at the farthest end of Singapore Archipelago"[25]

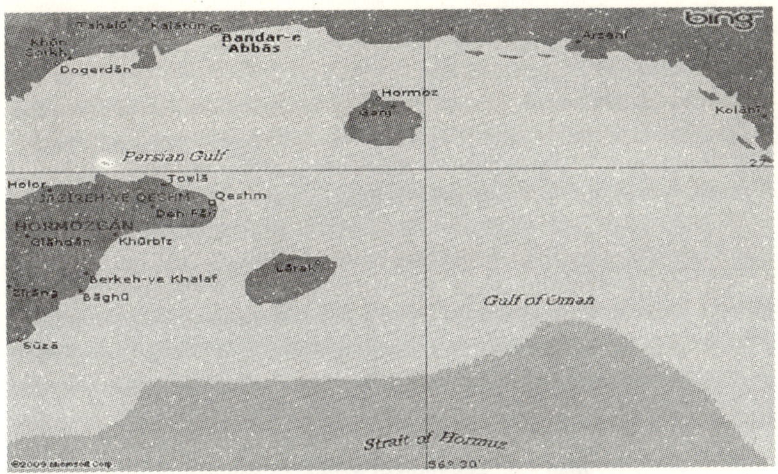

Map 4.5.: Location of the Hormuz Island

Source: MSN. Encarta

The area of the island is about 41 square kilometres and is located in the entrance of Persian Gulf and due to its strategic importance, the strait has been called Hormuz.

"In ancient Persian era, the Achaemenian had military bases on this island, and it was the commercial centre of Indian, Chinese and other eastern commodities. Spice route also passed through the island."[26]

To capture India, in 1507, Portuguese occupied Hormuz Island, where was the world's trade centre. By constructing military bases on the island, they assured their domination over Persian Gulf. Exploration of oil in the region in 20th century, the island's geographical conditions, its height, historical record and feasibility of approaching its southern offshore by huge ships (the depth is almost 14 meters) are the reasons which have made the island strategically very important, especially for Iran.

2.2.2. Larak Island

Larak Island, with 77 square kilometres area, is nearest Iranian island to the Strait of Hormuz. Its distance from Iranian coasts is 16 miles. Due to lack of drinking water, few people live there.

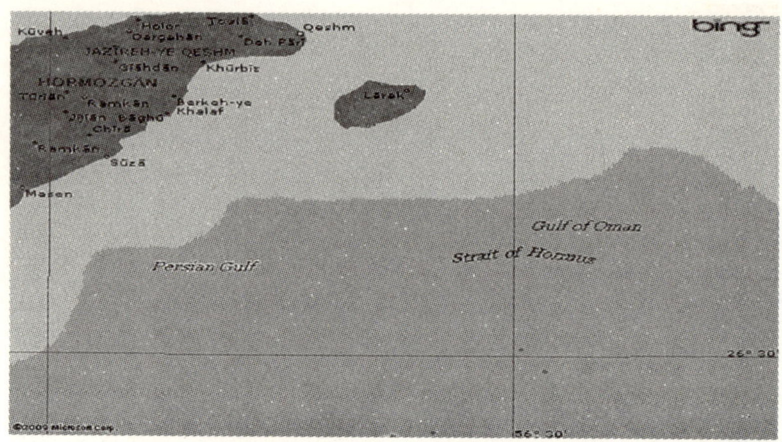

Map 4.6.: Location of the Larak Island

Source: MSN. Encarta

As the island is located in deep area of Strait of Hormuz where super-tankers cross, Larak Island to Iran, is being considered as the strait's defence front line.

2.2.3. Qeshm Island

Qeshm Island is the biggest with 2.5 times the size of Bahrain and 3 times that of Singapore, and one of the most populated Iranian Islands with area of "1093 square kilometres".[27]

Qeshm Island is located a few kilometers off the southern coast of Iran, opposite the port cities of Bandar Abbas and Bandar Khamir. The island by reason of its geographical conditions, vastness, bays, elevations, shape and coast-length "about 275 kilometres"[28] is strategically very important. Unlike most of the regions' islands, which have drinking water scarcity, Qeshm Island possesses drinking water and feasibility of developing cultivation. Due to its size and long coastal area, the island has the capacity to become naval headquarters. As the island is near to Bandar Abbas, strategic route into Iranian Plateau, it could play a significant role to protect Iran's southern coasts and most importantly to defend and protect the Strait of Hormuz.

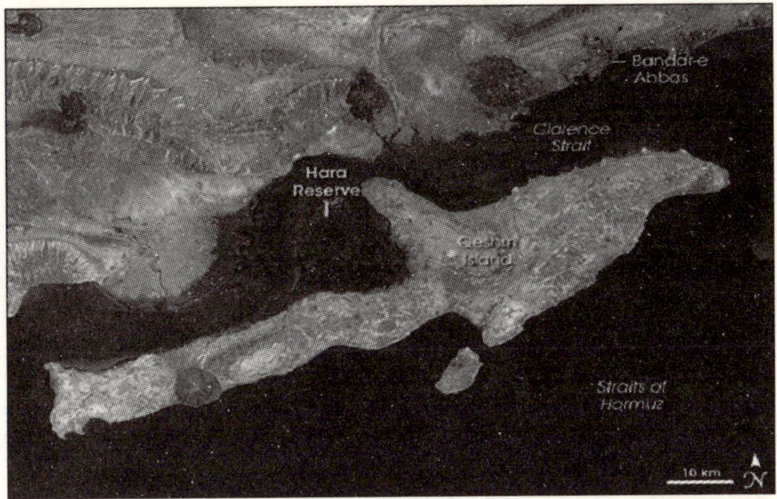

Map 4.7.: Location of the Qeshm Island

Source: NASA

As Qeshm Island is a Free Trade Zone, it is very important to international trade. In the year 1994, upon approval by the Iranian Majlis, the provision of this free trade zone was identified and as such, an area of 300 square kilometers on Qeshm Island received the designation of free trade zone. To that end, Qeshm Island was granted considerable leeway to set its own policies, independent of the central government, which had often been seen as an impediment to growth in many sectors of the economy. However, the Island retains the advantages associated with its connection to the mainland, including the rights to explore and develop oil and gas opportunities.

2.2.4. Hengam Island

The area of the island is 50 square kilometres. Hengam Island is located at south of Qeshm Island in the Persian Gulf. It has a truncated cone shape. The island is generally calcareous and low lying. The highest point on the island is Mitra Peak in Nakas Mountain that is about 106 meters. The distance between Hengam Island and Qeshm Island is about 2 km through the sea which is a proper shelter for ships against gales and hurricanes. The island's seashore depth is suitable for super-tankers to come near the coast.

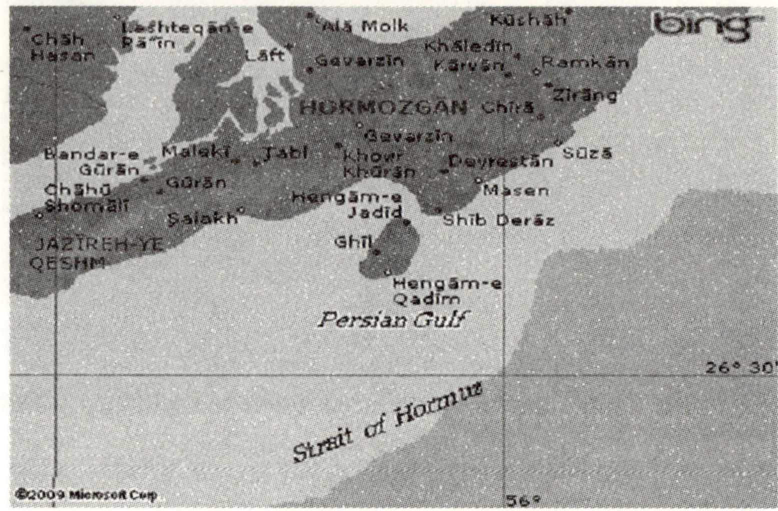

Map 4.8.: Location of the Hengam Island

Source: MSN. Encarta

Due to its location in Persian Gulf, the island could be the centre of naval operations to disturb traffic of Strait of Hormuz and also to prevent any warship from entering into Persian Gulf.

2.2.5. Tunb Islands

Two Tunb Islands (Greater Tunb and Lesser Tunb), due to depth of surrounding sea, form a very strong defensive base for Strait of Hormuz and also perfect stages for navy operations. They are being considered as observing and controlling platforms, from where the Persian Gulf's southern coasts could be watched. The Islands are administered by Iran as part of its province of Hormozgan, but are also claimed by UAE.

2.2.5.1. Greater Tunb

The area of the island is 11 square kilometres. It is known for its red soil. At present there is no native population, all local inhabitants have emigrated. "All establishment buildings are being used by military forces, who have taken possession of the island."[29]

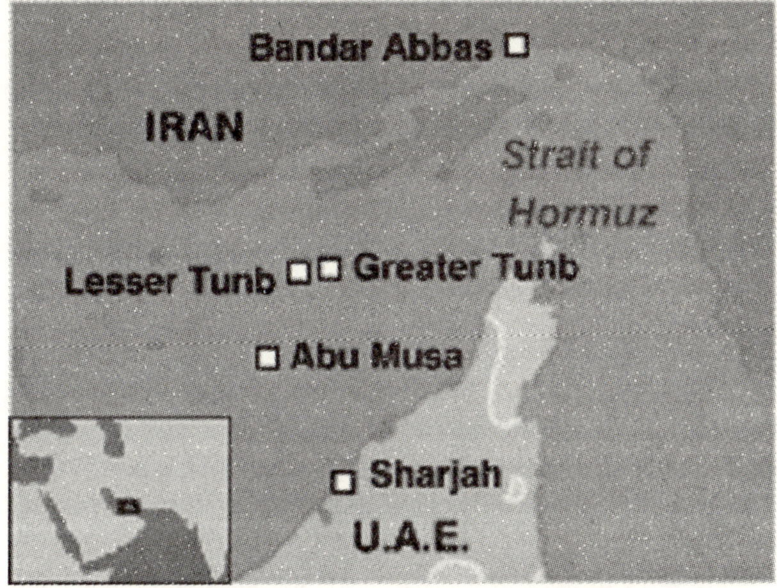

Map 4.9.: Location of the Tunb Islands

Source: BBC/ News Image/ Persian Gulf Islands

The island is located in the centre of navigation route, between inbound and outbound corridors of Traffic Separation Scheme. Tankers which enter the Persian Gulf pass the northern part of the island and tankers which exit Persian Gulf pass its southern part. Because of its location, the island is a proper place for observation and control over maritime traffic in the west side of Strait of Hormuz and east side of Persian Gulf.

Ample depth is needed for submarines' operations and manoeuvre. The depth of the most parts of Persian Gulf is not sufficient for submarine operation, as "the deepest point of the gulf is 93 meters."[30] Therefore, the deep water around the island, is a very suitable base for submarines. This has made the island very important, strategically.

2.2.5.2. Lesser Tunb

It has an area of 2 square kilometres. Because of lack of drinking water, the island is not habitable and only a few military forces are present there.

In spite of its size and geographical conditions, there are two reasons which have made the island strategically important:

1. The water around the island is deep enough for submarines' bases and movement of super-tankers,
2. It is located between the inbound and outbound corridors of TSS (Traffic Separation Scheme).

2.2.6. Abu Musa Island

Abu-Musa spans 14 square kilometres island and is located near the assumed western military-strategic boundary of Strait of Hormuz between Iranian port, Lengeh, and UAE's port, Dubai. Abu Musa lies in the Persian Gulf about halfway between Iran and the UAE.

For most of the recent years, it did not have more than a few dozen permanent residents. However, both Iran and the UAE desire to control the island. Abu Musa is full of oil reserves which fuel the economies of both Iran and the UAE. In addition, the island is located in the Strait of Hormuz, the mouth of the Persian Gulf. This strategic position could allow a country to influence the Gulf's valuable shipping lane, or even to close off the Gulf altogether.

Iran has controlled Abu Musa since 1971 when Britain ended its protectorate of the region. Since then, Iran has rejected any arbitration, claiming the island as part of its territory. The Island harbours a rich supply of untapped oil deposits.

Currently, oil is being extracted from a field close to the shores of Abu Musa. The dispute over the island is unresolved and could ignite an international crisis at some point. When Iraq made threatening moves toward Kuwait in October 1994, Iran increased its military presence on Abu Musa.

Neither the UAE nor GCC has contemplated an attack on Abu Musa because Iranian fortification would make it too difficult to invade or to hold the island. Not only would an invasion fail, but also Iran could respond by closing the Strait of Hormuz to all commerce, including the oil trade.

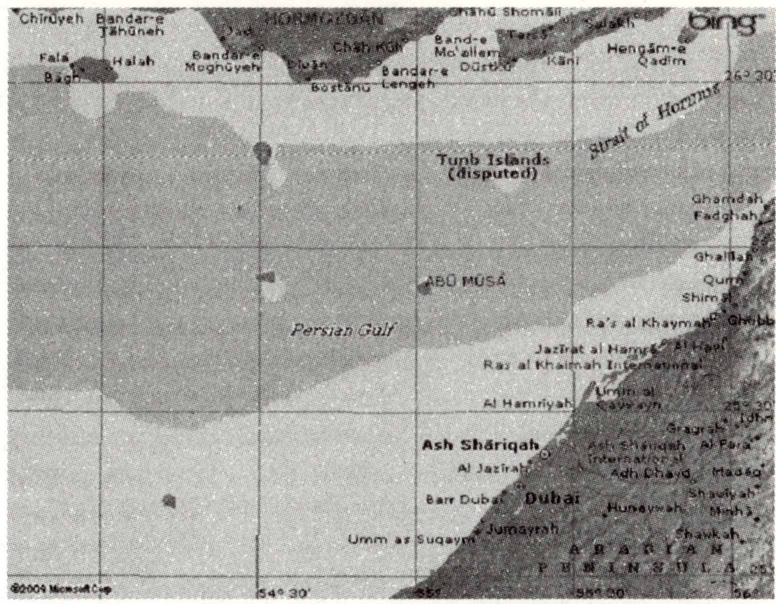

Map 4.10.: Location of Abu Musa Island*

*Source: MSN. Encarta

Its highest point, Halva Kooh, with 110 meters height, is used as sailor's guide. Control of Abu Musa also gives extra protection to the Iranian port Bandar Abbas, which is strategically important due to its oil industry and military base.

There are two groups of people who are living in the island:

1. Non-local Iranian, government's officers, military forces and constructors.
2. The island's roughly 500 inhabitants, "who are originally Iranian but Al-Sharjah's citizens."[31] They are supported by Al-Sharjah's government and are being paid a good amount

as monthly pensions. Drinking water and food are weekly brought to them by ships.

2.3. Arabian Strategic Islands

2.3.1. Musandam Peninsula

This island belongs to Oman. The Musandam Peninsula has an area of 1,800 square kilometers and a population of 28,727 people. There is no land way between Oman's main territory and this part of the country.

Map 4.11.: Location of the Musandam Peninsula

Source: MSN. Encarta

It is separated from the rest of the country by the United Arab Emirates. Connectivity has traditionally been a problem for the region, but this has greatly improved since August 2008 with the world's fastest passenger ferry launching service between Muscat, the capital of Oman, and Musandam. The island's cape is the nearest point to Iran (with only 39 km distance from Iranian island Larak). Majority of its residents are Iranian in origin.

Musandam Governorate has great strategic importance owing to its proximity to the Strait of Hormuz. Its location gives Oman partial control, shared with Iran, of the strategic strait. The most important part of Strait of Hormuz (its deepest part) is near to the island's coasts.

2.3.2. Bubiyan Island

This island is under Kuwait's sovereignty. It is the largest island in the Kuwaiti coastal island chain with an area of 863 square kilometers. It is separated from the mainland in the northeast by Khawr Abd Allah and from the mainland in the southwest by Khawr As-Sabiyah. The latter channel trends around the northern end of Bubiyan Island, separating it from Warbah Island.

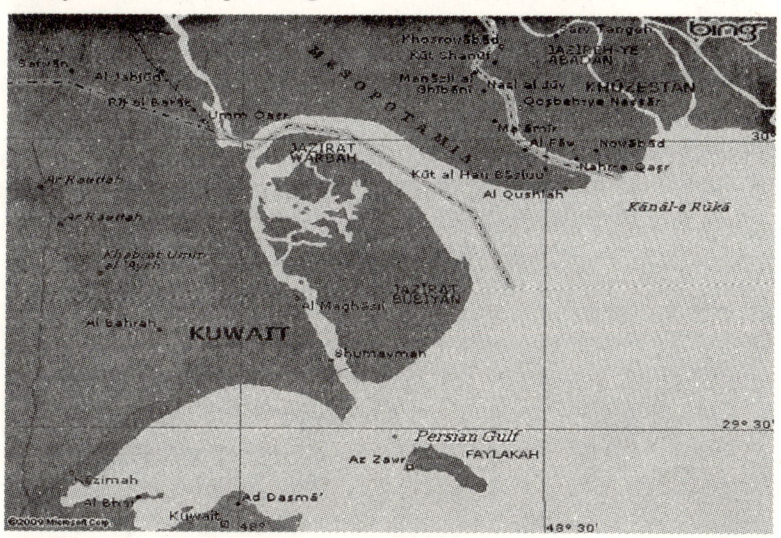

Map 4.12.: Location of Bubiyan Island

Source: MSN. Encarta

About 5.4 kilometers northwest of Ras Al Barshah, the southernmost point, Bubiyan is linked to the mainland by a concrete girder bridge over the Khawr as Sabiyah channel, 2.38 kilometers long, built in 1983, which is for military use only.

The island is situated in the north-western corner of the Persian Gulf. During the Persian Gulf War of 1991, the bridge was destroyed, but has been rebuilt.

In November 1994, Iraq formally accepted the UN-demarcated border with Kuwait which had been spelled out in Security Council Resolutions 687, 773 and 883 which formally ended an earlier claim to Bubiyan Island.

2.3.3. Hawar Archipelago

Hawar Islands used to be one of the settlements of the Bahraini branch of the Dawasir who settled there in the early 1800s and on the main island of Bahrain in 1845 in the areas of Zallaq and Budaiya.

The Hawar Islands are a group of islands situated off the west coast of Qatar in the Gulf of Bahrain of the Persian Gulf. The area is 50.6 square kilometers.

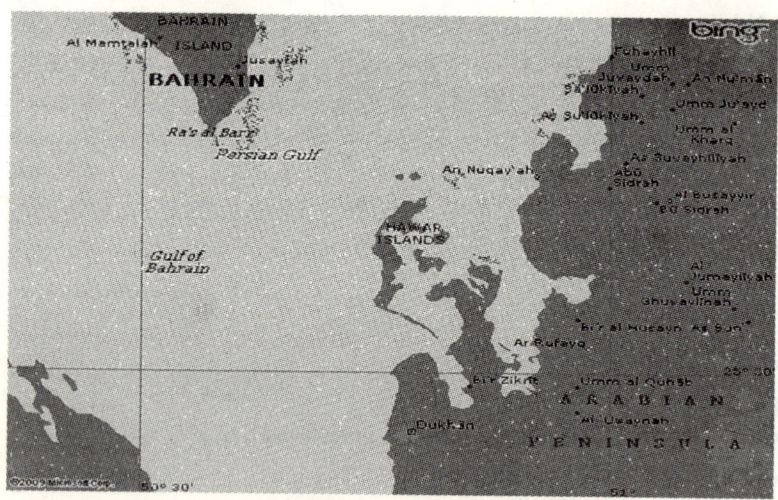

Map 4.13.: Location of Hawar Archipelago

Source: MSN. Encarta

Despite their proximity to Qatar (one of these islands is only 1.4 km from the Qatari mainland at the peninsula of Ras Abruq, while the closest island to the main island of Bahrain, lies at a distance of 19.7 km to it), the islands belong to Bahrain but were the subject of a dispute between Bahrain and Qatar. Resolution in 2001 of the dispute between Bahrain and Qatar over the Hawar Islands improved their already warming relations. In the 2001 census, the population numbered 3,875. A Hawari separatist movement exists in Europe but there is little evidence of support for their movement in the Hawar Islands. In 2002, Bahrain applied to have the Hawar islands recognized as a World Heritage Site, due to its unique environment and habitat for endangered species. This site is home to many wildlife species and a very interesting place for birdwatchers and divers.

2.4. Persian Gulf's Disputed Islands

Territorial disputes amongst the states that straddle the Persian Gulf have been a perennial feature of the region's geopolitical landscape ever since the retreat of British colonialism from the Middle East.

There have been, and continue to be, significant territorial disputes between Persian Gulf countries. Besides the Iraqi invasion of Kuwait in August 1990, and before that the Iran-Iraq War from 1980 to 1988, another important dispute is between the UAE and Iran over ownership of three islands; Abu Musa, Greater Tunb and Lesser Tunb Islands, all strategically located in the Strait of Hormuz.

In January 1968, Britain announced that it would withdraw all of its forces from east of Suez by the end of 1971. At that time, the Sheikdom of Sharjah (later part of the UAE) controlled Abu Musa. However, the Shah of Iran was very interested in the island. The Shah claimed that Abu Musa had been taken from Iran at a time when there had been no central government and that his father had tried unsuccessfully to recover the island and the British had assured him that the ownership of the island would be settled. Furthermore, the Shah is reported to have stated, "[Abu Musa is] of strategic importance to us as much as to the Persian Gulf states and to the peace and security of our region."[32]

"The Shah of Iran dropped Iran's claim on Bahrain in January 1969, in an effort to show accommodation and stave off strong condemnations of his military takeover of Abu Musa Island."[33]

By the end of November 1971, the conflict over the island reached a pitch. On November 29, 1971, Iran and Sharjah announced an agreement calling for Sharjah to maintain sovereignty over Abu Musa and Iran to station military forces on the island. "Oil revenues from the oil fields surrounding the island would be shared."[34]

The full text of Memorandum of Understanding signed by Iran and Sharjah, on November 29, 1971, is as follows:

"Neither Iran nor Sharjah will give up its claims to Abu Musa nor recognise the other's claim. Against this background the following arrangements will be made:

1. Iranian troops will arrive on Abu Musa. They will occupy areas, the extents of which have been agreed on the map attached to this memorandum.
2. (a) Within the agreed areas occupied by Iranian troops, Iran will have full jurisdiction and the Iranian flag will fly.

   (b) Sharjah will retain full jurisdiction over the remainder of the island. The Sharjah flag will continue to fly over the Sharjah police post and the Iranian flag will fly over the Iranian military quarters.
3. Iran and Sharjah recognise the breadth of the island's territorial sea as twelve nautical miles.
4. Exploitation of the petroleum resources of Abu Musa and of the seabed and subsoil, existing in agreement, which must be acceptable to Iran. Half of the governmental oil revenues, hereafter, attributable to the said exploitation, shall be paid directly by the company to Iran and half to Sharjah.
5. The nationals of Iran and Sharjah shall have equal rights to fish in the territorial sea of Abu Musa.

6. A financial assistance agreement will be signed between Iran and Sharjah."[35]

On November 30, 1971, a day before the termination of the treaty with Ras Al Khaimah, Iran sent military forces to Abu Musa, in accordance with its agreement with Sharjah, but then took control of the two nearby uninhabited Tunb islands.

Iran occupied the uninhabited Lesser Tunb Island and captured the Greater Tunb Island after some fighting. Britain also aided Iran to secure part possession of the island of Abu Musa from Sharjah in return for an annual grant. Iran added these three islands to the three it already possessed; Hormuz, Qeshm and Larak to control the six islands to the west and north of the Strait of Hormuz. Iran's seizure of these three islands caused a reaction in the Arab world. Iraq built up a port and naval facilities at Umm Al-Qasr, and the UAE was formed as a federation of five Trucial sheikdoms. However, the Arab states did not take any military action, and the US did not insist on an immediate withdrawal. "American non-interference can be attributed to Iran's strategic importance to the US at that time."[36]

"The dispute became a relatively dormant issue following the establishment of diplomatic relations between Iran and the UAE in October 1972".[37]

In 1980, however, the UAE submitted its claim on the Abu Musa island to the United Nations and joined with five other Gulf States to form the Gulf Cooperation Council (GCC). Throughout the rest of the 1980s, the dispute over the island was overshadowed by the Iran-Iraq war, until March 1992, when Iran expelled the foreigners from Abu Musa. The foreigners ran the UAE-sponsored school, medical clinic, and power-generating station.

"Then in April 1992, Iran took full control of the island."[38] After the UAE brought the issue up to the GCC in September of 1992, Iran declared full sovereignty over the three islands. However, the dispute was temporarily resolved again when Iran and Sharjah agreed to abide by the 1971 agreement. The reasons behind Iran's takeover in 1992 are still unclear. Youssef Ibrahim, of the New York Times, reported that "There have long been suspicions that the agreement between Iran and the Emirates included a secret annex that gave Iran control of the island in 1992."[39]

When Iraq made threatening moves toward Kuwait in October 1994, Iran increased its military presence on Abu Musa. Although even when the crisis subsided, Iranian troops remained on the island. Then in 1995, Iran increased its troops to "4,000 from 700 in just five months".[40] According to the Arab Press Service Organization, on May 25, 1996, Iran has opened an airport on Abu Musa in March 1996.

The UAE has been careful to maintain some contact with Iran because of the large number of Iranian expatriates in the UAE and because of Iran's proximity. The UAE has urged Iran to agree to take the dispute to the International Court of Justice in the Hague. "Iran has responded by stating that its sovereignty over the islands is not negotiable, although it has called for bilateral talks with the UAE to clear up any misunderstandings."[41]

2.4.1. Iran's Position

In late nineteenth and early twentieth centuries, the British occupied a number of Iranian islands in the Persian Gulf, either directly or through assumed sovereignty for the so-called Trucial Emirates. These included Tunbs and Abu Musa as well as Qeshm, Hengam and Sirri islands. Iran's case was further strengthened with the publication in 1892 of Lord Curzon's Persia and the Persian Question in which the map also showed the islands as Iranian territory.

During his tour of southern ports and islands in April 1904, Director of Iranian Customs found out that the Iranian flag was replaced in Tunb and Abu Musa by the flag of the Sheikh of Sharjah. He lowered that flag and ordered the Iranian flag to be re-hoisted. He also commissioned two armed guards at Abu Musa. The Iranian flag was lowered again and the two sides decided to maintain status quo pending further negotiations.

Meanwhile, Iran continued struggles for the recovery of its islands as Iranian Customs Office wrote to the government in July 1927, demanding action against illegal trade by establishing observation posts on the three islands. A small fleet of Iranian navy was sent to recover Abu Musa and the two Tunbs and to put an end to the problem there.

When Iran prepared in 1928 to take her territorial dispute with Britain to the League of Nations, the British agreed to negotiate the status of the Tunbs, Abu Musa and Sirri islands. These negotiations began in January 1929 and continued until mid-spring 1929 without much progress. "Baldwin's"[42] conservative government was replaced in May that year by a Labour government, and Arthur Henderson replaced Chamberlain as Foreign Secretary. Henderson showed a more protective line towards Britain's colonial role in the Persian Gulf and brought "Clive's"[43] negotiations with the Iranians on the issue of the Tunbs and Abu Musa to an abrupt end. This led the Iranians to try to recover the island in the 1930s through a series of actions.

When, at the end at the end of 1948, the Iranians expressed a wish to place administrative offices on Tunbs and Abu Musa, the British ignored it. In 1949 there were rumours, first that Iran was preparing to refer the case to the United Nations, later that they intended to occupy the islands by force. The Iranian government subsequently received a note from the British Embassy in Tehran reminding them of the clear attitude of the British Government in that respect.

The Iranians in return erected a Flagstaff on Lesser Tunb in August that year, which the Royal Navy promptly removed. Iran's protests and actions for the recovery of these islands continued until the British began withdrawing from the region.

The issue, however, was settled through negotiations that lasted throughout the year 1971 between Iran and Britain the latter acting on behalf of its protectorate Emirates. This was the outcome of about 68 years of Iranian protests and demands for the return of the islands.

As the legal guardian of the Emirates at the time, Great Britain concluded the issue by negotiating the legal instrument of 1971 Memorandum of Understanding (MOU) between Iran and Sharjah on Abu Musa and by agreeing to the unconditional return of the two Tunbs to Iran. "UK's permanent representative at the United Nations declared on December 9, 1971 the overall settlement of the issue of these islands as a model agreement for the settlement of similar territorial differences elsewhere in the world."[44]

Iranian authorities were reported in April 1992 to have prevented a group of non-nationals from Sharjah from entering Abu Musa. The High Council of the UAE met on May 12, 1992 to discuss the issue and agreed that commitments of each member states before 1971 were to be treated as commitments of the Union as a whole.

Again reports on August 24, 1992, indicated that Iranian authorities refused entry to Abu Musa of one hundred people of different nationalities. Iranian sources made it clear that activities were seen in the Arab part of Abu Musa involving a number of armed individuals from other countries, including, Western states.

The UAE, on the other hand, without officially denying these serious charges of breach of the 1971 MoU, accused Iran of preventing UAE nationals from entering Abu Musa demanding visas from them. Tension began to ease towards the end of 1992, but in late December, the closing statement of the 13th summit of the Arabic countries' Co-operation Council of the Persian Gulf, announced in Abu Dhabi, called on Iran to terminate 'occupation' of the Tunb islands.

2.4.1.1. Reasons of Iran's Interest in Abu Musa

1. One reason that Iran is interested in Abu Musa Island is oil. In April 1993, the Iranian Parliament passed a law extending the limits of the country's territorial waters to 12 miles. A

limit of 12 miles is significant considering the size of the Persian Gulf and the close proximity of the Gulf States. The Parliament also reasserted Iran's claims to the island, "this could be explained by the fact that there have been reports of large oil deposits under Abu Musa".[45]

Moreover, Iran has expressed displeasure over the amount of oil that it receives from the small, offshore oil field. The agreement between Iran and the UAE stated that the two countries were to share the income from the oil field, equally.

2. Control of Abu Musa could also directly affect shipping. All of Iran's oil tanker traffic must pass through this area; making the security of the area very important. Former Iranian Foreign Minister Abbas Ali Khalatbari, in post-revolution era, stated that his country occupied the islands so that another country could not "threaten navigation in the Strait of Hormuz to the detriment of all littoral states."[46]

   Iranian military deployments on the island could easily be used to control this shipping lane. During the Tanker War in the Gulf in the 1980s, Iran made considerable use of Abu Musa Island.

3. Control of Abu Musa also gives extra protection to Bandar Abbas, an Iranian port so important for its oil industry and military base. "If Iran wanted to deny the waterway to the US Navy, missile sites near Bandar Abbas would be more valuable since they are on the Iranian mainland and the US would be less willing to attack them for both political and military reasons."[47]

2.4.1.2. UAE's Claims and Iran's Counter claims

The following are the six main points argued by the United Arab Emirates and Iran's response to them:

1. Priority in Occupation
   1.1. Whereas the Emirates appeared on the political map of the region only in 19th century, Iran as an ancient nation

was the only government in the vicinity of these islands at the time. All historical documents verify that all islands of northern half of the Persian Gulf have always belonged to Iran.

1.2. Ras al-Khaimeh did not exist at the turn of 20th century, and Sharjah was not, at the time, an Emirate of territorial dimension to be able to claim offshore territories. The Sheikh was a tribal chief under British protection, whose authority was to the tribal people without territorial definition. One should not ignore the fact that British pretext for taking control in the Persian Gulf was to suppress the activities of the same tribes, and then referred to by them as 'pirates' of no political entity, let alone territorial dimension.

1.3. In the nineteenth century, Iran had lease arrangements with Oman, according to which Fath Ali Shah in 1811, and Nasser Ad-Din Shah in 1856, granted the Sultan of Oman, lease title to Bandar Abbas, Minab and southern Persian Gulf coastal areas from east to west as far as Bahrain. If all these areas belonged to Iran, the islands of Abu Musa and the two Tunbs situated in its geographical centre could not have been 'unoccupied'.

1.4. Iran's sovereignty and ownership of these islands, as well as all other offshore and inland areas of the country, were traditionally established without the display of flags of identity. Marking occupation or ownership of territory by hoisting flags was a new concept introduced to the region by European powers. Nevertheless, in 1887, Iran hoisted flags in Sirri and Abu Musa to mark her ownership of these islands after dismissing the Qasemi deputy governors of Bandar Lengeh.

2. Priority in Control

Britain claimed that "Qasemi family controlled Persian Gulf's southern part and also the islands, many years back."[48] But the 'many years back' is not clear. Also, an official British document states that after the establishment of one branch of the Qasemi family at Lengeh, the family occupied the Iranian islands, probably in the "confused period subsequent to the death of Nadir Shah of Iran."[49] This story is an admission that Tunbs, Abu Musa and Sirri islands belonged to Iran and were illegally occupied at a time when Iran in practice was leaderless.

"Sir E. Beckett, legal expert of British Government at the Foreign Office (who later served as a judge at the International Court of Justice) ruled in 1932 that the Iranians possessed sovereignty over Tunb and Abu Musa in 1887-88".[50]

3. Statute of Limitation

According to international law, statute of limitation is applicable only when a territory is being occupied ceaselessly and continuously. But a few months after Emirates' occupation of Tunbs and Abu Musa Islands in 1903, Iran not only started to protest but also in the end of 1934, succeeded to return Greater Tunb Island for a short period of time.

4. Arab-Origin Inhabitants

UAE claims that most of the people of the islands are originally Arab, but the fact is that, Abu Musa and Tunbs Islands' inhabitants are of mixed-race. In Abu Musa, some of the people are originally from Bandar Lengeh (Iran) and some from Sudan Tribe (Sharjah) and in Greater Tunb from Bani Yas Tribe.

Iranians were the first race who settled in Persian Gulf areas. Migration of Arab people started a little before rising of Islam. "The process of population intercourse between Persians and Arabs continued for many decades. Therefore, it is impossible to distinguish Persian and Arab races in the region."[51]

5. Coercion and Reluctance

UAE claims that the acceptance of 1971 MoU was under coercion and reluctance and they have informally, de facto, accepted that. But in the year of signing MoU (1971), Sharjah was under Britain's protection and, in fact, Iran signed the agreement with Britain not Sharjah, and as at that time Britain was a superpower and certainly most powerful than Iran, it could be more logical to claim that, Iran signed the MoU under coercion and reluctance.

6. Nineteenth-Century Correspondence

   The UAE bases its claims over these islands on a number of letters exchanged between the Qasemis of Bandar Lengeh, Sharjah and Ras al-Khaimeh. Some of these letters date as far back as 1864. They are contradictory and make fanciful claims on various localities up and down the region.

   "The most important of these letters was written by Shaikh Yusef Al-Qasemi of Bandar Lengeh to the Sheikh of Ras al-Khaimeh, in which Shaikh Yusef states: 'the island of Tunb actually or in reality is for you'. There is little doubt about the nature of this sentence as a standard oriental compliment. A few lines below this statement, Shaikh Yusef adds a further compliment: 'and the town of Lengeh is your town'. No one has ever been under any illusion, then or at any other time that Port Lengeh had ever belonged to any country but Iran. When this reference to Lengeh as belonging to the Sheikh of Ras al-Khaimeh has never been and cannot be taken as anything other than a courtesy/compliment, one must ask, how could a similar reference to Tunb Island be taken literally? When, in 1929, King Abdul-Aziz of Saudi Arabia wrote to the Sheikh of Bahrain complaining about the treatment of his subjects there, received a letter of from the Sheikh who states that 'Bahrain, Qatif, Hasa and Nejd were all one and belong to Your Majesty'. Certainly inclusion of Bahrain in that list could not have been but pure compliment."[52]

2.4.2. UAE's Position

The crisis concerning the three disputed islands is multidimensional.

1. Political Dimension: Politically, it reflects the hegemonic attitude of major regional powers (major in terms of population, area and wealth).
2. Economical Dimension: Economically it highlights the strategic importance of the islands' location as a toll booth to the Strait of Hormuz, controlling the passage of a vital regional commodity; oil, and even jeopardizing the very source of that commodity in a smaller state.
3. Historical Dimension: The crisis also has a historical-legal dimension.

Unfortunately, however, this third dimension has not been adequately probed by those concerned with, or interested in, the crisis. "This is probably due to the difficulty of research into the quagmire of history and international law, and to the scarcity of references and literature dealing with the dispute."[53]

Historical references point to a sharing of the Gulf islands by the two Qawasim factions:

The islands of Sirri and Hengam became the property of the Lengeh Qawasim, while Abu Musa, Greater and Lesser Tunbs, and Sir Abu Nuair came under the Qawasim of the southern coast (Ras Al-Khaimah and Sharjah). Such arrangements were already in being by 1835. Thus, the Qawasim of the coastal areas established and maintained unopposed legal and actual sovereignty over the islands.

The message of Qawasim ruler to British Resident in 1864 was the first document asserting the UAE's legal title to the islands.

Sovereignty was further demonstrated in various forms of protest against any intervention in the islands or violation of the agreement by the Lengeh Qawasim or neighbouring Emirates. This separation of the two Qawasim factions is further confirmed by the fact that, in 1873, the ruler of the Sharjah Qawasim, Sheikh

Salem Bin Sultan, dispatched 50 armed men to Abu Musa to drive away ships belonging to Lengeh Qawasim. Even earlier, in 1871, the Sheikh of the Qawasim of Ras al-Khaimah had denied Lengeh Qawasim entry into the Tunbs. He sent a message to the Lengeh Sheikh protesting against unauthorized visits to the islands by his subjects. The Lengeh ruler replied confirming that the islands actually belonged to the Qawasim of the southern coast.

The attitude of the then dominant colonial power (Britain, through the British government of India) was to consider the title to the islands and division thereof between the two Qawasim factions to be a purely local issue in which it had no desire to interfere. However, the British Political Agent, Haji Abdulrahman, who had broad commercial interests with the Lengeh Qawasim, tried to demonstrate, in his correspondence with the British government of India, that the islands belonged to the Lengeh Qawasim. He even ordered the ruler of Ras Al-Khaimah's Qawasim to quit them.

A further proof that the Qawasim of the southern Gulf had title to these islands is that they exercised all aspects of sovereignty over them. In 1879, for example, the ruler of Sharjah, Sheikh Salem ben Sultan, exiled his political opponents to Abu Musa Island. "In 1883, When he himself was overthrown by his nephew; Sheikh Saqr Bin Khaled, he chose to live on Abu Musa."[54]

Aside from the legal issues outlined above, there is a wealth of historical documentation to support the UAE's claim to sovereignty over the islands. Apart from short and interrupted periods in the seventeenth and eighteenth centuries, the three islands have been governed by Arab rulers since 1330. From then, until 1622, they were part of the Arab-ruled Kingdom of Hormuz, based on the island of the same name, which also included much of what is now the UAE and Oman.

From the middle of the eighteenth century, the islands were ruled by the Al Qawasim dynasty which today provides the Sheikhs of Ras Al-Khaimah and Sharjah. At that time the State of the Al

Qawasim included not only much of the northern UAE and the three islands but also extended along the southern coast of Iran to include the port of Bandar Lengeh. Treaties signed with the British in the early nineteenth century acknowledged that the Al Qasimi dominions extended to both sides of the Persian Gulf and, at the same time, represented an acknowledgement of their sovereignty under prevailing international law.

Bandar Lengeh remained under the rule of an Al Qasimi sheikh until 1886, at which time it was annexed by Iran, regardless of the fact that it had by then been part of the Al Qasimi state for over a century.

In 1887, Iran occupied a fourth island, Sirri, also part of the Al Qasimi dominions although administered by the Bandar Lengeh branch of the family. In a protest to Tehran, the British government, which had been in treaty relations with the Emirates since 1820, noted that Sirri, as well as the other islands, formed part of the hereditary estates of the Jowasimi (Qasimi) Arab Sheikhs. Many of Sirri's inhabitants, rejecting the occupation, and then moved to Abu Musa, which remained uncontested as part of the Al Qasimi state.

As late as 1903, the British Political Resident in the Gulf was able to state that, as far as he was aware, Iran had made no claim to the Tunbs. The next year, however, Iranian customs officials landed on both Abu Musa and Greater Tunb, although, after protests from the Ruler of Sharjah (which then included Ras Al-Khaimah) and from Britain, they withdrew. At the time, the government of Iran failed to respond to a request from Britain that it should produce documentation in support of its claim to the islands.

In 1920, the Al Qasimi state was divided into two, with Abu Musa becoming part of Sharjah, and Greater and Lesser Tunb becoming part of Ras Al-Khaimah.

Shortly afterwards in 1923, Iran once again put forward a claim to sovereignty over the three islands, but following protests from Sharjah, Ras al-Khaimah and Britain, the claim was dropped. Further incidents of Iranian interference took place, prompting more protests. In 1926, the Iranian customs were instructed by Tehran not to take any steps in Abu Musa or Tunbs, pending reply from the Ministry of Foreign Affairs regarding status of these islands, a clear indication that Iran was unsure of the legal validity of its claims.

The weakness of the Iranian position, in terms of international law, was underlined during negotiations between Iran and Britain in the late 1920s. Iran first offered to withdraw its claim to Abu Musa if its title over the Tunbs was recognized. Failing in that objective, in itself an acknowledgement that its claim to Abu Musa had no validity, Iran then offered to buy the Tunbs. The offer was rejected in 1930 by the Ruler of Ras al-Khaimah with the support of his colleague, the Ruler of Sharjah, following which Iran then offered to lease the Tunbs for a period of 50 years. Once again no agreement was reached.

Sharjah and Ras al-Khaimah continued to exercise their sovereignty over the three islands unchallenged until the late 1960s.

Following the announcement in 1968 by Britain of its intention to withdraw from the Persian Gulf by the end of 1971, the Government of Iran put forward a claim to the whole of the island of Bahrain. In the wake of a referendum conducted on Bahrain under UN supervision, Iran was obliged to abandon its claim which had no legal basis. It promptly revived its then-dormant claim to Abu Musa and Greater and Lesser Tunb. It is significant, in terms of international law that it did so not on the basis of providing historical evidence of its claim to sovereignty but through threat of coercion.

"On September 28, 1971 the Shah of Iran stated in an interview with the London Guardian that: 'we need them [the islands]; we shall have them; no power on earth shall stop us'."[55]

"Attempts by Britain to resolve the problem had mixed results. Sharjah, reserving its claim to sovereignty over Abu Musa but concerned about the obvious coercion from Iran, agreed to sign a Memorandum of Understanding."[56]

2.4.2.1. Reasons of UAE's Interest in Abu Musa

All of the sheikdoms in the UAE are attempting to acquire as many reserves as possible because it has been estimated that their current reserves may dry up within the next 30-50 years. Al-Sharjah is interested in the island because its economy depends heavily on its oil income. "Presently, the only oil that Sharjah has any claim to is located off Abu Musa".[57] The Mubarak offshore oilfield, 8x5 km, is about 20 km east of Abu Musa and is shared by Sharjah and Iran.

"The UK's Enterprise Oil entered into a joint venture with the UAE's Crescent Petroleum to increase production from the Mubarak oilfield, in 1996."[58]

2.4.2.2. Iran's Claims and UAE's Counterclaims

The five main points argued by Iran and the responses of the United Arab Emirates that an UAE scholar; Mohammad Abdullah Al Rokan has stated in his book, United Arab Emirates: A new Perspective, are as follow :[59]

1. Islands' Persian Names

   'Tunb' is a word of Persian origin meaning 'hill' and that it is derived from a local Persian dialect known as 'Tangistani Persian'.

   Apart from the legal invalidity of this evidence, because linguistic derivation is not a criterion for territorial title or sovereignty, it is also linguistically incorrect. 'Tunb' is a purely Arab word meaning 'a long rope used to erect a tent', while the name 'Abu Musa' leaves no doubt as to its being Arabic.

2. Priority in Occupation

   Iran claims that the three islands had for a lengthy period of time before the eighteenth century been under Persian occupation. Such a claim is disproved by historical fact. Moreover, the Persian occupation of the three islands lasted for a short while, and occurred as a result of internal conflicts and a subsequent period of weakness in the region. The Persians were soon driven out of the islands. The claim is also illogical in light of contemporary international relations.

If such a short period of occupation were to be taken as the basis of proving a state's title to any particular territory, it would result in the undermining of international peace and security.

3. Geographical Proximity

A third claim cited by Iran is based on geographical proximity. There is no factual basis for this claim, especially with regard to Abu Musa and, in any case, international law does not recognize geographical proximity as valid evidence supporting territorial claims.

4. Persian Officials as Rulers

The fourth claim is that the Qawasim had ruled Lengeh in their capacity as 'Persian officials', and hence the islands belonged to Iran. Historical facts refute this claim; the three islands had never been under the rule of Lengeh Qawasim. Throughout the years, they had always been ruled by Qawasim of Sharjah and Ras Al-Khaimah.

Unfortunately, however, many British legal advisers had labored under such a misunderstanding, drafting legal memoranda for the British government in which it was wrongly stated that the Lengeh Qawasim had exercised control over Greater and Lesser Tunb and Abu Musa. In fact, they only ruled the island of Sirri.

5. Britain's Geographical Maps

Britain's geographical maps, specially "a map which was presented to Iran's king in 1886,"[60] were used for sailing and are not authentic to determine borders. The mentioned map had been presented to Iranian king for the reason of gathering geographical information.

References

1. Nicholas John Spykman (1893 – 1943) was a Dutch-American geostrategist, known as the "Godfather of Containment".
2. Elahi Homayoun, "*The Persian Gulf and Its Problems*"; 8th edition, Ghoomes, Tehran, 2005, p.61
3. Ibid
4. Mahajan V.D. "*International Relations since 1900*", S. Chand and Company Ltd., New Delhi, 1989, p. 814
5. Till, Geoffrey, "*Maritime Strategy and the Nuclear Age*", McMillan; London,1984, p.130
6. N.2
7. The United Nations Convention on the Law of the Sea, www.un.org
8. OPEC Annual Report, 2007
9. Cutler J. Cleveland, Encyclopaedia of Earth, Last Updated: June 14th, 2007, www.eoearth.org
9. Hafeznia Mohammad Reza, "*Persian Gulf and Strategic Role of Strait of Hormuz*", 4th edition, Samt, Tehran, 2005, pp, 361-363
10. Aghai Diba Bahman, "*Closing the Strait of Hormuz*", Persian Journal, November 10th , 2006, www.iranian.ws
11. Al-Arabia.net, an Arabic-Language News Network, March 6th, 2009
12. This United States' Navy's ship was severely damaged by an Iranian mine in 1988.
13. Isenberg David, "A game of chicken in the Persian Gulf", Asia Times, January 10th , 2008
14. Iran's Jam-e Jam newspaper, June 1st, 2008
15. Ertan Fikret, "*Strait of Hormuz: The place to watch*", Turkish Today's Zaman Magazine, July 6th , 2008
16. "*Iran warns of closure of Hormuz Strait if threatened*" , China View, July 5th , 2008
17. N.10, pp. 343-351
18. Energy Information Administration, Country Analysis Briefs/ Persian Gulf Region , June 2007
19. James Baker Institute is an institute for public policy of the Rice University in Texas, USA.
20. China Daily News, March 21st, .2007
21. N.10, p. 353
22. N.10, p. 366
23. "*Canal to Bypass Strait of Hormuz*", Dow Jones, September 8th, 2008
24. N10, p. 220
25. N2, p.40

26. Dr. Hafeznia Mohammad Reza in his book, *"Persian Gulf and Strategic Role of Strait of Hormuz"*, has mentioned that the island's area is 1491 square kilometer .
27. N 2, p.41
28. N 10, p. 201
29. N 2, p. 68
30. Dr. Hafeznia Mohammad Reza in his book; "*Persian Gulf and Strategic Role of Strait of Hormuz"* (p. 199), has estimated the island's inhabitants; 618 persons.
31. Caldwell Dan, "*Flashpoints in the Gulf: Abu Musa and the Tunb Islands*" , Middle East Policy, Volume 4, Number 3, March 1st, 1996, p. 52
32. Amirahmadi Hooshang and Entessar Nader, editors., "*Iran and the Arab World*", St. Martin's Press, New York, 1993, p. 70
33. No. 31
34. Tabarsa Naghi, "*The Sovereignty Over Abu Musa, Lesser and Greater Tunbs Islands In The Iranian Foreign Policy"*, The Centre for Documents and Diplomatic History, Tehran, 2008, p. 729
35. No. 32, p. 127
36. Murphy Caryle, *"Iran Claims Sovereignty over Small, Oil- Producing Gulf Island"*, The Washington Post, September 25th, 1992, p. A31
37. No. 31, p. 53
38. Ibrahim Youssef, *"Iran Is Said to Expel Arabs from Gulf Island"*, The New York Times, April 16th, 1992, p. A7
39. No. 31, p. 54-55
40. No 31, p.56, referring to Reuter World Service, April 18th, 1996
41. He served three terms as Prime Minister of the United Kingdom, first from 1923-24, then 1924-1929 and again from 1935-1937.
42. Sir Robert Clive was the Britain's Minister to Tehran between 1926 and 1931.
43. Extracts from Dr. Piroz Mojtahedzade's letter to Mr. Javier Solana; Former High Representative of the European Union For Common Foreign and Security Policies, June 10th, 2004
44. No.31, p. 56
45. Shelly Alexander and Gould Deane, *"Factors in the Settlement of the Dispute Over Abu Musa and the Tombs"*, M.A. Thesis, The American University, 1979, p. 12
46. Hough Harold, *"Iranian Intentions-The Strait of Hormuz or Beyond?"* , Jane's Intelligence Review, Volume 7, Number 10, October 1st , 1995, p.454

47. "*Memorandum of August 24th 1928, India Office Library and Record, File No. L/P@ S/18/B 397,pp. 4512-4528*", Extracted from Wikipedia/ Territorial dispute in the Persian Gulf
48. Mojtahedzade Piroz, "*The Islands of Tunb & Abu Musa; An Iranian Argument in Search of Peace and Cooperation in the Persian Gulf,*" Translated by: Malek Mohammadi Nouri Hamid Reza, Institute of Political and International Studies, Tehran, 2007, p. 50
49. Ibid. p.92
50. Ibid. pp. 86-87
51. Ibid. pp. 94-95
52. Abed Ibrahim and Hellyer Peter, "*United Arab Emirates: A New Perspective*", Trident Press Ltd, London, 2001, p. 179
53. Ibid. pp. 180-181
54. "*Facts About the Three Occupied UAE Islands*", www.un.int/uae
55. www.emirates-islands.org.ae
56. No.45, p.25
57. *"Enterprise in UAE Project,"* Platt's Oilgram News, volume 74, number 132, July 10th , 1996, p.3
58. N. 52, p. 184
59. N 34, p. 559

5

Evolution of Regional Order of the Persian Gulf Region

1. Introduction

By virtue of its oil resources and consequent income, the Persian Gulf region is one of the world's key strategic areas. It has also been the scene of some of the most intensive geopolitical competition and violence. The location of the Persian Gulf has given the region a significant economic and strategic position. Due to the geostrategic changes during the last three decades the region suffered a prolonged period of tension and instability.

The geopolitics of the contemporary Gulf was dominated by a triangular conflict between the three most powerful states of the region; Iran, Iraq and Saudi Arabia. "For decades, the regional order in the Gulf was shaped by this triangle. If one of them gained too much weight, the other two tried to compensate."[1]

Emerging from an earlier history of western intervention, and from the process of state building within Gulf States in the post-1918 period, this conflict had dominated the region for the past quarter of a century, and showed no sign of abating: no stable resolution of the conflict, one in which each state felt itself to be at a potential disadvantage, had yet been achieved. Yet, if this instability was evident to all, the causes of it remained less evident. There was, at first sight, no insuperable international obstacle to peace between these three states; there were plenty of mechanisms that could resolve those issues; territorial, economic and political that divide them. The causes of instability in the Gulf, of past conflicts and probable future ones, lie much less in a continuous history or in the geopolitics itself, in past external intervention or relations between local states, and more in the contemporary domestic politics of these countries.

Yet the 2003 Iraq War has created an entirely new situation since the indefinite US presence has virtually transformed the triangle into a square. Yet in reality this impression is misleading because Iraq's role has actually been usurped by the United States. This has resulted in a new, artificial triangle comprising of the US, Iran, and Saudi Arabia. Strangely enough, within this new triangle, external, or at least non-Arab powers, i.e. the US and Iran, are the most powerful actors, even hinting at the emergence of a bilateral system. Nevertheless, history, tradition, and geography would suppose a renaissance of the traditional triangle. Washington would probably not object to an Iraq acting as its strategist partner in the region as imperial Iran did in the 1970s.

In large part, due to the growth of transportation, finance and information technologies since Second World War, global, regional and national security issues are impossible to separate.

Oil and natural gas are the primary drivers of the entire global economy, both in the developing and developed worlds. Regional security in the Gulf is, therefore, inherently tied to socioeconomic development throughout the world. And insofar as socioeconomic development has become a pre-eminent global security issue in the post 9/11 world.

Gulf security is inherently a global security problem. Gulf security is of primary concern for all poorer countries that are attempting to become middle powers, and all middle powers such as Brazil or India trying to become great powers. Regional security in the Persian Gulf constitutes a global public good.

1.1. Definition of Regional Order

Regional order can be defined as "a formal or informal arrangement that sustains rule-governed interactions among states in their pursuit of individual and collective goals in a specific region."[2]

The definition of regional order presupposes three following elements:

1. The first element is the idea of patterned regularity. Formal or informal arrangements of principles, rules, habits and institutions facilitate countries in the region to behave in patterned ways and anticipation of patterned behaviour in turn generates reciprocal reactions by other actors in the region. Such patterned regularity reduces chances for disorder and uncertainty.
2. Rule-governed behaviour is the second element. Reciprocal interactions and resulting patterned regularities are by and large a product of ruled-governed behaviour. Patterns of regularity would be inconceivable without corresponding rule-governed behaviour. Compliance with principles, norms and rules not only prevents any deviant behaviour but also creates and enhances purposive order.
3. The purposive regional order is in turn predicated on the satisfaction of normative conditions for coexistence of actors in the region. They involve, not only the reduction of the likelihood of regional violence, but also the creation of minimally acceptable conditions of economic well-being, social justice, ecological stability and participation in decision making in the region.

1.2. Theoretical Perspectives on Regional Order

Pathways to regional order differ among contending theoretical perspectives, which are as follows.

1.2.1. Realists

Realists argue that regional order is a function of power. Depending upon the configuration of power, regional order can take several forms:

1.2.1.1. Anarchical

Anarchical regional order, which resembles the "Hobbesian"[3] world of all against all, is rather rare in reality. However, diffused power deformed governance structure and individual maximizing behaviour for power, wealth and status can often lead to anarchical regional order. The only viable rule under the anarchical order is survival of the fittest. Actors in the region can avoid the violence and instability associated with anarchical order by resorting to a balance of power.

1.2.1.2. Hierarchical

The hierarchical form of regional order involves a differential arrangement of regional actors, depending upon their power and influence. A tributary system and patron-client relationship are classical examples of hierarchical regional orders. Although the tributary system no longer exists, hierarchical structure of patron-client relationships can be found in various forms of alliance.

1.2.1.3. Consortium

The consortium form of regional order refers to collective management of regional security and economic order by major powers.

1.2.1.4. Hegemonic

A hegemonic order can be envisaged. It can be either benign or malignant. While a benign hegemonic regional order refers to regional security and economic arrangements in which a hegemonic leader provides collective goods for the survival and prosperity of regional actors, a malignant one can be defined as a regional order in which a hegemonic leader engages in the practice of domination and subjugation. The malignant hegemonic order often involves the imposition of imperial order on a regional scale.

1.2.1.5. Balance of Power

As the Concert of Power in the post-Napoleonic era illustrates, such a regional arrangement can be undertaken through mutual consultation and consensus among major powers.

From the realistic point of view, balance of power arrangements best serve the pursuit of international security. Henry Kissinger, a *German* born *American political scientist* and *diplomat* that served as *National Security Advisor* and later, concurrently, as *Secretary of State* in the *Nixon administration*, argues that, "when working properly, the balance-of-power system is meant to limit both the ability of states to dominate others and the scope of conflicts... a balance of power arrangement cannot satisfy every member of the international system completely; it works best when it keeps dissatisfaction below the level at which the aggrieved party will seek to overthrow the international order."[4]

However, a balance of power can not always guarantee stable peace because of the fluidity of power and the dynamics of alliance politics.

1.2.2. Liberals and Constructivists

Liberals and constructivists suggest alternative views of regional order. They argue that regional order can evolve into several diverse forms, depending upon the configuration of interests and norms, not power. Actors in the region can show rule-governed behaviour, not only because of the salience of gain from patterned regularity and cooperation, but also because of norms, practices and even institutional inertia. Countries in a region can attempt to form a collective security system that can overcome the deficiencies of an alliance system, and this can surely be conducive to building and sustaining a stable peace.

2. Persian Gulf Region in Cold War Era

In Cold War era, Persian Gulf region was one of the most important centres of two superpowers' competition and contest. Some of the political analysts in late 1970s believed that Persian Gulf region was the only vital region of USA and USSR strife. Therefore, they were struggling to obtain higher position through increasing their influence on regional states.

The Persian Gulf was far more of an American than of a Soviet sphere of influence. While Moscow had a close relationship with Iraq, it never really penetrated the region. There was virtually no direct Russian presence. USA by strengthening Iran and USSR by supporting Iraq accomplished the mentioned policy.

In the Cold War years (1945–1991), the United States focused almost completely on building up strong local allies to dominate the region without taking account of the domestic side of security in the Gulf. Through the 60s and 70s, the United States increasingly relied on a strategy of 'local hegemony', via support for the Saudi Arabian monarchy and the Shah of Iran. This strategy failed when the Islamic revolution of Iran in 1979 ejected the Shah from power, and later when the rise of transnational terror groups with Saudi citizens as active members resulted in the terrorist attacks of September 11, 2001.

The United States had an alliance with Iran and Saudi Arabia, while US or British influence was pre-eminent in all the smaller Arab states of the region.

Iran was one of many 'third world' countries with which the United States has made arms trade agreements. From 1900 to the late 1940's, the United States had little involvement with Iran, but, both recognized that indeed the United States with its growing power would come to play some special beneficial role in rescuing Iran from its humiliating servitude and restore it to some semblance of its past history. During this period the United States had little national interest in the resources of Iran.

It was only after the mid 1950's that the United States began major arms shipments to Iran. Perhaps, it was a matter of strategy as reported by John L. Sutton and Geoffrey Kemp in Arms to Developing Countries 1945-1965, which states: "Only Iran confronts the Soviet Union directly, a fact which has been recognized in the supply of American aircraft to Iran as part of the American 'forward defence' strategy, through military grant and aid programmes."[5]

Following the restoration of the Shah of Iran to power in August 1953, the US began to encourage the formation of a regional military bloc, and this led in 1955 to the signing of the Baghdad Pact, comprising Iran, Iraq and Turkey. While this very much reflected the continued dominance of external, Western, strategic concerns, it also reflected the shared interests which the monarchs of Iran and Iraq had in facing a rising nationalist tide in the region.

Following the Iraqi revolution of 1958, Iran began to support the Kurds in northern Iraq, a commitment that reached its peak in the period 1969-1975 when Iran and Iraq fought a controlled, but at times intense, border war. Iraq, for its part, provided some assistance to Kurdish groups inside Iran, and from 1965, onwards began to champion the cause of the Arab population of south-west Iran. Much of the overt conflict between the two states involved the question of the frontier: an unfavourable settlement imposed by Britain on Iran in 1937 was rejected by Iran in 1969, but this border issue was less an issue of substance in itself, a reasonable compromise being possible at any time, and more a symbol around which inter-state and nationalist mobilization could occur.

The involvement in conflict with Iraq did not prevent Iran from asserting its position vis-à-vis other states in the region. Relations with the third powerful state in the Gulf, viz. Saudi Arabia, remained normal but there was suspicion between the two royal families owing to Tehran's closeness to the Hashemite in Baghdad.

USA, by reason of its dominance over Iran and the Persian Gulf's south shore states, got strongest and higher position in comparison with USSR. "Nevertheless, formation of regional balance of power was the main and basic part of USA and USSR foreign policy in the region."[6]

In the 1980s, the United States and local Arab monarchies of the Persian Gulf tried to create complete balance of power to keep the peace. This included US intelligence and financial aid to Iraq in its war with Iran, which kept both countries from growing too powerful and, thereby, provided immediate security to neighbouring Arab regimes.

However, this strategy allowed Iraq to build up offensive military power and turned a blind eye to the human rights transgressions of Saddam Hussein as well as to his use of chemical weapons against Iran.

In fact, the Iran-Iraq War did not validate the balance of power, but rather destroyed the natural Persian Gulf balance of power through the exhaustion and hollowing out of the region's two largest states. The 'northern' half of the Persian Gulf has been steadily enervated by so-called balance-of-power policies. Looking beyond superpower foibles, the largely pointless war between Iran and Iraq from 1980–88 also speaks against peace through armed victory in the region. In 1980, Saddam thought he could secure valuable geostrategic territories at the head of the Gulf waterway, as well as overall political, ideological and military hegemony throughout the Gulf, via a decisive defeat of an Iran that was internally weakened by its ongoing revolution. Saddam's dream was to become the indisputable leader of pan-Arabism and the natural geopolitical arbiter in conflicts between Arab states in the Gulf (and perhaps beyond).

Local and sub-regional issues predominated in setting the agenda for the Gulf States. The underlying power dynamic was a triangle with two strong and one weak side. The two strong sides were Iran and Iraq, each with large populations and relatively strong armies. Both countries have desired to dominate the Gulf in their own way, through different regimes and ideologies. This geostrategic framework seems a factor likely to shape the Gulf's future as well as its past. As suggested above, the Persian Gulf's Arab monarchies dealt with this competition in various ways. One technique was to use the United States as a protector against the more threatening regional power. Another was to appease Baghdad or Tehran. Finally, the monarchies could play off one of these stronger states against the other.

The key factor for regional states was that they wanted some level of American protection against local threats from radicals, internal upheavals, or perhaps, any Soviet actions. At the same time, though, they did not want to provoke their own highly traditional people or militant neighbours by showing too high a profile in their relationship with America. This balance of seeking a protector and appeasing potential threats, basically, worked for many years. There was no need for a Soviet role since its clients (Iraq, Syria, Egypt under the rule of Jamal Abdel Nasser, and South Yemen) were the very forces threatening the local regimes.

The monarchies cooperated to some extent by forming the Gulf Cooperation Council (GCC) but they could never defend themselves from external attack or intimidation without outside help.

2.1. Superpowers and the Region

2.1.1. United State of America

The United States concerns over the security and military defense of the Persian Gulf have steadily intensified during the last four decades.

USA interests in the Persian Gulf have been very palpable:

1. To ensure access by the industrialized world to the region's vast oil and gas resources,
2. To deny Soviet political and military control over those resources.

The significance of the region has tended to increase as a result of growing Western dependence on Persian Gulf and Middle East oil and the need to assure the continued access to the regions' vast resources. Preserving the stability and independence of the Gulf States and containing the threat of Islamic fundamentalism are other interests that have been expressed by American leaders from time to time. But, those are derivative concerns growing out of specific circumstances and are implicit in the two grand themes of oil and Soviet containment that have been the constants of expanding US policy.

Under the presidential administrations of Nixon, Carter, and Reagan, the United States went from a role of supporting the British to a major player in power responsibility in the Persian Gulf. The actions of these three presidents were in response to internal and external threats to the economic, political, and strategic interests of the United States in the Persian Gulf.

2.1.1.1. President Nixon Era: 1969-1974

He developed the initial US Persian Gulf policy to fill the void in Western participation by establishing Iran and Saudi Arabia, the 'twin pillars', as US surrogates for the region.

2.1.1.1.1. Twin Pillar Policy

Iran and Saudi Arabia, as two America's regional strategic pillars, were responsible for Persian Gulf's security and protector of its stability, respectively. Although, the US policy was known as the 'twin pillar', Saudi Arabia was clearly the less dominant partner. Saudi Arabia's importance was due to its possession of the world's largest oil fields and its emerging influence in pan-Arab politics and councils.

2.1.1.2. President Carter Era: 1977-1981

He took a more aggressive approach to safeguard US interests by designating the Persian Gulf as a 'vital interest' to the United States and threatened to repel any attempts by outside powers to gain control of the Gulf in the wake of the Soviet invasion of Afghanistan.

The new policy was articulated by President Carter in his 1980 State of the Union Address and became known as the Carter Doctrine.

2.1.1.3. President Reagan Era: 1981-1989

He affirmed the Carter administration policy and, though he saw the Soviets as the most significant threat to the region, he was concerned about internal Gulf instability serving Soviet objectives in the region.

With the Soviet threat as its focus, the Reagan administration at first embraced the idea of 'strategic consensus' in which a goal was to persuade the diverse countries of the region to put aside local parochial security concerns and unite with the US in an alliance type of relationship against the Soviet Union and its' clients states.

The Iran-Iraq war, along with the arms for hostages' sales to Iran presented the greatest challenges to US policy during the Reagan administration. The need to end the war, with its resultant attacks on shipping in the Gulf and the need to regain US credibility with Gulf friendly states resulted in over 30 US navy ships in the Gulf and the US leading peace efforts in the United Nations.

2.1.2. Soviet Union

The activities of the USSR's Western Allies in the Persian Gulf region and Middle East stimulated Soviet interests in the area.

The USSR focused its ties with Iraq upon its concern with Persian Gulf affair. Geopolitically, Vietnam, Somalia (later Ethiopia), South Yemen (the PDRY), Egypt, Syria, Angola and Cuba were all important regional actors which also, at one time or another, had made some of their land and air facilities available to the Soviet navy and air force.

Iraq ,too ,fell into this category, but its importance to the USSR was enhanced by its location in the Persian Gulf, a region which because of its enormous oil resources, had attracted a great deal of western attention. Diplomatic relation between Iraq and the USSR were first established in 1944, during the later stages of Second World War.

"When a military coup overthrew the Pro-Western monarchy in Baghdad in July 1958, the Kremlin, led by irrepressible Nikita Khrushchev, expressed a great deal of interest in the newly created republic."[7]This was not surprising.

Iraq had by then emerged as an important Arab State whose population base and economic potential, above all its huge oil reserves, propelled it into a position of leadership in a region engaged in shaking off the colonial tutelage and in asserting its political and, eventually, economic independence from the Western imperialist powers.

Baghdad's anti-Western credentials and policies directed at undermining 'imperialist' position and influence were in harmony with Moscow's own position. Last but not least, Iraq belonged to a small group of Third World clients which, because of their economic wealth, were able to secure Soviet military and industrial equipment in exchange for hard currency or oil.

All of these considerations made Iraq a particularly important attractive client, explaining the relative benevolence with which it was treated by Brezhnev's Kremlin in spite of occasionally grave provocations.

Politically, in the Gulf and elsewhere in the Middle East, Iraq had emerged as a staunch opponent of 'imperialism, colonialism and Zionism', a line which, in the main, corresponded with the Soviet position.

Militarily, the Soviet gained less than was commonly assured in the West. Contrary to reports circulating in the early 1970; no Iraqi bases were placed at the USSR's disposal. In October 1976, the USSR and Iraq concluded another arms agreement, providing for the delivery of tanks and of additional Scud missiles.

Economically, after 1973 Oil Crisis, the USSR was receiving Iraqi petroleum at the pre-increase price of below US$ 3 per barrel and, given the oil shortages in the West, proceeded to make a killing.

Iraq was, first of all, the closest of all the Arab nations to Soviet borders. Because of that proximity the threat of Soviet expansion, could have been seen as being much more realistic and likely by its leaders, as compared with the leaders of the other *Arab states*.

In short, in the late 1970s, relations between Iraq and USSR were marked by a significant coincidence of interest with respect to American policies in the Arab-Israeli sector as well as in the Persian Gulf and by concurrent conflicts over Moscow's own political and military activities in the Horn of Africa, the Persian Gulf and Afghanistan.

The centre of gravity in Iraq's international economic relations in the period between 1976 and 1979 clearly and overwhelmingly shifted to the industrial West.

The policy of the *Soviet Union* towards the two powers of the region, *Iran and Iraq,* varied. *This could be seen in USSR policy towards Iran-Iraq War* of 1980 to 1988, beginning with a stance of 'strict neutrality' and moving towards massive military support for Iraq in the final phase of the war. The war was inconvenient for the USSR, which had aimed to ally itself with both Iran and Iraq.

In the first period of the war, the Soviets declared a policy of 'strict neutrality' towards the two countries, at the same time urging a negotiated peace. Iraq had been an ally for decades and the Soviets now tried to win over Iran as well, but their offers of friendship were rebuffed by the Iranian leadership, whose slogan was 'Neither East nor West'. In 1982, the war turned in Iran's favor and the Iranian leader, *Ayatollah Khomeini*, pledged not to stop the conflict until he had overthrown the Iraqi president *Saddam Hussein*. Such a prospect was unacceptable to the Soviet Union which now resumed arms sales to Iraq while still maintaining an official policy of neutrality. The Soviets also feared losing Saddam's friendship to the West. After further Iranian gains in 1986, the Soviet Union massively increased its military aid to Iraq. The Soviets were now afraid of the Iranians encouraging Islamic revolution in *Central Asia.* Soviet aid allowed the Iraqis to mount a counteroffensive which brought the war to an end in August, 1988.

The lack of materials from Soviet archives led to a situation in which many of the conclusions about the USSR policy in this region were necessarily based on speculation.

2.2. Regional Order of Persian Gulf Region in Cold War Era

Hostility between Arabs and Iranians has been an enduring feature of the Gulf for centuries, if not millennia. Ever since the *Islamic (Arab) conquest of Persia*, in 644, Iranian–Arab relations have sometimes been mixed. *Arabs* and *Iranians* share bitter cultural, historical, political, economical rivalries which fuel prominent *mutual contempt* between both sides.

It is in this way that contemporary nationalists, and those who see the region in terms of timeless cultural forces, often present current conflicts. But, such an approach is questionable. History is not univocal: for all the conflicts and conquests, and insults and divergences, there has been at least as much to unite and bring together the Arabs and Iranians as there has to divide them. Language, religion, pilgrimage, migration and trade have tied the regions of both peoples together for all of history. For much of the time, they have lived in peace, not war.

Moreover, the very formulation of the issue in terms of two opposed and conflicting 'nations' is misleading: the political boundaries have not corresponded to neat ethnic and linguistic divisions. Within, what is today the Arab domain, there have always been communities with Iranian characteristics; in Iraq, open for centuries to Iranians influence, not least in the period of the Persian-influenced Abbasid Empire, the very culture of the Arab speakers is suffused with Iranian influence.

Iranian–Arab relations have always been very mixed. Within the *region*, historical conflicts have always coloured neighbouring *Arab countries*' perceptions about *Iran*; sometimes peacefully coexisting, while at other times in bitter conflict.

In short, during the 20th century, the Persian Gulf seems to have gone through at least three distinctly different regional orders, including Pax Britannica, Pax Saudi-Iranica, and Pax Americana.

2.2.1. Pax Britannica

The era lasted from 1918, the conclusion of the First World War to 1971, which marked the withdrawal of British forces from the East of Suez. The destruction of the Ottoman Empire and the transfer of Iraq, Trans-Jordan, and Palestine to Britain as League of Nations mandates, inaugurated this period.

In 1925, Reza Khan established a new dynasty in Iran, and in 1926, the Saudi dynasty had emerged in the Arabian Peninsula. Albeit, this probably caused little concern in Tehran at the time, it was later to do so, to both Shah and Imam; for the Iraqis, on the other hand, this rebel regime, which had ousted the Hashemite from the Arabian Peninsula, was to remain a rival, and at best an uneasy ally, for decades to come.

For the following four decades, the dominant power in the Gulf was neither Arab nor Persian, but British, in formal control of Iraq and much of the Peninsula's coastline, from Kuwait to Aden. The strategic situation was, therefore, one in which Britain maintained its military and administrative dominance. Local states; Iran included, conducted their relations largely with Britain and other major powers. There was very little contact of substance between the regional states. Iran and Saudi Arabia formally recognized each other.

2.2.2. Pax Saudi-Iranica

The era of Pax Britannica ended with the post-war dismemberment of the British Empire and the rise of nationalist regimes in Iran, Iraq, Syria, Palestine/Israel, and Egypt. A new era emerged in 1971 when the British forces were withdrawn from the East of the Suez. Under the circumstances, Pax Americana could have effectively replaced Pax Britannica. However, the United States defeat in Vietnam had led to the emergence of the Nixon Doctrine calling for the establishment of proxy powers in various regions of the world to act on behalf of the United States interests. In the Persian Gulf, the monarchist regimes of Saudi Arabia and Iran presented themselves as candidates for this role. The two regimes were, thus, bolstered by extensive US political and military aid. The USA tried to promote a loose alliance, the 'twin pillar' policy, involving Iran and Saudi Arabia in a formal 'Gulf Pact', however, this never reached fruition and the Saudis, because of lacking a significant military capability, were suspicious of the Iranians.

For its part, Iran continued to press for recognition of the 'Persian' character of the Gulf and was to a considerable extent hostile to the constitutional plans made for the British withdrawal from the smaller Gulf States between 1968 and 1971. Thus, Iran at first opposed the independence of Bahrain, and only accepted its sovereignty after a UN 'consultation' of the islands' population. Less officially, but in unmistakabe terms, it also insisted that its yielding on Bahrain should be compensated for by the acquisition of three small islands, the Tunbs and Abu Musa, belonging to the Emirates. When no agreement was forthcoming, London acquiesced in the Iranian seizure of the islands in November 1971, on the eve of the British withdrawal. Iran also took advantage of crises in other regional states to assert its military influence by dispatche several thousand troops to assist the Sultan of Oman against the Marxist guerrillas in its southern province Dhofar between 1973 and 1975, and provided the Bhutto government in Pakistan with helicopter gunship to help suppress the guerrillas operating, with some Iraqi support, in Baluchistan in the early 1970.

The emergence of a Pax Saudi-Iranica had anticipated and unanticipated consequences. It led to Saudi-Iranian rapprochement on the Shiite-Sunni conflicts, the Organization of Islamic Conference, but also to a new unity in the Organization of Petroleum Exporting Countries (OPEC) that quadrupled the price of oil in 1973.

Some boundary disputes were resolved, including the Iranian abandonment of sovereignty claims over Bahrain, an understanding between Iran and Sharjah on Abu Musa Island and continental shelf agreements among the littoral states.

In 1975, Iran and Iraq also reached an agreement in Algiers regarding their boundary dispute over Shatt Al Arab, Arvand River, and the withdrawal of Iranian support for the Kurdish rebellion in Iraq. As part of the new security regime, Iran also assisted the government of Oman to successfully defeat a Marxist rebellion in the Dhofar Province. The Islamic Revolution of 1979 in Iran brought Pax Saudi-Iranica to an end.

2.2.3. Pax Americana

With the tacit support of Saudi Arabia and Kuwait, as well as Western powers, Iraq invaded Iran in 1980. A historical pattern was repeating itself. As in the case of modern revolutions in France, Russia, China and Cuba, the new revolutionary regime in Iran presented an ideological threat to its neighbouring conservative governments. Although, the rhetoric far outweighed the power of a newly established and disorganized government, it was considered opportune by Iraq and its Arab and Western allies to nip the revolution in the bud. However, as in other historical instances, the Iraqi invasion had a counter-intuitive effect. It unified a divided revolutionary regime against the enemy in a patriotic war which was imposed on the country. The consequence was an eight-year tug of war in which both sides suffered incalculable material and human costs. Initially, Iraq had the upper hand, but as the Iranians better organized themselves, the tide turned against Iraq in roughly 1987. During a tanker war that threatened oil exports from the Gulf, Kuwait also requested the United States to protect its ships.

These dual circumstances brought the United States with full force into the region. A third period, thus, began under the aegis of Pax Americana. The approaching end of the Cold War had made it possible for the US and Soviet Union to jointly pressure Iran and Iraq to accept a cease-fire in 1988. Under the threat of great power intervention, Ayatollah Khomeini had no choice but to accept the ceasefire declared by United Nations. The invasion of Kuwait by Iraq on August 2, 1990 ensured that intervention. The United States response was a rapid deployment of forces to oppose the Iraqi invasion. It is not entirely certain if this turn of events was premeditated.

The Cold War ended in the Gulf area earlier than in other parts of the world. Neither the Iranian revolution nor the Iran-Iraq war, much less the Iraqi invasion of Kuwait and subsequent US-led attack on Iraq were part of the Cold War. On the contrary, it could be claimed that, it was the absence of competition of Cold War's superpowers and standoff which made these events possible.

2.3. Major Regional Pacts in Cold War Era

2.3.1. CENTO

In the Cold War era, the original American plan for the Middle East was to form a defensive perimeter along the north of the region, including Iran and Iraq; two Persian Gulf's dominant powers.

The Central Treaty Organization (also referred to as CENTO, original name was Middle East Treaty Organization or METO, also known as the Baghdad Pact) was adopted in 1955 by *Iran*, *Iraq*, *Pakistan*, *Turkey*, and the *United Kingdom*. Its main purpose was to block possible expansion by the Soviet Union into the region.

US pressure and promises of military and economic largesse was the key in the negotiations leading to the agreement though the *United States* could not initially participate for purely technical reasons of budgeting procedures. Some (particularly nationalist radicals) saw the pact as an attempt by the British to retain influence in the Middle East as a substitute for the loss of their empire in *India*.

In 1958, the United States joined the military committee of the alliance. It is generally viewed as one of the least successful of the *Cold War* alliances. The organization's headquarters were initially located in *Baghdad* (*Iraq*) 1955–1958 and *Ankara* (*Turkey*) 1958–1979.

Modeled after the *North Atlantic Treaty Organization* (NATO), CENTO committed the nations to mutual cooperation and protection, as well as non-intervention in each other's affairs. Its goal was to *contain* the *Soviet Union* by having a line of strong states along the USSR's southwestern frontier. Unlike NATO, CENTO did not have a unified military command structure, nor were many US or UK military bases established in member countries, although the US had communications and electronic intelligence facilities in Iran, and operated *U-2* intelligence flights over the USSR from bases in Pakistan.

The United Kingdom had access to facilities in Pakistan and Iraq at various times while the treaty was in effect. In addition, Turkey and the US agreed to permit American access to Turkish bases, but this was done under the auspices of NATO.

On July 14, 1958, the Iraqi monarchy was overthrown in a military coup. The new government was led by General *Abdul Karim Qasim* who withdrew from the Baghdad Pact, opened diplomatic relations with Soviet Union and adopted a non-aligned stance. In 1958, when Iraq withdrew from the Baghdad Pact, the pact was known as CENTO pact. The organization dropped the Baghdad Pact moniker in favor of CENTO at that time. The *Middle East* and *South Asia* became extremely volatile areas during the 1960s with the ongoing *Arab-Israeli conflict* and the *Indo-Pakistani wars*. CENTO was unwilling to get deeply involved in either dispute.

In 1965 and 1971, Pakistan tried unsuccessfully to get assistance in its wars with *India* through CENTO, but this was rejected under the idea that CENTO was aimed at containing the USSR, not India.

CENTO did little to prevent the expansion of Soviet influence to non-member states in the area. Whatever containment value the pact might have had was lost when the Soviets 'leapfrogged' the member states, establishing close military and political relationships with governments in *Egypt*, *Syria*, *Iraq*, the *People's Democratic Republic of Yemen*, *Somalia*, and *Libya*. Indeed, by 1970, the USSR had deployed over 20,000 troops to Egypt and had established naval bases in Syria, Somalia and PDR Yemen.

The *Islamic revolution* of Iran in 1979, spelled the end of the organization. It was dissolved in 1979. However, in reality; it had been as good as finished after 1974, when Turkey invaded *Cyprus*, leading the United Kingdom to withdraw forces that had been earmarked to the alliance. With the fall of the Iranian monarchy, whatever remaining rationale for the organization was lost.

Future USA and British, defense agreements with regional countries, such as Pakistan, Egypt, and the Gulf States, were conducted bilaterally.

2.3.2. Gulf Cooperation Council (GCC)

The Gulf Cooperation Council (GCC) was established in an agreement concluded on May 25, 1981 in Riyadh (Saudi Arabia) between Bahrain, Kuwait, Oman, Qatar, Saudi Arabia and UAE. Saudi Arabia had taken the lead in forming the GCC. These countries declared that the GCC is established in view of the special relations between them, their similar political systems based on Islamic beliefs, joint destiny and common objectives.

The GCC which consists of six countries vary in size and attitudes. Saudi Arabia has successfully served as the GCC leader shaping its policies in the Gulf. As relatively rich but less populated countries, the GCC governments also have been looking for protection from the United States against any possible threats.

However, feelings about the presence of the US forces are mixed. Too close an identification with the US opens the GCC regimes to accusations of complicity with un-Islamic and imperialist powers. Although the recent rapprochement with Iran is not universal among the GCC members, Saudi Arabia has led the way. The United Arab Emirates continues to have a serious conflict with Iran on the issue of sovereignty over the three Gulf islands (Abu Musa, Greater and Smaller Tunbs). Bahrain has accused the Iranian regime of subversive activities within its borders. Oman and Qatar seem to enjoy the best relations with Iran. Expanding commercial relations between Iran and the southern Gulf States, however, are paving the way for greater common and enduring interests. Saudi Arabia and the UAE are currently at odds over the GCC opening to Iran. Symbolic issues such as the name of 'the Gulf' and practical issues such as the control of the three Gulf islands continue to divide the two sides of the Gulf.

The GCC is a regional common market with a defence planning council as well. The geographic proximity of these countries and their general adoption of free trade economic policies are factors that encouraged them to establish the GCC.

The Gulf Cooperation Council (GCC) was formed to confront security challenges of the member states collectively. The immediate objective was to protect them from the threat posed by the Iran-Iraq War and Iranian-inspired activist Islamism. In a series of meetings, chiefs of staff and defence ministers of the Gulf States developed plans for mutual defence and launched efforts to form a joint command and a joint defence network. Ground and air units of the six member states carried out several multilateral exercises between 1983 and 1987 under the code name of Peninsula Shield.

Based on their conviction about the connected nature of their security and that an aggression against any one of them is deemed an aggression against all of them, cooperation in the military field has received the attention of the GCC states. Such conviction stems from the facts of geopolitics and faith in one destiny. Moreover, the security challenges in an unstable regional environment, like the Gulf area, impose on the GCC States coordination of their policies and mobilization of their capabilities.

Military assistance, funded mainly by Saudi Arabia and Kuwait, was extended to Bahrain for up-to-date fighter aircraft and a modern air base, and to Oman to improve its defensive capability at the Strait of Hormuz.

The GCC planned to integrate naval and ground radar systems and to create a combined air control and warning system based on Saudi AWACS aircraft. Problems of compatibility with different communication and electronic systems, however, delayed the introduction of these programs. In 1984, the GCC defence ministers agreed on the creation of a two-brigade (10,000-man) Peninsula Shield Force. This joint intervention force was based in Saudi Arabia near King Khalid Military City at Hafar Al Batin under the command of a Saudi officer. In addition to a headquarters staff, the force consisted of one infantry brigade of about 5,000 men with elements from all GCC states in 1992.

Its mission, however, had not been publicly defined. It was not clear, for example, whether the joint force would have authority to intervene in a domestic emergency. The force could be enlarged at a time of threat; it was apparently reinforced prior to the Persian Gulf War in 1991 but did not take part in the war as a distinct unit.

The GCC States seek to build up their defence forces according to a common conception. In this context, they have unified operational procedures, training, and military curricula. They also endeavour to accomplish compatibility of their military systems.

Moreover, the armed forces of the GCC States carry out joint military exercises with the Peninsula Shield Force, as well as joint air and sea manoeuvres. Among the important achievements in the military field is the resolution taken during Kuwait summit in 1997, which entailed to link the GCC Member States with a military communication network for early warning.

In March 1991, after the conclusion of the Persian Gulf War, the six members of the GCC, together with Egypt and Syria, declared their intention to establish a deterrent force to protect Kuwait, with Egypt and Syria to provide the bulk of the troops and the GCC states to provide the financing. The plan subsequently encountered a series of setbacks. At year's end, there appeared little chance that the Arab deterrent force would be installed.

In the meantime, Kuwait had succeeded in obtaining security commitments from the United States and Britain and arranged for the propositioning of United States military equipment.

2.4. Regional States' Relations in Cold War Era

2.4.1. Iran-Saudi Arabia

These two opposing countries' struggle for dominance in the region goes back decades and draws on a deep well of sectarian hatred. Even before 1979, the year of Iranian revolution, Riyadh and Tehran competed for geopolitical influence in the Persian Gulf. With the ascent of Ayatollah Khomeini's clerical regime, however, the competition became far nastier. Both countries portrayed themselves as defenders of the faith and based their political legitimacy on their religious bona fides. The difference was more than just Sunni vs. Shiite, or Arab vs. Persian. Iran purported to represent revolutionary Islam. The result was a "Cold War within Islam."[8]

Of late, after years in the shadows, Saudi Arabia had suddenly become a very important country. It was thought to have the largest oil reserves by far in the world, as much as that of the United States, Iran and Libya taken together.

Until very recently, Saudi Arabia had been rather isolated, a conservative regime increasingly out of tune with the radical forces in the Middle East. Its only potential ally was Iran, but, in view of the traditional distrust between Arabs and Persians, not to mention certain conflicting interests in the Persian Gulf, relations between Riyadh and Tehran were not in fact very friendly; the Saudis would turn to Tehran only in a grave emergency.

Historically, relations with non-Arab Iran had been normal although the Saudis tended to distrust Iranian intentions and to resent the perceived arrogance of the Shah of Iran. Nevertheless, the two countries had cooperated on regional security issues despite their differences over specific policies such as oil production quotas.

The Islamic Revolution of Iran in 1979, disrupted their shared interest in regional political stability. From a Saudi perspective, the rhetoric of some Iranian revolutionary leaders, who called for the overthrow of all monarchies as being un-Islamic, presented a serious subversive threat to the regimes in the area. Political disturbances in the kingdom during 1979 and 1980, including the violent occupation of the Grand Mosque in Mecca by Sunni religious extremists and riots among Saudi Shiites in the Eastern Province, reinforced the perception that Iran was exploiting, even inciting, discontent as part of a concerted policy to export its revolution.

The Saudi government, consequently, was not displeased when Iraq invaded Iran in September, 1980. Nevertheless, Saudi Arabia remained officially neutral throughout the Iran-Iraq War, even though in practice its policies made it an effective Iraqi ally.

Following the outbreak of the *Iran–Iraq War*, Iranian pilgrims felt they had to hold a political demonstration against Saudi support for *Iraq* during the *Iran–Iraq War*; during the *Hajj* in *Mecca* in which they succeeded in 1987. Efforts by Saudi security forces to suppress an unauthorized demonstration in front of Mecca's Grand Mosque led to the deaths of more than 400 pilgrims, at least two-thirds of whom were Iranians. Immediately following the riot, Ayatollah Khomeini called for Muslims to avenge the pilgrims' deaths by overthrowing the Saudi royal family. In early 1988, Riyadh cut its diplomatic relations with Tehran.

The Persian Gulf War, however, significantly altered Saudi perceptions of Iran. The unexpected emergence of Iraq as a mortal enemy refocused Saudi security concerns and paved the way for a less hostile attitude toward Iran.

Reopening of embassies in Riyadh and Tehran in 1991, accompanied the resolution of the Hajj and other outstanding issues.

2.4.2. Iran-Iraq

Iran and Iraq both are located in the north of the Persian Gulf. Much more powerful than the comparatively insignificant Sheikhdoms of the southern Gulf, the northern duo constantly was brawling.

Fortunately for the southerners, Iran and Iraq most often fought with each other in the modern period. These fights started in the 1950s, when Iraq became a republic and acquired arms from Russia. Iran, which was then ruled by the Shah, found this objectionable and throughout the 1960s and 1970s, Tehran supported Kurdish rebels fighting in the north of Iraq, with the intent of destabilizing the regime in Baghdad. Then, in the 1980s, followed the Iran-Iraq War.

Iraq and Iran were the Persian Gulf's main anti-status quo powers. In 1980, Iraq initiated a war against Iran which lasted eight years. Iraq's motives were both from fear of Iranian subversion and from the sense of an opportunity to defeat Iran and easily dominate the Gulf. Baghdad had, of course, underestimated Iran's ability. Instead, the war went on for eight years and resulted in a million casualties, as well as high costs for both combatants. For the Gulf Arab monarchies, Iraq was essentially fighting as their defender against the radical Islamic threat emanating from Iran. They subsidized its war effort with billions of dollars of aid, albeit often concealed as loans, and lobbied for other countries, especially the United States, to back Iraq.

Iraqi-Iranian relations have remained cool due to both participants having fought the worst war in modern history, within the region. Outstanding issues from that war, including prisoner of war exchanges and support of armed opposition parties operating in each other's territory, remained to be solved until 1990. On August 17, 1990, days after Saddam invaded *Kuwait*, Saddam told Iran he would withdraw from occupied Iranian territory and formally settled the 1980–88 war. The two countries then restored diplomatic relations in October 1990.

2.4.3. Iran-GCC States (except Saudi Arabia)

2.4.3.1. Iran-Bahrain

In 1970, Iran simultaneously laid claim to both *Bahrain* and three other *Persian Gulf* islands (Lesser and Greater Tunb Islands and Abu Musa Island). However, in an agreement with the *United Kingdom,* it agreed to 'not pursue' its irredentist claims on Bahrain if its other claims were realized. The British withdrew from Bahrain in August 1971, making Bahrain an independent Emirate; meanwhile, the strategic Persian Gulf Islands were returned to Iran in exchange. After 1979 *Islamic revolution* in Iran, Bahraini *Shiite* fundamentalists, orchestrated a *failed coup attempt* under the auspices of a front organization, the *Islamic Front for the Liberation of Bahrain* in 1981. The Bahraini government unofficially regarded the coup as Iran attempting to overthrow their *Sunni* government. Iran denied all knowledge saying the fundamentalists were inspired by the Iranian revolution but had received no support from Iran.

Bahraini suspicions of the Iranian role in local unrest in the mid-1990s remained. However, with the decline of Iraq as a regional powerbroker, Bahrain has begun taking steps to improve relations with Iran and increase regional harmony. These efforts have included encouraging Bahrain-Iran trade. Both the countries are beginning to enjoy closer relations again and have engaged in many joint economic ventures, although, Iran has been severely critical of Bahrain hosting the *US* navy Fifth Fleet within the *Persian Gulf.*

2.4.3.2. Iran-Kuwait

After the *Shiite* Islamic Revolution in Iran in 1979, the then Kuwaiti Prime Minister, *Sabah Al-Ahmad Al-Jaber Al-Sabah* (now the Amir of Kuwait), visited Iran and congratulated the Islamic Revolution, yet the *Sunni* led government of *Kuwait* became fearful of its large *Shia* population and of possible Iranian hegemony in the

Persian Gulf and began to regard Iran with increasing suspicion. When the *Iran–Iraq War* broke out with Saddam Hussein's invasion of Iran, Kuwait deeply supported the Iraqi move. It was an action that was bitterly resented by Iran. Throughout the war, Kuwait provided Iraq with billions of dollars in military and social aid as well as logistical support by allowing Iraqi use of its ports. Iran, consequently, led a failed attempt to attack a Kuwaiti refinery complex in 1981 (intercepted and blocked by Iraqi air force), which inspired subsequent acts of sabotage in 1983 and 1986. In 1985, a member of the underground pro-Iranian Iraqi radical group, *Al-Dawah*, attempted to assassinate the Kuwaiti ruler, *Sheikh Jaber Al-Ahmad Al Sabah*. In September 1986, while the *Iran–Iraq War* was still raging on, Iran began to concentrate its attacks on Persian Gulf shipping, largely on Kuwaiti tankers in an effort to dissuade Arab support for *Iraq*. This led Kuwait to invite both the *Soviet Union* (with which it had established diplomatic relations in 1963) and the *United States* to provide protection for its tankers in early 1987. Political tensions between Tehran and Kuwait increased significantly after the United States agreed to reflag Kuwaiti oil tankers.

Iran's neutral stand during the 1991 Gulf War that ended Iraq's brief occupation of Kuwait brought the countries closer.

2.4.3.3. Iran-Oman

Since 1970, Oman has pursued a moderate foreign policy and expanded its diplomatic relations dramatically. During the Cold War period, Oman avoided relations with communist countries because of the communist support for the insurgency in Dhofar. Iran and *Oman* have always had close ties covering economic, cultural, political, and military spheres.

Between 1970 and 1975, the ruler of Oman; *Sultan Qabus*, acknowledged Iran's regional strength and obtained Iranian military assistance in fighting the *Saudi* backed *Dhofar Rebellion*. During the same period, an Omani-Iranian border agreement was also signed regarding the *Strait of Hormuz*. During the *Iran–Iraq War*, Oman remained neutral, preferring to take no sides. This allowed it to be in the position to attempt to bring Iran and Iraq into a negotiated settlement after the war, in 1994. Since then, peaceful ties have continued and expanded.

2.4.3.4. Iran-Qatar

Relations between Iran and *Qatar* have partially been based on proximity and partly on mutual interests. The relationship between Iran and Qatar had become cold during Iran-Iraq conflict as Qatar was backing Iraq. However, the Iran-Qatar relations have been normalized and cordial and both are crucial members of the OPEC.

2.4.3.5. Iran-United Arab Emirates

Since its release from the *United Kingdom* as a British protectorate on December 1, 1971, Iran has had frayed, but cordial, relations with the *United Arab Emirates*. Throughout the 1980s, the UAE had striven with difficulty to maintain neutrality in the Iran-Iraq War. That conflict was also a source of internal UAE tension because Abu Dhabi tended to support Iraq while Dubai was more sympathetic to Iran. After the war ended in 1988, Iran appeared to single out the UAE for special and friendly attention.

2.4.4. Iraq-Saudi Arabia

Saudi relations with Iraq have been the most problematic, vacillating from tension to *de facto alliance* to war. Throughout the 1960s and into the early 1970s, Riyadh suspected Baghdad of supporting political movements hostile to Saudi interests, not only in the *Arabian Peninsula* but also in other *Middle Eastern* countries, due to which Saudi-Iraqi ties were strained. The kingdom tried to contain the spread of Iraqi radicalization by strengthening its relations with states such as *Iran*, *Kuwait*, *Syria* and the *United States*, all of which shared its distrust of *Baghdad*. Beginning about 1975, however, Iraq began to moderate its foreign policies, a change that significantly lessened tensions between *Riyadh* and Baghdad. Saudi Arabia's diplomatic relations with Iraq were relatively cordial by the time the *Islamic Revolution* erupted in Iran in 1979. The Saudis and Iraqis both felt threatened by the Iranian advocacy of exporting Shiite Islamic revolution, and this shared fear fostered an unprecedented degree of cooperation between both countries.

Although Riyadh declared its neutrality at the outset of the *Iran–Iraq War* in 1980, it helped Baghdad in non-military ways.

On the contrary, in August 1990, only two years after Baghdad and *Tehran* had agreed to cease hostilities, Iraqi forces unexpectedly invaded and occupied *Kuwait*. Saudi Arabia took action against Iraq, claiming Iraq's actions posed a serious threat to its security and requested the *United States* to bring troops into the kingdom to help containing Iraq.

2.4.5. Iraq-GCC States (except Saudi Arabia)

The competition for leadership in Arab world reached its peak during the Iraqi invasions of Iran and Kuwait. During the Iran-Iraq war, Iraq enjoyed the support of Arab countries except Libya and Syria. In the 1990 Gulf War, however, it was isolated except for Jordanian and Palestinian support. Having been subjected to nearly a decade of economic sanctions, the Iraqi regime suffered from intense insecurity. It viewed itself as the victim of Western imperialism, conservative Arab perfidy, and Iranian hostility. Dominated by Sunni Arab leadership, the Baath regime's suspicion of its own Shia and Kurdish population added to this sense of insecurity.

The cessation of fighting between Iran and Iraq led to the realization of the GCC's deepest fears that a militarily strong Iraq would try to intimidate its neighbours. By the end of 1988, Iraq had begun to pressure Kuwait for the rights to use Kuwaiti islands that controlled access to Iraqi ports. Tension between Iraq and Kuwait escalated, culminating in August 1990 with Iraq's invasion, occupation, and annexation of the small country. The aggression revealed to a stunned GCC that the alliance had insufficient power to deter or repel an attack on one of its members. All other GCC members provided military contingents for the coalition that was formed to confront Iraq.

2.4.6. Saudi Arabia –Rest of the GCC States

In contrast to its relations with Iran or Iraq, Saudi Arabia's ties with the small Arab oil-producing states along its eastern flank have been historically close. The outbreak of the Iran-Iraq War in September 1980 had provided the impetus Riyadh needed to convince its neighbours to join in a defensive pact. Despite their distrust of the revolutionary regime in Tehran, Iraq's early successes alarmed the Saudis because they feared a defeat of Iran would embolden Baghdad to adopt an aggressive posture against other countries, especially in the Arabian Peninsula.

Saudi Arabia has played a leading role in Gulf Cooperation Council. Its relation with other GCC states has been cordial, despite some border disputes which mostly have been solved.

3. Persian Gulf Region in Post-Cold War Era

The end of the cold war and the disappearance of the threats the Soviet Union posed to the Persian Gulf have presented the United States with an opportunity to pursue a fundamentally different type of strategy in that region; a policy of friendly but more detached and contingent relations with the regional states, in distinction to the existing US policy of close and enduring political, military, and personal ties with friendly regimes. The former can be termed 'insulating strategies' because they are intended to distance the United States from the risks attendant to the endemic political instability of the region. The latter can be termed 'controlling strategies' because they focus on managing and subduing those risks.

There have been multiple variations on two central themes in the approach to security by both local Gulf States and the United States as an external security guarantor for the region. One such theme is simply peace through 'victory', whether defined as local hegemony, global hegemony, and unconditional surrender of an opponent during war, or transformation of societies and political regimes in favour of one version of state interests and values. The other theme is peace through a rough balance of power.

The Clinton administration, almost the first USA administration after the end of Cold War, identified both Iraq and Iran as significant threats to America's interests in the region. It developed a policy, known as 'dual containment', to deal with those threats by isolating both countries regionally, cutting them off from the world economic and trading system, and encouraging a regime change in Iraq. It strongly supported the continuation of UN sanctions against Iraq, made efforts to persuade Europe, Russia and Japan to deny Iran access to international capital and arms markets, and continued American military commitments to Saudi Arabia and the smaller monarchies that form the Gulf Cooperation Council (GCC). According to Professor Gregory Gause, a prominent Professor of Political Science at the University of Vermont, "if there is one part of the world where the Clinton administration cannot be accused of lacking a clear foreign policy, it is the Persian Gulf."[9]

The USA strategies in the Persian Gulf region, in post-cold war era, have been examined in seventh chapter; Role of USA in the Region, in details.

3.1. Regional Order of Persian Gulf Region in Post-Cold War Era

Regional order of the Persian Gulf, during 1990s had a three axis structure, as it was formed by three power axis; Iran, Iraq and Saudi Arabia. This power relation between these three powers was altered by the UN sanctions against Iraq. But based on the table shown from the power point of view, Iran, Iraq and Saudi Arabia were the superpowers in the region respectively, during 1990s. After regime change in Iraq, since 2003, this triangle has lost one of its facets Iraq.

Table 5.1.: Ranking of the Regional Powers in 1990s

Countries	*Population*	*Wealth*	*Military Power*
Iran	1	2	1
Iraq	2	3	2
Saudi Arabia	3	1	3

Source: "Extracted from a reference book" [10]

"In 1990s, Saudi Arabia and other GCC countries started to strengthen their military power and armament. It seems there were two reasons to do so. First, they had no other choice to protect and defend themselves against any possible threats. Second reason could be to satisfy USA. As they requested USA to establish the security of the Persian Gulf, they wanted to accomplish their own share."[11]

3.2. Regional States' Relation in Post-Cold War Era

3.2.1. Iran-Saudi Arabia

Saudi Arabia's post-war (Iran-Iraq War) concerns about Iraq led to a rapprochement with Iran during 1991. A rapprochement between Saudi Arabia and Iran is paving the way for a potential balance of power between the triumvirate of Iran, Iraq, and the Gulf Cooperation Council (GCC) consisting of Saudi Arabia, Kuwait, Qatar, Bahrain, United Arab Emirate, and Oman. This needs to be seen whether these propitious circumstances can lead to the establishment of an indigenous security regime guaranteed by the great powers and how and when this may be achieved.

Saudi-Iranian ties began to improve only after the Iraqi invasion of Kuwait and its subsequent 1991 Persian Gulf War. Iran's taking sides with the Kuwaitis and the anti-Iraqi coalition of the Arab States of the Persian Gulf helped to put Iran's ties with its southern Arab neighbours on a friendly path. In particular, Saudi-Iranian relations, especially their diplomatic ones, began to improve, as reflected by exchanges of high-ranking delegates between the two countries in the 1990s, even though various remaining grievances on both sides prevented their rapid expansion.

The 1997 election of Mohammad Khatami as Iranian president acted as a catalyst in Iranian-Saudi relations. His pursuit of a foreign policy aimed at tension reduction and improving ties with foreign countries paved the way for a rapid expansion of ties between Iran and its southern Arab neighbours. In particular, that policy put Iranian-Saudi relations on a stable and friendly path. Their bilateral relations encompassing various fields, such as political, economic, educational and security have since grown on a steady basis. Their well-coordinated policies within the Organization of Petroleum Exporting Countries over issues such as oil pricing and production quotas for the member states have clearly reflected the depth of their closeness.

A major indicator of warming relations between the two former foes has been their cooperation on security affairs, including regional security. As the largest and the richest Persian Gulf countries with certain influence, Iran and Saudi Arabia have the capabilities to affect the pace of events in their region. Thus, their cooperation is a necessity for ensuring security in the region, which contains over 60 percent of the world's proven oil reserves in addition to a phenomenal amount of gas deposits.

"In *2001*, *Iran* and Saudi Arabia have signed an agreement on cooperation in combating crime, terrorism, money laundering, surveillance of borders and territorial waters"[12], Iran's IRNA (Islamic Republic News Agency) reported. After two years of negotiations, the agreement was signed by former Iranian Interior Minister, Abdolvahed Mousavi Lari, and visiting Saudi Interior Minister, Nayef Ibn Abdul-Aziz, the official news agency said. "This agreement promises peace and friendship and Iran has always reached out hand of friendship to its neighbours," Lari said after the signing of the pact. He added that Iran and Saudi security is 'akin' and the agreement would "initiate a new chapter in the Tehran-Riyadh relations." Nayef said that the agreement was within the framework of confidence-building, adding that "the region should enjoy full security and the agreement should benefit the whole region."[13]

Iran's arrest and extradition to Saudi Arabia of 16 suspected members of al-Qaeda, in 2002, illustrates that, in addition to their expanding political and economic relations, security ties between Iran and Saudi Arabia are also growing.

In 2008, the Saudi King Abdullah invited former *Iranian President, Ali Akbar Hashemi Rafsanjani* to visit Saudi Arabia for the purpose of attending an Islamic conference. Rafsanjani responded by saying that "the opportunity was a way that Iran and Saudi Arabia can resolve differences in the Muslim world."[14]

Saudi-Iranian cooperation is not a new development and thus, its continuation is perfectly understandable within the context of relations between the two largest nations on the northern and southern shores of the Persian Gulf.

3.2.2. Iran-Iraq

In 1991 war, Iran took side with the Kuwaitis and anti-Iraq coalition of the Arab States of Persian Gulf, even in February 4, 1991, Iran offered to mediate peace talks.

Since 2000, Iran-Iraq relations visibly improved. After the US-led war on Iraq started in 2003, *Tehran* strongly opposed the invasion, calling for a key role of the UN in Iraq's reconstruction. Iran then offered assistance to Iraq's post-war reconstruction and bilateral relations began to improve. *Tehran* supported the Interim Governing Council in *Iraq*, but it strongly advocates a prompt and full transfer of state authority to the Iraqi people.

In May 2005, a transitional government led by Ibrahim Al-Jaafari of the pro-Iran Islamist Dawa party was established in Iraq. In mid May 2005, former Iranian Foreign Minister, eq:*Kamal Kharazi*, visited Iraq and Jaafari paid a visit to Iran in July 2005.

Iraqi president, *Jalal Talabani*, visited Iran In November 2005, becoming the first Iraqi head of state to visit Iran in almost four decades.

Iran-Iraq relations have been strengthening up since 2006 by the exchange of high level visits; Iraqi Prime Minister *Nouri Al-Maliki* has made frequent visits, along with Jalal Talabani visiting numerous times to help boost bilateral cooperation in all fields.

Relations appear to have further improved since March 2008, when "Iranian president, *Mahmoud Ahmadinejad*, made a two-day visit to Iraq."[15] He became the first Iranian president to visit Iraq since Iran's 1979 *Islamic revolution*.

3.2.3. Iran-GCC States (except Saudi Arabia)

3.2.3.1. Iran-Bahrain

Bahrain is a former Persian territory, and an Iranian desire to reclaim it arose again recently, shocking the island state's leadership. Bahrain's crown prince became the first Arab leader to publicly accuse Tehran of trying to develop nuclear weapons. His kingdom is also the base for the US Navy's Fifth Fleet, which could play an important role if hostilities erupt between Iran and the United States.

According to the *United Press International*, Bahrain said on May 15, 1999 that Iran continues to be a 'potential threat' to Arab security and that its refusal to give up three disputed islands to the United Arab Emirates would obstruct its reconciliation with the Arab States of the Persian Gulf.

On May 15, 1999, the London-based 'Al-Hayat' daily quoted "Bahrain's Defence Minister, Sheikh Khalifa Bin Ahmad Al-Khalifa, as saying that although his country has diplomatic ties with Iran, Bahrain is waiting for positive signs, especially since Iran is still sheltering dissidents who are hostile to Bahrain."[16]

In August 2007, tension developed between Iran and the Gulf States, particularly Bahrain, in the wake of an article written by the editor of the Iranian daily 'Kayhan', Hussein Shariatmadari, who is an associate of Iranian Supreme Leader Ali Khamenei. "It depicted the Gulf regimes as not legitimate and claimed that Bahrain is an inseparable part of Iran and should be returned to it, provoked angry reactions in the Gulf."[17]

Iran's official response to Shariatmadari's piece was that it did not express Iran's official position but only a personal view. Nevertheless, Iran attempted to alleviate the resulting tension with the Gulf States through diplomatic channels. In a visit to Bahrain during which he met with Bahraini Foreign Minister, Sheikh Khaled Bin Ahmad Al Khalifa, Iranian Foreign Minister, Manouchehr Mottaki, refused to apologize for the piece, saying that the Iranian government did not accept Shariatmadari's statements, and that "Iran and Bahrain respect each other's national sovereignty and territorial integrity."[18] The Bahraini Foreign Minister responded that Bahrain had received official guarantees from Iran alleviating concerns aroused by Shariatmadari's statements, and that there was no need for any apology from Iran.

According to Arab News Agency, on February 3, 2009, Gulf neighbours Bahrain and Iran said that they will maintain good relations, indicating that the diplomatic row that erupted between them, was over. Iranian President, Mahmud Ahmadinejad, who met with the visiting Bahrain's Foreign Minister, Sheikh Khaled Bin Ahmad Al Khalifa, in Tehran, called for more closeness and cooperation between the two nations, Iranian state television's website reported. "This friendship and closeness will not leave any opportunity for the mischief of evil people,"[19] the president said. In a short statement, the two men indicated that the diplomatic row was over.

Iran's former Majlis (parliament) Speaker, Ali Akbar Nateq-Nouri, who is now the advisor of Iranian Supreme Leader Ayatollah Ali Khamenei, addressing Bahrain's history on the 30th anniversary of the Iranian revolution on February 10, 2009, said that "Bahrain was the 14th province of Iran, until 1970."[20] A number of other Iranian officials have also reportedly claimed that Bahrain was an integral part of the Islamic republic and questioned its Arabic identity.

Iranian officials' sovereignty claim has drawn strong criticism from Bahrain and other Arab countries. Bahrain paused negotiations with Iran regarding gas imports in response, and the *Gulf Cooperation Council* (GCC) condemned the remarks.

The *Iranian foreign minister*, Manouchehr Mottaki, immediately commented on the controversy and stated that Mr. Nateq Nouri's remark about the history of Bahrain was misinterpreted by the media and that Iran respects Bahrain's sovereignty, saying that "Iran-Bahrain relations have always been upon mutual respect to their sovereignty, which would never be affected by insignificant issues."[21]

"Nategh Nouri himself told *Al-jazeerah* TV channel that his remarks about the history of the region was misunderstood and his comment is not relevant to today's Iran-Bahrain relationship"[22], Islamic Republic News Agency; *IRNA*, reported.

3.2.3.2. IRAN-KUWAIT

Kuwait's relations with Iran deteriorated during the 1980-88 Iran-Iraq war because of Kuwait's support for Baghdad.

In 1990, following the *Persian Gulf War,* Iraqi-Kuwaiti relations suffered bitterly and consequently, Kuwaiti-Iranian relations began to improve. Bilateral relations were gradually strengthened, with exchanges of Iranian and Kuwaiti political and economic delegations leading to the signing of several economic and trade agreements.

Since the end of the Iran-Iraq War more than two decades ago, however, Kuwait and Iran have been working to better their political relationship. In 2005, Iran's Foreign Minister, Manoucher Mottaki, met with Kuwait's Prime Minister, Sheikh Sabah Al Ahmad Al Sabah, conveying Iran's message of peace, friendship and willingness to expand friendly ties with all regional countries, particularly with Kuwait. The Kuwaiti Prime Minister responded that "blossoming Iran-Kuwait ties would definitely have positive effects on regional peace and stability, particularly between Iran and the other Persian Gulf Cooperation Council (PGCC) member-states."[23] Since this friendly encounter, greater bilateral economic cooperation has helped improve the political atmosphere between the two countries, even as Kuwait has complied with the UN Security Council against Iran's nuclear enrichment program.

In February 2006, Iranian President, *Mahmud Ahmadinejad*, visited Kuwait opening a new chapter in relations between the two countries. The well reported visit was the first to Kuwait by a high-ranking Iranian official in 27 years.

According to Iran News Agency, IRNA, in June, 2009, "Emir Sheikh Sabah al-Ahmad al-Jaber al-Sabah congratulated Iranian President Mahmud Ahmadinejad on his re-election. He described Iran as a friend of Kuwait and expressed hope that Kuwait and Iran would continue to expand their relationship in all fields. The Kuwaiti crown prince and prime minister, Nasir al-Muhammad al-Ahmad al-Sabah, also extended his congratulations to Ahmadinejad".[24]

3.2.3.3. Iran-Oman

Oman is an ally of the United States, but also maintains friendly relations with the Islamic Republic of Iran.

In 2006, the two countries agreed to cooperate in their national healthcare programs. According to Manouchehr Takin of the Centre for Global Energy Studies in London, "of all the Persian Gulf Cooperation Council (PGCC) countries, Oman had historically been closest to the region's neighbor to the north."[25]

"In March 2008, US Vice President Richard Cheney visited Oman to discuss cooperation over Iran's nuclear program."[26]

"In August 2008, Iran and Oman discussed developing joint military programs."[27] These were addressed in a meeting of the Iran-Oman joint military committee and would involve joint training and military exercises.

In December 2008, former Omani Foreign Minister, Yousuf Bin Alawi, said that Iran's nuclear enrichment is "no cause for concern."[28]

In January 2009, Omani Foreign Minister Yahya bin Abdullah Al Feneh al-Arimi described Iran as a "great and powerful neighbor and called for the two to expand bilateral ties in regional issues."[29]

In May 2009, Iran and Oman began drafting a security agreement, with Omani Crown Prince, Malik Bin Suleiman Al Moammari, saying that "the Omani government and nation are willing to further expand ties with the Islamic Republic of Iran in all fields."[30]

According to the Iranian Press TV, "In June, 2009, Sultan Qaboos Bin Said Bin Taimur, sent a letter of congratulations to newly re-elected President Mahmud Ahmadinejad."[31] Taimur congratulated Ahmadinejad for his victory despite heated public demonstrations against the election results that still disrupted Tehran.

3.2.3.4. Iran-Qatar

Throughout the *Iran–Iraq War* (1980-1988), Qatar supported Saddam Hussein's *Iraq* financially by providing large loans and cash gifts.

In 1991, following the end of the *Persian Gulf War*, *Sheikh Hamad ibn Khalifa* welcomed Iranian participation in Persian Gulf security arrangements; however, due to resistance from other *Arab States* of the Persian Gulf, these never came into fruition. Additionally, plans were being formulated in 1992 to pipe water from the Karun River in Iran to Qatar, but after local resistance in Iran, this was laid to rest.

The Emir of Qatar since 1995, *Sheikh Hamad bin Khalifa Al-Thani*, has lately been going on an expansive boost to promote Qatar as a foreign player. Iran's claim in May 1989 that one-third of Qatar's North Field gas reservoir lay under Iranian waters, apparently, was resolved by an agreement to exploit the field jointly.

The Iranian community in Qatar, although large, is well integrated and has not posed a threat to the regime. Iran and Qatar have made pledges over the past few years to further develop their economic relationship, most specifically their oil and gas cooperation, both within and outside of OPEC. Today relations between the two countries are cordial.

"The Iranian President, Mahmud Ahmadinejad, paid a visit to Doha on the 3rd and 4th of December 2007 as a guest to the GCC summit."[32]

3.2.3.5. Iran-United Arab Emirates

Following the Islamic Revolution in Iran, the UAE has been pushing for the return of the three disputed islands; Abu Musa and Greater and Lesser Tunbs. By 1992, the UAE was the Arab country with which Iran had the closest commercial relations. Thus, the crisis that erupted in April 1992 over disputed islands in the Persian Gulf seemed unexpected.

The dispute was rekindled in 1992 when Iranian officials in Abu Musa refused to permit UAE contract workers to disembark, in apparent contravention of a shared sovereignty agreement. In the midst of the 1992 crisis over Abu Musa, Ras al Khaymah resurrected its grievance over Greater Tunb and Lesser Tunb, thus enflaming an already delicate situation. At the end of the year, Iran and Sharjah quietly agreed to a restoration of the status quo ante the crisis, but the incidents left the UAE feeling wary of Iranian intentions. Despite of the dispute, the countries maintain very close economic ties and the UAE has a significant Iranian expatriate community. Iranian investors have a wide presence in the UAE accounting for 10 percent of the Arab country's population.

"Relations between the UAE and Iran are strong and based on the cultural relations between the people of the two countries"[33], Khalifa Shahin Al Merri, the UAE's Ambassador to Iran, said in a statement on July 16, 2008.

3.2.4. Iraq-Saudi Arabia

Saudi Arabia's relationship with Iraq has been tense historically, although periods of Saudi-Iraqi cooperation have occurred when supported by convergent interests, most notably during the Iran-Iraq war of the 1980s.

Saudi Arabia publicly opposed the US-led invasion of Iraq in 2003, but provided logistical support to US forces.

Saudi Arabia's principal interests with regard to the conflict in Iraq are as follows:

1. To prevent instability and conflict in Iraq from threatening Saudi Arabia's internal security and stability,
2. To prevent the repression of Iraq's Sunnis by newly dominant Shiites,
3. To limit the regional influence of Iran.

Saudi Arabia's longer term interests include ensuring that the revival of Iraq's oil industry does not threaten Saudi pre-eminence and preferences in global energy markets and that Iraq does not re-emerge as a strategic military threat to the Arab States of the Persian Gulf. The Saudi Arabian government has refrained from overt political-military intervention in Iraq since 2003, in spite of the threat that instability in Iraq has posed to Saudi Arabia's national security.

In August 2007, Saudi Foreign Minister, Prince Saud Al Feisal, during a joint news conference with US Defence Secretary, Robert Gates and former US Secretary of State, Condoleezza Rice, stated that "Saudi Arabia promises to continue working with its Gulf neighbours to support Iraq's new government and promote stability in the region."[34]

3.2.5. Iraq-GCC States (except Saudi Arabia)

The Iraqi invasion and occupation of Kuwait and the resulting threat to other small Gulf States forced other Gulf States to alter significantly its defence and foreign policy priorities. For example, whereas Qatar had supported Iraq financially in its 1980-88 war against Iran, it quickly joined the anti-Iraq coalition in the 1991 war.

During the *Persian Gulf War* in 1990-91, Bahrain also, was part of the coalition that fought to liberate *Kuwait*. Bahraini pilots flew air strikes in Iraq from the *Sheik Isa Air Base*, while coalition navies operated out of *Manama*, the capital. Bahrain was hit by Scud missiles fired from Iraq. A number of Bahraini students studying in Iraq and Kuwait at the outbreak of hostilities went missing and are presumed the victims of Saddam Hussein's secret police. After the liberation of Kuwait, Bahrain and the *United States* strengthened their already good ties by signing a ten-year agreement in October 1991, which granted American forces access to Bahraini facilities and allowed the US to pre-position war material for future crises. However, the Kingdom opposed unilateral action against *Iraq* in 2003, and to the annoyance of Washington, in the run up to the war, sought to defuse the crisis by offering *Saddam Hussein* asylum as a way of avoiding war.

In sum, the GCC, which for years had been aimed, in part, at dealing with a perceived Iranian threat (both external and, in the cases of Kuwait, Bahrain, and Saudi Arabia, internal), became a forum for condemnation of Iraq and a venue for building a concerted defence against further Iraqi advances.

After the regime change of Iraq, in 2003, all the GCC members focused their energies on improving cooperation and coordination on mutual defence issues while also continuing to work together in social, cultural, political, and economic spheres. They have been historically sensitive to outside military intervention in the gulf and were eager to bolster regional security measures.

3.2.6. Saudi Arabia–Rest of the GCC States

In 1992, the kingdom was allied with its fellow monarchies and Sheikhdoms of Bahrain, Kuwait, Oman, Qatar, and the United Arab Emirates (UAE) in the Gulf Cooperation Council (GCC), a regional collective security and economic organization. Saudi Arabia had taken the lead in forming the GCC.

According to the Ministry of Foreign Affairs of Saudi Arabia, "the country's foreign policy in the Persian Gulf; exclusively in GCC, is based on the following principles:

1. The security and stability of the region is the responsibility of the states of the region.
2. The Gulf States have the right to defend their security and maintain their independence according to their own discretion and as guaranteed by the international law to confront any internal or international challenges.
3. Decline the interference in internal affairs of these countries, and work out to cooperate and stand against any aggression on one of the state members, with regard to any aggression; at the same time, member states consider aggression on one country as aggression on all member states.
4. Strengthen cooperation between the Kingdom and the member states of the GCC in different political, economical, security, social, cultural fields and others, through deepening and consolidating relations and ties among member states.
5. Coordinate policies of the GCC when possible, especially toward the regional and international momentous issues. Such cooperation and coordination were obvious during the crisis witnessed by the region, especially during the Iraq-Iran war, and the Iraqi invasion to Kuwait.
6. Take serious and persistent action to solve all disputes (especially border disputes) among the countries of the region through understanding that is based on brotherhood and good neighbouring principles.
7. Sound enthusiasm on the importance of economic coordination among member states through continuous support for unifying economic policies and establish suitable integrated contexts, paying special attention to coordination with regard to oil policies of the member states in a manner that serves their interests, considering that oil is the strategic source of these countries."[35]

4. Persian Gulf Region in Post-Iraq War Era

While political and security elites in Gulf countries are trying to perfect an international power balance in the region, the entire Middle East is undergoing a socio-political transformation that is largely bypassing traditional forms of "Realpolitik"[36]. Amid the hyperbole regarding Iran's nuclear program and Iraq's continuing chaos, a much larger and potentially more explosive phenomenon has been steadily developing from Northern Africa to the Persian Gulf; the transition from authoritarian, controlled states to more open societies, alongside a population boom that could lead to high rates of unemployment and economic stagnation throughout the region over the next several years.

Although nearly all high-level Gulf Arab political leaders expect the United States to continue its role as 'external balancer' in the region indefinitely, popular support within the region for this 'security environment' does not exist. And, given the rapid growth of international, trans-national and domestic media in the Gulf region, this situation is unlikely to get any better without a strong reassessment of current policies by regional governments, the United States and other external powers.

Meanwhile, Arab monarchies of the Persian Gulf point out that both historically and today, external powers are often by default local powers. This is true whether one is talking about the naval presence and contributions of Portuguese, Dutch and British imperial forces to the security of coastal tribal networks in past decades and centuries, or whether one is considering the current American economic and security agreements (and military deployments) in regard to states in the Gulf over the past few decades. Whether as tribes or states, coastal Arab leaders have purposely relied on 'security-economic trades' with external powers that have ensured a modicum of authority and order for local elites while meeting the larger, more global concerns of great powers who wish to keep sea lanes open and access to natural resources predictable.

The UAE, Oman, Qatar, Bahrain and Kuwait are all signing their own non-transparent deals with the United States and trying to build their economies apart from each other via economic reliance on an external power, rather than transforming economic relations with each other via the GCC. And all five countries are signing these strictly bilateral deals in a way that radically weakens Saudi Arabia's reigning local hegemony, essentially taking away its once-dominant regional role on matters of trade and finance with its Arab neighbours in the Persian Gulf region.

After Iraq War (2003), the order of Persian Gulf has been changed and due to that, the following new conditions are dominating the region:

1. Strategic equilibrium order and balance of power have been entirely disrupted and regional states' place in power equations has totally been changed.
2. The states which were powerfully ordaining the Gulf's affairs, are under internal and external pressures and instead of them, small states that could not play any important role in regional order, have been USA's political and martial bases.
3. Some of the regional states, especially Iran, consider invasion of Iraq by USA as a preface of spoiling their political structure and social order.
4. The regional states' cultural sphere which was deeply static and restricted to religious rites has become strongly political.
5. "Iraq as a threat to regional states with a regard to clash with USA's interest is changing to a threat against their (regional states), interests and to USA's advantage".[37] This issue is important as Iraq's inherent abilities and potentials were significant factures in balance of power in the region and now with occupation of Iraq by USA and its allies, the balance of power in the region has been altered to USA and Israel's advantage.
6. The presence of American forces in the region has caused expanded opposition in cultural and political spheres.

7. Trust building policy between Iran and other Gulf States has been very difficult as new phenomena, such as falling of Saddam, have occurred.
8. Shiite community is getting more strength in Iraq and as the other Gulf States are anxious of its effects, they try to weaken and defeat this process.
9. Gulf States are considered to Iran's influence in Iraq and USA's serious problems in that country. The possibility of any collaboration between USA and Iran so as to obtain mutual benefits, has worried Gulf States. They assume that kind of cooperation will not be wholesome for their security, especially, considering progressive process of Shiite geopolitics in the region.
10. There is no suitable sphere of mutual trust between Gulf States yet. Saudi Arabia is not pleased with Qatar and Kuwait's dependence on USA. Kuwait is very anxious about Saudi Arabia due to their historical backgrounds. UAE has serious problem with Saudi Arabia on their oil rich border lines. Border disputes between UAE and Qatar have not been solved yet. Kuwait considers itself as the main loser of Iraq war (2003 onwards). Qatar is considered as USA's new political and martial base.

Considering above mentioned issues, it appears that there is no reliable and confirmed regional order in the region. As any instability and disorder in the region will definitely spread out all over the Middle East, a stable order; accepted by the all actors of the region, seems vital.

References

1. Halliday Fred, "*Arabs and Persians Beyond the Geopolitics of The Gulf*", Le Monde Journal, No 22, July-December 1996
2. Ikenberry John and Moon Chung-in, " *The United States and Northeast Asia: Debates, Issues and New Order*", Rowman and Littlefield Publishers, USA, 2008, pp. 194-196

3. Thomas Hobbes, an English philosopher and political theorist, 1588-1679, argued that the only way to secure civil society is through universal submission to the absolute authority of a sovereign. His idea's followers are called Hobbesians.
4. Laos Nicolas K., "*International Security In The Post-Cold War Era*", Journal of International Affairs, December 1999- February 2000, Volume IV, Number 4
5. Sutton, John L. and Kemp Geoffrey, "*Arms to Developing Countries 1945-1965*" , The Institute for Strategic Studies, London, 1966
6. Asadian Amir, "*US Policy in Persian Gulf*", Strategic Studies' Research Centre, Tehran, 2001, pp. 95-96
7. Smolansky Oles M., "*The USSR and Iraq*", Duke University Press, USA, 1991, p. 13
8. Byman Daniel L., "*Saudi Arabia's Own Iraq Nightmare*", Saban Centre for Middle East Policy (Brooking Institute), February 8w:th, 2007
9. Gause III Gregory F., "*The Illogic of Dual Containment*" Foreign Affairs Journal, *March/April 1994*
10. Haji Yusefi Amir Mohammad, "*Iran's Foreign Policy Based on Regional Transitions:1991-2001*", Iran's Foreign Office's International and Political Studies Office, Tehran, 2005, p. 160
11. Ibid, pp. 161-162
12. IRNA; Iran News Agency, April 18th, 2001
13. Ibid.
14. Al Issawi Tarek, "*Saudi King Abdullah invites Iran's Rafsanjani to Saudi Arabia*", Bloomberg, May 15th, 2008
15. IRNA; Islamic Republic News Agency, March 15th, 2008
16. "*Bahrain: Iran a Potential Threat*," United Press International, May 15th , 1999
17. "*Tension in Iran-Bahrain Relations after Kayhan Editor Claims Bahrain is Inseparable Part of Iran*", The Middle East Media Research Institute, August 3rd, 2007
18. Akhbar Al-Khaleej (Bahrain), July 15th, 2007
19. "*Bahrain-Iran Eye Good Relations*", Arab News Agency, February 4th, 2009
20. Ali Khan, Ghazanfar, "*GCC warns Iran against making hostile remarks, Arab News*, February 23rd, 2009

21. "*Iran-Bahrain relations*", BBC News, *BBC Persian* (in Persian), April 5th, 2009
22. No. 21
23. "*Kuwait Supports Peaceful Nuclear Program*" Iran Daily, October 5th, 2005
24. "*Kuwaiti Emir Congratulates Ahmadinejad On Re-election*", IRNA, June 14th, 2009
25. "*Omani Plants Likely To Process Gas for Iran,*" , Thai Press Reports, September 5th, 2008
26. "*Cheney To Meet Oman's Sultan for Talks on Iran,*" Voice of America, March 19th, 2008
27. "*Iran, Oman Discuss Military Cooperation,*" , Middle East News line, August 27th, 2008
28. "*Oman Dismisses US Concerns on Iran Nuclear Issue,*" , Fars News Agency, December 28th, 2008
29. "*Larijani, Omani Ambassador Call for Regional Cooperation*", Iranian Student News Agency, January 27th, 2009
30. "*Iran, Oman Prepare Security Pact*", Middle East News line, May 20th, 2009
31. "*More congratulations for Ahmadinejad on election win*", Iranian Press TV, June 15th, 2009
32. CNN News Agency, December 5th, 2007
33. "*UAE-Iran relations strong, says top envoy*", Gulf News, July 17th, 2008
34. Miles Donna, "*Saudi Arabia Pledges to Support Iraq, Promote Regional Stability*", American Forces Press Service, August 1st, 2007
35. Ministry of Foreign Affairs of Saudi Arabia/ foreign policy the country
36. Realpolitik refers to politics or diplomacy based primarily on practical considerations, rather than ideological notions and is a depiction of foreign policy that should be based on considerations of power, not ideals, morals, or principles. *Henry Kissinger* was a proponent of this belief as demonstrated in the Nixon administration's dealings with Communist China.
37. Ferdosipour Mojtaba (Collector), "Collection of Monographs of Fourteenth Persian Gulf's International Conference in 2004, Persian Gulf; Regional Transitions after Iraq's Occupation", Foreign Ministry's Publication Centre, Tehran, 2004, pp.137-139

6

Wars of the Persian Gulf Region Post 1979

1. Introduction

Conflict and change in the Persian Gulf region has been a way of life since the ending of "Pax Britannica"[1] in 1971. This momentous change in the regional power base began a new era in which the local powers have attempted to create a regional balance which would secure their future peace and prosperity. The Gulf States' hopes for stability have been severely challenged in recent years, first by Shiite Islamic Revolution in Iran and then by Hussein in Iraq. Result from these and other threats during this period has been the formation of closer more involved relationships between the Gulf States and the United States. The Gulf States see this as a source of encouragement, yet, are still concerned about the long term impact of a Western presence.

Sources of conflict and change in the Gulf region are many. Most often discussed have been the external threats posed by Iraq. Each state also has existing or potential conflicts with its neighbours and fellow Gulf Cooperation Council (GCC) members. Potential for internal conflict is also present. Pressures for more representative forms of government are increasing and may become serious as monarchs' abilities to satisfy the needs and desires of their subjects are reduced. Other internal pressures created by population makeup and economic difficulties are posing interesting challenges.

The Persian Gulf region has a history of armed conflict and major threats to the regional states' national security and has seen three major wars in the past two decades.

1. The Persian Gulf was the focus of the Iraq-Iran War that lasted from 1980 to 1988.
2. In 1991, the Persian Gulf again was the background for what was called the 'Persian Gulf War' or 'The Gulf War' when Iraq invaded Kuwait and was subsequently pushed back.
3. On March 19, 2003, American and British forces began the third Persian Gulf War. Since 2003, Persian Gulf region has become the scene of US-led invasion of Iraq; which caused regime change in Iraq. Its consequences such as instability and violence in Iraq, have had direct and indirect impacts on the regional security.

The 'No-Fly Zone War' (1991-2003) pitted the air and naval forces of the United States and the United Kingdom against the air defences of Iraq. To ensure that Iraq could not use its still formidable conventional forces against its neighbours, the United States and Britain patrolled 'no fly zones' over northern and southern Iraq in the 'Northern Watch' and 'Southern Watch' operations, respectively. Together, the zones cover approximately 62% of Iraq's territory. US-led Coalition wars with Iraq (the 1990-1991 Gulf War, and the 2003 Gulf War) can really be seen as one long, extended conflict, but for classification purposes, are seen as separate conflicts.

2. Iran-Iraq War; 1980-1988

2.1. Introduction

The Iran-Iraq War was multifaceted and included religious schisms, ethnic schism, border disputes, and political differences.

2.1.1. Religious Schism; Sunni versus Shiite

Iraq and Iran have had a long history of conflict fuelled by religious differences between the Sunni Muslim Iraqi government and the mainly Shiite Muslim Iraqi population and the Shiite religious government of Iran. The most violent reaction to Iran's Shiite revolution came from Saddam Hussein in Iraq.

Despite Iraq's aggression, it had no trouble attracting the support of all of the Sunni Muslim leaders in the region.

2.1.2. Ethnic Schism; Arab versus Persian

Viewed from a historical perspective, the outbreak of hostilities in 1980 was, in part, just another phase of the ancient Persian-Arab conflict that had been fuelled by 20th century border disputes. Many observers, however, believe that Saddam Hussein's decision to invade Iran was a personal miscalculation based on ambition and a sense of vulnerability. Saddam Hussein, despite having made significant strides in forging an Iraqi nation-state, feared that Iran's new revolutionary leadership would threaten Iraq's delicate Sunni-Shia balance and would exploit Iraq's geostrategic vulnerabilities—Iraq's minimal access to the Persian Gulf, for example.

In this respect, Saddam Hussein's decision to invade Iran has historical precedent; the ancient rulers of Mesopotamia, fearing internal strife and foreign conquest, also engaged in frequent battles with the peoples of the highlands.

But Saddam did not cast the conflict in sectarian terms. "Saddam largely represented himself as the bastion of Arab nationalism resisting Persian hordes."[2]

Iraq launched the war in an effort to consolidate its rising power in the Arab world and to replace Iran as the dominant Persian Gulf state. Phebe Marr, a noted analyst of Iraqi affairs, stated that "the war was more immediately the result of poor political judgment and miscalculation on the part of Saddam Hussein," and the decision to invade, taken at a moment of Iranian weakness, was Saddam's."[3]

Iraq claimed territories inhabited by Arabs, the South-western oil-producing province of Iran called Khuzestan. The Iraqis also perceived revolutionary Iran's Islamic agenda as threatening to their pan-Arabism.

2.1.3. Border Disputes

The relation between two states was inflamed by a dispute over the ownership of the Arvand River (Shatt al Arab) waterway. This strategic waterway is the confluence between the Tigris and Euphrates rivers and forms the southern boarder between Iraq and Iran. Iran claimed the border was the middle of the river while Iraq claimed the border was on the Eastern bank giving them complete ownership of this navigable waterway. In addition "between 1961 and 1975, Iran gave assistance to Kurdish rebels fighting in northern Iraq draining Iraqi resources."[4]

In 1975, an agreement was finally reached in which Iran withdrew support for the Kurds in return for Iraq recognizing its claims on the Shatt al Arab waterway.

Iraq and Iran had engaged in border clashes for many years and had revived the dormant Shatt al Arab waterway dispute in 1979. Iraq claimed the 200-kilometer channel up to the Iranian shore as its territory, while Iran insisted that the thalweg; a line running down the middle of the waterway, negotiated last in 1975, was the official border. The Iraqis, especially the Baath leadership, regarded the 1975 treaty as merely a truce, not a definitive settlement. The Iraqis saw the treaty as a defeat.

2.1.4. Political Differences

Iraq's relations with Iran grew increasingly strained after the Shah was overthrown in 1979. Iraq recognized Iran's new Shiite Islamic government, but the Iranian leaders would have nothing to do with the Baath regime, which they denounced as secular. The most violent reaction to Iran's Shiite revolution came from Saddam Hussein in Iraq. Ayatollah Ruhollah Khomeini, the spiritual leader of the Iranian revolution, proclaimed his policy of "exporting the revolution,"[5] and Iraq was high on the list of countries whose governments were to be overthrown and replaced by a replica of the Islamic regime in Iran. In addition, Iran still occupied three small pieces of territory along the Iran-Iraq border that were supposed to be returned to Iraq under the treaty of 1975. In 1979 and 1980, border clashes occurred frequently.

Despite the Iraqi government's concern, the eruption of the 1979 Islamic Revolution in Iran did not immediately destroy the Iraqi-Iranian rapprochement that had prevailed since the 1975 Algiers Agreement. As a sign of Iraq's desire to maintain good relations with the new government in Tehran, former Iraqi President; Bakr sent a personal message to Ayatollah Khomeini offering "his best wishes for the friendly Iranian people on the occasion of the establishment of the Islamic Republic."[6] In addition, as late as the end of August 1979, Iraqi authorities extended an invitation to Mehdi Bazargan, the first Prime Minister of the Islamic Republic of Iran, to visit Iraq with the aim of improving bilateral relations. The fall of the moderate Bazargan government in late 1979, however, and the rise of Islamic militants preaching an expansionist foreign policy soured Iraqi-Iranian relations.

2.2. Events of Eight Years War of Attrition (1980-1988)

On September 17, 1980, Saddam Hussein announced that he was abrogating the 1975 agreements because they had been violated by Iran and he was ending the treaty with Iran that had been agreed in 1975, five days later the Iraqi armed forces had started a massive offensive and by the end of October 1980 Khorramshar; the largest port in Iran had fallen to Iraqi forces, who were now threatening the Iranian oil capital of Abadan and the regional capital of Khuzestan.

Iraqi leader Saddam Hussein claimed as a reason for the invasion a territorial dispute over the Shatt al-Arab, the waterway which forms the boundary between the two countries. However, the conflict was rooted in regional rivalry.

In September 1980, border skirmishes erupted in the central sector near Qasr-e Shirin, with an exchange of artillery fire by both sides.

Saddam Hussein felt directly threatened by the Islamic revolution which had brought Ayatollah Khomeini to power in Iran in 1979. The ayatollah, for his part, saw Saddam as a brutal Sunni tyrant oppressing his country's Shiite majority, and did not disguise his desire to see him toppled.

Thus, for Saddam Hussein, the war's purpose was pre-emptive: to overthrow the Khomeini regime before that regime could overthrow him. He believed that Iran was in turmoil and that his forces could achieve quick victory. Saddam became more confident as it watched the once invincible Imperial Iranian Army disintegrate, as most of its highest ranking officers were executed.

The war was fought initially in Iran's oil-rich region, then on the other side of the border in southern Iraq, where Iraq's Shiite population was concentrated.

Baghdad possessed fully equipped and trained forces. Morale was running high. Against Iran's armed forces, including the Pasdaran (Revolutionary Guard) troops, led by religious leaders with little or no military experience, the Iraqis could muster twelve complete mechanized divisions equipped with the latest Soviet materials.

In addition, the area across the Shatt al Arab posed no major obstacles, particularly for an army equipped with Soviet river-crossing equipments. Iraqi commanders correctly assumed that crossing sites on the Karkheh and Karun rivers were lightly defended against their mechanized armour divisions; moreover, Iraqi intelligence sources reported that Iranian forces in Khuzestan, which had formerly included two divisions distributed among Ahvaz, Dezful, and Abadan; now, consisted of only a number of ill-equipped battalion-sized formations.

Tehran was further disadvantaged because the area was controlled by the Regional 1st Corps headquartered at Bakhtaran (formerly Kermanshah), whereas operational control was directed from the capital. In the year following the Shah's overthrow, only a handful of company-sized tank units had been operative, and the rest of the armoured equipment had been poorly maintained.

For Iraqi planners, the only uncertainty was the fighting ability of the Iranian air force, equipped with some of the most sophisticated American-made aircrafts. Besides enlisting the Iranian pilots, the new revolutionary regime also recalled veterans of the old Imperial army, although many experienced officers; most of them had been trained in the United States, had been purged.

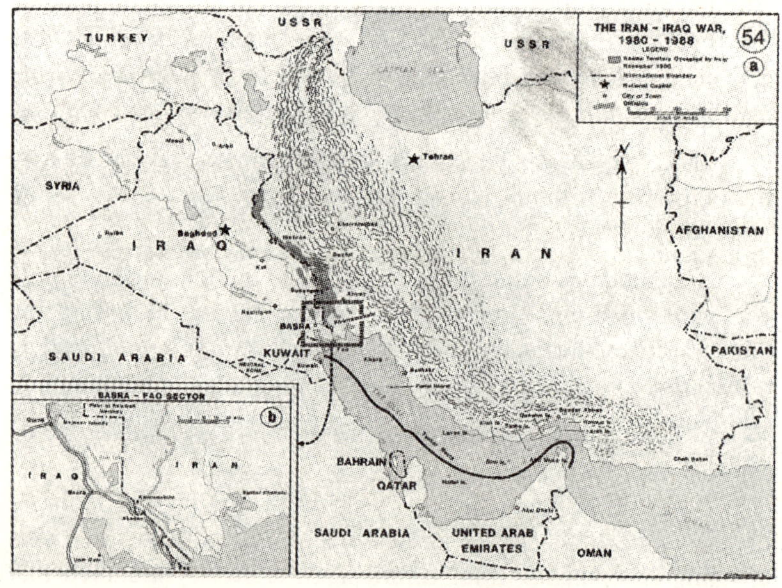

Map 6.1.: Map of Iran-Iraq War; 1980-1988

Source: US Military Academy

The air force was active in the wake of the failed United States attempt to rescue American hostages in April 1980. This show of force had impressed Iraqi decision makers to such an extent that they decided to launch a massive pre-emptive air strike on Iranian air bases in an effort similar to the one that Israel employed during the June 1967 Arab-Israeli War. On September 22, 1980, formations of Iraqi MiG-23s and MiG-21s attacked Iran's air bases at Mehrabad and Doshen-Tappen (both near Tehran), as well as Tabriz, Bakhtaran, Ahvaz, Dezful, Urumia, Hamadan, Sanandaj, and Abadan. Their aim was to destroy the Iranian air force on the ground.

On September 28, 1980, the UN Security Council called for a cease-fire and appealed to Iran and Iraq to 'settle their dispute by peaceful means'. Saddam Hussein replied, saying that Iraq would accept a cease-fire provided Iran also did so. Iran's response, however, was negative. "Further attempts at mediation in 1980 and 1981 also were rejected by Iran."[7] The war thus continued and in succeeding years was extended to the gulf area, leading to foreign intervention. It has been aptly called the Gulf War.

Approximately 200,000 Iranian soldiers were sent to the front by the end of November 1980. They were ideologically committed troops (some members even carried their own shrouds to the front in the expectation of martyrdom) that fought bravely despite inadequate armour support. For example, on November 7, 1980, commando units played a significant role, with the navy and air force, in an assault on Iraqi oil export terminals at Mina Al Bakr and Al Faw.

With the Iraqi military build-up in the late 1970s, Saddam Hussein had assembled an army of 190,000 men, augmented by 2,200 tanks and 450 aircrafts.

Iran hoped to diminish Iraq's financial resources by reducing its oil revenues. Iran also attacked the northern pipeline in the early days of the war and persuaded Syria to close the Iraqi pipeline that crossed its territory. Iran's resistance at the outset of the Iraqi invasion was unexpectedly strong, but it was neither well organized nor equally successful on all fronts. Iraq easily advanced in the northern and central sections and crushed the Pasdaran's scattered resistance there. Iraqi troops, however, faced untiring resistance in Khuzestan.

Saddam Hussein of Iraq had thought that the approximately 3 million Arabs of Khuzestan would join the Iraqis against Tehran. Instead, many allied with Iran's regular and irregular armed forces and fought in the battles at Dezful, Khorramshahr, and Abadan. Soon after capturing Khorramshahr, the Iraqi troops lost their initiative and began to dig in along their line of advance.

The Iraqi advance into Iran was stopped in November 1980. There followed a stalemate that continued until September 1981, when Iran began a series of successful offensives.

In May 1982, Iranian units finally regained Khorramshahr, but with high casualties and the Iraqis had been driven from most of the captured territory. "Iranian forces began to penetrate into Basra province."[8]

After this victory, the Iranians maintained the pressure on the remaining Iraqi forces, and Saddam Hussein announced that the Iraqi units would withdraw from Iranian territory. Saddam ordered a withdrawal to the international borders, believing Iran would agree to end the war. Iran did not accept this withdrawal as the end of the conflict, and continued the war into Iraq.

In late June 1982, Baghdad stated its willingness to negotiate a settlement of the war and to withdraw its forces from Iran. Iran refused. The Iranians sustained an immense number of casualties, but they enabled Iran to recover some territory before the Iraqis could repulse the bulk of the invading forces.

By the end of 1982, Iraq had been re-supplied with new Soviet materiels, and the ground war entered a new phase.

Throughout 1983, both sides demonstrated their ability to absorb and to inflict severe losses. Iraq, in particular, proved adroit at constructing defensive strong points and flooding lowland areas to stymie the Iranian thrusts, hampering the advance of mechanized units. Both sides also experienced difficulties in effectively utilizing their armour. Rather than manoeuvring their armour, they tended to dig in tanks and use them as artillery pieces. Furthermore, both sides failed to master tank gun sights and fire controls, making themselves vulnerable to antitank weapons.

Beginning in 1984, Baghdad's military goal changed from controlling Iranian territory to denying Tehran any major gain inside Iraq.

Furthermore, Iraq tried to force Iran to the negotiating table by various means which are as follows:

1. First, Saddam Hussein sought to increase the war's manpower and economic cost to Iran. For this purpose, Iraq purchased new weapons, mainly from the Soviet Union and France. Iraq also completed the construction of what came to be known as 'killing zones' (which consisted primarily of artificially flooded areas near Basra) to stop Iranian units. In addition, according to Jane's Defence Weekly and other sources, Baghdad used chemical weapons against Iranian troop concentrations and launched attacks on many economic centres.

   Despite Iraqi determination to halt further Iranian progress, Iranian units in March 1984 captured parts of the Majnun Islands whose oil fields had economic as well as strategic value.

2. Second, Iraq turned to diplomatic and political means. In April 1984, Saddam Hussein proposed to meet Ayatollah Khomeini, personally in a neutral location to discuss peace negotiations. But Tehran rejected this offer and restated its refusal to negotiate with President Hussein.

3. Third, Iraq sought to involve the superpowers as a means of ending the war. The Iraqis believed this objective could be achieved by a new series of attacking Iranian shipping on February 1, 1984.

The major development in 1985 was the increased targeting of population centres and industrial facilities by both combatants. In May 1985, Iraq began aircraft attacks, long-range artillery attacks, and surface-to-surface missile attacks on Tehran and on other major Iranian cities. The Iraqi Air Force's first real strategic bombing campaign, the so-called war of the cities, aimed at breaking civilian morale and disrupting military targets.

Iraq's two efforts early in 1985, from March 14th to April 7th and May 25th to June 15th, were reportedly very effective. Iraq's air force and "Scud"[9] strikes at Iranian cities pushed the Islamic Republic to look for a comparable response. Between August and November, Iraq raided Khark Island forty-four times in a futile attempt to destroy its installations.

Iran responded with its own air raids and missile attacks on Baghdad and other Iraqi towns. In addition, Tehran systematized its periodic stop-and-search operations, which were conducted to verify the cargo contents of ships in the Persian Gulf and to seize war materiel destined for Iraq.

Iran began the Iran-Iraq War with no "SSM"[10] capability but "managed to import SS-1 'Scud Bs' (R-17Es) in 1985 from Libya and in 1986 from Syria."[11]

The Revolutionary Guard Corps, which took charge of the weapons, used them against Iraq between 1985 and 1988.

One of the major ground offensives, codename Operation Badr, involving an estimated 60,000 Iranian troops, occurred on March 11, 1985, near Basra; once again, the assault proved inconclusive except for heavy casualties.

The Iraqis, perhaps for the first time since the outbreak of hostilities, began a concerted air-strike campaign in July 1986.

Heavy attacks on Khark Island forced Iran to rely on makeshift installations farther south in the Gulf at Sirri Island and Larak Island. Thereupon, Iraqi jets, refuelling in midair or using a Saudi military base, hit Sirri and Larak. The two belligerents also attacked 111 neutral ships in the Gulf in 1986. Meanwhile, to help defend it, Iraq had built impressive fortifications along the 1,200-kilometer war front. Iraq devoted particular attention to the southern city of

Basra, where concrete-roofed bunkers, tank- and artillery-firing positions, minefields and stretches of barbed wire, all shielded by an artificially flooded lake 30 kilometres long and 1,800 meters wide, were constructed.

On January 8, 1987, Operation Karbala Five began, with Iranian units pushing westward between Fish Lake and the Shatt al Arab. This operation captured the Iraqi town of Duayji.

In this intensive operation, Baghdad lost forty-five airplanes. Attempting to capture Basra, Tehran launched several attacks, some of them well-disguised diversion assaults such as Operation Karbala Six and Operation Karbala Seven. Iran finally aborted Operation Karbala Five on February 26, 1987.

In late May 1987, just when the war seemed to have reached a complete stalemate on the southern front, reports from Iran indicated that the conflict was intensifying on Iraq's northern front. This assault, Operation Karbala Ten, was a joint effort by Iranian units and Iraqi Kurdish rebels. They surrounded the garrison at Mawat, endangering Iraq's oil fields near Kirkuk and the northern oil pipeline to Turkey. Believing, it could win the war merely by holding the line and inflicting unacceptable losses on the attacking Iranians, Iraq initially adopted a static defensive strategy. This was successful in repelling successive Iranian offensives until 1986 and 1987, when the Al-Faw peninsula was lost and Iranian troops reached the gates of Al-Basrah.

Embarrassed by the loss of the peninsula and concerned by the threat to his second largest city, Saddam ordered a change in strategy. From a defensive posture, in which the only offensive operations were counterattacks to relieve forces under pressure or to exploit failed Iranian assaults, the Iraqis adopted an offensive strategy.

On July 20, 1987, the Security Council of the United Nations passed the US-sponsored Resolution 598, which called for an end to fighting and a return to pre-war boundaries. Iraq, which had lost important pieces of land over the course of the war, accepted the resolution. "Iran, however, was loathed to surrender its gains when total victory seemed close at hand, and so the fighting continued."[12]

Finally, both Iran and Iraq accepted United Nations (UN) Security Council Resolution 598, on August 20, 1988.

"When the foreign ministers of Iraq and Iran met for the first time in Geneva in August 1988 and later in 1989, there was no progress on how Resolution 598 was to be implemented. Iraq demanded the full exchange of prisoners as the first step, while Iran insisted that withdrawal of Iraqi forces from Iran should precede the exchange of prisoners."[13] It was not until 1990 that both Iraq and Iran finally agreed to settle their differences on the basis of the 1975 agreement and carry out the terms of UN Resolution 598.

2.2.1. The Tanker War

The Tanker War started properly in 1984 when Iraq attacked Iranian tankers and the vital oil terminal at Khark Island. Iran struck back by attacking tankers carrying Iraqi oil from Kuwait and then any tanker of the Gulf States supporting Iraq.

The tanker war seemed likely to precipitate a major international incident for two reasons, as follows:

1. First, some 70 percent of Japanese, 50 percent of West European, and 7 percent of American oil imports came from the Persian Gulf in the early 1980s.
2. Second, the assault on tankers involved neutral shipping as well as ships of the belligerent states.

The tanker war had two phases. The relatively obscure first phase began in 1981, and the well-publicized second phase began in 1984.

2.2.1.1. First Phase

As early as May 1981, Baghdad had unilaterally declared a war zone and had officially warned all ships heading to or returning from Iranian ports in the northern zone of the Gulf to stay away or, if they entered, to proceed at their own risk. The main targets in this phase were the ports of Bandar-e Khomeini and Bandar-e Mahshahr; very few ships were hit outside this zone. Naval operations came to a halt, presumably because Iraq and Iran had lost many of their ships by early 1981. The lull in the fighting lasted for two years.

2.2.1.2. Second Phase

In March 1984, the tanker war entered its second phase when Iraq initiated sustained naval operations in its self-declared 1,126-kilometer maritime exclusion zone, extending from the mouth of the Shatt al Arab to Iran's port of Bushehr.

Neutral merchant ships became favourite targets. Seventy-one merchant ships were attacked in 1984 alone, compared with forty-eight in the first three years of the war. Iraq's motives in increasing the tempo included a desire to break the stalemate, presumably by cutting off Iran's oil exports and by, thus, forcing Tehran to the negotiating table.

However, repeated Iraqi efforts failed to put Iran's main oil exporting terminal at Khark Island out of commission. The new wave of Iraqi assaults, however, led Iran to reciprocate. In April 1984, Tehran launched its first attack against civilian commercial shipping by shelling an Indian freighter. Iran attacked a Kuwaiti oil tanker near Bahrain on May 13, 1984, and then a Saudi tanker in Saudi waters five days later, making it clear that if Iraq continued to interfere with Iran's shipping, no Gulf State would be safe.

"These sustained attacks cut Iranian oil exports by half and reduced shipping in the Gulf by 25 percent."[14]

The Saudi decision in 1984 to shoot down an Iranian Phantom jet intruding in Saudi territorial waters played an important role in ending both belligerents' attempts to internationalize the tanker war.

Iraq and Iran accepted a 1984 UN-sponsored moratorium on the shelling of civilian targets, and Tehran later proposed an extension of the moratorium to include Gulf shipping, a proposal the Iraqis rejected unless it were to include their own Gulf ports.

Iraq began ignoring the moratorium soon after it went into effect and stepped up its air raids on tankers serving Iran and Iranian oil-exporting facilities in 1986 and 1987, attacking even vessels that belonged to the conservative Arab States of the Persian Gulf. Iran responded by escalating its attacks on shipping serving Arab ports in the Gulf.

As Kuwaiti vessels made up a large portion of the targets in these retaliatory raids, the Kuwaiti government sought protection from the international community in the fall of 1986. The Soviet Union responded first, agreeing to charter several Soviet tankers to Kuwait in early 1987.

Washington, which had been approached first by Kuwait and which had postponed its decision, eventually followed Moscow's lead. United States involvement was sealed by the May 17, 1987, Iraqi missile attack on the USS Stark, in which thirty seven crew members were killed. Baghdad apologized and claimed that the attack was a mistake and this was accepted.

Ironically, Washington used the Stark incident to blame Iran for escalating the war and sent its own ships to the Gulf to escort eleven Kuwaiti tankers that were re-flagged with the American flag and had American crews.

To ensure a repeat of the incident didn't happen again US, Iraqi and Saudi forces collaborated. Iran with some justification accused the US of helping Iraq and this was not helped when on July 3, 1988, an American warship shot down an Iranian airliner in error. Iran then started sowing the Gulf with anti ship mines and several ships were hit, including the USS Samuel B. Roberts in April 1988. Once again the US retaliated by destroying Iranian warships and patrol boats further demonstrating to the Gulf States the American support of Iraq, embittering Iran, and illustrating how vulnerable military and civilian shipping is to attack in the Persian Gulf.

2.2.2. Using Chemical Weapons by Iraq

To avoid defeat, Iraq sought out every possible weapon. This included developing a self-sustaining capability to produce militarily significant quantities of chemical warfare agents.

During the Iran-Iraq War, Iraq developed the ability to produce, store, and use chemical weapons. These chemical weapons included H-series blister and G-series nerve agents. Iraq built these agents into various offensive munitions including rockets, artillery shells, aerial bombs, and warheads on the Al Hussein Scud missile variant.

"With more than 100,000 Iranian victims of Iraq's chemical weapons during the eight-year war, Iran is one of the countries most severely afflicted by weapons of mass destruction. Iraq used chemical weapons on Iranian civilians, killing many in villages and hospitals. Many civilians suffered severe burns and health problems, and still suffer from them."[15]

The official estimate does not include the civilian population contaminated in bordering towns or the children and relatives of veterans, many of whom have developed blood, lung and skin complications, according to the Organization for Veterans of Iran.

Plate 6.1.: Iranian Soldier with Gas Mask in the Battlefield•

•Source: Sajed; Imposed War Official Website

According to a 2002 article in the Star-Ledger, "Nerve gas killed about 20,000 Iranian soldiers immediately, according to official reports. Of the 90,000 survivors, some 5,000 seek medical treatment regularly and about 1,000 are still hospitalized with severe, chronic conditions."[16]

A series of offensives in 1984 allowed the Iranians to cross the border in Kurdistan and move towards the Tigris River. Finally, the Iranians seized Majnoon Island in southern Iraq. This marshy region was notoriously difficult to move troops into. It was during this phase of the war that the Iraqis made use of poison gas to repel Iranian attacks; both mustard gas and the more modern nerve gas were used demonstrating the Iraqi capability to manufacture and deploy such weapons of mass destruction.

In March 1986, the former UN secretary general, Javier Perez de Cuellar, formally accused Iraq of using chemical weapons against Iran. Citing the report of four chemical warfare experts whom the UN had sent to Iran in February and March 1986, the secretary general called on Baghdad to end its violation of the 1925 Geneva Protocol on the use of chemical weapons. The UN report concluded that "Iraqi forces have used chemical warfare against Iranian forces and Iraqi chemical warfare was responsible for about 10,000 casualties. The weapons used included both mustard gas and nerve gas."[17]

The spring of 1988 saw the last major offensive; Iranian troops broke through in Kurdistan and nearly captured the hydro electric dam at Dukan, capturing 400 square miles of Iraq. Iraq, which was on the verge of defeat and backed into a corner, used poison gas to stop the Iranians. In March 1988, a war crime was committed when the Kurdish village of Halabjah under Iranian occupation was hit by gas.

"Iraqi planes carried out twenty bombing missions, dropping one of the most lethal toxic gases, hydrogen cyanide, on civilians. It left about 5000 dead and more than 7000 seriously injured."[18]

"A UN report later confirmed the use of poison gas on a civilian target by the Iraqis".[19]

"In July 1988 Iraqi airplanes dropped chemical cyanide bombs on the Iranian Kurdish village of Zardan (as they had done four months earlier at their own Kurdish village of Halabja). Hundreds were killed at once, and the survivors are still suffering from a variety of physical and mental disorders."[20]

The US Defense Intelligence Agency also accused Iran of using chemical weapons. These allegations however, have been disputed. Joost Hiltermann, who was the principal researcher for Human Rights Watch in 1992–1994, conducted a two year study, including a field investigation in Iraq, capturing Iraqi government documents in the process. According to Hiltermann, the literature on the Iran–Iraq War reflects a number of allegations of chemical weapons use by Iran, but these are "marred by a lack of specificity as to time and place, and the failure to provide any sort of evidence."[21]

"At his trial in December 2006, Saddam Hussein said he would take responsibility 'with honour' for any attacks on Iran using conventional or chemical weapons during the 1980–1988 war but he took issue with charges he ordered attacks on Iraqis."[22]

2.2.3. Attacking Nuclear Reactors

Iran launched an unsuccessful attack on the Iraqi Osirak nuclear reactor on September 30, 1980. On June 7, 1981, Israel initiated an air attack on the same Iraqi Osirak reactor; destroying it. Iraq launched seven air attacks on the Iranian nuclear reactor at Bushehr between 1984 and 1988 during the Iran-Iraq War, ultimately destroying the facility.

2.2.4. War of Cities

Iraq first bombed Iranian cities in 1984 starting with "Dezful and moving on to Tehran"[23] and other cities, although neither side had enough bombers to do much damage. Iraq's air force soon began strategic bombing against Iranian cities, chiefly Tehran, in 1985. To minimize losses from the superior Iranian Air Force, Iraq rapidly switched to Scud and Al-Hussein improved Scud launches.

In retaliation, Iran fired Scud missiles acquired from Libya and Syria against Baghdad and Basra. During this first war of the cities, Iran's strategic depth prevented Iraq's missiles from reaching major targets such as Tehran.

"In all, Iraq launched 520 Scuds and Al-Husseins against Iran and received only 177 in exchange. In October 1986, Iraqi aircraft attacked civilian passenger trains and aircraft, including an Iran Air Boeing 737 unloading passengers at Shiraz International Airport. In retaliation for the Iranian Operation Karbala-5; an early 1987 to attempt capturing Basra, Iraq attacked 65 cities in 226 sorties over 42 days, bombing civilian neighborhoods. Eight Iranian cities came under attack from Iraqi missiles. The bombings killed 65 children in an elementary school in Borujerd alone. The Iranians also responded with Scud missile attacks on Baghdad and struck a primary school there. These events became known as the war of the cities."[24]

1987 saw the first use of missiles against civilian populations with Iraqi Scud missiles modified to reach Tehran being used by the Iraqis. Many fled the city and some put the number of refugees at 4 million, half the city's population; in that time. Iran retaliated by using missiles against Baghdad.

In response to Iranian missile attacks against Baghdad, some 190 missiles were fired by the Iraqis over a six week period at Iranian cities in 1988 and took Iran by surprise with its strikes on key urban conurbations, Tehran, Qom and Isfahan. The Iraqi missile attacks caused little destruction, but each warhead had a psychological impact and caused panic in the populace and hundreds of thousands fled the cities.

The threat of rocket attacking the Iranian capital with missiles capable of carrying chemical warheads is cited as a significant reason why Iran accepted a disadvantageous peace agreement.

2.2.5. Casualties of War

The Iran-Iraq war was extremely costly in lives and material, one of the deadliest wars since Second World War. Both countries were devastated by the war's effect.

Because both Iran and Iraq used irregular military units, attacked civilian populations, and played down their own losses while playing up those of their opponents, reliable casualty figures do not exist. For example, Iran claimed to have lost 200,000 or fewer of its own citizens, while Iraq claimed to have killed 800,000 Iranians. Neutral estimates come closer to the Iranian claim but are uncertain. Because of different battlefield techniques, Iraq's deaths were probably about half those suffered by Iran. The total number of people killed almost certainly exceeds 300,000. Wounded and captured soldiers push the casualty totals over one million, and some estimates of total casualties exceed two million.

A variety of unresolved humanitarian issues from the Iran-Iraq war include a failure to identify combatants killed in action and to exchange information on those killed or missing.

About 60,000 Iraqi were taken prisoner by the Iranians. Iran agreed to the release of 5,584 Iraqi Prisoners of War; (PoW) in April 1998, and news organizations reported intermittent meetings throughout the remainder of the year between Iranian and Iraqi government officials toward reaching a final agreement on the remaining PoW's held by each side. "The Iranian government pledged to settle the remaining PoW issues with Iraq in 1999."[25] And joint Iran-Iraq search operations were initiated to identify remains of those missing in action.

2.2.6. Superpowers and Gulf States' Involvement in the War

After Islamic revolution of Iran in 1979, Iraq turned the tide portraying itself as a modern secular state fighting against a fanatical religious enemy. Relations with other Arab states started to normalize and diplomatic relations and possibly arms shipments, resumed with America. Certainly the Americans allowed European arms dealers' access to Iraq such as the French, whereas Iran still had an arms embargo. Europe supplied the arms and the moderate Arab states fearful of Islamic fundamentalism supplied the money for Iraqis war effort.

Part of the Iran-Iraq war of the 1980's, the Tanker War, attracted much international interest and some US intervention. With Iran blocking Iraqi exports of oil via the Shatt-al-Arab waterway, the war against Iran was turning against the Iraqis. Syria closed Iraq's pipeline to the Mediterranean and it looked like economics would straggle the Iraqi war effort. Despite the unpopularity of Iraq's government, the other Arab states feared the fundamentalism of Iran much more and came to Iraq's rescue. Jordan opened Aqhaba to Iraqi imports (mainly weapons) and new pipelines were constructed across the desert to the Red Sea and to Turkey. "Iraqi exports went through Kuwait also and the Arab states also directly funded Iraq to the sum of about US$ 60 billion."[26]

Iranian military gains inside Iraq after 1984 were a major reason for increased superpowers' involvement in the war. In February 1986, Iranian units captured the port of Al Faw, which had oil facilities and was one of Iraq's major oil-exporting ports before the war.

In early 1987, both superpowers indicated their interest in the security of the region. "Soviet deputy foreign minister from 1986 to 1991, Vladimir Petrovsky, made a Middle East tour expressing his country's concern over the effects of the Iran-Iraq War. In May 1987, United States Assistant Secretary of State from 1983 to 1989, Richard Murphy, also toured the Gulf emphasizing to friendly Arab states the United States commitment in the region."[27]

In a USA bid to open full diplomatic relations with Iraq, the country was removed from the US list of state sponsors of terrorism. Ostensibly, this was because of improvement in the regime's record, although former United States Assistant Secretary of Defense Noel

* Chronology of the Iran-Iraq war has been presented in Appendix C.

Koch later stated, "No one had any doubts about [the Iraqis'] continued involvement in terrorism... The real reason was to help them succeed in the war against Iran."[28]

In another diplomatic effort, both superpowers supported the UN Security Council resolutions seeking an end to the war.

The war appeared to be entering a new phase in which the superpowers were becoming more involved. For instance, the Soviet Union, which had ended military supplies to both Iran and Iraq in 1980, resumed large-scale arms shipments to Iraq in 1982 after Iran banned the Tudeh; a communist party, and tried and executed most of its leaders. Subsequently, despite its professed neutrality, the Soviet Union became the major supplier of sophisticated arms to Iraq.

By late spring of 1987, the superpowers became more directly involved because they feared that the fall of Basra might lead to a pro-Iranian Islamic republic in largely Shia-populated southern Iraq. They were also concerned about the intensified tanker war.

3. Persian Gulf War; 1990-1991

3.1. Introduction

After ending the Iran-Iraq War in 1988, peace in the Persian Gulf lasted for just two years. And then, Saddam embarked on another ill-fated military adventure: the seizure of Kuwait.

Kuwait had been part of the Ottoman Empire's province of Basra, and although its ruling dynasty, the al-Sabah family, had concluded a protectorate agreement in 1899 that assigned responsibility for its foreign affairs to Britain, it did not make any attempt to secede from the Ottoman Empire. For this reason, Iraqi governments had always refused to accept Kuwait's separation, and its borders were never clearly defined or mutually agreed. The British High Commissioner drew lines that deliberately constricted Iraq's access to the ocean so that any future Iraqi government would be in no position to threaten Britain's domination of the Persian Gulf.

In 1961, Iraq (under President Qasim) threatened Kuwait, invoking old Ottoman claims. Britain supported Kuwait and Iraq backed down. In March 1973, Iraq occupied As-Samitah, a border post on Kuwait-Iraq border and demanded the right to occupy the Kuwaiti islands of Bubiyan and Warbah but Saudi Arabia and the Arab League convinced Iraq to withdraw.

Kuwait was a close ally of Iraq during the Iraq-Iran war and functioned as the country's major port once Basra was shut down by the fighting. Following the end of the war, relations between Iraq and Kuwait deteriorated; with a lack of gratitude from the Baghdad government for help in the war and the reawakening of old issues regarding the border and Kuwaiti sovereignty.

After the Iraq-Iran War ended, the friendly relations between the two neighboring Arab countries, Iraq and Kuwait, turned sour due to several economic and diplomatic reasons which finally culminated in an Iraqi invasion of Kuwait.

In late July 1990, as negotiations between Iraq and Kuwait stalled, Iraq massed troops on its border with the Emirate and summoned US ambassador, April Glaspie, to a meeting with former Iraqi President Saddam Hussein. Two transcripts of that meeting have been produced, both of them controversial. In them, Saddam Hussein outlined his grievances against Kuwait, while promising that he would not invade Kuwait before one more round of negotiations.

Amid growing tension between the two Persian Gulf neighbours, Iraq and Kuwait, Saddam Hussein concluded that the United States and the rest of the outside world would not interfere to defend Kuwait.

According to the research being conducted by UK's Norwich University's Military College, there are three basic causes to the Iraqi invasion of Kuwait in 1990, which are as follows:

1. First, Iraq had long considered Kuwait to be a part of Iraq. This claim led to several confrontations over the years, and

continued hostility. Also, it can be argued that with Saddam Hussein's attempted invasion of Iran defeated, he sought easier conquests against his weak southern neighbours.

2. Second, rich deposits of oil straddled the ill-defined border and Iraq constantly claimed that Kuwaiti oil rigs were illegally tapping into Iraqi oil fields. Middle Eastern deserts make border delineation difficult and this has caused many conflicts in the region. Also Iraq claimed that Kuwait was responsible for reducing the oil prices, which lead to economic difficulties for Iraq, which itself had no other substantial export product and which already was producing close to its capacity. Kuwait did not accept any of Iraq's claims for compensation for Iraq's economic losses.

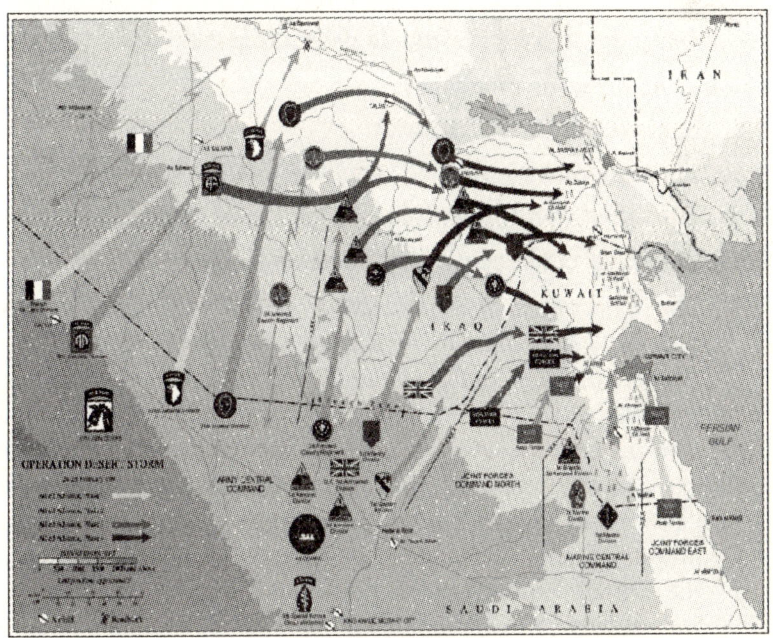

Map 6.2.: Map of Persian Gulf War; 1990-1991•

•Source: Suite 101

3. Finally, the fallout from the First Persian Gulf War between Iraq and Iran strained relations between Baghdad and Kuwait. This war began with an Iraqi invasion of Iran and degenerated into a bloody form of trench warfare as the Iranians slowly drove Saddam Hussein's armies back into Iraq. Kuwait and many other Arab nations supported Iraq against the Islamic Revolutionary government of Iran, fearful that Saddam's defeat could herald a wave of Iranian-inspired revolution throughout the Arab world.

The Persian Gulf War, January–February 1991, was an armed conflict between Iraq and a coalition of 36 nations led by the United States. It was a result of Iraq's invasion of Kuwait on August 2, 1990; Iraq then annexed Kuwait, which it had long claimed.

War fought between Iraq and allies of Kuwait, from January 16 to February 28, 1991, lasted 44 days altogether.

The war had three main phases:

1. Iraq's occupation of Kuwait,
2. The diplomatic game and sanctions against Iraq,
3. The allied war against Iraq.

The third phase could be divided into two phases:

3.1. The first phase was Operation Desert Shield, a largely defensive operation in which the United States and Saudi Arabia rushed to build up the defensive forces necessary to protect Saudi Arabia and the rest of the gulf, and the United Nations attempted to force Iraq to leave Kuwait through the use of economic sanctions. The United States then led the UN effort to create a broad international coalition with the military forces necessary to liberate Kuwait, and persuaded the United Nations to set a deadline of January 15, 1991 for Iraq to leave Kuwait or face the use of force.

3.2. The second phase, known as Desert Storm, was the battle to liberate Kuwait when Iraq refused to respond to the UN deadline. The fighting began on January 16, 1991 and ended on March 1, 1991.

3.2. Events of 1990

On August 2, Iraqi forces invaded Kuwait and quickly seized control of the small nation.

On August 3, the Arab League passed its own resolution. The resolution called for a solution to the conflict from within the League, and warned against outside intervention.

On August 4, after two days of intense combat, most of the Kuwaiti Armed Forces were either overrun by the Iraqi Republican Guard or escaped to neighboring Saudi Arabia.

On August 6, UN Resolution 661 placed economic sanctions on Iraq.

On August 8, Iraq declared parts of Kuwait to be extensions of the Iraqi province of Basra and the rest to be the "19th province of Iraq."[29]

Iraq was eventually persuaded by the Soviet Union to a full and unconditional withdrawal from Kuwait without having won any concessions, but the US insisted on a timeframe that did not allow Iraq to remove all its ordnance. As this would have seriously weakened it militarily, Iraq pressed for more time, but was rebuffed. The US was determined not only that Iraq pulled out of Kuwait, but that its ability to threaten its neighbors be reduced.

The decision by the US and its allies to fight Iraq had more to do with discouraging a future attack on Saudi Arabia, a nation of considerable importance owing to its oil reserves, than with liberating Kuwait. The rapid success of the Iraqi army had brought it within easy striking distance of the Hama oil fields; one of Saudi Arabia's largest. Iraqi control of these fields as well as Kuwait and Iraqi reserves would have given it control of the majority of the world's reserves.

The Iraqi armoured divisions would have encountered the same difficulties that Saudi forces faced defending the oil fields, namely traversing large distances across inhospitable desert. This would have been exacerbated by intense bombing by the Saudi Air Force, by far the most well- equipped arm of the Saudi military.

The United States Navy mobilized two naval battle groups, the aircraft carriers USS Dwight D. Eisenhower and USS Independence and their escorts, to the area, where they were ready by August 8. A total of 48 F-15s of US Air Force landed in Saudi Arabia and immediately commenced round the clock air patrols of the Saudi–Kuwait–Iraq border areas to discourage further Iraqi advances.

The US also sent the battleships USS Missouri and USS Wisconsin to the region. Military buildup continued from there, eventually reaching 5,43,000 troops, twice the number used in the 2003 invasion of Iraq. Much of the material was airlifted or carried to the staging areas via fast sealift ships, allowing a quick buildup.

"The United States, especially former Secretary of State James Baker, assembled a coalition of forces to join it in opposing Iraq."[30] Although they did not contribute any forces, Japan and West Germany made financial contributions totaling US $10 billion and US $6.6 billion respectively. US troops represented 73% of the coalition's 9,56,600 troops in Iraq.

Many of the coalition forces were reluctant to join; some felt that the war was an internal Arab affair, or did not want to increase US influence in the Middle East. "In the end, many nations were persuaded by Iraq's belligerence towards other Arab states, fear of the US, offers of economic aid or debt forgiveness, and threats to withhold aid."[31]

3.3. Events of 1991

3.3.1. January 1991

By January of 1991, over half a million allied troops were deployed in Saudi Arabia and throughout the Gulf region.

On January 12, 1991, the United States Congress authorized the use of military force to drive Iraq out of Kuwait. Soon after, the other states in the coalition also followed suit.

The coalition launched a massive air campaign which began the general offensive codenamed Operation Desert Storm with more than 1,000 sorties launching per day. Iraqi antiaircraft defenses, including shoulder-launched ground-to-air missiles, were surprisingly effective against coalition aircraft and "the coalition suffered 75 aircraft losses."[32]

The Persian Gulf War started with an extensive aerial bombing campaign. The coalition flew over 100,000 sorties, dropping 88,500 tons of bombs, and widely destroying military and civilian infrastructure.

The next coalition targets were command and communication facilities. Coalition planners hoped Iraqi resistance would quickly collapse if deprived of command and control.

The third and largest phase of the air campaign ostensibly targeted military targets throughout Iraq and Kuwait; Scud missile launchers, weapons research facilities, and naval forces. About one-third of the Coalition airpower was devoted to attacking Scuds, which were on trucks and therefore difficult to locate.

Some US and British Special Forces teams had been covertly inserted into western Iraq to aid in the search and destruction of Scuds. However, the lack of adequate terrain for concealment hindered their operations, and many of them were killed or captured. Iraqi fighters tried to stop these attacks, but they suffered many losses.

Allied bombing raids were successful in destroying Iraqi civilian infrastructure. 11 of Iraq's 20 major power stations and 119 substations were totally destroyed; while a further six major power stations were damaged. Bombs destroyed the utility of all major dams, most major pumping stations and many sewage treatment plants, turning Iraq from one of the most advanced Arab countries into one of the most backward.

"Telecommunications equipment, port facilities, oil refineries and distribution, railroads and bridges were also destroyed."[33]

The effect of the air campaign was to devastate entire Iraqi brigades deployed in the open desert in combat formation. The air campaign also prevented effective Iraqi resupply to forward deployed units engaged in combat, as well preventing a large number (450,000) of Iraqi troops from achieving the force concentration essential to victory. The air campaign had a significant effect on the tactics employed by opposing forces in subsequent conflicts.

Intense diplomacy between US and Iraqi officials failed to bring an Iraqi withdrawal, so, on January 16, 1991; Allied forces began the devastating bombing of Iraq and her forces in Kuwait. The Allied bombing sought to damage Iraq's infrastructure so as to hinder her ability to make war while also hurting both civilian and military morale.

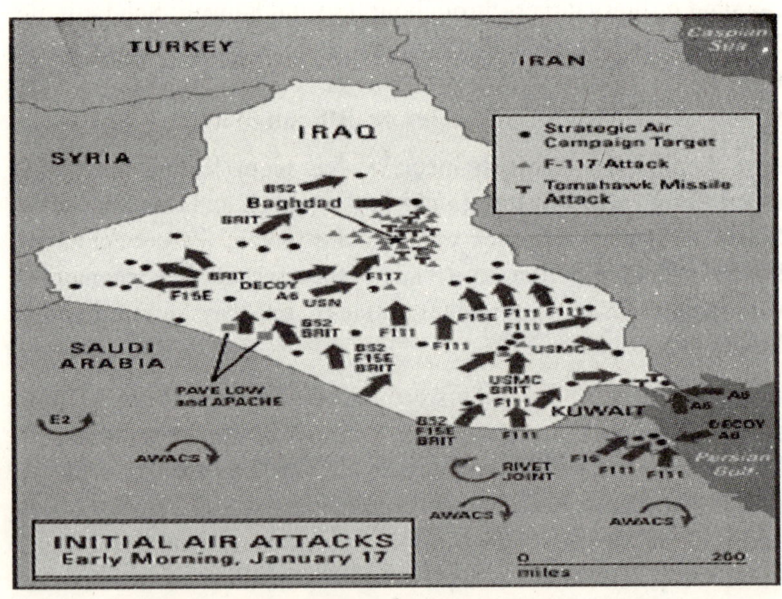

Map 6.3.: Map of Persian Gulf War's Air Campaign•

•Source: PBS Channel

To counter the air attack, Saddam ordered the launching of his feared Scud missiles at both Israel and Saudi Arabia. He hoped to provoke the Israelis into striking back at Iraq, which he theorized would split the Arab nations from the anti-Iraq coalition due to the ongoing hostility between Israel and the Arab world.

Israel came very close to retaliating, but held back due to President George Bush's pledge to protect Israeli cities from the Scuds. "Israeli Prime Minister, Yitzhak Shamir, hesitantly refused any retaliatory measures against Saddam Hussein, due to increasing pressure from the United States to remain out of the conflict."[34] As a result of Bush's promise, US Patriot missile batteries found themselves deployed in Israel to shoot down the Scuds. Another result of the Scud launches was to divert Allied air power from hitting the Iraqi army to hunting for the elusive mobile missile launchers. Even so, the Allied air strikes and cruise missile attacks against Iraq proved more devastating than expected.

On January 29, Iraq attacked and occupied the lightly defended Saudi city of Khafji with tanks and infantry. However, the Battle of Khafji ended when Iraqis were driven back by Saudi and Qatari forces supported by US Marines with close air support over the following two days. The coalition forces dominated the air with their technological advantages, but the ground forces were considered to be more evenly matched up between Iraqis and coalition infantry. Coalition ground forces had the significant advantage of being able to operate under the protection of superior air cover that had been achieved by the Air Forces prior to start of the main ground offensive.

"The ground phase of the war was given the official designation Operation Desert Sabre".[35] The first units to move into Iraq were three patrols of B squadron of the British Special Air Service, call signs Bravo One Zero, Bravo Two Zero, and Bravo Three Zero in late January. The patrol, including eight men, were tasked with observing the main supply route (MSR) between Baghdad and North-West Iraq, along with locating and destroying Scud missile launchers.

Coalition forces had two key technological advantages:

1. The Coalition Main Battle Tanks such as the American M1 Abrams, British Challenger 1 and Kuwaiti M-84AB were vastly superior to the export version Soviet-built T-72 tanks used by the Iraqis, with crews better trained and armoured doctrine better developed.
2. The use of "GPS"[36] made it possible for Coalition forces to navigate without reference to roads or other fixed landmarks. This allowed them to fight a battle of maneuver rather than a battle of encounter; they knew where they were and where the enemy was.

3.3.2. February 1991

A peace conference was held in Iraqi territory occupied by the coalition. At the conference, Iraq won the approval of the use of armed helicopters on their side of the temporary border, ostensibly for government transit due to the damage done to civilian transportation. Soon after, these helicopters, and much of the Iraqi armed forces, were refocused toward fighting against a Shiite uprising in the south.

"The rebellions were encouraged on February 2, 1991, by a broadcast on CIA run radio station; the Voice of Free Iraq broadcasting out of Saudi Arabia. The Arabic service of the Voice of America supported the uprising by stating that the rebellion was large and that they soon would be liberated from Hussein."[37]

In the North, Kurdish leaders took heart in American statements that they would support an uprising and began fighting, in the hopes of triggering a coup. However, when no American support was forthcoming, Iraqi generals remained loyal and brutally crushed the Kurdish troops. Millions of Kurds fled across the mountains to Kurdish areas of Turkey and Iran. These incidents later resulted in "No-Fly Zones"[38] being established in both the North and the South of Iraq.

In Kuwait, the Emir was restored and suspected Iraqi collaborators were repressed. Eventually, over 400,000 people were expelled from the country, including a large number of Palestinians (due to their support of and collaboration with Hussein). There was some criticism of the Bush administration for its decision to allow Saddam Hussein to remain in power, rather than pushing on to capture Baghdad and overthrowing his government.

On February 13, 1991, two laser-guided smart bombs destroyed the Amiriyah blockhouse, which was a civilian air shelter, killing hundreds of civilians. US officials claimed that the blockhouse was also a military communications centre, a claim that has never been verified.

On February 22, 1991, Iraq agreed to a Soviet-proposed ceasefire agreement. The agreement called for Iraq to withdraw troops to pre-invasion positions within six weeks following a total ceasefire, and called for monitoring of the ceasefire and withdrawal to be overseen by the UN Security Council. The Coalition rejected the proposal but said that retreating Iraqi forces would not be attacked, and gave twenty-four hours for Iraq to begin withdrawing forces. It was said at the time that Iraqi troops numbered approximately 5,45,000 (even 6,00,000). The Coalition committed approximately 5,40,000 troops. In addition to these, a further 1,00,000 Turkish troops were deployed along the common border of Turkey and Iraq. This caused significant force dilution of the Iraqi military by forcing it to deploy its forces along all its borders. This allowed the main thrust by the Americans to not only possess a significant technological advantage but also superiority in force numbers. Saddam Hussein bought military equipment from almost every major dealer of the World's weapons market.

When the Allied armies launched the ground war on February 23, the Iraqi occupation forces in Kuwait were already beaten. Cut off from their supply bases and headquarters by the intense air campaign, thousands of Iraqi soldiers simply gave up rather than fight, as the Allies pushed through Iraq's defences with relative ease.

In the few cases where the more elite Iraqi forces, such as the Republican Guard, stood and fought, superior American, British and French equipment and training proved the undoing of the Soviet-equipped Iraqis.

On February 24, the main coalition forces invaded Kuwait and south Iraq.

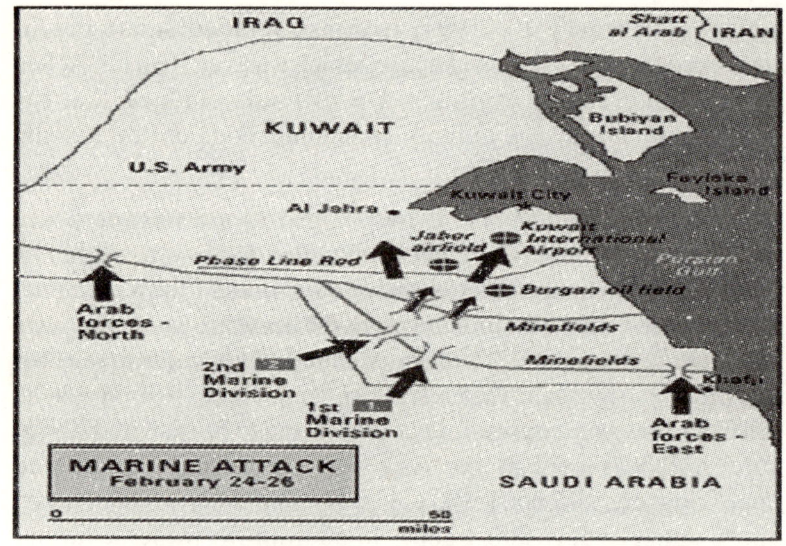

Map 6.4.: Map of Persian Gulf War's Ground Campaign•

•Source: PBS Channel

On February 25, the Scud missiles used by Iraq generally caused fairly light damage, although their potency was felt as 28 US soldiers were killed when a Scud destroyed their barracks in Dhahran.

By February 26, USA and Allied Arab forces, along with the underground Kuwaiti Resistance, controlled Kuwait City and Allied air forces pounded the retreating Iraqi occupation army. In southern Iraq, Allied armoured forces stood at the Euphrates River near Basra, and internal rebellions began to break out against Saddam's regime.

On February 27, President Bush ordered a ceasefire and the surviving Iraqi troops were allowed to escape back into southern Iraq.

On February 28, when US President George H. W. Bush declared a ceasefire; most of the Iraqi forces in Kuwait had either surrendered or fled.

3.3.3. March 1991

On March 3, 1991, Iraq accepted the terms of the ceasefire and the fighting ended. Although, the war was a decisive military victory for the coalition, Kuwait and Iraq suffered enormous property damage, and Saddam Hussein was not removed from power. In fact, Hussein was free to turn his attention to suppressing internal Shiite and Kurd revolts, which the US-led coalition did not support, in part, because of concerns over the possible breakup of Iraq if the revolts were successful. Coalition peace terms were agreed to by Iraq, but every effort was made by the Iraqis to frustrate implementation of the terms, particularly UN weapons inspections.

As a result of the ceasefire terms, Iraq had to accept the imposition of 'no-fly zones' over her territory and United Nations weapons inspection teams sifting through her nuclear and other weapons programs.

In their co-written 1998 book, "A World Transformed"[39], Bush and Brent Scowcroft argued that such a course would have fractured the alliance and would have had many unnecessary political and human costs associated with it.

In 1992, the United States former Secretary of Defense, Dick Cheney, made the same point: "I would guess if we had gone in there, I would still have forces in Baghdad today. We'd be running the country. We would not have been able to get everybody out and bring everybody home. And the final point that I think needs to be made is this question of casualties. I don't think you could have done all of that without significant additional US casualties, and while everybody was tremendously impressed with the low cost of the (1991) conflict, for the 146 Americans who were killed in action and for their families, it wasn't a cheap war. And the question in my mind is how many additional American casualties is Saddam (Hussein) worth? And the answer is, not that damned many. So, I think we got it right, both when we decided to expel him from Kuwait."[40]

Saddam's second war of foreign conquest ended even worse than the first one. Iraq again stood defeated with the liberation of Kuwait.

3.4. Casualties of War

3.4.1. Combat Casualties

3.4.1.1. Allied Forces

The US Department of Defence reports that US forces suffered 148 battle-related deaths (35 to friendly fire), plus one pilot listed as MIA, Missing In Action (his remains were found and identified in August 2009). "A further 145 Americans died in non-combat accidents. The UK suffered 47 deaths (9 to friendly fire), France two and the Arab countries, not including Kuwait, suffered 37 deaths (18 Saudis, 10 Egyptians, 6 from the UAE, and 3 Syrians)."[41]

"In 2001, at least 605 Kuwaiti soldiers were still missing 10 years following their capture."[42]

"The number of coalition wounded in combat seems to have been 776, including 458 Americans."[43] About 30 percent of the 7,00,000 men and women who served in US forces during the Gulf War still suffer an array of serious symptoms whose causes are not fully understood.

3.4.1.2. Iraqi Forces

The exact number of Iraqi combat casualties is unknown, but known to be heavy. Immediate estimates said up to 1,00,000 Iraqis

** Chronology of the Persian Gulf War (1990-91) has been presented in Appendix D.

were killed. Some now estimate that Iraq sustained between 20,000 and 35,000 fatalities. "A report commissioned by the US Air Force, estimated 10,000-12,000 Iraqi combat deaths in the air campaign and as many as 10,000 casualties in the ground war."[44] "According to the Project on Defense Alternatives study, 3,664 Iraqi civilians and between 20,000 and 26,000 military personnel were killed in the conflict. 75,000 Iraqi soldiers were wounded in the fighting."[45]

3.4.2. Civilian Casualties

The Iraqi government claimed that 2,300 civilians died during the air campaign. Saddam Hussein's government gave high civilian casualty figures in order to draw support from the Islamic countries. The US claimed the Iraqi government fabricated numerous attacks on Iraqi holy sites in order to rally the Muslim community. One such instance had Iraqis reporting that coalition forces attacked the holy cities of Najaf and Karbala.

Within the first 24 hours of the war, more than 1,000 sorties were flown, many of them against targets in Baghdad. The city received heavy bombing due to being the seat of power for Saddam Hussein and the Iraqi forces' command and control. However, this also led to substantial civilian casualties. During the long bombing campaign prior to the ground war, many aerial attacks led to civilian casualties.

4. Iraq War; 2003 Onwards

4.1. Introduction

"Fighting an irregular war is an extremely difficult conversion for any regular army, even a superpower."[46]

The Iraq War of 2003 was a most important event affecting the world leadership of the United States and international relations in general in the first part of the 21st Century.

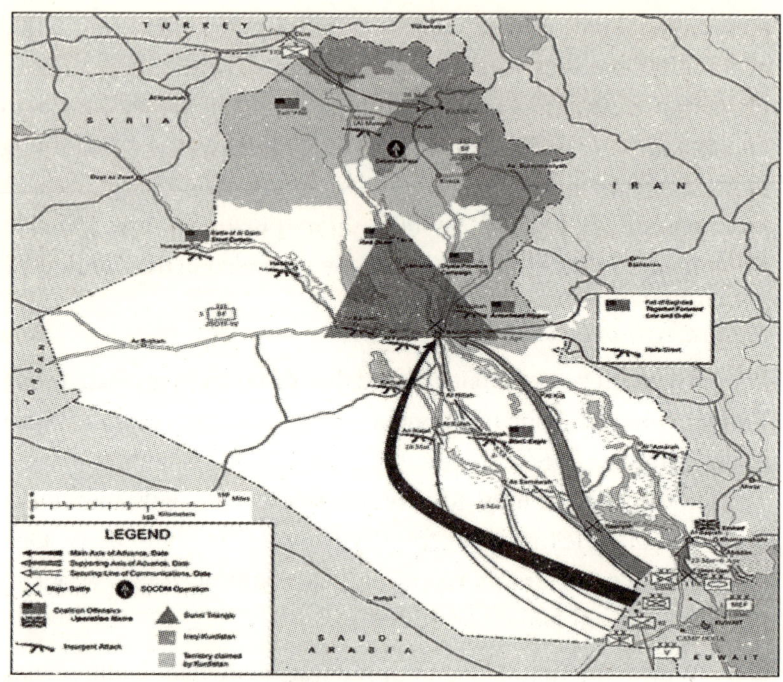

Map 6.5.: Map of Iraq War; 2003 Onwards•

•Source: Wikipedia

On March 19, 2003, American and British forces began the third Persian Gulf War, a conflict which may become popularly known as 'Gulf War 2' or the 'Second Iraq War', or 'Iraq War". The US government already calls this conflict Operation 'Iraqi Freedom.'

Regardless of what it is called, this conflict is by far the first truly major war of the 21st Century. While considered by many to be another part of the 'War on Terror', it is in many ways separate and unique in its own right.

In scope of preparation and potential consequences, the new war in Iraq by far overshadows the earlier invasion of Afghanistan. Former US president George W. Bush had openly threatened war for months prior to the US invasion. Bush argued that in the aftermath of the September 11 attacks, Saddam Hussein's regime posed a grave threat to US security and peace in the region because of its alleged pursuit of weapons of mass destruction and links to international terrorism.

The war was between the Iraqi military and a coalition of multinational forces. The United States and the United Kingdom were the two major components of the occupation that invaded and deposed Saddam Hussein's regime. This was done on claims which included Hussein had failed to comply with UN resolutions requiring a full accounting of its weapons of mass destruction and full cooperation with UN inspections. The forces opposing the coalition units were the conscript Iraqi Regular Army. They were reinforced and strengthened by the Republican Guard and Fedayeen Saddam.

The invasion led to a protracted US occupation of Iraq and the birth of a guerrilla insurgency against the occupation. The resulting destabilization of Iraq also created conditions for a civil war to break out between Iraq's majority Shiite Muslim population and its minority Sunni Muslim population. In addition to attempting to quell the insurgency, US forces was trying to police the civil war. By 2007, the US war in Iraq had lasted longer than US involvement in Second World War.

According to Global Security Organization, the military objectives of Operation 'Iraqi Freedom' consisted of:

1. Ending the regime of Saddam Hussein.
2. To identify, isolate and eliminate Iraq's weapons of mass destruction.
3. To search for, to capture and to drive out terrorists from the country.
4. To collect intelligence related to terrorist networks.
5. To collect such intelligence as is related to the global network of illicit weapons of mass destruction.
6. To secure Iraq's oil fields and resources, that belongs to the Iraqi people.

7. To help the Iraqi people create conditions for a transition to a representative self-government.

Allied military strategy in Iraq was based on several expectations. All along, the intent of coalition commanders had been to bypass most of the major cities in the south and focus on taking Baghdad, the seat of Hussein's power, where the regime appeared determined to make a final stand. Six of Hussein's elite Republican Guard divisions guarded the approaches to the city, while a division of the Special Republican Guards, among other security forces, protected its interior. Military planners expected that advancing forces would be met by grateful, cheering Iraqis, especially among the Shiite Muslims of the south, who had been long oppressed by the Hussein regime. In addition, coalition commanders also believed that Iraq would use chemical or biological weapons as US troops closed in on Baghdad. For this reason, US soldiers had received vaccinations against smallpox and anthrax before the war and donned protective suits as they advanced. None of these expectations proved accurate. Iraqi forces never used chemical or biological weapons during the fighting, and none were found in the months following the war.

4.2. Post 1991 War

The seeds for the US-Iraq War were sown by the 1991 Persian Gulf War, which took place during the administration of former US President George Herbert Walker Bush, George W. Bush's father. During the Persian Gulf War, allied forces evicted Iraqi troops from Kuwait, which Iraq invaded in 1990. After allied forces defeated the Iraqi army, armed rebellion against Hussein's rule broke out among the Shiite Muslims of the south, who had suffered years of oppression under Hussein's Sunni Muslim regime .The Bush administration had encouraged Iraqis to rebel in the hope that Hussein would be overthrown, but removing him from power was not an explicit objective of the allies. The administration was wary of involving itself in the fighting inside Iraq and was apprehensive about the consequences of a Shiite victory. It decided not to intervene. Lacking international aid, the rebellion was crushed by Hussein's remaining forces.

In 1993, the United States, France, and Britain launched several air and cruise-missile strikes against Iraq in response to provocations, including an alleged Iraqi plan to assassinate former US President George H. W. Bush.

An Iraqi troop build up near Kuwait in 1994 led the United States to send forces to Kuwait and nearby areas. Continued resistance to weapons inspections led to bombing raids against Iraq, and trade sanctions imposed on Iraq remained in place, albeit with an emphasis on military-related goods until the second Gulf conflict.

In 1997, some thinkers joined a Project for a New American Century (PNAC), a Washington think tank that argued openly for the United States to play a dominant role, militarily and diplomatically, in the world. The PNAC wrote a letter to President Clinton in January 1998 calling for 'the removal of Saddam Hussein's regime' from power and urging Clinton to use 'a full complement of diplomatic, political and military efforts to accomplish this. The letter warned that if Hussein acquired weapons of mass destruction, "the safety of American troops in the region, of USA friends and allies like Israel and the moderate Arab states, and a significant portion of the world's supply of oil will all be put at hazard."[47]

A month later, the same signatories joined a broader group of foreign policy and defence experts known as the 'Committee for Peace and Security in the Gulf' in another open letter to President Clinton advocated for the use of military force, including a call for a 'systematic air campaign' to destroy Iraq's Republican Guard divisions. These efforts helped lead to the Iraq Liberation Act, passed by Congress and signed by Clinton in 1998, which made regime change in Iraq official US policy.

4.3. United Nations' Sanctions against Iraq

Saddam had a record of violent aggression, externally against Iran, Kuwait and Israel, internally against Kurds and Shiite Muslims. This history had led, after the 1991 Gulf War, to an ongoing conflict between the UN Security Council (in which the USA and the UK were the main protagonists) and Iraq.

The conflict led the UN to continue economic sanctions, which combined with Saddam's policies led to terrible impoverishment. "In 2001-2, many believed that inspections, military action and sanctions had worked."[48]

As part of the ceasefire arrangements after the Persian Gulf War, the United Nations Security Council (UNSC) ordered Iraq to eliminate its programs to develop biological, chemical, and nuclear weapons. A system of UN inspections was established to oversee this process. Over the next decade, UN inspectors made important strides in disarming Iraq, but faced resistance from Iraqi authorities to their requests that all information about the destruction of stockpiles be made available. Iraq denied inspectors access to some sites within the country, and much of the information Iraq provided about its weapons programs was viewed as incomplete, inaccurate or misleading. Some inspectors believed that Iraq had destroyed 85 percent of its stockpiles, and in retrospect they were more nearly correct, but others remained suspicious that Iraq was hoarding biological and chemical weapons or capabilities.

Frustrated by Iraq's apparent refusal to cooperate, former US president, Bill Clinton, ordered a series of air strikes in 1998 aimed at destroying Iraq's weapons-making capability; called 'Operation Desert Fox'. Following this, Iraqi forces significantly increased attempts to challenge the Allied planes patrolling the No-Fly Zones, thereby also causing an increase in the Allied bombing of Iraqi targets. UN weapons inspectors were withdrawn shortly before the United States and Britain carried out three days of air attacks. Following the air strikes, Iraq resisted the resumption of UN inspections. No inspections were conducted for four years, a development that led to considerable uncertainty in Washington about the status of Iraq's weapons programs.

The United Nations Security Council passed nearly 60 resolutions on Iraq and Kuwait since Iraq's invasion of Kuwait in 1990. "Resolution 1441, in November 2002, was most prominent during the run up to the war and formed the main backdrop for US Secretary of State Colin Powell's address to the Security Council one month before the invasion."[49] At the same time, Bush Administration officials advanced a parallel legal argument using the earlier resolutions, which authorized force in response to Iraq's 1991 invasion of Kuwait. Under this reasoning, by failing to disarm and submit to weapons inspections, Iraq was in violation of UN Security Council Resolutions 660 and 678, and the US could legally compel Iraq's compliance through military means.

4.4. Events of 2001

Subsequent disclosures by former high-level officials within the Bush administration revealed that Bush had been preparing for the use of military force against Iraq almost as soon as he took office in January 2001. For example, Paul O'Neill, the administration's former treasury secretary, has said that planning for war with Iraq began almost as soon as Bush took office. Bush's former head of counterterrorism, Richard Clarke, later wrote that immediately after the September 11, 2001 terrorist attacks, Bush approached him with a demand to learn if Iraq could be linked to the attacks. And on the day of the attacks Cheney, Rumsfeld, and "Wolfowitz"[50] all raised the question of whether to attack Iraq, not just Osama bin Laden's al-Qaeda, with Rumsfeld calling it 'an opportunity', according to an account by Washington Post journalist Bob Woodward.

The election of George W. Bush to the US presidency returned to government many officials from his father's administration who had favoured removing Saddam Hussein from power in the first war. After the September 11, 2001 attacks on the World Trade Centre and Pentagon, the United States moved toward a doctrine of first-strike, pre-emptive war to eliminate threats to national security.

As early as October 2001, US Defence Secretary; Rumsfeld, publicly suggested that military action against Iraq was possible, and in November President Bush asked Rumsfeld to undertake a war-plan review.

4.5. Events of 2002

In January 2002, President Bush accused Iraq, along with North Korea and Iran, as being part of 'an axis of evil' and with the Taliban forced from power in Afghanistan, the administration's attention turned to Iraq. All three nations, Bush said, were threatening global security. The Bush administration viewed Iraq as a rogue state and Hussein as a regional troublemaker in the volatile Middle East.

Accusing Iraq of failing to abide by the terms of the 1991 ceasefire (by developing and possessing weapons of mass destruction and by refusing to cooperate with UN weapons inspections) and of supporting terrorism, the president and other officials suggested that the 'war on terrorism' might be expanded to include Iraq and became more forceful in their denunciations of Iraq for resisting UN arms inspections, called for 'regime change' in Iraq, and leaked news of military planning for war. President Bush also called on the United Nations to act forcefully against Iraq or risk becoming 'irrelevant'.

Iraq announced in September 2002 that UN inspectors could return, but, Iraqi slowness to agree on inspection terms and US insistence on stricter conditions for Iraqi compliance stalled the inspectors' return.

In October, US Congress approved the use of force against Iraq, and in November, the Security Council passed a resolution offering Iraq a 'final opportunity' to cooperate on arms inspections. A strict inspections timetable was established, and active Iraqi compliance insisted on. Inspections resumed in late November.

In December 2002, a declaration by Iraq that it had no weapons of mass destruction was generally regarded as incomplete and uninformative, but by January 2003, UN inspectors had found no evidence of forbidden weapons programs. However, they also indicated that Iraq was not actively cooperating with their efforts to determine if previously known or suspected weapons had been destroyed and weapons programs had been ended.

Despite much international opposition, including increasingly rancorous objections from France, Germany, and Russia, the United States and Britain continued their military build-up in areas near Iraq insisting that Iraq was hiding weapons of mass destruction. Turkey, which the allies hoped to use as a base for a northern front in Iraq, refused to allow use of its territory.

4.6. Events of 2003

4.6.1. March 2003; Beginning of the Operation Iraqi Freedom

After failing to win the explicit UN Security Council approval desired by Britain (because Britons were otherwise largely opposed to war), President Bush issued an ultimatum to Iraqi president Hussein on March 17, 2003.

The military plan for Operation Iraqi Freedom differed from that for the 1991 Persian Gulf War. Unlike the Persian Gulf War, coalition military commanders did not plan for a long bombing campaign prior to introducing ground forces. The plan was for the air campaign and a ground attack to begin nearly simultaneously. In the 2003 war, the United States also used a far smaller ground force than it used in 1991.

On March 17, in a nationally televised speech, Bush said, "Intelligence gathered by this and other governments leaves no doubt that the Iraq government continues to possess and conceal some of the most lethal weapons ever devised."[51] But "in March 7, Hans Blix, head of the UN Monitoring, Verification and Inspection Commission (UNMOVIC), indicated that he believed the inspectors should have been given more time to investigate Iraq's weapons programs."[52]

Bush gave Saddam Hussein and his immediate family 48 hours to leave the country or face a military attack. It was later disclosed that Hussein had offered to leave Iraq and go into exile but under conditions that were not acceptable to the Bush administration.

On March 19, the United States conducted an air strike in an attempt to kill Hussein. It involved an attack on the Dora Farms area of Baghdad where Hussein was believed to be holding a meeting in a bunker. After the war, the US military determined that there was no bunker at this location. A number of civilian casualties resulted from this attack.

After the bombing attack on March 19, which was intended to kill Hussein, Iraqi forces responded by firing surface-to-surface missiles at US bases in Kuwait. Iraqis also set fire to a small number of oil wells in the Ar-Rumaylah oil field in south-eastern Iraq. Coalition officials were concerned that Iraq might set the entire oil field ablaze. As a result, plans for the allied ground invasion were advanced one day and took place on March 20 before the main air assault, which came a day later.

The war began on March 20. The invasion of Iraq, dubbed Operation Iraqi Freedom by the White House, was led by General Tommy Franks, then head of the US Central Command. On the night of March 21, as coalition forces streamed into southern Iraq, the United States unleashed air strikes against Baghdad.

The air attack, referred to as a 'shock and awe' campaign, was intended to provoke an Iraqi surrender early in the conflict. Bombs destroyed key targets in the capital, but the bombardment failed to lead to the collapse of the Hussein regime.

On March 21, US Special Operations Forces seized two airfields in western Iraq in an effort to prevent the Iraqis from attacking Israel with Scud missiles, as they had done during the Persian Gulf War. The Bush administration feared that if Israel entered the war, it would be more difficult to maintain the quiet support of some Arab and Muslim nations.

According to the former President of the United States, George W. Bush, and former Prime Minister of the United Kingdom, Tony Blair, the reasons for the invasion were "to disarm Iraq of weapons of mass destruction (WMD), to end Saddam Hussein's support for terrorism and to free the Iraqi people."[53]

The Hussein regime sought to block the coalition advance by ordering paramilitary-style attacks using fighters based in An-Nasiriyah, An-Najaf and other southern towns. These irregular troops, in fact, played a more important role in Iraq's strategy than did the Republican Guard. The paramilitary's presence in the south, combined with the memory of the US failure to support the 1991 Shiite rebellion, discouraged the population there from welcoming coalition forces and rising up against Hussein.

The unexpected Iraqi strategy led to a change of tactics on the coalition side. The coalition decided that it needed to defeat the paramilitary forces in and around the southern cities before taking Baghdad. This delayed for several days the push toward Baghdad, but military officials said the step was necessary to protect the coalition's lengthening supply lines.

On March 26, more than 1,000 American soldiers from the Army's 173rd Airborne Brigade parachuted into northern Iraq. They quickly secured an airfield about 300 km north of Baghdad. Controlling the airfield allowed the United States to use air transport to deploy tanks and other fighting vehicles in the area. The main aim was to stabilize the region and discourage ethnic violence and Turkish intervention. But the forces were also able to open a second northern front.

4.6.2. April 2003; Fall of Baghdad

In early April, the US force with its supply lines secured, moved in on Baghdad. On April 4, Army forces seized Saddam

International Airport, west of the city, and renamed it Baghdad International Airport.

On April 5, a battalion from the second Brigade of the 3rd Infantry Division drove through Baghdad in a raid. More than 1,000 Iraqis were reported killed during the operation, according to a US estimate.

On April 7, the second Brigade attacked into central Baghdad. The same day, US B-1 bombers dropped four 900-kg bombs on a building in western Baghdad where Hussein was believed to be hiding. Local residents later reported that neither Hussein nor his family were present at the time of the attack, which levelled the building and reportedly killed 14 civilians. Nevertheless, Hussein's grip on power was gone.

US Marines arrived in Baghdad on April 9, and helped Iraqi civilians tear down a massive statue of Saddam Hussein that towered over a major city square. Within a few days Marines captured Tikrit, a city north of Baghdad and Hussein's ancestral home, with little struggle. With the fall of government control, came widespread looting in many cities; particularly Baghdad.

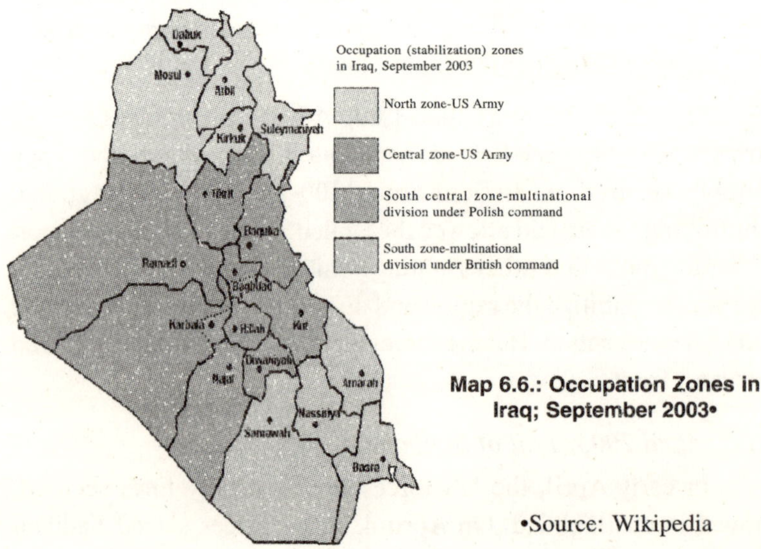

Map 6.6.: Occupation Zones in Iraq; September 2003•

•Source: Wikipedia

Overstretched US forces were unable to stop the looting, undermining two key aspects of US strategy:

1. First, while most Iraqis were glad to see Hussein deposed, the disorder and lack of services undermined popular support for US intervention.
2. Second, the United States had limited its air strikes to avoid extensive damage to Iraq's electrical system and other infrastructures that would be needed for Iraq's recovery. But in the increasing chaos, many important infrastructures and related government offices were looted or destroyed. Iraqi saboteurs, presumably loyalists of Hussein's Baath Party, also attacked power plants, oil pipelines, and bridges.

On April 10, encountering very little resistance, Kurdish fighters and a small number of US Special Operations Forces took control of the northern city of Kirkuk. Iraqi army units retreated in the face of the coalition advance after confronting an uprising among the city's Kurds. Kurdish and USA forces continued to advance rapidly, taking Mosul, the largest city of the north, on April 11. In the absence of local government or police forces, Mosul descended into chaos, with rampant looting and violence.

In December 2003, US forces captured Saddam Hussein in a night-time's raid on a farmhouse near Tikrit. Hiding in a small underground chamber, the deposed leader was apprehended without a fight. Members of the Iraqi Governing Council pledged to try Hussein for crimes against humanity in a public trial. In 2004, he was transferred to Iraqi legal custody; tried and convicted of crimes against humanity, and was executed in 2006.

As a result of the insurgency that followed the US conquest of Iraq, President Bush has subsequently declared that "a successful US-led pacification of the anti occupation resistance in Iraq would be an essential victory in the war on terror and that continued US military involvement in Iraq is necessary because we must recognize Iraq as the central front in our war on terror."[54]

Iraq War was supposed to be a short war, but it became protracted and expensive in both manpower and money. "Alliances were crumbling, and the most powerful nations, save the United Kingdom, rejected the war from its inception; plans for reforming the US military were in abeyance; and the goals and doctrines the Bush administration had when it took office and retained after September 11 were in tatters. Something went wrong for the United States, as it has for virtually every ambitious warring nation before it: there are countless, surprises."[55]

Even though declared by Bush on May 1, 2003, major combat ended, the escalating guerrilla war damaged American public, and even some of its allies' support for the war.

4.7. Events of 2004

The Sunni Arab regions of Iraq increasingly went into the hands of the guerrillas, a mixed assortment of ex-Baathists, nationalists, Sunni religious revivalists and tribal groupings.

In the western city of Fallujah on March 31, 2004, four private security guards; three Americans and one South African, were killed and their bodies desecrated.

The Bush administration ordered an assault on the city, but as word of heavy civilian casualties leaked out, public opinion in Iraq turned against the operation and members of the interim governing council threatened to resign. The Bush administration then backed off, attempting to reach a political settlement with the city's elites.

Also in early April 2004, US authorities decided to attempt to 'kill or capture' Muqtada al-Sadr, whose Shiite militia; the Mahdi Army, was viewed as an impediment to law and order, though it had not come into conflict with US troops. Al-Sadr eluded the Americans and ordered a general uprising. Mahdi Army militiamen took over most police stations in East Baghdad and in cities throughout the south, such as An-Najaf and An-Nasiriya. They expelled the Ukrainian troops from their base at Al-Kut and took it over. The US military lost control of much of Baghdad and its supply and communications lines to the south, as large-scale fighting broke out.

This conflict led to the deadliest month of the war to date for both sides. About 1,361 Iraqi civilians and 1,000 insurgents were killed, while 136 US troops died in April. Public opinion polls showed that a majority of Iraqis opposed the US occupation and wanted US troops to leave. Support declined further following the disclosure that US military and civilian personnel had abused some Iraqi prisoners by subjecting them to sexual humiliation and other acts of degradation. Public opinion polls in the United States also showed waning support for the war among Americans.

US former Secretary of State, Colin Powell, admitted in September 2004 that "we have seen an increase of anti-Americanism in the Muslim world,"[56] a point that Saudi Arabians, who have experienced growing extremism, made even more strongly the following month. The insurgency in Iraq was getting stronger; the Muslim world was being radicalized, and it became more anti-American than ever.

4.8. Events of 2005

In 2005, former US President, Bush, began to receive low approval ratings for his conduct of the war in Iraq. US military commanders kept about 1,40,000 US troops in Iraq through 2005. Facing growing public discontent with the war, the Bush administration said it planned to reduce US forces in 2006, but in the fall of 2006, US military commanders said a force of 1,40,000 would be required until 2010. Spain's decision to withdraw its 1300 troops after April 2004 was a harbinger of the departure of large numbers of small coalition units in 2005 such as Norway and Thailand. Other countries concluded that their original peacekeeping mission threatened to become more of a military mission. In December 2005, Bulgaria and Ukraine withdrew the last of their troops; about 1500 soldiers.

"In April 2005, the Central Intelligence Agency (CIA) released a report saying that no weapons of mass destruction had been found in Iraq."[57]

4.9. Events of 2006

In June 2006, Japan began withdrawing its force of about 600 soldiers, who were engaged in humanitarian and noncombatant duties. As US and British forces play the principal combat role in Iraq, the departure of smaller forces was believed to have more of a political than a military impact. In addition to the US force, Britain maintained a force of about 7,000 troops in Iraq in 2006, mainly around the city of al Basra.

In October 2006, British participation came into question when Britain's new Army Chief, General Sir Richard Dannatt, called for a withdrawal of British troops 'sometime soon' because, he said, "the presence of foreign troops was worsening the situation."[58] In what was regarded as an unusual critique of a foreign policy position by a military commander, Dannatt also said he believed the presence of British troops in Iraq affected domestic security within the United Kingdom.

Britain was not alone in having leading military figures question the ongoing occupation. October 2006 also saw a number of recently retired US generals make public statements against US strategy and policy in Iraq. The wartime dissents by such figures as Major General, Charles Swannack Jr., and Major General, John Batiste; both of whom had commanded combat troops in Iraq were regarded as unprecedented in US history.

Much of the criticism was directed at former US Defence Secretary, Rumsfeld, and his decision to ignore the original recommendation of the Joint Chiefs of Staff for an initial invasion force of about 4,00,000 troops.

But some of the criticism expressed opposition to the decision to invade. Marine Lieutenant General, Gregory Newbold, revealed that he had purposely retired prior to the war, which he called 'unnecessary', because of his opposition to "those who used 9/11's tragedy to hijack our security policy."[59]

Retired Lieutenant General William Odom called the Iraq war "the worst strategic mistake in the history of the United States."[60]

Rumsfeld announced his retirement. He was replaced by Robert M. Gates, a former CIA director and a member of the bipartisan Iraq Study Group. Gates was known as a protégé of former US National Security Adviser, Brent Scrowcroft, who had opposed the US invasion.

4.9.1. Iraq Study Group

In December 2006, the Iraq Study Group, which was created and funded by the US Congress in 2005 to provide an assessment of the war, released its much-awaited report. The report said that the situation in Iraq was 'grave and deteriorating'.

Headed by former US Secretary of State, James Baker, and former Congressman, Lee Hamilton, the Iraq Study Group found that the principal cause of instability was sectarian conflict and that the collapse of Iraq's government and a humanitarian catastrophe could result if stability was not restored. The report made 79 recommendations envisioning ways in which a national reconciliation could occur among Iraq's Kurds, Shiite and Sunni Muslims, paving the way for US combat forces to leave by early 2008 while retaining a smaller US force that would become embedded in the Iraqi Army.

The report also called for a comprehensive peace settlement throughout the Middle East involving Israel and its conflict with the Palestinians, Lebanon and Syria. The Study Group recommended that the United States should negotiate with Syria and Iran without preconditions with the goal of enlisting their aid to bring stability to Iraq.

Finally, the report warned that a failure to bring peace and stability to Iraq would result in a diminished international and regional standing for the United States and a propaganda victory for Al Qaeda, which it said was trying to instigate a wider sectarian war in Iraq.

4.10. Events of 2007

On January 10, 2007, in a nationally televised address, Bush largely rejected the recommendations of the Iraq Study Group and put forward many of the recommendations made in the report of the AEI; American Enterprise Institute for Public Policy Research. The report suggested a troop escalation and a renewed emphasis on reconstruction, economic development, and jobs. Bush called for an additional 21,500 soldiers to be deployed in Iraq, mostly in Baghdad to halt sectarian violence by both Sunni insurgents and Shiite militias. Most of the US troops were to be embedded with Iraqi army forces.

A smaller number of the new troops would go to Al Anbar province, where foreign and native fighters, some aligned with a group known variously as Al Qaeda in Iraq or Al Qaeda in Mesopotamia, were active. The group did not exist prior to the September 11 attacks, and some intelligence officials doubted whether it had organizational ties to Al Qaeda itself.

Bush accused Iran and Syria of allowing terrorists and insurgents to use their territory to move in and out of Iraq and he charged Iran with providing material support for attacks on American troops. He said, "We will disrupt the attacks on our forces. We will interrupt the flow of support from Iran and Syria. And we will seek out and destroy the networks providing advanced weaponry and training to our enemies in Iraq."[61]

Bush warned that he was ordering a second aircraft-carrier battle group and Patriot antimissile batteries to the Persian Gulf. During his speech, Bush acknowledged that mistakes had been made in Iraq and said that he took responsibility for them. Asked in interviews what mistakes had been made, Bush cited among other incidents the abuse at Abu Ghraib prison.

In a background briefing for reporters prior to his January 10 speech, Bush also mentioned an apparent massacre of 24 Iraqi civilians by US marines in Haditha in 2005.

Bush's decision to introduce more troops to Iraq, which he characterized as a "Surge Strategy"[62] not an escalation, met with opposition in Congress.

In September 2007, General David Petraeus, the commander of US forces in Iraq, and Ryan Crocker, the US ambassador to Iraq, gave the first formal presentation on the administration's progress since the surge began. In his testimony, Petraeus asserted that the surge was successfully reducing the level of violence in Iraq. He said that "the 30,000 troops added to US forces by the surge, bringing it to a peak level of 1,69,000, would no longer be needed by July 2008."[63] However, he cautioned that about 1,30,000 remaining US troops would need an indefinite amount of time to help stabilize Iraq and that it would be premature to discuss further withdrawals. Petraeus said he foresaw a long-term need for the presence of US forces in Iraq.

In October 2007, another significant military voice cast doubt on the effectiveness of the surge strategy. Retired Lieutenant General Ricardo Sanchez, who headed US combat forces in Iraq from 2003 to 2004, called the US mission in Iraq "a nightmare with no end in sight."[64] Sanchez called the surge a desperate attempt to make up for failed US policies in Iraq. In November, Sanchez allied himself with Democratic legislation to withdraw most US troops from Iraq by the end of 2008.

Opponents of the war challenged Petraeus's assessment of the surge's success. They pointed to a nonpartisan report released just prior to Petraeus's testimony by the Government Accountability Office (GAO), an independent agency that advises Congress. The report maintained that the Iraqi government was failing to meet the chief political benchmarks needed for political reconciliation in Iraq and an end to sectarian fighting.

"Former US President Bush followed up Petraeus's testimony with a national TV address in which he called for an 'enduring' US relationship with Iraq that would require a US troop presence long after his presidency ended. Bush proposed a defence pact with Iraq along the lines of the defence treaties that have kept US forces in South Korea since the Korean War ended. Bush said a long-term US force was needed to prevent a victory by Al Qaeda and to counter Iran, thereby preventing extremists from gaining control of a key part of the global energy supply."[65]

In July 2007, Britain announced plans to begin withdrawing its remaining 5,500 troops from the centre of Al Basra to an airport headquarters outside the city. Britain also shifted some of its forces from Iraq to Afghanistan.

In December 2007, Britain handed over control of al Basra to Iraqi forces and withdrew its remaining 4,500 troops to its airport headquarters.

4.11. Events of 2008

As 2008 began, attention focused on the US presidential election year with the two major political parties taking nearly opposite positions on the Iraq war. The leading Democratic presidential candidates promised to begin phased withdrawals of US combat forces from Iraq if elected, while leaving some troops there indefinitely to help train the Iraqi military in counterinsurgency efforts. The leading Republican candidates supported the war, insisting that the war could still be won.

Many political commentators have questioned how the surge has shaped the 2008 presidential election. Although, the American economy had been considered to be the top issue in the election, Voice of America stated on February 28, 2008, that the war in Iraq had 'reemerged as a central issue'.

Republican candidate, John McCain, called for an increase in troops before the idea was brought before Congress, and backed Bush when he called for the troop surge. Some commentators have suggested that increased Republican support for the surge has been a boon for McCain, whose campaign had gone through a midsummer implosion and looked to be on its way out, but during the primaries emerged as the presumptive Republican presidential nominee. McCain stated that his prospects are tied to the success or failure of the surge.

Conversely, Democrat candidate; Barack Obama, opposed the surge in the beginning. Obama no longer stated that "the surge is not working."[66] He promised to begin taking US forces out if he is elected president. Senator Barack Obama called the war in Iraq a "dangerous distraction"[67] and said more emphasis must be placed on the battle in Afghanistan.

In June 2008, Australia ended its combat role in Iraq and withdrew its troops. Poland ended its involvement in October 2008, withdrawing its force of 900 troops. The same month the Czech Republic announced that it would be withdrawing its contingent of 100 troops who were being used mainly in coordination with British troops.

On August 22, while negotiating a security pact that will govern US involvement in Iraq, the United States said it will withdraw combat troops from Iraqi cities by June 2009, followed by the removal of all combat troops by the end of 2011 as long as Iraq being stable and secure.

On September 1, the US transferred to the Iraqi military and police responsibility for maintaining security in Anbar Province, which was the cradle of the Sunni insurgency.

On October 17, Iraq and the US completed a draft of a security agreement that called for all US troops to be withdrawn from Iraq by the end of 2011, depending on the conditions in Iraq. Plan also gave US military personnel immunity from Iraqi law except for serious premeditated felonies committed outside their duty status.

On October 31, General David Petraeus became the head of Central Command to oversee military operations in 20 countries spreading from Egypt to Pakistan including Operation Iraqi Freedom.

4.12. Events of 2009

During his presidential transition, President-elect Obama announced that he would retain the incumbent Defence Secretary, Robert Gates, in his Cabinet.

Early in his presidency, Mr. Obama moved to change US war strategy by increasing troop strength in Afghanistan and reducing troop levels in Iraq.

On February 27, Mr. Obama declared that combat operations would end in Iraq within 18 months. His remarks were made to a group of Marines preparing for deployment to Afghanistan. Obama said, "Let me say this as plainly as I can; by August 31, 2010, our combat mission in Iraq will end."[68]

On June 30, US troops formally handed over security duties to Iraqi forces and withdrew from towns and cities in Iraq. US troops continue to be embedded with Iraqi forces.

4.13. Casualties of War

4.13.1. Coalitions Casualties

While estimates on the number of casualties during the invasion in Iraq vary widely, the majority of deaths and injuries have occurred after former US President Bush declared the end of "major combat operations on May 1, 2003."[69]

According to CNN News Agency, the US government reported that 139 American military personnel were killed before May 1, 2003; of these, 115 died in combat while the rest died due to traffic accidents, drowning, illness or other causes "while over 4,000 have been killed since 2003."[70] However, coalition forces continued to suffer casualties after May 1, 2003, as an urban guerrilla resistance began to develop.

By late April 2003, a serious and persistent guerrilla struggle had been launched in the Sunni Arab heartland against the foreign military presence in the country. The total US military death toll had doubled by late August 2004 and reached more than 4,000 following the fifth anniversary of the invasion in 2008.

"At least 22,565 US troops have been wounded in action, according to the Pentagon."[71]

The year 2007 was the deadliest year for US forces since the war began, with 894 US soldiers killed in that year alone. The number of US troops wounded totalled about 30,000 by March 2008, the beginning of the sixth year of the US occupation. "As 2008 came to a close, the US death toll was more than 4,200 and the number of wounded was nearly 31,000."[72]

4.13.2. Iraqi Casualties

Tens of thousands, if not hundreds of thousands, of Iraqis have been killed in the war, although US military officials do not publicly keep a count of Iraqi military or insurgent or civilian casualties. Estimates on civilian casualties are more variable than those for military personnel. "In November 2006 Iraq's Health Minister, Ali Al Shemari, said that since the March 2003 invasion between 100,000 and 150,000 Iraqis have been killed."[73] Al Shemari based his figure on an estimate of 100 bodies per day brought to morgues and hospitals, such a calculation would come out closer to 130,000 in total.

The Lancet surveys of casualties of the Iraq War, conducted by researchers at Johns Hopkins University, estimates much higher civilian casualties, but does not differentiate between the invasion phase (March-May 2003) and the occupation phase (post May 2003). "The Lancet survey estimates that over 6,50,000 Iraqi civilians have died as a result of the conflict, with the vast majority of these deaths occurring after May 2003."[74] These studies were highly controversial at their time of publication, attracting considerable criticism from predominantly non-scientific sources. Both the US and the Iraqi governments disputed the Lancet study, but the researchers based at Johns Hopkins University defended their results. They said the study was based on a widely accepted scientific method known as Cluster Sampling and that a majority of the deaths in the sample were substantiated by death certificates.

According to Iraq Body Count, a group that relies on Western press reports to measure civilian casualties, approximately 7,500 civilians were killed during the invasion phase, "while more than 60,000 civilians have been killed as of April 2007."[75]

A September 14, 2007 estimate by ORB (Opinion Research Business); an independent British polling agency, suggests that the total Iraqi violent death toll due to the Iraq War since the US-led invasion is in excess of 1.2 million (1,220,580). "Although higher than the 2006 Lancet estimate, this result, which were based on a survey of 1499 adults in Iraq from August 12-19, 2007, is more or less consistent with the figures that were published in the Lancet study."[76]

In January 2008, researchers with the World Health Organization and the Iraqi Ministry of Health, in a study published in the New England Journal of Medicine estimated that 1,51,000 Iraqis; both civilians and fighters, died violently from March 2003 to June 2006. The study was reportedly the largest to date because it was based on a survey of 10,000 Iraqi households.

On January 28, 2008, Opinion Research Business (ORB) published an update based on additional work carried out in rural areas of Iraq. "Some 600 additional interviews were undertaken and as a result of this the death, estimate was revised to 10,33,000 with a given range of 9,46,000 to 11,20,000."[77]

4.13.2.1. Iraqi Refugees

The war also led to a refugee crisis in Iraq. By the end of 2007, the Office of the United Nations High Commissioner for Refugees estimated that 2.3 million Iraqis had fled their country and another 2 million had been displaced from their homes within Iraq "with nearly 1,00,000 Iraqis fleeing to Syria and Jordan each month."[78]

Roughly 40% of Iraq's middle class is believed to have fled, the UN said. Most are fleeing due to systematic persecution and have no desire to return. All kinds of people, from university professors to bakers, have been targeted by militias, insurgents and criminals. An estimated 331 school teachers were slain in the first four months of 2006, according to Human Rights Watch report in 2006, and at least 2,000 Iraqi doctors have been killed and 250 kidnapped since the 2003 US invasion.

4.14. Criticism of War

According to some opinion polls, the war was unpopular from the outset in many occupation countries; including the largest worldwide protest in human history, a day of Global Protests against War on Iraq on February 15, 2003.

The Iraq War was widely viewed by many critics as counterproductive. Many viewed the war as improper (being a moral and ethical violation) and, at the extreme, illegal under international law. By the summer of 2005, there was an increase in the number of individuals in the United States that felt the same way. Opponents of military action against Iraq challenged the Bush administration's case. They argued that an invasion to overthrow Hussein would pull resources away from the US campaign against terrorist groups such as al-Qaeda and the war in Afghanistan.

Generally, the criticism of war could be classified as follows:

1. No evidence of weapons of mass destruction was found.
2. No evidence linking Iraq to Al Qaeda or the September 11, 2001 attacks was found. In September 2006, the US Senate Intelligence Committee led by Republican senator, Pat Roberts of Kansas, concluded that there was no evidence linking the Iraqi government to Al Qaeda or the September 11 attacks. In March 2008, the US Department of Defence released a study that concluded there was no direct connection between the Saddam Hussein regime and al-Qaeda. "The study was based on an analysis of 6,00,000 Iraqi government documents seized by US forces after the invasion and the

interrogations of former top officials in Hussein's government."[79]

3. Post-war planning was inadequate. In the absence of a clear plan of action for creating a democratic and sovereign Iraq, the insurgency grew.
4. The war has tarnished the reputation of the United States in Muslim countries.
5. The war has endangered United States' national security by bringing Al Qaeda elements into Iraq and establishing a network of terrorists where none existed before the American invasion.
6. Civilian infrastructure has been destroyed including water, sewage and electricity as a result of the invasion; much of which has never been repaired.
7. There have been heavy civilian casualties. Critics have cited that the human cost is simply too great and thus it should instead make diplomatic concessions to radical Islamists in lieu of military confrontation.
8. Critics have cited that, economically, the various engagements in Iraq have cost the United States about US$ 4,000,000,000 per month. Critics of the present war can make the tactical argument that it is wiser to fight Al Qaeda in Pakistan than in Iraq. Or that money spent in the frontline Iraqi offensive theatre would be better invested on defence and security of the United States of America.

** Chronology of the war has been presented in Appendix E.

References

1. Pax Britannica is a multiplayer game of empire, diplomacy, and global confrontation set in the Victorian era. The Great Powers — Great Britain, France, Germany, Italy, Russia, Japan, and the United States — vie throughout the world for the wealth and esteem conferred by vast colonial holdings in the far-flung corners of the earth.
2. Shuster Mike, "*Export of Iran's Revolution Spawns Violence*", National Public Radio, USA, February 14, 2007, www.npr.org

3. Global Security, www.globalsecurity.org/ Iraq-Iran War
4. Military History Encyclopedia On The Web; www.historyofwar.org /Iran Iraq War
5. www.angelfire.com/ Iraq-Iran War
6. Global Security, www.globalsecurity.org / Iraq-Iran War
7. www.angelfire.com /Iraq-Iran War
8. Ibid.
9. Scud is a series of tactical ballistic missiles developed by the Soviet Union during the Cold War and exported widely to other countries.
10. Surface to Surface Missiles
11. Global Security, www, globalsecurity.org/ Iran-Iraq War
12. "*Iran–Iraq War: Diplomacy and International Involvement*" , MSN Encarta Encyclopedia
13. www.angelfire.com, Iraq-Iran War
14. Global Security, www.globalsecurity.org, Iraq-Iran War
15. Center for Documents of The Imposed War; Tehran, Iran
16. Fassihi Farnaz , "*In Iran, grim reminders of Saddam's arsenal*", New Jersey Star-Ledger, October 27, 2002
17. Coddy Eric and Wirtz James J. and Larsen Jeffery A., " *Weapons of Mass Destruction: An Encyclopedia of Worldwide Policy, Technology and History*", ABC-CLIO, USA, 2004, p.165
18. Rajaee, Farhang, "*The Iran–Iraq War: The Politics of Aggression*", University Press of Florida, USA, 2001, p.33
19. Military History Encyclopedia On The Web; www.historyofwar.org
20. www.srilankadot.com/ Iran-Iraq War
21. Potter Lawrence, "*Iran, Iraq, and the legacies of war*", MacMillan, USA, 2004, p. 153
22. Rasheed Ahmed, "*Saddam admits Iran's gas attacks*", The Australian, December 19, 2006
23. Military History Encyclopedia On The Web; www.historyofwar.org
24. No 18, p.235
25. Global Security, www.globalsecurity.org
26. Military History Encyclopedia On The Web; www.historyofwar.org
27. www.Iranian.ws/ Iraq-Iran War
28. Borer Douglas A., "*Inverse Engagement: Lessons from U.S.-Iraq Relations, 1982–1990*", US Army Professional Writing Collection. US Army, 2003

29. "*15 Years After Desert Storm, US Commitment to Region Continues*", February 22, 2006, www.defenselink.mil/news
30. *"The Unfinished War: A Decade Since Desert Storm"*, CNN In-Depth Specials, January 15, 2001
31. www.washingtonpost.com/wp-dyn/content/article/2006
32. No. 30
33. *"Iraqi Air Force Equipment — Introduction"*, www.globalsecurity.org/military/world/iraq/air-force- equipment- intro
34. Freedman Lawrence, Karsh Efraim, "*The Gulf Conflict: Diplomacy and War in the New World Order 1990-1991*", Princeton, USA, 1993, p. 331
35. http://www.globalsecurity.org/military/ops/desert_sabre
36. The Global Positioning System (GPS) is a global navigation satellite system.
37. Fisk Robert, "*The Great War for Civilization*", Vintage, UK, 2007 reprint, p. 646
38. A no-fly zone is a territory over which aircraft are not permitted to fly. Such zones are usually set up in a military context, somewhat like a demilitarized zone in the sky. In 1992, The United Kingdom and the United States intervened in Kurdish-Iraqi dispute in northern Iraq by establishing a no -fly zone in which Iraqi aircraft were prevented from flying. The intent of the no-fly zone was to prevent possible bombing and chemical attacks against the Kurdish people by the Iraqi regime.
39. "*A World Transformed*" is a 1998 book (*ISBN 0-679-43248-5*) by former President George H. W. Bush and Brent Scowcroft, Bush's National Security Advisor, documenting foreign relations during the Bush administration.
40. Pope Charles, "*Cheney changed his view on Iraq*", Seattle Post-Intelligencer, September 29, 2004
41. No. 30
42. Blanford Nicholas, "*Kuwait hopes for answers on its Gulf War POWs*", Christian Science Monitor, 2001
43. MSN Encarta/ Persian Gulf War
44. Thomas Keaney, Cohen Eliot. A, "*Gulf War Air Power Survey*", United States Department of Air Force, 1993
45. Conetta Carl, " *Wages of War*", Project on Defense Alternative; Appendix 2, October 20, 2003

46. Major General Webster William G.; Commander of Task Force Baghdad, November 2005 (AFJ, Armed Forces Journal), www.armedforcesjournal.com
47. Encarta Encyclopedia/ Iraq War 2003
48. Shaw Martin, "*The New Western Way of War*" , Polity Press, UK, 2005,p.35
49. "*Transcript of Powell's UN Presentation*", CNN News Agency, February 6, 2003
50. US Deputy Secretary of Defense in 2001
51. "*Bush gave Saddam Hussein and his sons 48 hours to leave Iraq*", Global Policy Forum, March 18, 2003
52. Transcript of Blix's UN presentation, CNN News Agency, March 7, 2003
53. "President Discusses Beginning of Operation Iraqi Freedom", www.whitehouse.gov, March 22, 2003
54. Former US President Bush, a nationally televised address, September 2003
55. Kolko, Gabriel, "*The Age of War; Things Go Wrong*", Lynne Rienner Inc., USA , 2007, p.161
56. Ibid.p.155
57. *CIA's final report: No WMD found in Iraq - Conflict in Iraq*, Msnbc.msn.com. April 25, 2005
58. *"Army Chief Says British Troops Should Be Pulled Out of Iraq."* The Independent, UK, October 13, 2006
59. *"Why Iraq Was a Mistake"*, Times, April 9, 2006
60. "*Despair not an Option in Iraq War"*, CNN, October 17, 2006
61. "President's Address to the Nation", USA Office of the Press Secretary, January 10, 2007
62. In the context of the Iraq War, the surge commonly refers to United States President George W. Bush's 2007 plan to increase the number of American troops in order to provide security to Baghdad and Al Anbar Province.
63. "*General Petraeus's Testimony to Congress"*, defenselink.mil, September 10, 2007
64. BBC News Agency, October 13, 2007
65. "*Bush to Endorse Petraeus Plan"*, Washington Post, September 12, 2007

66. "*Iraq War*", New York Daily News, July 14, 2008
67. CNN, July 15, 2008
68. Guardian News, February 27, 2009
69. "*Getting amputees back on their feet*", Washington Post, October 25, 2005
70. Ibid
71. Pentagon's Report on Iraq War Casualties, page 5 , December 2006
72. Encarta Encyclopedia
73. *"Iraqi health minister estimates as many as 1,50,000 Iraqis killed by insurgents"*, ww.iht.com, November 9, 2006
74. Parsons, Tim, *"Updated Iraq Study Affirms Earlier Mortality Estimates"*., The JHU Gazette, October 16, 2006
75. *"Iraq Body Count: A Dossier of Civilian Casualties in Iraq, 2003 – 2005"*, CNN News Agency, May 2nd, 2007, www.iraqbodycount.org
76. *"More than 1,000,000 Iraqis murdered"*, Opinion Research Business, September 2007, Susman Tina, *"Poll: Civilian Death Toll in Iraq May Top 1 Million"*, Los Angeles Times, September 14, 2007
77. "*Update on Iraqi Casualty Data*", Opinion Research Business, January 2008
78. Higgins Alexander G., "*U.N.: 100,000 Iraq refugees flee monthly*", Boston Globe, November 3, 2006
79. "*US Department of Defense' Study on Iraq War*", White House official site, March 2008

7

Role of USA in the Persian Gulf Region

1. Introduction

Prior to 1971, the responsibility for the region's security fell with the British, with the United States maintaining a supportive role. However on January 18, 1968, British Prime Minister, Harold Wilson, announced to the House of Commons that the British had decided to withdraw their forces from the Persian Gulf by the end of 1971. That action set the stage for America's future involvement in the Persian Gulf.

The British generally represented United States' interests and created and fostered conditions of calm and stability. The British role in the Gulf coincided with a period in which the United States did not take a major position in the political/security affairs of the sector and focused its activities in unofficial, non-political and nonstrategic spheres that might best be described as philanthropic, missionary, humanitarian, educational, cultural, and commercial in nature.

As the world's pre-eminent economy and military power, the US has always had a vital interest in helping to create the internal conditions that will be necessary for the Persian Gulf Suppliers to increase their oil production to meet global demand.

The policies and priorities developed in response to these interests and concerns have varied with each administration. There has been a desire to ensure the maintenance of open sea lanes for transporting the oil and the development of political and economic cooperation with the Arab world. The US has also sought to limit regional conflicts (such as the Iran-Iraq war) that might affect other interests.

Before Iraq's invasion of Kuwait in 1990, the United States was already regarded as a main defender of the Persian Gulf region but had little physical or institutional involvement in defence schemes. Until 1990, the United States stuck to the British approach of maintaining a low-cost security system by relying on regional allies and a naval presence. After the Gulf War, this approach was replaced by one involving extensive forward basing and regular military engagements, sometimes escalating into large-scale deployments.

Former USA President Clinton's Defense Secretary, William Perry, said to the Council on Foreign Relations on May 18, 1995, that: "*Roosevelt* was the first US president to declare that the United States has vital interests in the region."[1]

The importance of the Persian Gulf to US strategic interests is beyond question. While the United States draws only a small portion of its oil from the Gulf, other regions; including Europe and Asia, are more heavily dependent.

Several overriding factors have dominated the United States' approach to the Persian Gulf since Second World War. The interests of the United States in the Persian Gulf region have been very simple and consistent:

1. First, to ensure access by the industrialized world, including itself, to the vast resources of the region.

Oil has remained an element of United States' strategic/political concern in the region, and as United States oil dependency grows, so does the significance of the Persian Gulf. The United States has had a gradual increase in oil and energy consumption in recent years and with it have come increases in net oil imports. Because of declining American reserves and production, as well as a price that has not been sufficiently high to promote alternative energy sources and development of new oil finds in the United States, there is a growing need to import oil from abroad. The increasing dependence on imported oil necessarily links the United States to a growing need for other regions, especially the Persian Gulf region's oil since this is where most of the world's oil reserves, excess production capacity and available oil for export are located.

2. Second, to prevent its rivals from acquiring political and military control over those resources.

Despite Perestroika; the political and economic reforms introduced in June 1987 by the *Soviet* leader, *Mikhail Gorbachev*, and Glasnost; the policy of maximal publicity, openness, and transparency in the activities of all government institutions in the *Soviet Union*, together with freedom of information, introduced by *Mikhail Gorbachev* in the second half of 1980s, the USA had been concerned about Soviet diplomatic advances in the region. The Soviet Union had maintained its embassies in four of the six Gulf Cooperation Council countries: Kuwait, Oman, Qatar, and the United Arab Emirates and there had been growing contacts with Saudi Arabia despite the absence of formal diplomatic links during 1980s. While increasing its diplomatic relationships with the moderate Arab states, Moscow continued to maintain a military presence and influence in Ethiopia, Libya, Iraq, Syria, South and North Yemen. In June 1989, the Soviet Union formalized its developing relationship with Iran during the Moscow visit of former President of Iran, Ali Akbar

Rafsanjani. During Rafsanjani's visit, formal economic and military agreements were signed between the two countries. The military agreement was undertaken by the Soviet Union with "the explicit understanding that this will not injure the security of third countries nor make for a change in the power balance in the region."[2]

As Professor Sokolsky, Policy Advisor at US Department of State, has discussed in his book; The United States and Persian Gulf, "the involvement of outside powers in the Gulf scene creates two sets of problems for US regional security strategy.

First, it opens up opportunities for regional states to balance American influence by appealing to European countries, Russia or China. Indeed, in many cases, the external great powers may be just as dissatisfied with the regional status quo as the regional rogues are themselves. Any of regional states might find support and encouragement for its efforts to overturn the status quo from great powers looking to remake the Gulf political order more to its liking. In short, adding more players to the Gulf mix could easily encourage the more adventurous tendencies of Gulf rogues.

Second, and potentially of much greater significance, some of these great powers could furnish Gulf States with highly sophisticated weaponry."[3]

3. Preserving the stability and independence of the Gulf States and containing the threat of Islamic fundamentalism are other interests that have been expressed by American leaders from time to time.

   21st century started with the United States preserving stability in the Persian Gulf via an extensive forward military presence. The US build-up is also a reflection of the fact that efforts to create a security system that did not require a major presence had failed. At the same time, given the practical and political difficulty of building a forward presence large enough to meet worst-case military needs, the United States has also increased investment in its ability to launch massive expeditionary operations.

2. USA Policy on the Persian Gulf Region

As has been mentioned in the introduction section of this chapter, the visible and direct role of USA in the Persian Gulf region started from the time of withdrawal of the British from the region.

Although American President, Roosevelt, was the first American president which declared USA's vital interest in the region, but Great Britain's withdrawal of military forces from east of Suez, Iran's revolutionary excesses and the Soviet Union's maritime penetration of the Indian Ocean and invasion of Afghanistan during the 1970s and 1980s prompted the USA's administrations' policies in the region. American policy on the Persian Gulf has been progressively expanded by three presidential administrations; Nixon, Carter and Reagan and became an important part of the succeeding administrations.

In this section, the policy of USA administrations is discussed. As the withdrawal of the British forces and strongest presence of the USA happened in the term of President Nixon, this section has been started with explaining his administration's policy on the region.

2.1. President Richard Nixon (Republican); 1969-1974

Significant events in Persian Gulf region in this period could be classified as follows:

1. British Withdrawal from the Persian Gulf
2. Concern over Regional Balance of Power
3. The USA's 'Twin Pillar' Policy on the region

Under the guidelines of the Nixon Doctrine, Assistant Secretary of State for Near Eastern and South Asian Affairs, Joseph Sisco, stated before Congress in August 1972, that "US interests and policies toward the Persian Gulf region were the following:

1. Supporting orderly political development and regional cooperation to assure the tranquility of the area,
2. Supporting local governments in maintaining their independence and ensuring peace, progress, and regional cooperation without USA interfering in the domestic affairs of the friendly countries,
3. Encouraging Iran, Saudi Arabia, Kuwait and the smaller states to cooperate wholeheartedly with one another to assure that the region remains secure,
4. Assisting in the modernization of the armed forces of Iran and Saudi Arabia to enable them to provide effectively for their own security and to foster the security of the region as a whole,
5. Extending Washington's diplomatic presence in the area,
6. Continuing to maintain a small naval contingent at Bahrain, this has for a quarter of a century carried out the mission of visiting friendly ports in the region to symbolize American interests."[4]

2.1.1. Twin Pillars Policy

President Nixon term in office was the height of Cold War rivalry with the Soviet Union, and the United States was deeply involved in Vietnam. Consequently, the United States decided instead of direct intervention to build up its two regional allies, Iran and Saudi Arabia, as local powers that could protect the region from the spread of Soviet influence. As the 'Twin Pillars' of US policy, both countries were encouraged to acquire billions of dollars of the most advanced arms during the 1970s. Iran embraced the Twin Pillars policy more enthusiastically than Saudi Arabia and intervened militarily with US approbation in Iraq and Oman.

"Considering its population and powerful military, the role of military power was given to Iran, and Saudi Arabia became an influential economic power."[5]

The post Second World War attitude of the United States towards Iran was not as a capitalist nation. But USA, more as a big brother, assured Iran that the United States would go as far as necessary to maintain its independence. The United States chiefly wanted to stabilize the Gulf region, to assure the oil supply without interference. Each of the Gulf States was supplied with various types of arms and equipment to resist interference by any of the great power nations.

USA also strengthened Iranian king's power in the Strait of Hormuz and empowered him the right of using Al-Ghanam Island; in the mouth of the strait. Iran's geographical condition; locating in Rimland and in the narrowest point of the security fortification due to "Containment Policy"[6], caused Iran to be the centre of security belt around USSR. "The belt initiated by USA included Iran, Turkey and Pakistan under the title of Central Treaty Organization (CENTO)."[7]

The policy collapsed suddenly in 1979, when the Shah (king) of Iran was overthrown in a revolution that brought to power a republican regime opposed to US influence in the region.

2.2. President Gerald Ford (Republican); 1974-1977

This administration continued Nixon policy on the Persian Gulf region; the Twin Pillars Policy.

Indeed, President Gerald Ford and Henry Kissinger, his National Security Advisor, believed that the Shah of Iran should survive a sufficient number of years to play a controlling role among the regional powers in helping to assure stability in the Persian Gulf area. On May 13, 1975, Henry Kissinger stated in the Oval Office, the office of the President of the United States, that: "It has been a cardinal point in our policy over the past several years to encourage Iran to intensify its cooperation with other moderate anti-communist states in the Gulf region, particularly, Saudi Arabia."[8]

2.3. President James Earl Carter (Democrat); 1977-1981

A series of events in the region beginning in 1979 started the end of the Nixon Doctrine and a more aggressive US policy towards the Persian Gulf region. These events included:

1. The downfall of the Shah's regime in Iran and the revolution that followed,
2. The short border war between the two Yemens,
3. The Soviet invasion of Afghanistan,
4. The outbreak of the Iran-Iraq war.

The Carter administration wanted to prevent a communist take over in Iran which would further unsettle the Gulf region. More importantly, the USA was concerned about the continuation of the export of oil to the Western world. Therefore, Carter administration officials attempted to 'normalize' relations and to avoid offending the new regime or giving the impression that the USA was intent on containing or isolating the new regime. However, in late 1979, after the Iranian revolutionary regime condoned the seizure of 52 US diplomatic personnel, relations with Teheran were ended.

The Soviet invasion of Afghanistan in late December 1979 made a new policy inevitable.

To Carter, the Soviet invasion of Afghanistan represented but one more step in a broader Soviet move towards the Persian Gulf. The Iranian revolution and the hostage crisis supported the USSR's achievement of this goal by reducing American influence in the area and by distracting the administration from the immediate threat posed by the USSR to Americans' interests in the region.

The image of a Soviet drive to the Persian Gulf and the Indian Ocean dominated analysis by the Carter administration.

2.3.1. Carter Doctrine

The new policy was articulated by President Carter in his January 23, 1980 State of the Union Address and became known as the Carter Doctrine. In a definitive statement of US policy to meet the threat posed by the Soviet invasion of Afghanistan, President Carter stated:

"Let our position be absolutely clear: any attempt by outside force to gain control of Persian Gulf region will be regarded as an assault on vital interests of the United States of America, and such an assault will be repelled by any means necessary including military force."[9]

The Carter Doctrine was accompanied by the establishment of the Rapid Deployment Joint Task Force (RDJTF) at Mac Dill Air Force Base in Florida on March 1, 1980. In November 1979, the Carter administration defined the Gulf as vital to US interests and established the Rapid Deployment Joint Task Force as the principal tool for its defense. This was a permanent military force designed to deploy rapidly into the region to respond to contingencies threatening US interests, specifically threats to Persian Gulf oil. The RDJTF evolved from a planning concept which was then called the Rapid Deployment Force (RDF). At its inception, the RDJTF (commonly referred to as the Rapid Deployment Force) was frequently criticized as a 'paper tiger' lacking the force structure and firepower to engage effectively projected Soviet forces in the region and facing severe problems in strategic mobility to get them into the battle. The RDJTF later became the United States Central Command (CENTCOM) during the Reagan Administration.

2.4. President Ronald Reagan (Republican); 1981-1989

The Reagan Administration affirmed the Carter Doctrine and saw the Soviet Union as the most significant threat to the Persian Gulf region.

Unlike Carter, Reagan assumed the main focus of American interest in the Middle East to be in the Persian Gulf sector. The Soviet invasion of Afghanistan represented a direct threat to the security of the Gulf.

President Reagan's Secretary of State, Alexander Haig, expressed the administration's view as follows:

> "We confronted a situation where strategic passivity during the Ford administration and excessive piety of the Carter administration's human rights crusade had sapped the will of authoritarian anti-communist governments, eroded confidence of Western allies and encouraged risk taking by the Soviet Union and by Soviet manipulated totalitarian regimes."[10]

2.4.1. Strategic Consensus Policy

With the Soviet threat its focus, the Reagan administration at first embraced the idea of 'strategic consensus' in which the goal was to persuade the diverse countries of the region to put aside local parochial security concerns and unite with the US in an alliance type of relationship against the Soviet Union and its' client states.

The aim of such a consensus was to contain a revolutionary Iran and an Iran-Iraq war that, in the words of the most prominent advocate of 'strategic consensuses', Secretary of State Alexander Haig, had exposed "deeply rooted rivalries and historic animosities."[11]

He was referring, in particular, to what the New York Times then called the dangers of the Iran-Iraq war's broadening into a clash between Shiite Muslims in Iran, Syria and parts of Iraq and Sunni Muslims who rule Iraq, Jordan, Saudi Arabia and the Persian Gulf States.

The assumption behind 'strategic consensus' was that Arab states, including even Iraq, would be more concerned about the supposed threats posed by Moscow or Tehran than by Israel's refusal to recognize Palestinian rights and return to its 1967 borders.

The challenge for the Reagan administration was to convince the regional states that their primary security threat came from the Soviet Union. Strategic consensus required access and a regional network of support facilities for US military forces. A principal incentive of strategic consensus was to be the expansion of US arms sales to cooperative countries.

However, the idea of 'strategic consensus' did not agree with the Gulf States' perceptions. Regional and domestic concerns were of far more interest to the Gulf States than external Soviets threats. They had formed the Gulf Cooperation Council (GCC) in 1981 to enhance prospects for security cooperation and to contend with economic and political concerns of the region. Though the GCC states recognized the need for US diplomatic support, and for guarantee of American intervention, they were reluctant to become more overtly aligned with the US than necessary.

Despite Reagan administration urgings, the Gulf States remained uninterested in an anti-Soviet regional coalition. Thus, the US moved to a policy that included strengthening its relations with the regional states and improving the Rapid Deployment Joint Task Force (RDJTF). Saudi Arabia appeared to be regarded as the primary instrument of US policy in the Gulf as the result of the new policy change.

Additional arms sales to the Saudis reflected the change. Saudi policy preferred to keep the US forces 'over the horizon' so as not to cause antagonism with other Gulf States and possible disruptions within its own traditional society.

The Carter Doctrine was expanded to say that the US would deal with any kind of threat to the Saudi regime and would keep open the Strait of Hormuz if the Iranians should try to stop shipping through the waterway.

The Reagan administration was also concerned by the negative effects of the Iran-Iraq war and it adopted the view that US interests in the region would not be served by a decisive victory by one side or the other.

A victory by Iraq might encourage a Soviet military intervention into Iran. A victory by Iran would risk the spread of

Iranian Islamic fundamentalism into the Gulf and the Arabian Peninsula. As the Iran-Iraq war expanded into the Gulf and attacks against non-belligerent shipping increased in 1987, the US agreed to the reflagging of Kuwaiti oil tankers and providing them with US naval protection in "Operation Earnest Will."[12]

Force levels of the Middle East Force (MIDEASTFOR) which had been operating in the Persian Gulf since the 1940s, routinely with a flag ship and four surface combatants were substantially increased in size with the deployment of the Joint Task Force Middle East (JTFME) in support of Earnest Will. At the height of the protection action, as many as 40 US naval vessels were operating in the Persian Gulf and the Arabian Sea.

As the Iran-Iraq war continued, US policy-makers were more occupied with events occurring in other areas of the Middle East involving Israel and Lebanon. However, as Iran won a series of victories in its war with Iraq, American concern shifted back to the Persian Gulf region.

The Reagan administration's policy towards the war was clearly stated to support America's strategic, economic and political interests which were as follows:

1. Strict neutrality, including refusal to sell weapons to either side and appeal to other countries to similarly refrain,
2. Determination to maintain freedom of navigation in the Gulf,
3. Support for international efforts to mediate the conflict,
4. Support for the security of the Gulf nonbelligerent states against the spread of hostilities.

2.4.2. Iran-Contra Affair

The Iran-Contra Affair was a *political scandal* which was revealed in November 1986 as a result of earlier events during the *Reagan administration*. It began as an operation to increase US-Iranian relations, wherein *Israel* would ship weapons to a moderate, politically influential group of Iranians; the US would then re-supply

Israel and receive payment from Israel and funding Contra militants in Nicaragua. "The Israeli ambassador to the US says that the reason weapons were eventually sold directly to Iran was to establish links with elements of the military in the country."[13]

At the time, Iran was in the midst of the *Iran–Iraq War* and could find few Western nations willing to supply it with weapons. The moderate Iranians agreed to do everything in their power to achieve the release of six US hostages, who were being held by *Hezbollah* in Lebanon.

The affair has two elements:

1. Arms sales to Iran,
2. Funding of Contra militants in Nicaragua. Direct funding of the Nicaraguan rebels had been made illegal through the "*Boland Amendment*."[14]

The plan eventually deteriorated into an arms-for-hostages scheme, in which members of the *executive branch* sold weapons to *Iran* in exchange for the release of the American hostages, a portion of the proceeds from the weapon sales was diverted to fund anti-*Sandinista* and *anti-communist* rebels; *Contras*, in *Nicaragua* "without the direct authorization of President *Ronald Reagan*."[15] While President Ronald Reagan was a supporter of the Contra cause, there has not been any evidence uncovered showing that he authorized this plan.

After the weapon sales were revealed in November 1986, Ronald Reagan appeared on national television and stated that "the weapons transfers had indeed occurred, but that the United States did not trade arms for hostages."[16] On March 4, 1987, Reagan returned to the airwaves in a nationally televised address, taking full responsibility for any actions that he was unaware of, and admitting that "what began as a strategic opening to Iran deteriorated, in its implementation, into trading arms for hostages."[17]

"Many investigations ensued, and in the end, fourteen administration officials were charged with crimes, and eleven convicted, including then-*Secretary of Defense Caspar Weinberger*."[18] "They were all pardoned in the final days of the *George H.W. Bush* presidency, who had been vice-president at the time."[19]

The 'arms-for-hostages' is important because of its significance for the Persian Gulf region and US policy-making for strategic regions. The sale of arms to Iran can be traced to two strategic reasons, as follows:

1. Israel, who reportedly first suggested the value of arms to Iran to US government officials, apparently acted on the basis of its long-standing 'periphery policy' whereby it has tried to maintain good relations with Iranian governments.
2. There was strategic merit in the US creating an 'opening' with Iran. As with his predecessors, President Reagan was concerned with the Soviet Union, in the wake of its invasion of Afghanistan, would turn its sights on Iran and control of the Persian Gulf region.

2.5. President George H. W. Bush (Republican); 1989-1993

President Bush and his National Security Advisor, Brent Scowcroft, acknowledged in their Joint Memories that "the Persian Gulf region had not been among US major concerns early in the Administration. Despite a number of sometimes exasperating differences with Iraq, developments in the region had begun to return to normal following the 1980-88 Iran-Iraq conflict and occupied the attention of US specialists rather than the policy-making team."[20]

The Bush administration possessed two fundamental strengths that enabled it to develop and implement foreign policies and take the necessary decisions to safeguard US interest within and outside of the Persian Gulf.

First, Bush and the members of the inner circle of his foreign policy team had lengthy records of public service in the federal level.

Second, in working together in the past, they developed an excellent rapport and resultant ability to avoid the types of intra-administration disputes that have the potential to complicate policymaking during international crises.

The Administration recognized that the US had vital interests in the Persian Gulf to protect in 1989-1990.

It defined those interests in terms of their interconnected issues areas, those pertaining to economics, politics and security.

Economically, the US remained dependent on the Gulf's vast oil resources .Thus, avoiding a prolonged Middle Eastern crisis on the scale of those that impeded Western access to the region's petroleum resources during the 1970, was a paramount concern.

Politically, the instability that any such crisis would entail within the Gulf, and along its periphery, was likely to have disastrous consequences.

From the security point of view, preventing regional destabilization, in turn, demanded the use of Washington's diplomatic and military assets to maintain a secure environment in the Persian Gulf.

In brief, the Bush administrations enunciated the followings as US interests in the Persian Gulf area:

1. The security of the oil and its free passage out of the Gulf,
2. The security and stability of friendly regional states,
3. Containing Soviet advances because of uncertainty concerning Soviet intentions.

These interests did not deviate substantially from those of earlier administrations, but US goals appeared to reflect the changed circumstances in the region and beyond. Stated goals included; maintaining stability in the region, preventing either Iran or Iraq from dominating the region, preventing the spread of radical Islamic fundamentalism and reducing the threat of terrorism from and in the region.

The Bush administration continued to rely on both diplomatic and military approaches in its Gulf strategy. The Gulf sector posed a number of interrelated policy issues in the political-military arena for the United States. These tended to revolve around America's past and future relationship with Iran and Iraq and their roles and activities in the region.

The Bush administration chose to maintain the strategy of the Reagan administration, which had tilted toward Baghdad during the Iran-Iraq war.

On Iraq, Bush administration policy was to try to alter Iraq's behaviour and to seek to influence Iraq to move in a more positive direction rather than to penalize it.

Iraq-US relations remained a dilemma. Iraq's poor human rights record, American concerns about its development of weapons of mass destruction and its use of chemical warfare weapons during the war with Iran and against dissident Iraqi Kurds contributed to problems that heightened by the execution of Farzad Bazoft; an Iranian-born journalist living in Great Britain accused of spying on Iraq, Iraq's attempt to acquire krytons (nuclear trigger devices) and Saddam Hussein's threats to retaliate against an Israeli strike on Iraq with chemical weapons.

From the Bush administration point of view, the US-Iran relationship revolved around a range of issues including the restoration of diplomatic and other relations, the Iranian threat to regional (and other) states, Iranian support of international terrorism and the Iranian role in the continued captivity of American hostages in Lebanon. The adversarial role of the United States during the later stages of the Iran-Iraq War remained a factor in poor relations. To limit Iran's ability to pursue the Iran-Iraq war, the United States initiated "Operation Staunch"[21] with its allies to embargo the flow of weapons to Iran. These sanctions were to continue in force until Iran accepted UN resolution 598 in the end of the war. The sanctions have remained in place and Iran sees these continued war-related sanctions as evidence of US hostility toward Iran. The Bush administration sought to contain Iran's Islamic fundamentalism to keep it from spreading to the Arabian Peninsula and to convince Iran to end its support of international terrorism.

The stability of the moderate regional states has been a concern of previous administrations in light of Islamic fundamentalism, expatriate Palestinians, terrorism and the minority ruling elites in some of the regional states. With a ceasefire in the Iran-Iraq war, the Bush administration was concerned with the potential for instability in the region created by Iran and Iraq; the region's most dominant powers. Iraq now had the largest and most battle experienced military force in the Arab world and had the capability to create significant tensions in the region. Iran continued to possess the capability to disrupt maritime traffic in the Persian Gulf and to destabilize regional states through the export of its Islamic revolution.

The Gulf Cooperation Council was not strong enough to confront effectively either Iran or Iraq without external assistance. Kuwait did sign an official defence pact with the United States, on September 18, 1991, and followed it up by pacts with Britain and France. Bahrain also concluded a defence accord with the United States in the same month and, "according to unconfirmed reports, its rulers also agreed to house the regional headquarters of the US Central Command."[22]

The members of the Gulf Cooperation Council (Saudi Arabia, Kuwait, Qatar, Bahrain, Oman and the United Arab Emirates) generally have had positive relations with the United States. These were enhanced by the United States' role during the later stages of the Iran-Iraq War and particularly by the United States' reflagging of Kuwaiti ships and actions to assure freedom of navigation in the Persian Gulf.

Concurrent with American efforts to maintain stability in the Persian Gulf through the economic inducements, Iraqi President; Saddam, spent the opening months of 1989 pressuring Kuwait and the UAE to reduce their oil production to avoid reductions in the oil price.

In the early hours of August 1, 1990, Iraqi forces crossed the border into Kuwait, firing the proverbial opening shot in the 1990-1991 Persian Gulf War. Bush responded to Iraq's invasion of Kuwait with equal measures of prudence and resolve. From the outset, he was determined not to allow Saddam's aggression to stand. However, Bush also recognized the need to avoid unilateral American action in a region generally averse to Western culture and influence. Eventually, the American-led Coalition forces surged into Kuwait and South-western Iraq and within 100 hours of ground war obtained a clear victory over Saddam.

The US presence was still considered to be offshore and over the horizon, with no bases or home porting rights, except for Bahrain and Oman, where access agreements had been established to allow pre-positioning of military equipment. The Iraqi invasion of Kuwait shattered the myth of US over-the horizon presence and exposed the Arabs to their inability to prevent their large, powerful and angry neighbours from taking out their wrath or seeking succour in the oilfields of Kuwait and the Gulf at large. Also, to the relief of the rulers and the concern of the ruled, it brought the US military into the region with a reshaped strategic doctrine and security perceptions. For a while after the war, it seemed as if the United States would maintain a significant military footprint and the GCC would stay under an American security umbrella to protect the regimes, their oil and sea lanes from hegemonic threats from any aggressive state.

2.6. President William Jefferson Clinton (Democrat); 1993-2001

President Clinton took office at a time when conducting diplomacy in the Persian Gulf region was increasingly complicated. Beginning with the Carter administration, US policy sought a balance of power between Iran and Iraq.

American policy in the Gulf was changed from indirect involvement and using the region as a setting for Cold War confrontation, to very direct US intervention and war with Iraq. In addition to American presence in the Gulf, the US strategy called for helping the Gulf Cooperation Council (GCC) nations maintain a collective defence.

The Clinton Administration's primary focus in the Persian Gulf area was to reduce the chances of any nation's threat to the sovereignty of any of the GCC states.

In the aftermath of the 1991 Gulf war, the Gulf states, with the exception of Saudi Arabia, renewed or formalized defence agreements with the United States. The agreements have provided not only for facilities access for US forces, but also for US advice, training and joint exercises; lethal and non-lethal US equipment pre-positioning; and arms sales. The pacts did not formally require the United States to come to the aid of any of the Gulf States if they are attacked nor did the pacts give the United States automatic permission to conduct military operations from Gulf facilities; the United States must obtain permission on a case by case basis.

As an example, the UAE did not have close defence relations with the United States prior to the 1991 Gulf war. After that war, the UAE determined that it wanted a closer relationship with the United States, in part to deter and balance out Iranian naval power. On July 25, 1994, the UAE announced it had signed a defence pact with the United States. The UAE has allowed some US pre-positioning, as well as US ship port visits at its large man-made Jebel Ali port. It also has hosted US refuelling aircraft participating in the southern no fly zone enforcement operation (Al Dhafra air base).

2.6.1. Dual Containment Policy

A significant part of President Clinton's strategy to safeguard US interests in the Persian Gulf was Dual Containment. In conjunction with dual containment, the United States tried to maintain US long-standing presence which was centred on naval vessels in and near the Persian Gulf and pre-positioned combat equipment.

The United States followed Dual Containment policy toward Iran and Iraq since May 1993. The object of dual containment was to isolate these regimes politically, economically and militarily. The policy was supposed to constrain the two most powerful area states; Iran and Iraq, by imposing harsh economic sanctions on them. The innovators of the policy decided to commit American resources to repressing Iran and Iraq when the two were already accomplishing that task on their own.

The Clinton administration identified both Iraq and Iran as significant threats to America's interests in the region. It developed dual containment policy, to deal with those threats by isolating both countries regionally, cutting them off from the world economic and trading system and encouraging a regime change in Iraq. It strongly supported the continuation of United Nations' sanctions against Iraq, made efforts to persuade Europe, Russia and Japan to deny Iran access to international capital and arms markets and continued American military commitments to Saudi Arabia and the smaller monarchies that form the Gulf Cooperation Council (GCC).

On May 18, 1993, Martin Indyk, the special assistant to President Clinton for Near East and South Asian affairs at the National Security Council, outlined the dual containment policy in a speech to the Washington Institute for Near East Policy. He said that "the United States would no longer play the game of balancing Iran against Iraq. The strength of the United States and its friends in the region, Egypt, Israel, Saudi Arabia, Turkey and the GCC, would allow Washington to counter both the Iraqi and Iranian regimes. US will not need to depend on one to counter the other."[23]

In the decade between the Gulf War and the terrorist attacks on the World Trade Centre and the Pentagon in September 2001, the strategy of dual containment of Iraq and Iran was a key driver of American military planning and force posture for the region.

During these years, the overriding US concern was; preserving access to Gulf oil at reasonable prices as both Iran and Iraq possessed only a limited ability to project power and influence beyond their borders. The Persian Gulf states acquiesced to a significant US military presence on their soil despite the domestic costs and the United States was reasonably successful in insulating its relationships with key Gulf States from the Israeli-Palestinian conflict.

American allies in the region and elsewhere showed no enthusiasm for dual containment, making its implementation highly problematic.

For example, the United States and Europe share a number of common goals and interests in the Gulf. These include; securing access to Persian Gulf oil supplies at reasonable prices, preventing the spread of terrorism and weapons of mass destruction (WMD) and fostering peace, stability, and prosperity.

Nonetheless, over the years some of the most acute tensions in the transatlantic relationship have stemmed from US and European disagreements in the Persian Gulf, especially over the most effective policies to achieve these goals. The most contentious disputes have revolved around the American use of military force and the imposition of sanctions to moderate the behaviour of Iraq and Iran (dual containment policy).

Both Iran and Iraq are potentially quite rich countries. They both have oil, to which the Europeans, among others, would like to gain access; France, in particular, has been keen to acquire oil concessions from either of the two countries for a number of years going back to just after First World War.

As it turned out, the Europeans were amenable to boycotting Iraq, but they would, under no circumstances, cooperate where Iran was concerned.

Dual containment offered no guidelines for dealing with change in the Persian Gulf region, and it tied American policy to an inherently unstable regional status quo. Worse yet, it assigned to the United States a unilateral role in managing gulf security issues at a time when the American capacity to influence events in Iran and Iraq was at best limited.

The United States had to deploy significant resources in the Gulf to enforce the dual containment policy, and "some US military officials believed that US resources could be severely strained in the event of a major crisis in the Gulf and a simultaneous crisis in another world's region."[24]

The Clinton Administration sought dialogue with former Iranian president, Khatami, to advance US interests and to press US concerns, which it defined primarily as Iran's attempt to acquire weapons of mass destruction and delivery means, opposition to the Arab-Israeli peace process and support for international terrorism. However, Iran refused direct dialogue with the United States until the September 11, 2001 attacks brought the United States, in force, into Iran's immediate neighbourhood, Afghanistan.

2.7. President George W. Bush (Republican); 2001-2009

For the Gulf States and their people, the critical objective has been to move through a period of economic and political transition in the post-Saddam era, while maintaining internal stability. It was critical that the region remains free from external threats during this period. "A credible security architecture that protects the region from external threat, while promoting collective security and regional military integration, would certainly support this overall strategic objective."[25]

In spite of their objective, good feelings about the US presence did not survive the decade after the end of the war for the liberation of Kuwait.

First months after taking office by President Bush were coincident with the change of regional states' policy towards the presence of US in the region. While the Arab States of Persian Gulf acknowledged the need for US protection and monitoring of the uneasy set of relationships between the GCC states, Iraq and Iran; those governments that were pro-Western or pro-American in orientation began to feel uneasy about life with only one superpower. They welcomed a US created and sustained coalition when Iraq invaded Kuwait for its ability to provide protection against real and potential aggressors and to help the Gulf return to peace and stability. But Gulf governments, in particular the Saudi ruling family, began to come under domestic criticism for hosting the US military presence and for spending riyals on expensive military hardware while the government remained unable to defend the country.

2.7.1. Counter Proliferation Policy; Before September 11, 2001

The most important feature of Bush administration's foreign policy before September 11, 2001 was; "building missile defence capability and transforming the military."[26]

"Such a unilateral and idealist approach stemmed from the neo-conservatives' longstanding exaggeration about the threats facing the US and their determination to eliminate them through the 'overweening use of American Power', their assertion of the 'superiority of American Values' and the insistence that their brand of morality is universal."[27]

This doctrine marked a dramatic shift away from those times during the Cold war when containment and deterrence sporadically prevailed and thus called into question US reliance on the UN and other multinational coalitions, including even NATO and the Organization of American States.

The key issues that shaped Bush administration policy in the Persian Gulf included:

1. Eliminating Iraq's regime as a threat to the security and stability of the region,
2. Maintaining support for the war on terrorism,
3. Securing access to reasonably priced oil,
4. Preventing Iran from acquiring weapons of mass destruction (WMD) or taking actions that are hostile to US interests.

In fact, the United States' strategy in the region was based on the following elements:

1. A military-based counter proliferation approach based upon a flexible mix of deterrence, coercive diplomacy and global military superiority,
2. The preventive or pre-emptive use of military force, alongside the spread of US-defined democratic and free-market values.

2.7.2. War on Terror Policy; After September 11, 2001

After September 11, 2001 attacks on World Trade Centre and Pentagon, the Bush administration's previous security focus on rogue states and Weapons of Mass Destruction (WMD) proliferation, particularly in the context of missile defence, was broadened to encompass the new war on terrorism.

Indeed, Bush directly linked the proliferation and terrorism issues in a speech three months after the attacks, declaring that "rogue states are clearly the most likely sources of chemical and biological and nuclear weapons for terrorists."[28]

United States was back in the business of extensive global involvement in what became known as 'the war on terror'.

The war on terror has never attracted that kind of international allegiance. China and Russia welcomed it because it distracted the United States' strategic focus away from them, and because both saw utility in a war on terror that for Moscow meant a war on the Chechens and for Beijing a war on the Uighurs. But to most of the United States' traditional allies, it was at best an unwelcome distraction from the issues they care about more.

The Bush Administration, in the aftermath of the September 11 attacks, moved policy toward Iraq from containment to regime change, as part of the overall War on Terrorism.

2.7.3. Policy on Iraq

In his January 29, 2002, State of the Union message, President Bush called Iraq part of an 'axis of evil', along with North Korea and Iran. He identified the key threat as Iraq's potential to deliver WMD against the United States and its friends and allies, or to transfer WMD technology to terrorist groups.

For Washington, Saddam was the issue. He was seen as the prime threat to regional security. US policymakers assumed his objectives and behaviour were unlikely to change while he was in power and that only his removal would offer hope for change.

In the wake of 9/11, the Bush administration developed its own grand design for the region. The centerpiece of the plan was to replace the repressive regime of Saddam Hussein in Iraq with a thriving democracy. A successful US intervention in Iraq, in 2003, was supposed to intimidate anti-American actors in the Middle East, start a democratic chain reaction throughout the region, encourage Arab-Israeli peace and reduce the threat of terrorist attacks against the United States.

But despite some modest successes, the Bush administration's 'forward strategy of freedom', much like Clinton's efforts at engagement, ultimately failed to remake the Middle East. As Iraq became weaker, Iran grew stronger and both the fundamentalist parties within Iraq and Islamic groups elsewhere, such as Hamas and Hezbollah, gained political ground.

The United States paid a huge price for the years of stumbling. Whatever damage was done to the United States' reputation by the invasion itself, the damage done by four years of failure; from 2003 to 2007, including the more spectacular manifestations of that failure, such as the "Abu Ghraib prison scandal"[29], was incalculably greater. In a fracturing world, the only thing worse than a self-absorbed hegemony is an incompetent self-absorbed hegemony.

The hoped-for transformation of Iraq through a 'war of choice' resulted in a potential civil war based on a complex mixture of transnational terror groups, local insurgencies, ethnic and religious divides and tense exchanges between independent armed militias.

2.7.4. Policy on Iran

The Bush Administration came into office espousing much the same policy toward Iran as the preceding administration, offering dialogue but repeating US concerns and insisting those concerns be addressed. President Bush characterized Iran as part of an 'axis of evil', in his January 29, 2002 State of the Union message.

Then September 11 attack happened. "Off all the countries of the Persian Gulf region, Iran's reaction was the most extraordinary, expressing an empathy with the US position that contradicted the stereotype so frequently presented to the American people."[30] Rather than celebrate, as some insensitively did in the full glare of the Western media, or indulge in formal pronouncements of commiseration, both state officials and important sections of Iranian society publicly expressed their solidarity with the victims of the outrage.

After the September 11 attacks, there was substantial optimism for a major breakthrough in relations when Iran largely cooperated with the US effort to defeat the Taliban and install a new government. Some note that Iran had long wanted the Taliban ousted, so that backing the US effort was in Iran's own interests and did not necessarily represent a new effort to reach out to the United States or a turning away from support for international terrorism.

The attempt of the Bush administration to stop Iranian nuclear proliferation through coercive diplomacy; involving economic isolation, diplomatic pressure and even veiled threats of conventional military strikes, utterly failed to do more than cause a temporary halt to Iranian pursuit of a fully-indigenous fuel cycle via uranium-enrichment facilities. If anything, these coercive techniques, alongside a US refusal to formally recognize the legitimacy and sovereignty of the Islamic Republic of Iran simply hardened the resolve of conservative Iranian leaders to secure a nuclear-weapons option. Moreover, US pressure and threats were even turning the issue of a peaceful nuclear-energy program into an issue of national pride for all Iranians, liberal, moderate and conservative alike.

2.7.5. Policy on GCC (Gulf Cooperation Council) States

The September 11, 2001 attacks introduced new frictions in US relations with the Gulf States. The revelation that fifteen of the nineteen September 11 hijackers were of Saudi origin led to additional strain in US-Saudi relations; which had already been tense because of the Israeli-Palestinian dispute, and to speculation that US forces might be asked to leave the Kingdom. There were also reports that the hijackers had used financial networks based in the UAE in the September 11 plot.

Indeed, the United States remained highly engaged in the Gulf because the September 11 attacks added a new dimension to US relations with the Gulf States beyond the need to contain longstanding threats from Iran or Iraq. After the September 11 attacks, the United States began pressing the Gulf States for their cooperation against Al Qaeda activists and financial channels located in the Gulf States themselves. The need for the United States to deal with all the security threats emanating from the Gulf gave the United States a stake in the political stability of the Gulf regimes. Many of the Gulf monarchies faced potential threats to political stability.

The September 11 attacks offered a new opportunity to exercise the longstanding defence cooperation with the Gulf States. The Gulf States were asked, and most of them agreed, to host US forces performing combat missions in Afghanistan in Operation Enduring Freedom (OEF, the war against the Taliban and Al Qaeda). For example, Qatar publicly allowed the United States to locate its forward US Central Command (CENTCOM) headquarters at the Army pre-positioning site at Saliyah for the war with Iraq, and Kuwait hosted virtually the entire US ground invasion force.

From Operation Desert Storm in 1990 until the US overthrow of the Saddam Hussein regime in 2003, the Kingdom of Saudi Arabia was the United States' key Arab partner in confronting the problems to international stability emanating from Iraq. Over that decade and more, however, the demands associated with containing

Iraq and Saddam Hussein began to place unprecedented strains on the US-Saudi relationship, particularly after the terrorist attacks of September 11, 2001, and the run up to the US invasion. The abnormal situation that bound Saudi Arabia to the United States in having to face a common threat from Iraq gave way to a more normal situation in which the two countries' interests and approaches toward Iraq will converge or diverge, depending on the issue concerned.

Saudi Arabia did not offer to allow US pilots to fly missions in Afghanistan from Saudi Arabia, but it did permit the United States to use the Combined Air Operations Centre at Prince Sultan Air Base; south of Riyadh, to coordinate US air operations over Afghanistan.

2.8. President Barak Obama (Democrat); 2009 Onwards

President Obama took office in January 2009, with 'Change We Can Believe In' as his slogan. Since starting his presidency term, he has faced very complicated issues; especially in the Persian Gulf region.

For decades, US national security policy has dedicated significant resources and attention to the Gulf region for one primary reason; to ensure the safe export of the region's considerable oil and gas resources that are vital for global economic growth and security.

According to the experiences gained in the recent years, military power, of course, is not the only instrument for pursuing US goals in the Persian Gulf.

Indeed, diplomacy and multilateral economic policies are probably more important and defence of the Persian Gulf will remain a high US strategic priority.

The Obama administration seems to have more realistic goals in the Persian Gulf region and Middle East than its successors. It seems that President Obama's major plans in the Persian Gulf region are to withdraw troops from Iraq and hold talks with Iran without preconditions.

President Obama's major policy for the Middle East, specifically Persian Gulf region, have signalled that the new US administration is thinking ambitiously and creatively about the opportunities and threats for global security emanating from this strategically important region of the world.

In his first two months in office, President Barack Obama moved rapidly to set the contours of a new strategy to address multiple security challenges in the Middle East, especially in the Persian Gulf and South Asia. As the administration continues to define its policies on complicated issues like counterterrorism, the Arab-Israeli conflict, Iraq, Iran, Afghanistan and Pakistan in the future, it should consult closely with its Persian Gulf Arab allies, who serve as a key link between nearly all of the pieces of the broader puzzle of the Middle East and South Asia.

But as for the chronic power imbalance in the Gulf region, it is most likely that President Obama's policies will not differ significantly from those of his predecessors.

2.8.1. Policy on Iraq

Early in his presidency, President Obama moved to change US war strategy by increasing troop strength in Afghanistan and reducing troop levels in Iraq.

The President set a new tone aimed at fostering cooperation for greater stability in the region in his inaugural address, his first televised interview as president with the Arabic language satellite television channel; Al Arabia, on January 26, 2009, and his announcement of a plan for a phased and responsible redeployment of US troops from Iraq that provided the broad outlines of the diplomatic and development assistance goals and efforts that will help mitigate the risks of a US troop drawdown.

In his speech at Camp Lejeune; North Carolina on February 27, 2009, President Obama declared that combat operations would end in Iraq within 18 months. His remarks were made to a group of Marines preparing for deployment to Afghanistan. Obama said, "Let me say this as plainly as I can: By August 31, 2010, our combat mission in Iraq will end."[31]

US officials, while praising improvement in Iraqi security forces, remain deeply concerned that Al Maliki's Shiite Muslim-dominated government has been unable or unwilling to reconcile with the country's minority Sunni Muslims and Kurds. The Sunnis had run Iraq until the US ouster of Saddam Hussein in 2003 and are still smarting over their loss of power in politics, the economy and military. Aware of Sunni hard feelings and Kurdish desires for autonomy in an oil-rich section of the northeast of Iraq, Obama enjoined al-Maliki to be more flexible about sharing power and allowing provincial governments a greater role in decision-making.

"In a speech after his meeting with Iraqi prime minister in the White House, President Barack Obama said that he pressed Iraq's prime minister to make room in his government and security forces for all ethnic and religious groups to prevent a resurgence of the violence and turmoil that took the country to the verge of civil war."[32]

Al Maliki, contrary to past practice, said he shared Obama's goal. "Iraq has suffered a great deal from being marginalized, from the policies of sectarianism and from wars. We will work very hard in order not to allow any sectarian behavior an opportunity to flourish," Mr. Al Maliki said in the same meeting.

Though the United States currently has stationed about 130,000 troops in Iraq, its strategic focus in the country has been shifting from combating against insurgents to training Iraqi security forces, as well as supporting political reconciliation process.

2.8.2. Policy on Iran

During his presidential campaign, Mr. Obama called the idea of a nuclear Iran unacceptable, and offered to meet with the Tehran regime without precondition to persuade it to change course. And his advisors agree that there is still a window for diplomacy. The new team realizes that the Iranian leadership has to be engaged rather than isolated in the hope that it might just go away.

President Obama promised in his Inaugural Address, on January 20, 2009, "a new relationship with nations willing to unclench their fists"[33], an offer which he repeated at his news conference on February 9, 2009.

In his speech on February 10, 2009, President of Iran; Mr. Ahmadinejad, promised that if the United States was truly serious about changing the countries' relations, then Iran was ready to respond in kind. "It is clear that change should be fundamental, not tactical, and our people welcome real changes,"[34] he said. "Our nation is ready to hold talks based on mutual respect and in a fair atmosphere", he added.

President Obama said he expected his administration would be looking for openings through which the two countries can start "face-to-face diplomatic overtures"[35] in a press conference on February 9, 2009. A diplomatic thaw won't occur overnight because of the mistrust that has built up over the years, he said.

"The Status of Forces Agreement"[36] of Iraq, which has been recently approved, may provide the umbrella for a possible total pull-out plan. President Obama could use such total pull-out as a bargaining chip in talks with Iran based on following proposals :

1. US withdrawal from Iraq,
2. International security guarantees for Iran,
3. Acceptance of the growing Iranian influence in Iraq and of its regional role.

All of the above mentioned proposals are in exchange for a halt to Iran's nuclear program.

But Tehran is most likely to reject the deal because these are only short-term guarantees that would make Iran dependent on the US and European arrangements.

President Obama is working against time to untangle more than 30 years of enmity and prevent Iran from building a nuclear bomb, but even his own advisors know the chance of success is slim.

Even as the White House engages in direct diplomacy, President Obama has said "we are very clear about certain deep concerns that we have as a country, that Iran understands that we find the funding of terrorist organizations unacceptable, that we're clear about the fact that a nuclear Iran could set off a nuclear arms race in the region that would be profoundly destabilizing."[37]

The transformation of Iran into a nuclear power will change the balance of power in the entire Middle East. One of the consequences will be a serious arms race, at least if Israel does not launch a pre-emptive strike on the Iranian nuclear plant. It is, therefore, difficult for the Obama administration to accept Iran as a nuclear state.

However, it seems that talks with Iran will be tough and direct, and will put on the table the same deal that the international community has been trying to get Tehran to accept for the past four years: extensive economic and diplomatic help if uranium enrichment is suspended whereas, further economic pressure and diplomatic isolation if it does not. Iran has resisted this carrot-and-stick approach so far, despite four sets of UN sanctions, but Western diplomats hope that direct engagement by Washington will help break the impasse.

President Obama released a special video message for all those celebrating Nowruz on March 19, 2009. It is translated 'New Day' and it is the beginning of the new year, for millions in Iran and other communities around the world. The US President wanted to send a special message to the people and government of Iran on Nowruz, acknowledging the strain in Iran and USA relations over the last few decades. "At this holiday we are reminded of the common humanity that binds us together,"[38] he said. After committing his administration to a future of honest and respectful diplomacy, he continued on to address Iran's leaders directly:

"You, too, have a choice. The United States wants the Islamic Republic of Iran to take its rightful place in the community of nations. You have that right. But it comes with real responsibilities, and that place cannot be reached through terror or arms, but rather through peaceful actions that demonstrate the true greatness of the Iranian people and civilization. And the measure of that greatness is not the capacity to destroy, it is your demonstrated ability to build and create," he added.

As reports of political violence in Iran intensified after fiercely disputed election on June 12, 2009, the Obama administration insisted that it would not interfere with the struggle for power between regime-backed Mr. Mahmud Ahmadinejad and the thousands of demonstrators who contend the election was stolen. Administration officials, on and off the record, said that "President Obama would offer support for human rights in Iran generally and would not back away from his diplomatic outreach to the long-time US adversary, regardless of the ultimate outcome of the election."[39]

In an interview on ABC's 'This Week' on June 7, 2009, US Vice President, Joe Biden, was asked whether the US would stand in the way if Israel; viewing the prospect of an Iranian nuclear bomb as a threat to the existence of the Jewish state, decided to launch a military attack. "Look, we cannot dictate to another sovereign nation what they can and cannot do,"[40] he said.

US Vice President, Joe Biden, told to the ABC News Agency on July 4, 2009, that 'everything is on the table' when it comes to protecting the interests of the US and Israel against the threat of an Iranian nuclear attack. He also signalled that the Obama administration would not stand in the way if Israel chose to attack Iran's nuclear facilities, even as the top US military officer said any attack on Iran would be destabilizing.

US President, Barack Obama, has suggested that the consequences of post-election violence and demonstrations in Iran could shadow possible Washington-Tehran talks.

"My hope is that they continue to see [the US diplomatic effort vis-à-vis the Iranian government] as an opportunity, but obviously what's happened over the past several weeks raises serious questions,"[41] President Obama said in an interview with CNN's '360 Degrees' on July 15, 2009.

"The United States could extend a 'defence umbrella' over the Arab States of Persian Gulf if Iran develops a nuclear weapon,"[42] says Secretary of State; Hillary Clinton, on July 23, 2009. Mrs. Clinton told a town hall meeting in Bangkok that Iran should know that acquiring a nuclear capability would not enhance the Islamic republic's security. "We want Iran to calculate what I think is a fair assessment that if the US extends a defence umbrella over the region, if we do even more to support the military capacity of those in the Gulf, it's unlikely that Iran will be any stronger or safer, because they won't be able to intimidate and dominate, as they apparently believe they can, once they have a nuclear weapon," she added.

2.8.3. Policy on GCC (Gulf Cooperation Council) States

President Obama's policy in the region seems to be based on changing the traditional policy of 'balance of power', which seems to be a source of tension and war in the region. The Iran-Iraq War was likely the result of an arms race which had begun due to this policy.

If the US president changes this policy to 'balance of interests' in which all actors' interests (regional or trans-regional) are secured, the policy might be more acceptable by the regional states. Making it work will require strong US coordination with the key Persian Gulf's Arab allies.

On the one hand, even as the Persian Gulf's Arab countries continue to build their military defences by acquiring weapon systems such as "Patriot missile batteries"[43], there is virtually no support for military action by the United States or any other country to address the possible Iranian threat.

Yet, on the other hand, while most of the Gulf States support the type of diplomatic engagement with Iran that the Obama administration has discussed, there is a great deal of scepticism that diplomacy will yield any tangible results. Even those in the Persian Gulf's Arab countries who support US engagement with Iran worry that the Obama administration may be too naive when it comes to negotiating with Iran; that the United States won't have the right negotiators or strategy to strike a good bargain that doesn't undermine the interests of these countries.

In sum, as for US–Iran relations and their implications for the region, in principle Arabs and GCC countries do not find Obama's plan to hold direct talks with Tehran a source of threat. On the contrary, they regard restoring normal ties between the two countries as a positive development that will maintain regional stability and security. What might be a cause of concern for Arabs and GCC countries is a US–Iranian deal that comes at the expense of their strategic interests.

It seems that President Obama is going to open "a new chapter between the United States and the Muslim world."[44] His trip to Saudi Arabia and visiting King Abdullah on June 3, 2009, before his historic speech in Cairo on June 4, 2009, indicates the important role of the leaders of the Persian Gulf States not only in the region but also in the Middle East issues; which US is involved, and in the Muslim world.

References

1. US Department of Defence, May 18, 1995, *www.defenselink.mil/speeches*
2. Reich Bernard and Major Gotowicki Stephen H., "*The United States and the Persian Gulf in the Bush Administration*", *Royal United Services Institute and Brassey's Defence Yearbook*, London, 1991
3. Sokolsky Richard D., "*The United States and the Persian Gulf: Reshaping Security Strategy for the Post-Containment Era*", National Defence University Press, USA, 2003, p. 147

4. Major Randy B. Bell, "*Expansion of American Persian Gulf Policy By Three Presidents*", 1990, globalsecurity.org
5. Asadian Amir, "*US Policy in Persian Gulf*", Strategic Studies' Research Centre, Tehran, 2001, p. 96
6. Containment was a *United States* policy using military, economic, and diplomatic strategies to temper the spread of *Communism*, enhance America's security and influence abroad, and prevent a "*domino effect*".
7. Hafeznia Mohammad Reza, *Persian Gulf and Strategic Role of Strait of Hormuz*; 4th edition, Samt, Tehran, 2005, p 67
8. Little Douglas, "*American Orientalism: The United States and The Middle East since 1945*", University of North Carolina Press, USA, 2002, p. 146
9. Encyclopaedia of American Foreign Policy/ Carter Doctrine
10. Major Randy B. Bell, "*Expansion of American Persian Gulf Policy By Three Presidents*", 1990, globalsecurity.org
11. "*Politics-USA/Middle East, Strategic Consensus*", Inter Press Service News Agency, October 4th, 2006
12. It was the *US military* protection of *Kuwaiti* owned oil tankers from *Iranian* attacks in 1987 and 1988, two years into the *Tanker War* phase of the *Iran–Iraq War*. It was the largest naval *convoy* operation since Second *World War.*
13. "*The Contras, cocaine, and covert operations: Documentation of official US knowledge of drug trafficking and the Contras*", The National Security Archive/George Washington University/ Iran-Contra Affair
14. The Boland Amendment was the name given to three *US legislative amendments* between 1982 and 1984, all aimed at limiting *US government* assistance to the rebel *Contras* in *Nicaragua.*
15. "*Reagan's mixed White House legacy*", BBC News, June 6, 2004
16. *Reagan, Ronald*, "*Address to the Nation on the Iran Arms and Contra Aid Controversy*", "Reagan Presidential Foundation, November 13, 1986
17. *Reagan, Ronald*, "*Address to the Nation on the Iran Arms and Contra Aid Controversy*", Reagan Presidential Foundation, March 4, 1987
18. Dwyer, Paula, "*Pointing a Finger at Reagan*", Business Week, June 23, 1997

19. "*Pardons and Commutations Granted by President George H. W. Bush*", United States Department of Justice/ Iran-Contra Affair
20. Pauly Robert J. , *"US foreign policy and the Persian Gulf*", Ashgate, London, 2005, p. 41
21. It was a campaign initiated by the US, on December 14, 1983, to stop the flow of arms to Tehran from the US allied states.
22. Al Rumaihi Mohammad, "*The Gulf Monarchies, Testing Time,*" Middle East Quarterly, December 1996, pp. 45-61
23. Gause III *F. Gregory,* "*The Illogic of Dual Containment*", Foreign Affairs Magazine, March-April 1994
24. Katzman Kenneth, "*Searching for Stable Peace in the Persian Gulf*", US Army War College, USA, 1998, p.12
25. Loveman Brian, "*Strategy for Empire: US. Regional Security policy in the Post Cold War Era*", Rowman and Little Field, USA, 2004, p.117
26. Hodge Carol C. and Nolan Cathal J., "*US presidents and foreign policy: From 1789 to the Present*", Abc-Clio Inc., USA, 2006, p.379
27. Hoff Joan, "*A Faustian Foreign Policy from Woodrow to George W. Bush*", Cambridge University Press, USA, 2008, p. 169
28. Litwak Robert, *"Regime Change: US Strategy Through the Prison of 9/11*", Woodrow Wilson press, USA, 2007, p.61
29. Beginning in 2004, accounts of *physical*, *psychological*, and *sexual abuse*, including *torture*, *rape*, *sodomy*, and *homicide* of *prisoners* held in the *Abu Ghraib prison* in *Iraq* came to public attention.
30. No. 31, p. 181
31. Feller Ben, "*Obama sets firm withdrawal timetable for Iraq*", The Detroit News, February 27th , 2009
32. Associated Press News Agency, July 22nd ,2009
33. White House website/ President Obama's Inaugural Address
34. New York Times, February 11th , 2009
35. "*Obama: Policy on Iran to be different*", United Press International Journal, February 9th, 2009
36. A Status of Forces Agreement (SOFA) is an agreement between a country and a foreign nation stationing *military* forces in that country.
37. *"Obama: Policy on Iran to be different"*, United Press International Journal, February 9th ,2009
38. White House website, March 19th, 2009

39. The Washington Independent Journal , June 15, 2009
40. Associated Press, July 6, 2009
41. Iranian Press TV Channel, July 15, 2009
42. "*US Warns Iran of Defense Umbrella Over Gulf States*", Irish Times Agency, July 23, 2009
43. It is Patriot Missiles' semi-trailer launcher platform and missile canister.
44. "*Obama Visits Saudi King Before Speech*", CBS News, June 3, 2009.

8

Conclusion and Recommendations

Middle East and its sub-region, Persian Gulf region, have long been amongst the most volatile regions of the world and major centers of world affairs; strategically, economically, politically, culturally, and religiously. The location of the Persian Gulf has given the region a significant economic and strategic position. Both the Middle East and Persian Gulf region remain areas of unresolved and dangerous conflict involving the external powers, arms proliferation and ethnic and religious hatred that go back centuries.

World demand for energy continues to grow propelled in part by the booming economies of Asia. Furthermore, oil and natural gas are the primary drivers of the entire global economy, both in the developing and developed worlds. The world, therefore, faces the coincidence of increasing demand for energy and growing dependence on dangerous and unstable regions. Furthermore, the new patterns of Asian demand will invariably mean that different Asian countries will establish their own political and economic ties with the Persian Gulf countries.

As geological exploration and new extraction technologies become more sophisticated, it is clear the world is well endowed with fossil fuels; coal, oil and natural gas. The problems of getting new energy to market are, primarily, economic and political. For the foreseeable future, the importance of Middle East oil and natural gas supplies will increase and the Persian Gulf will continue to be the most significant repository for reasonably priced energy. Persian Gulf States hold 55 percent (728 billion barrels) of the world's crude oil reserves and access to the region's oil is critical to Western, indeed global, prosperity. Yet, because of the expected untapped energy resources of the region, the local players and the key external powers realize that if political conflicts can be resolved, an economic bonanza could transform the region.

The Geostrategic and Geopolitical Importance of Persian Gulf are based on two facts, as follows:

1. Iran and USA as Two Major Powers of the Region

· This region has been the centre of conflicts in the Middle East. Due to the geostrategic changes in the last three decades the region suffered a prolonged period of tension and instability, with reference to Iran-Iraq War; 1980-1988, Gulf War;1990-1991 and Iraq War; 2003 onwards.

Iran is an important player in the Persian Gulf region; taking into consideration its nuclear policy, its dispute about Persian Gulf islands with UAE, with repeated threats to close the Strait of Hormuz and its significant role in the Iraq security. Since 9/11, the Middle East issues have been the focus of international politics. Among the Middle Eastern countries, Iran's role has also been at the centre of related issues, especially since the disintegration of the Soviet Union and the containment of Iraq after the First Gulf War. As the conflict in the Middle East continues, attention turns to the influence of Iran over there.

Considering Iran's political, cultural and geopolitical realities without focusing on any particular predominant factor, it can be seen as a nation that critically affects international politics in the Middle East because of its centuries-long profile in the region. A nation of 70 million, Iran is one of the largest oil exporters in the world. And with its long coastline, good highways and railroad links to Central Asia, it is a natural crossroads and trading partner. For Iran to hold that position, however, it must contend with some significant drawbacks; it is a Persian state in a region dominated by Arabs, and a Shiite Muslim nation surrounded, for the most part, by Sunni states.

In the years since the September 11 attacks and the onset of crisis in Iraq, Iran's consolidation of its political-security role in the Middle East, and its impact upon regional and international security systems has been the focus of attention in international and Middle East security studies. The prevailing view in the West and the Arab world is that new political-security and geopolitical developments have changed the balance in regional power and political structure in favour of Iran. Accordingly, this situation has had negative effects on the United States' strategic interests, its regional allies in the Arab world, and on Israel's position.

It also began forming alliances with its oil-rich neighbors along the Caspian Sea as well as with Russia and China to counter-balance US power in the region.

USA as an extra-regional state is a major power in the region with strong influence on the region's politics. USA is present in the region since 1991. From 2001, its presence became stronger by invading Iran's eastern neighbour Afghanistan, where its troops are deployed and going to be increased. And since 2003, the western neighbour of Iran, Iraq, also has been occupied by USA and its allies' troops.

The Gulf War has taught a number of lessons about the effective use of military power. Military force can capture territory and destroy enemy forces, but it can not guarantee peace. Even a military-weakened Saddam Hussein had remained a threat to stability in the Persian Gulf region and Middle East.

Invading Iran or any surgical strikes against Iran's nuclear facilities are not logical and viable options. These actions would most likely lead to a protracted retaliation by Iran and its becoming more determined to become a nuclear power, greater instability in Afghanistan, Iraq, Lebanon and the Persian Gulf region and higher oil prices. General David Petraeus, the head of the US Central Command region which includes Iran, has stated another reason in not invading Iran. In an interview with Reuters on February 3, 2010 he said that, "It's possible (a strike) could be used to play to nationalist tendencies."[1] "A military strike on Iran could have the unintended consequence of stirring nationalist sentiment to the benefit of Tehran's hard-line government," he added.

On the other hand, the United States is providing Ballistic Missile Defence (BMD) to four countries on the Arabian Peninsula. "The New York Times carried a front-page story on the United States providing anti-missile defences to Kuwait, the UAE, Qatar and Oman, as well as stationing BMD-capable, Aegis-equipped warships in the Persian Gulf."[2]

Meanwhile, the front page of The Washington Post carried a story saying that "the Obama administration is quietly working with Saudi Arabia and other Persian Gulf allies to speed up arms sales and rapidly upgrade defences for oil terminals and other key infrastructure in a bid to thwart future attacks by Iran."[3]

Iraq's invasion of Kuwait in 1990 had a tremendous impact on the regional politics. It proved that the Gulf's many small oil-producing states are largely incapable of defending themselves against larger players in the region. The US was working together with Saudi Arabia and this was followed by the forging of ties with individual Gulf Cooperation Council (GCC) countries. Iran's decision to remain neutral during the Iraq-Kuwait crisis resulted in an improvement in Iran's relations with the West and the GCC countries. Iraq remained weakened after its defeat in the Gulf War and until removal of Saddam's regime in 2003, it was the biggest threat to the region's stability.

The removal of Saddam has not removed all enmity towards the region, and it seems that a large continued extra-regional military presence and intervention threat has perpetuated that enmity. So there is a need of constructing a regional order that works and lasts. On the other hand, this presence could be used to deter any state from violating the security and stability of the region. Maintaining a determined presence would demonstrate to any aggressive state that the United States and its allies, take the region's security commitments seriously. Moreover, Saudi Arabia and its partners in the GCC are consumers of security and vulnerable to attack from larger, more powerful neighbors. The memory of Iraq's invasion of Kuwait should be sufficient reminder that threatening neighbors cannot be ignored.

Involving extra-regional states with a stake in a peaceful and stable Gulf, most notably the US, Europe, South Asian and China, will be important for achieving long-term stability. Their geographical proximity to the Gulf, growing dependence on Gulf oil, importance to counterterrorism and non-proliferation, and abiding proclivities to be a partner with the United States on global problems all point to the need for including them in a stable structure in this sub region.

This proves that the United States is an important extra-regional power that has considerable influence in this region. Since the disintegration of Soviet Union, the United States has played a significant role in the region, especially with reference to the Gulf War (1990) and the Iraq War (2003).

The United States has placed substantial forces, to the east and the west of Iran, in Afghanistan and Iraq. For the Iranians, the current situation has posed a dangerous scenario. Iran is not concerned about these troops invading Iran. That is not a military possibility. Iran's concern is that the United States will use current situation as platform to foment ethnic dissent in Iran. This concern has been strengthening after the disputed Iranian presidential election in June 2009.

As USA has committed itself to the security of its regional Arab allies, no political settlements of Gulf conflicts are possible as long as these two countries, Iran and USA, remain adversarial.

Hostility between the two states has been intensified and a Manichaean paradigm has been developed in both of them. Each one came to perceive the other as a mortal enemy in a zero-sum game. Anti-Americanism and anti-Iranian feelings became two sides of the same coin; of course these are the feeling of governments and not nations. The walls of mistrust have been built over decades and need to be deconstructed, brick by brick. This is not an easy task, but it is an essential one. The United States has also to assure the Gulf States that negotiation with Iran does not mean withdrawal of its forces from the region and their security is not the price of US-Iran rapprochement.

It is a fact that every American president since the Islamic Revolution has been unable to deal successfully with the question of Iran. President Carter was the most visible casualty, losing the presidency in the shadow of the hostage crisis. His popular successor, President Reagan, was himself held hostage by the Iran-Contra scandal, as was his heir, President George H.W. Bush, whose political woes were multiplied by allegations of further covert dealing with Iran. The Democrats returned to power in 1993, and President Clinton could be forgiven for concluding that it would be better to be safe than feel sorry and avoided Iran altogether. Yet Iran refused to be ignored, and by the middle of his first term, Clinton was persuaded to take decisions that would draw him inexorably towards the Iranian question, a question that would come to the fore with the election of President Khatami in Iran in 1997. Contrary to expectations, Clinton found himself increasingly engaged with Iran, only to be disappointed by the end of his presidency with the lack of progress. With the inauguration of President George W. Bush, and the tragedy of September 11, 2001, the policy of neglect was shelved. He declared Iran as a part of axis of evil. To avoid Iran to reach to the nuclear power, he used the policy of carrot-and-stick frequently. But none did work out. Again the Democrats have come to power and President Obama is running the United States. He has declared his policy a kind of engagement with Iran and is trying to bring the relation of the two countries to normal. But in his first year in the office, the disputed presidential election in Iran, has suspended all the efforts in this regard. As President Obama has backed the Iranian people who are protesting against the result of the election, having direct and face to face negotiation with the Iranian government seems impossible, so far.

Amongst the obstacles in direct talk between two sides, Iran in one side and Western states lead by USA in other side. In this regard, two issues, which are interrelated seem more important:

1.1. Iran's nuclear program

Currently there is a standoff between Iran and international community on the question of nuclear development. The creation of an Iranian nuclear program serves two functions.

1. First, if successful, it further deters external threats.
2. Second, simply having the program enhances Iranian power.

Since the consequences of a strike against these facilities are uncertain and raise the possibility of Iranian attempts at interdiction of oil from the Persian Gulf, the strategic risk to the attacker's economy discourages attack. The diplomatic route of trading the program for regional safety and power becomes more attractive than an attack against a potential threat in a country with a potent potential counter.

Iran is secure from conceivable invasion. It enhances this security by using two tactics.

1. First, it creates uncertainty as to whether it has an offensive nuclear capability.
2. Second, it projects a carefully honed image of ideological extremism that makes it appear unpredictable. It makes itself appear threatening and unstable.

Paradoxically, this increases the caution used in dealing with it because the main option, an air attack, has historically been ineffective without a follow-on ground attack. If just nuclear facilities are attacked and the attack fails, Iranian reaction would be unpredictable and potentially disproportionate. Iranian posturing enhances the uncertainty. The threat of an air attack is liable to be deterred by Iran's threat of an attack against sea lanes. Such attacks would not be effective, but even a low-probability disruption of the world's oil supply is a risk not worth taking.

The Iranian government claims that its nuclear program is designed for peaceful purposes. It says that using nuclear weapons would violate Islamic law, but Washington and much of the West accuse it of having a secret program to build the bomb. So far, the International Atomic Energy Agency has found no smoking gun or any evidence that Iran has diverted its nuclear program towards military purposes. But, nor has it been able to confirm Tehran's peaceful intentions, because the Iranian government has refused to answer some major questions. Now that Iran has joined a small club of countries that can enrich uranium to a low level of purity, it seems unlikely to cave in to international pressure and accept zero enrichment in the future. The existing nuclear impasse could create an excellent bargaining chip for Tehran in future negotiations. This may be the reason that Iran's leaders are cultivating uncertainty about the country's actual capability. Iran and the United States seem to be engaged in a game of poker, with Tehran not showing its cards about its nuclear capabilities and Washington refusing to exclude the possibility of attacking Iran.

During the Cold War, Iran and Israel actually cooperated on many security issues. With a threat from the Soviet Union gone, the Iran-Israel relationship changed. Suddenly after the Cold War, Iran and Israel found themselves being the two most powerful states in the region of Middle East. And rather than potential security partners, they started to view each other as rivals. In late 1992, Israel made a sudden U-turn and started to depict Iran as a global and existential threat. At the same time, the United States rebuffed Iran's attempts to come out of its isolation and play a bigger role in regional security. So, Tehran began to see the Middle East peace process as a threat to its influence in the region and began to support Palestinian radicals such as Hamas and Hezbollah in Lebanon.

The Lebanon conflict of 2006, also called the 2006 Israel-Hezbollah War, was an indication of an assertive Iranian posture in this region, especially considering the support given by Iran to the Hezbollah in Lebanon. Hezbollah; literally '*Party* of *God*', is a *Shiite Islamist* political and *paramilitary* organization based in *Lebanon*. Its leaders were inspired by *Ayatollah Khomeini*, and its forces were trained and organized by a contingent of *Iranian Revolutionary Guards*. Some experts believe that this group is Iran's local proxy group, while some others say that Hezbollah is more of an equal partner than a proxy in the alliance with Iran.

Hezbollah is now also a major provider of social services, which operate schools, hospitals, and agricultural services for thousands of Lebanese Shiites, and plays a significant role in *Lebanese politics*. It is regarded as a *resistance movement* throughout much of the *Arab* and *Muslim world*. Many governments, including Arab ones, have condemned actions by Hezbollah while other states, such as Iran and Syria, have praised the party. Several western countries regard it in whole or in part as a terrorist organization. It seems that Hezbollah has broadened its motives from fighting Israel in Lebanon to fighting Israeli and US influence in the region.

Israel is more concerned with Iran's nuclear program than USA. The Americans have seen a number of apparently extreme and dangerous countries develop nuclear weapons. The most important example was Maoist China. Once China developed nuclear weapons, it behaved quite cautiously. Furthermore, the United States is a big country with widely dispersed population and a massive nuclear arsenal. A reckless country that launched some weapons at the United States would do minimal harm to the United States while the other country would face annihilation. But, Israel's geography forces it to see things differently. Iranian President, Mahmud Ahmadinejad, has said Israel should be wiped off the face of the Earth while simultaneously seems working to attain nuclear weapons. Moreover, the United States is outside the range of *the Iranians' current ballistic missile arsenal* while Israel is not. And a nuclear strike would have a particularly devastating effect on Israel. Israel is small country with a highly concentrated population. A strike with just one or two weapons could destroy Israel. Therefore, Israel has a very different threshold for risk as far as Iran is concerned. For Israel, a nuclear strike from Iran is improbable, but would be catastrophic if it happened. For the United States, the risk of an Iranian strike is far more remote, and would be painful but not catastrophic if it happened.

Besides, it is believed that if Iran succeeds in getting a bomb, it will also create a potential arms race as Arab states see the need to obtain weapons to deter the Iranians. In fact, since 2006, twelve Middle East countries (Saudi Arabia, Algeria, Egypt, Jordan, Morocco, Tunisia, Turkey, Syria, Yemen, Iraq, Libya, and the Gulf Cooperation Council) have either announced plans to explore atomic energy or signed nuclear cooperation agreements. All say they are only interested in peaceful uses of nuclear technology. As Iran is demonstrating, it is not so easy to achieve a nuclear capability, especially with the whole world watching, but the region will become far more dangerous as the number of countries engaged in nuclear activities grows.

1.2. The Sanctions Imposed by the Western Countries on Iran

After Islamic revolution in Iran and start of the existing hostility between Iran and USA, the country has been suffering from the sanctions imposed by the Western states, particularly USA.

Recently, the Iranian government has rejected, at least for the moment, a proposal from the P-5+1 to ship the majority of its low-enriched uranium abroad for further enrichment. But in January 21, 2010, Iranian Foreign Minister said that "Iran has not rejected an UN-brokered offer to exchange enriched nuclear fuel but it wants a staged swap rather than a wholesale handover of most of its stockpile."[4]

The group is now considering the next step in the roadmap that it laid out in April 2009. The next step to force Iran to change its attitude and policy seems to be a new round of sanctions, this time meant to be crippling. The only crippling sanction available is to cut off the supply of gasoline, since Iran imports 35 percent of its refined gasoline products. That would theoretically cripple the Iranian economy and compel the Iranians to comply with US demands over the nuclear issue. But it seems that even all of them are not committed to the idea of sanctions, referring to negative vote by China to impose new sanctions and favor to continue dialogue. China and Russia, both members of 5+1 group, seem to be not eager to impose more sanctions on Iran.

In case of China, there are two important reasons :

1. First, China is the world's second biggest oil consumer, 6.39 million barrel consumption per day, after USA. Therefore, it is trying to keep its good relations with Iran, resulting in continued oil export from Iran. USA is encouraging key Arab states to boost oil exports to China in order to reduce Beijing's reliance on Iranian energy.
2. Second, relates to Taiwan and an arms sale to this country. "USA has announced the sale of US$ 6.4 billion worth arms to Taiwan."[5] This has sparked China's anger. It is expected to prompt China to slow or even break military relations with the United States. It seems that if Western states, especially USA, want to have full coordination of China in dealing with Iran's nuclear program and sway its support from Iran side to their side, Taiwan issue and China's oil consumption must be somehow managed.

In Russia's case, according to Reuters, US Secretary of State, Hilary Clinton, was speaking in London after talks with Russian Foreign Minister, Sergei Lavrov; part of a series of meetings held on the sidelines of international conferences on Afghanistan and Yemen focused on Iran. Russia, which along with China has been less eager to push for new UN sanctions on Tehran, was now 'very willing' both to work with the United States and to consider 'appropriate pressure' as a next step, she said, While Lavrov stated

"It is clear that one can't wait forever, and our partners are already talking about the need to discuss further measures in the UN Security Council."[6] He warned that patience with Tehran was running out, according to remarks quoted by state-run Russian Information Agency (RIA) Novosti.

In his first State of the Union address on January 27, 2010, President Obama warned Iran's leaders of the nuclear programme. President Obama said that "Iran's leaders continue to ignore their obligations. Iranian leaders would face growing consequences. That is a promise."[7] The Senate bill targets non-Iranian companies that export fuel to Iran or help expand Tehran's oil refining capacities by denying them US loans and other financial assistance. The Senate backing follows legislation approved in the House of Representatives and the two must be reconciled before becoming law.

There have been three rounds of UN sanctions against Iran and the US and its allies on the Security Council have been pushing for a fourth. In 2006, the council called on states to block Iran's import and export of 'sensitive nuclear material and equipment' and to freeze the financial assets of those involved in Iran's nuclear activities. In 2008, the council banned all of Iran's arms exports. Further restrictions, imposed in March 2008, encouraged scrutiny of the dealings of Iranian banks.

Moreover, the sanctions have already hurt Iran badly. Its plan for gas and oil pipelines that would connect the Persian Gulf to the Caspian Sea has stalled because of the restrictions. Its oil industry has been deprived of access to important modern technologies as a result of which Iran's oil production today remains significantly below what it was in 1979 (6 million barrels per day) falling to 4 million barrels per day in 2008.

But it should not be ignored that any new sanctions against Iran will cause further suffering to Iranian people, who are already affected by the consequences of existing embargoes. It is strongly recommended that if any new sanctions are in agenda, the best way to aid Iranian people is maintaining or even increasing military sanctions and dropping economic sanctions.

On the other hand, it is a fact that historically, sanctions have not succeeded so far. For example, the United States placed sanctions on the sale of grain to the Soviet Union during the Cold War. It is learnt that while the sanctions were hurting the Soviets, they were hurting American farmers as well. The sanctions which USA imposed on Japan in 1941 could be another example. As another example, the United States halted the shipment of oil and scrap metal to Japan in an attempt to force it to reshape its policies in China and Indochina. The sanctions were crippling, as the Americans expected; however, the Japanese response was not capitulation, but Pearl Harbor.

Furthermore, the sanctions have been lose-lose economic proposition for both United States and Iran. Not only Iran has to bear the consequences of imposed sanctions, but also USA. Nor should one underestimate the negative long-term implications for US interests of increasing involvement of China and Russia in the Persian Gulf, which Iran has facilitated, or of Tehran's recent move to use Euro in its international transactions.

Considering above mentioned issues shows that a strategy of full engagement will be the best option to eliminate or at least diminish the problems in the two states' relations. This strategy which gradually increases economic, educational and cultural exchanges between the two states, will exploit the commonalities shared by two governments and establish concrete institutional mechanism to manage their remaining differences. But normalizing Iran-USA relations will be a long and difficult process.

As a first step, there needs to be held direct, comprehensive and unconditional negotiations to learn firsthand about the two government's shared interests on all the important issues, such as defeating Al Qaeda and stabilizing Afghanistan, Iraq security, Iranian nuclear program and etc.

Meanwhile, USA has to assure its Arab allies of the region and also Israel that any direct negotiation with Iran does not mean that Iran's disputed nuclear policy is being neglected and it will remain the main item on the agenda.

It seemed that both states were ready for negotiation in 2009, but the disputed presidential election and its following unrest and crises in Iran halted all efforts and Iranian government's suspicions about Western countries, mostly USA, to support and help the oppositions to change the regime has made the possibility of any future direct dialogue very unlikely.

2. Essential Regional Order

It is also argued that order in the Persian Gulf is a critical necessity for stability in the Middle East. Such an order would be a product of the policies of two important players; Iran and United States, besides the other states of the Persian Gulf. Order in the Persian Gulf would ensure stability for the region of the Middle East and also in the long run, provide for containing the so-called Civilization Clash, which is emerging in the World today.

An unstable regional balance of power is likely to force the United States to remain militarily active and could accelerate Iran's pursuit of nuclear weapons. A failure to reform governance in the Gulf States and the Middle East could permit political instability and in the end undermine any security system.

Before Islamic Revolution in Iran, in 1979, regional order of the Persian Gulf region was triangular comprising Iran, Iraq and Saudi Arabia. Iran's policies in the region and Middle East, as a pro-Western state, were in favour of USA and its allies. Iraq, as a pro-Soviet state, also was a dominant country of the region and Saudi Arabia due to its huge oil reserves, one of the highest in the world, had and still has the power of influence on regional policies.

Iran and Iraq have had conflicted relationship since Second World War. They have fought a prolonged conflict in 1980s and continued to have strained relationship until Saddam Hussein was in power.

Iran and Saudi Arabia, the other dominant and powerful state of the region, never had a direct confrontation. But they were struggling to get ahead of each other and become the superpower of the region.

The Islamic Revolution changed Iran's governmental structure as a result of which Iran's regional and foreign policies also altered. In 1979, besides Islamic revolution in Iran some other important events happened; such as Camp David Treaty, dissolution of CENTO, Russia's aggression against Afghanistan and establishment of USA's embassy in Tehran followed by hostage crisis. On the other hand, Islamic Revolution in Iran was the reason of turning some of Islamic States' back to Western Ideologies, as the Revolution casted doubts about the legitimacy of Persian Gulf's monarchies'. A threat to the monarchies' legitimacy indicated their weakness of security establishment since Iranian Islamic revolutionaries called specifically for the overthrow of monarchies and their replacement with Islamic republics, much to the alarm of its smaller Sunni-run Arab neighbors *Iraq*, *Kuwait*, *Saudi Arabia* and the *Persian Gulf States*.

Then, the Iran-Iraq War started in 1980 and lasted for eight years. Iran and Iraq, the states which were powerfully ordaining the Gulf's affairs and had dominated the security picture of the Persian Gulf for more than two decades, were under internal and external pressures and instead of them, small states that could not play any important role in regional order, became USA's political and martial bases.

After Islamic Revolution and due to a prolonged war with Iraq, Iran became weak and almost lost its position as a dominant state of the region. Iraq also had been weakened by the long period of sanctions imposed by USA and most of the Western countries; therefore it seemed that the stage was set for Saudi Arabia to become the region's unique dominant power. The invasion of

Kuwait by Iraq altered the situation and to respond to the Gulf States' demand, USA entered the region.

During recent decades, preserving a 'balance of power' policy between the regional actors has been the basis of American foreign policies in the region, especially in the Persian Gulf. The recent developments have unbalanced power equations in favour of Iran.

The US, by regime change in Iraq, helped Iran become the biggest military power in the region after Israel. On the other hand, the US presence in the region which firstly was in response to the Gulf States demand for confronting Iraq, and now to maintain the stability of the region, is being opposed by the government of Iran. It believes that this will intensify the tension and instability in the region and the regional disputes must be solving by the regional states. But regional states have accepted that US and its allies force has removed the greatest source of insecurity to the Gulf and in doing so, the regional balance of power has again been shifted as a consequence of the action, although US presence has caused expanded opposition in the cultural and political spheres. It is essential that Tehran accept it so, because Iraq was the major threat to Iran, in particular.

Washington surrounds Iran with bases in Bahrain, Kuwait and Qatar and massive troop's build-ups in Afghanistan and Iraq. It makes friends with the leaders of Iran's neighbours and its nuclear-equipped naval force carries patrol of the Persian Gulf region.

The Iranian counter could be the following actions:

1. Maintain a military force capable of protecting the surrounding borders so that major American forces cannot penetrate.
2. Move to create a nuclear force, very publicly, in order to deter attack in the long run and to give Iran a bargaining chip for negotiations in the short term.

In this new environment, Iran faces a stark choice: either continue to resist US penetration of the region by heavy investment in what has become a shrinking circle of allies or exploit its considerable tactical advantages to broaden its policy of detente and diplomacy for greater economic and political gains.

It seems that Iran legitimately demands that Washington recognize its important role in Afghanistan, Iraq, Lebanon and the Palestinian territories and also Tehran's new role as a major regional power.

To set right the imbalance of power, America and others reacted by following an eminently realist script. They banded together to support a largely US operation that pushed Saddam back within his own borders, freeing Kuwait. This correction of the balance of power weakened and enervated Saddam's Iraq more, followed by over a decade of economic sanctions, that by 2003, had already gutted the once-powerful Iraqi state, for balancing potential future aggression by an unpredictable Iraq.

When the United States eventually implemented its new doctrine and took military action against Iraq in 2003, Iran, which under other circumstances would have welcomed any effort to remove the Iraqi regime, was unprepared and unwilling to lend any direct support to the US effort. The reason was simple and understandable; Iran itself was in the US crosshairs as an evil power.

Since 2003, the year of removal of Saddam and regime change in Iraq and most importantly USA's more firmed presence in the region, another triangle was formed; including USA, as an extra-regional state which replaced Iraq, Iran and Saudi Arabia.

Saudi Arabia and Iran have continued their relations conservatively and are trying to avoid any kind of confrontation despite their desire to increase influence in the region. Iran does not pose a military threat to Saudi Arabia, and the Saudis do not see Iran as such. While Riyadh worries about the Iranian nuclear program, that is an issue for the future, not the immediate present. Iranian President, Mahmud Ahmadinejad, visited Saudi Arabia in 2007 and the two countries have kept lines of communication open. The Iranians are not trying to destabilize the Saudi regime in its own domestic politics, as they tried to do in the 1980's. The Saudis do not want to see an American-Iranian military confrontation, because they fear that the Arab side of the Gulf will be targeted for Iranian retaliation.

For their part, the Iranians do not seek out a direct confrontation with Saudi Arabia, hoping to avoid a sectarian Sunni-Shiite polarization that might benefit them in Iraq but could hobble their influence elsewhere in the Muslim world. Their contest for influence is more subtle, played out in the domestic politics of Iraq, Lebanon, the Palestinian territories and in Arab public opinion. But it is very real.

The Saudi leadership realizes that Iran has more cards to play in Iraq than it does and believes that the Iranians have a wider array of local allies, particularly armed allies, in Iraq. They created and continue to support Islamic Supreme Council of Iraq (ISCI), which was formerly the Supreme Council of the Islamic Revolution in Iraq. They have ties with other Shiite groups, including the Sadrist movement. They have good relations with Kurdish parties, particularly the Patriotic Union of Kurdistan led by Iraqi President; Jalal Talabani. They have a thriving trade with Iraq; tens of thousands of Iranian pilgrims visit the holy sites in Iraq every year. While the Shiite religious establishments in Najaf and Qom have something of a historical rivalry for leadership in Shiite theology, one should not discount the personal and family ties and corporate identity which link the Shiite Ulama across the Iran-Iraq border. Saudi Arabia does not seek to reverse the reality of post-Saddam Iraq, that the Shiite Arab majority has a central role in Iraqi politics. What Riyadh seeks is to prevent Iraq from becoming an Iranian client state. It sees the current Iraqi government of Nouri Al Maliki as, in effect, an Iranian client regime. Saudi opposes the proposal by the Islamic Supreme Council of Iraq to create a regional government in the centre and south of Iraq; a Shiite ruling region on the model of the KRG (Kurdistan Regional Government). Riyadh views that prospect as the end of Iraq as a state, with the Shiite-dominated regional government as a permanent client of Iran.

One of Iran's foreign policy challenges has been regulating its relations with the Arab world. This is, firstly, due to the various religious-cultural, historical and geographical connections between Iran and its Arab neighbours as well as (more significantly) to the fact that the particular issues pertaining to the Arab world also impact Iran. Secondly, by its presence in the Arab world politics especially in the Persian Gulf region, Iran has balanced its relations with the great powers.

Iran's newly significant roles in shaping international politics of the Middle East include:

1. Acting as a balancing political power in regional crises such as Afghanistan, Iraq and Lebanon.
2. Its geopolitical posture in the battle against global terrorism and being situated between the two major bases of global terrorism; Afghanistan and Iraq.
3. Its influence among the Shiite factions who are currently at the centre of the Middle East's shifting politics.

Three fundamental factors shape Iran's self-image: Iran as national identity and regional power, Islam as faith and ethical code and Persia as source of history and future national prestige. Iran's foreign and security policy goals under the ayatollah or shah have remained the same: security of Iran's territorial and political integrity, recognition of regime legitimacy, acknowledgment of the country's security concerns and historic regional leadership role.

Affairs pertaining to the Middle East and Persian Gulf region are very complicated and their detailed examination is a difficult task. After reviewing the conditions of the Persian Gulf region, in Cold War and Post-Cold War eras, it seems that the greatest danger in the Gulf is not a nuclear Iran or a traditional threat of conventional invasion, but rather internal socioeconomic and political changes that might be increasingly hard for leaders to direct or control.

Regionally, the greatest threat is not strategic Weapons of Mass Destruction attacks, but the fragmentation and weakening of the central Saudi state, Iraqi civil war and dissolution, recent disputed presidential election in Iran which may lead to violence and overshadow other issues related to Iran and growing radicalism via violent forms of politicized Islam in Persian Gulf's Arab states; including increased levels of trans-national violence and terrorism.

Recommendations

The followings are some of the findings and recommendations proposed for resolution of the complex issues involved :

1. To restore the peace in Persian Gulf Region and ultimately in the Middle East, two major actors; Iran and USA, must cooperate. To re-establish stability and security in Middle East and Persian Gulf region, both USA and Iran should change their policies.

   USA needs to give more offerings in its carrot and stick policy. As a first step, the imposed sanctions, which are causing hardships to Iranian people, should be lifted. Washington should consider the extent of Iranian role in the region that the US and its allies can agree to. This may necessitate a paradigm shift in Washington's approach to Iran and the Middle East, but failure to reconcile with Iranian demands justified by the new balance in the region will likely disable USA administration from turning political opportunities into real diplomatic breakthroughs; irrespective of their positive intentions.

   Iran has to modify and moderate its policies, especially its nuclear policy. Without these main actors' cooperation, any attempt to establish and maintain stability in the region will fail.

2. The existing border disputes, dilemma over the sovereignty of some of the Persian Gulf islands, interfering in each others' internal issues by the regional states and existing hostility between some of them must be solved and removed, immediately, as any of the mentioned issues could become the source and reason of another conflict or even a devastating war in this critically sensitive region.

3. A stable regional order in the Persian Gulf is a dire necessity for the Middle East. Such an order would be an outcome of the policies of Iran, United States and the other states of the Persian Gulf. Order in the Persian Gulf would ensure stability for the region and eventually for the Middle East.

The Gulf States' hopes for stability have been severely challenged in recent years, first by Shiite Islamic Revolution in Iran and then by Hussein in Iraq. Results from these and other threats during this period has been the formation of closer, more involved, relationships between the Gulf States and the United States. The Gulf States see this as a source of encouragement, yet, are still concerned about the long term impact of a western presence.

Today, the security preference of most Gulf governments is to re-establish the kind of balance of power in the Persian Gulf they once felt comfortable under, a balance maintained by friendly relations with a major regional power and backed up by a more distant US presence.

Further, it is felt that the best path to establish regional order in the Persian Gulf region is to restore a sort of balance of power consisting of Iran, Saudi Arabia and US as an extra-regional power.

USA has two advantages in doing so which are as follows :

1. This would enable it to create a very strong influence on regional politics.
2. It will have power to deter any aggressive state which may have tendency to violate the peace and stability of region.

It is hoped that the findings and recommendations propounded provide food for thought to the readers and lead to further seminal works on this so critical issues having global ramifications.

References

1. "*Petraeus says strike on Iran could spark nationalism*" , Reuters, February 3, 2010
2. "*US Speeding Up Missile Defences in Persian Gulf*", New York Times, January 31, 2010

3. "*US Steps Up Arms Sales to Persian Gulf Allies*", Washington Post, January 30, 2010
4. France Press News Agency, Tehran, January 21, 2010
5. "*US sells weapons to Taiwan, angering China*", Washington Post, January 30, 2010
6. "*Clinton sees consensus forming on Iran steps*", Reuters, January 28, 2010
7. "*US Senate Backs New Sanctions Against Iran*", BBC News Agency, January 29, 2010

Appendices

Appendix A

Disputed Islands' Chronology According to Iran

Antiquity

Studies show that, in 1000 BC. Abu Musa Island was administered by Iranians, like other islands of Pars Sea (Persian Gulf), and "was a part of Iranian territory."[1]

138-171 BC

In Parthians (Arsacides) era and in the time of Mehrdad the First (138-171 BC.), Abu Musa was under the dominance of this Iranian dynasty.

Sasanian Dynasty

In Sasanian time (another Iranian dynasty); these islands were a part of Iranian territory.

1147

In 1147, Karim Xane Zand ruled over the ports and islands of the Persian Gulf.

1811

Fath Ali Shah, in 1811, granted the Oman's Sultan lease title to Bandar Abbas, Minab and southern Persian Gulf coastal areas from east to west as far as Bahrain where the islands of Abu Musa and the two Tunbs are situated.

1840

The Anglo-Iranian territorial contention began in 1840s with declaration of "Haji Mirza Aghasi"[2] opposition to the British annexation of ports and islands of lower Persian Gulf.

1865

Nasser Al Din Shah, in 1856, granted the Oman's Sultan lease title to Bandar Abbas, Minab and southern Persian Gulf coastal areas from east to west as far as Bahrain where the islands of Abu Musa and the two Tunbs are situated.

1885

The challenges of the modern world forced the Iranian government to abandon the old Safavid federative administrative system and introduce a new system of state organisation based on the division of the country into 27 provinces. The 26th province incorporated the ports and islands of the Persian Gulf.

1887

British, under the pretext of creating security in the Persian Gulf by fighting pirates, and to take advantage of the weak state of the Iranian government of the day, took over the three islands. Iran hoisted flags in Sirri and Abu Musa to mark her ownership of these islands after dismissing the Qasemi deputy governors of Bandar Lengeh.

1888

A War Office map, presented by the British Minister in Tehran to the Shah of Iran, confirmed these three islands as Iranian-owned.

1892

In "Lord Curzon's"[3] 'Persia and the Persian Question', the map showed the islands as Iranian territory.

July 1903

Citing fears of growing Russian influence in the Persian Gulf, the British occupied all the strategic islands of the southern Persian Gulf, including the Tunbs and Abu Musa. British occupation forces hoisted the flag of Sharjah in Greater Tunb and Abu Musa immediately after their occupation.

1908

British occupation forces hoisted the flag of Sharjah in Lesser Tunb.

1928

British agreed to negotiate the status of the Tunbs, Abu Musa and Sirri islands with Iran.

January 1929

Britain and Iran began negotiations and continued them until mid-spring 1929 without much progress.

1934

Governor of Bandar Abbas and other Iranian officials visited Greater Tunb. This visit was the result of a secret Iranian arrangement with the Sheikh of Ras Al Kheimah according to which the Sheikh lowered his flag in Greater Tunb and the Iranian flag was hoisted instead.

1948

Iranians expressed a wish to place administrative offices on Tunbs and Abu Musa, the British ignored it.

1950

The Iranian Government had, from the year 1950, imposed visa requirement for the inhabitants of the lower Persian Gulf travelling into Iran. Before that year, they carried an Iranian identity document that allowed them to travel freely between the opposite coasts.

1965

Negotiations began between Iran and Britain for a north-south maritime division in the Persian Gulf.

November 1971

Britain settled the issue Islands through negotiations between Iran and Sharjah and a Memorandum of Understanding was signed between Iran and Sharjah on Abu Musa, Sharjah to maintain sovereignty over Abu Musa and Iran to station military forces on the island. Oil revenues from the oil fields surrounding the island was shared and by agreeing to the unconditional return of the two Tunbs to Iran.

November 30, 1971

The *Iranian Navy* seized the Islands. There was only resistance of a tiny Arab Police force. Iranians were instructed not to open fire and didn't. The only shots fired were by the Arab police which killed 4 Iranian marines and injured one.

December 9, 1971

UK's permanent representative at the United Nations declared the overall settlement of the issue of these islands as a model agreement for the settlement of similar territorial differences elsewhere in the world.

October 1972

The dispute became a relatively dormant issue following the establishment of diplomatic relations between Iran and the UAE.

1980s

The dispute over the islands was overshadowed by the Iran-Iraq war.

April 1992

Iran prevented a group of non-nationals from Sharjah from entering Abu Musa.

May 12, 1992

The High Council of the UAE met to discuss the issue of the islands and agreed that commitments of each member states before 1971 were to be treated as commitments of the Union as a whole.

Supreme Council of the United Arab Emirates; the Emir of Sharjah who was Iran's original partner in the 1971 Memorandum of Understanding, refused to pass his Emirate's authority over the issue of Abu Musa Island to the UAE leadership and left the meeting.

August 24, 1992

Iranian authorities refused entry to Abu Musa of one hundred people of different nationalities.

Autumn of 1992

Negotiations between Iran and Sharjah to arrive at a final status for Abu Musa were scuppered by the UAE foreign minister who linked any settlement on Abu Musa to the subjection of the Tunbs to UAE sovereignty. This stance destroyed any prospects for real negotiations.

April 1993

Iranian Parliament passed a law extending the limits of the country's territorial waters to 12 miles. The Parliament also reasserted Iran's claims to Abu Musa Island.

1996

Iran has built an airport on Abu Musa and a power station on Greater Tunb.

November 1999

Gulf Cooperation Council backs the UAE in its dispute with Iran over Greater and Lesser Tunb and Abu Musa.

June 3, 2004

Abu Dhabi made an armed assault on the Iranian boat in the territorial waters of Abu Musa in spite of the fact that Abu Musa's territorial waters are under joint Iranian-Sharjah sovereignty.

References

1. www.geocities.com
2. Hajj Mirza Aghasi worked as the Prime Minister of Iran during 1835-1848.
3. Between 1911 and 1921, he was a *British Conservative* statesman who was *Viceroy of India* and *Foreign Secretary*.

Appendix B

The Disputed Islands' Chronology According to UAE

1624–1741 AD

On the fall of the Yaaruba state in Oman, a new Arab maritime power (the Qawasim state based in Ras Al Khaimah) rose to fill the vacuum.

1750

A faction of the Qawasim moved northward where they settled down in the area of Lengeh.

1864

Southern coast ruler sent an official message to the British Resident informing him that the islands of Abu Musa, Greater and Lesser Tunbs, and Sir Abu Nuair had been ruled by his ancestors, and would, therefore, remain under his rule.

1870s

Abu Musa Island had become an agricultural centre and a resort for the Qawasim rulers of Sharjah.

February 1873

The ruler of Ras Al Khaimah stressed that the three islands (Abu Musa, Greater and Lesser Tunbs) were under his jurisdiction and also asserted that Sirri Island belonged to the Lengeh Qawasim.

1877

The Lengeh Qawasim admitted that title to the Tunbs belonged to Ras Al Khaimah Qawasim.

1879

The ruler of Sharjah exiled his political opponents to Abu Musa Island.

1883

When the ruler of Sharjah himself was overthrown by his nephew, he chose to live on Abu Musa.

1887

Persian armies invaded Lengeh and expelled the Qawasim governors who had ruled it for over 125 years. The Persians occupied the island of Sirri.

March 11, 1888

Britain demanded an explanation for the hoisting of the Iranian flag on Sirri Island.

1904

Iran began to challenge Sharjah's sovereignty over Abu Musa Island.

1912

Britain and the ruler of Sharjah agreed to establish a lighthouse on Greater Tunb, with the assurance that this would not entail any encroachment on the ruler's sovereignty over the island.

August 24, 1928

British administration issued a memorandum on the status of the three islands. In that memorandum it was stated that the islands of Greater and Lesser Tunbs had belonged to Ras Al Khaimah since its emergence as an entity independent of Sharjah, while Abu Musa belonged to Sharjah.

1929-1930

This period witnessed negotiations between Britain and Iran aimed at reaching an Anglo-Iranian treaty. During these negotiations, evidence emerged supporting the Qawasim's title to the three islands, and hence highlighting the weakness of the Iranian claims. In the draft of the treaty, it was decided to recognize Iran's title to the island of Sirri, while the three other islands (the Tunbs and Abu Musa) would remain Arab.

February 1935

The ruler of Sharjah signed an agreement with Golden Valley Ochre and Oxide Company Ltd to exploit red oxide in Tunbs Islands.

1935

The same company, Golden Valley Ochre and Oxide Company Ltd, was granted exploration concessions to exploit red oxide in Abu Musa. The company continued to function until 1968.

March 3, 1964

The ruler of Ras Al Khaimah granted oil exploration concessions in the Tunbs to two companies: Union Oil Exploration and Production Company and The Southern Natural Gas Company (American company). Meanwhile, Sharjah granted similar concessions in Abu Musa and its territorial waters extending twelve nautical miles to Buttes Gas and Oil Company (American company).

1969

British Foreign Office documents for 1969 (released early in 2000) indicated that the rulers of Sharjah and Ras Al Khaimah continued to refuse to hand over the three islands, in spite of repeated British and Iranian pressures on them to accept an amicable settlement of the issue; one that would prevent direct military occupation by Iran depriving the two rulers of their sovereignty over the islands.

1971

The six Persian Gulf states; Abu Dhabi, Ajman, Al Fujairah, Ash Sharjah, Dubai and Umm al Qaiwan, merged to form the United

Arab Emirates (UAE). They were joined in 1972 by Ras Al Khaimah.

November 30, 1971

British endeavours ultimately resulted in a Memorandum of Understanding which was signed by Iran and Sharjah. Under this agreement, Iranian troops could land on the northern part of Abu Musa.

Ras Al Khaimah, maintained its position of rejecting any concessions with regard to its title to the Tunbs. Consequently, the Shah of Iran ordered troops to land on the two islands and to occupy them by force.

July 17, 1972

The UAE sent a note to the President of the United Nation Security Council in which it affirmed that the three islands; Tunbs and Abu Musa were Arab territories.

October 5, 1972

A statement was read out before the twenty-seventh session of the General Assembly, in which the UAE reaffirmed its sovereignty over the three islands; Tunbs and Abu Musa.

February 20, 1974

A similar statement was read out before the Security Council.

November 19, 1974

A third statement was read out before the UN Special Political Committee.

August 6, 1980

A similar statement was sent to the UN Secretary General in which the UAE reaffirmed its unchanging policy of affirming its sovereignty over the islands.

December 1, 1980

A similar statement was read out before the Secretary General.

1987

Iran moved its troops to the southern side of Abu Musa, and occupied it following an abortive coup in Sharjah.

1991

Iran imposed restrictions on third party citizens wishing to enter the UAE zone of Abu Musa by requiring entry permits.

April 1992

As the UAE rejected that measure, Iran ordered all foreigners to leave off the Abu Musa Island.

August 1992

Iran prevented teachers working in Abu Musa, as well as some UAE nationals, from entering the island, and returning them to Sharjah harbours following three nights aboard ship.

January 2, 1994

The United Nations Secretary General stated that the world organization was ready to play any role in resolving the dispute over the three islands within the context of diplomacy, mediation and arbitration, should the two parties seek its mediation.

December 29, 1994

Iran launched off an air route linking Bandar Abbas and Abu Musa, an action that violated UAE's sovereignty over the island.

1996

UAE adopted a permanent constitution.

March 4, 1998

Leading Iranian newspapers stated that "Tehran has offered the Lesser Tunb and a joint administration of Abu Musa to Abu Dhabi in exchange for the UAE's acceptance of Iran's sovereignty over the Greater Tunb."[1]

February 27, 1999

Iran conducted military manoeuvres in the UAE's territorial waters around Abu Musa Island and constructed military and civilian establishments on Abu Musa Island, and the deployment of medium-range missiles therein.

July 3, 1999

Foreign Ministers of the member states of the Gulf Cooperation Council (GCC) announced the formation of a tripartite committee that would set up a mechanism to start direct negotiation for settling the issue of Iran's occupation of the three islands by peaceful means.

December 31, 2001

The GCC issued a statement reiterating its support for the UAE's sovereignty over Abu Musa and the Tunbs, declared Iran's claims on the islands as 'null and void', and backed 'all measures by the UAE to regain sovereignty on its three islands peacefully'.

November 11, 2005

A British couple and an Australian yachtsman ran into trouble when they sailed towards a disputed island in the Strait of Hormuz, between Iran and the United Arab Emirates. The trio was released without any charge or even knowing why they had been apprehended. "Initial questioning by the officials focused on spying and the possibility that it was 'a subtle probe' into ownership of the island. Iranians were clearly being cautious about the unwelcome visitors."[2]

References

1. Foley Sean, "*The UAE: Political Issues and Security Dilemmas*", MERIA Journal, Volume 3, Number 1, March 1999
2. BBC News Agency, November 11th, 2005

Appendix C

Chronology of the Iran-Iraq war; 1980-1988

September, 1980

Start of Iraq-Iran war, Iraq invaded Iran after alleged Iranian artillery bombardment on Khonqin and Mandali (September 4), Iraqi abrogation of 1975 treaty (September 17), Iraq quickly captured Khoramshahr (November 10) and Abadan. Both attacked each others' oil facilities.

June 17, 1981

Israel bombed Iraqi Osirak nuclear plant near Baghdad.

April 12, 1982

Under strong Iranian counterattack, despite flow of arms from US and France and money from GCC to Iraq, Saddam Hussein offered to withdraw from Iran in order to end the conflict. Iran made peace conditional on payment of reparations and launched major offensive in the south (from April 29), but failed in bid in to take Basra (July) and Mandali (October).

February 1984

Iran and Iraq shelled each others' cities; UN-mediated agreement to cease fire, with UN observers posted in Baghdad and Tehran to monitor (from June 12). Meanwhile, Iran captured Iraq's oil-rich Majnun islands. Iraq turned to attacking Khark Island oil terminal and Iranian ships in the Gulf, using French-purchased Exocet missiles (March 27). Iran retaliated with strikes on Saudi and Kuwaiti ships (May 13). UN condemned the shipping war (June 1); Saudi shot down an Iranian jet fighter, allegedly in its airspace (June 5).

1985:

March

Iraq began bombing Ahvaz and Bushehr; Iran responded with missiles on Baghdad and then Iranian troops crossed Tigris, closing

Basra-Baghdad road (March 17); unable to hold it and ceasefire arranged in the war of the cities (April 6).

May

Iraq broke ceasefire again on May 26. Shah Hussein (Jordan) and Mubarak (Egypt) visited Saddam to show their support.

September 13

Iran received 508 US-made Tow missiles, as part of secret arms-for-hostages deal with US.

Jan 17, 1986:

4000 more missiles for Iran authorized by Reagan were supplied through Israel.

February

Iran captured Faw peninsula; in South Iraq, many Iranians set the objective of capturing Najaf and Karbala, and installing an Islamic government in Baghdad.

April 22

US arrested 10 officials involved in Iran arms sales.

November 2

US/Iran Arms sales were finally revealed by Al-Shiraa newspaper (Beirut), creating the international 'Iran gate' scandal.

1987:

USS Stark attacked in Gulf by two Iraqi Exocet missiles; killing 37. United States blamed Iran.

Feb 18

Iraq resumed war on Iranian cities. Moscow pressured Iraq to end it.

May 21

Reports of chemical warfare attacks on Kurdish villages and guerrilla fighters became more frequent and detailed. Clinical evidence as well as soil samples, confirmed the use of mustard gas and the nerve agent tabun against the Kurdish population.

1988:

Feb 27

Iraq resumed 'war of the cities'. Iraq replied to Iranian attacks on Baghdad, by hitting Tehran by missiles for the first time.

March 16

Iraq used chemical weapons against Kurds supporting Iran in Halabja; killing 5000, an attack which began the Anfal campaigns against Kurdish villages. 1276 villages were destroyed.

April 16-18

Iraq recaptured Faw peninsula, using large quantity of chemical weapons; similar attack on Mehran (17-22 June).

April 18

US blew up two Iranian oil rigs, destroyed an Iranian frigate and immobilised another.

July 3

USA's Vincennes shot down an Iranian Airbus passenger aircraft, killing 290.

July 20

Iran accepted ceasefire after UN-brokered agreement in Geneva.

August 20

Formal ceasefire in Iraq-Iran war, UN monitoring force established for Iran-Iraq border. Confirmation by UN that Iraq did use mustard gas against Iranian civilians.

Appendix D

Chronology of the Persian Gulf War; 1990-1991

1990:

August 2

Iraq invaded Kuwait.

August 3

Iraqi forces reached Kuwaiti-Saudi border. The Arab League condemned Iraq.

August 5

President Bush declared invasion will not stand.

August 6

Saudi King, King Fahd, met with US Vice President, Richard Dick Cheney, requested US military assistance.

UN resolution 661 banned the importation of Iraqi goods.

August 7

Operation Desert Shield began.

First Contingent of US forces arrived in Saudi Arabia.

August 8

Initial batch of US Air force fighter planes arrived in Saudi Arabia,

Iraq declared a 'comprehensive and eternal merger' with Kuwait and annexed it as its 19th province.

August 9

UN resolution 662 found the annexation of Kuwait had no legal validity.

August 12

Iraq offered to withdraw in exchange for an Israeli withdrawal from Palestinian territory (the Gaza Strip and the West Bank) and a Syrian withdrawal from Lebanon,

First Operation Desert Shield-related US death.

August 18

UN resolution 664 asked Iraq to release foreign nationals who were being detained in Iraq.

August 21

Syria joined earlier Egyptian commitment to defend Saudi Arabia.

August 25

UN resolution 665 strengthened the economic embargo against Iraq.

August 28

Secret Israeli delegation flied to Washington to stress likelihood of Iraqi attack on Israel if war begins.

September 5

Iraq called for the overthrow of leaders in Saudi Arabia and Egypt.

September 9

Joint US-Soviet statement issued that "we must demonstrate beyond any doubt that aggression can not and will not pay."

September 13

UN resolution 666 asked for continuous information on the humanitarian situation within Kuwait and Iraq.

September 16

UN resolution 667 condemned Iraqi violation of diplomatic compounds in Kuwait and demanded the immediate release of foreign nationals captured from Kuwait.

September 18

Schwarzkopf, the USA General who led Operation Desert Storm, asked four Army planners to begin work on ground offensive.

September 24

UN resolution 669 imposed an air embargo on Iraq.

October 21

US Secretary of State, Colin Powell, fled to Riyadh to discuss offensive plans.

October 29

UN resolution 674 reiterated the condemnation of Iraqi treatment of foreign nationals and demanded their release.

October 31

Bush decided to double US forces in Saudi Arabia; decision kept secret until November 8.

November 8

The United States announced that it would double its troop presence in the region to over 4,00,000.

November 19

Iraq began significant reinforcement of its troops in Kuwait.

November 29

UN Security Council authorized use of 'all means necessary' to eject Iraq from Kuwait.

December 6

First ship carrying VII Corps equipment arrived in Saudi Arabia from Germany. Iraq decided to release all foreign nationals who had been held since the invasion.

1991:

January 9

US Secretary of State, James Baker, met Iraqi Foreign Minister, Tariq Aziz, in Geneva in unsuccessful effort to find a peaceful resolution to the conflict. Baker delivered a letter from President Bush to President Hussein. Aziz read but refused to forward it.

January 12

The US Congress authorized the use of force. The Senate vote was 52–47 in favour.

January 15

UN deadline for Iraqi withdrawal, Schwarzkopf accused Air Force of ignoring orders by not including Republican Guard in initial bombing sorties.

January 17

The allied attack; Operation Desert Storm, began with an Apache helicopter strike at 2:38 A.M.,

US Patriot missiles successfully intercepted first Scud over Dhahran; Saudi Arabia.

Iraq attacked Israel with seven Scud missiles.

January 18

First American air attacks were launched from Turkey.

January 19

USA Department of Defence announced deployment of Europe-based Patriot missiles and crews to Israel.

January 23

Intense attack against Iraqi aircraft shelters began.

January 25

Iraq created massive oil slick in Persian Gulf.

January 26

US Marines in Oman participated in Sea Soldier IV; rehearsal for amphibious landing on Kuwaiti coast.

January 29

Iraqis attacked Khafji and other border positions.

Allied pilots began flying combat air patrols to thwart Iraqi flights to Iran.

January 30

US Vice President, Richard Dick Cheney, dispatched "Delta Force"2 to Saudi Arabia to hunt for Scuds.

January 31

Khafji was recaptured. Iraq captured first US female prisoner of war.

February 1

Last "Tomahawk missiles"3 were launched in attack on Baghdad airfield.

February 2

Schwarzkopf formally decided against amphibious landing in Kuwait.

February 3

First battleship gunfire against targets in Kuwait started.

February 5

First "Tank Plinking"4 mission was flown.

February 7

CIA in daily intelligence brief, noted large discrepancy between claims of Washington and Riyadh, regarding destruction of Iraqi armour in air attacks.

February 8

Cheney, US Vice President and Powell, US Secretary of State, flied to Riyadh for final review of ground war plans.

February 11

Al Firdos bunker in Baghdad suburb added to master attack plan. Moshe Arens, Israel's Defence Minister, complained about ineffectiveness of Patriot missile against Scuds in Washington. "Yevgeny Primakov"5 arrived in Baghdad to urge Iraqi withdrawal.

February 13

Strike on Al Firdos bunker killed more than two hundred civilians and led to restrictions on strategic bombing campaign.

February 15

Radio Baghdad suggested Iraq willing to withdraw. Bush rejected proposal as a 'cruel hoax'.

February 18

USS Tripoli and USS Princeton stroke mines. Army complaints about insufficient air support led to confrontation with Air Force.

February 21

CIA and Pentagon officials met at White House to air differences over battle-damage assessment. Bush set deadline of noon of February 23 for Iraqi withdrawal.

February 23

Iraqis ignited estimated 700 oil wells in Kuwait,

Stealth fighters attacked Iraqi intelligence headquarters, unaware that allied Prisoner of Wars were inside.

Army Special Forces teams inserted deep into Iraq.

February 24

Ground attack began.

February 26

Iraqis fled Kuwait City.

February 28

Ceasefire took effect at 8 A.M.

March 1

Ceasefire terms negotiated in Safwan; Iraq.

March 3

Schwarzkopf met Iraqi generals at Safwan.

March 5

Most of the prisoners of war were released.

March 17

US Department of Defence announced first troop redeployment home.

April 5

President Bush announced US relief supply airdrops to Kurdish refugees in Turkey and northern Iraq.

April 6

Iraq officially accepted ceasefire terms.

June 8

Victory parade took place in Washington.

References

1. Bush George and Scowcroft Brent, "*A World Transformed*", Knopf, New York, 1998, p. 368
2. It is the United States Army's Tier One Special Operations Unit, categorized as a Special Missions Unit (SMU) and its existence is denied by the United States Department of Defense.
3. It is a long-range, all-weather, subsonic cruise missile.
4. Tank Plinking is a term that was given by pilots during the Gulf War to the practice of using guided munitions to destroy artillery, armored personnel carriers, tanks, and other targets.
5. He was a former KGB general and a former Prime Minister of Russia in 1998.

Appendix E

Chronology of the Iraq War; 2003 Onwards

2003:

January 16

UN inspectors discovered 11 undeclared empty chemical warheads in Iraq.

January 27

The UN's formal report on Iraqi inspections was highly critical with chief UN weapons inspector, Hans Blix, stating that Iraq appeared not to have come to a genuine acceptance of the disarmament that was demanded of it.

January 28

In his State of the Union Address, President Bush, announced his readiness to attack Iraq even without a UN mandate.

February 14

In a February UN report, chief UN inspector, Hans Blix, indicated that slight progress had been made in Iraq's cooperation. Both pro-war and anti-war nations felt the report supported their point of view.

February 15

Massive peace demonstrations took place around the world.

February 22

Hans Blix ordered Iraq to destroy its Al Samoud 2 missiles by March 1. The UN inspectors had determined that the missiles have an illegal range limit. It was believed Iraq could have missiles that reach neighbouring countries, but not ones capable of reaching Israel.

February 24

The US, Britain and Spain submitted a proposed resolution to the UN Security Council which stated that Iraq had failed to take the final opportunity afforded to it in Resolution 1441 and that it was the perfect time to authorize use of military force against the country.

France, Germany and Russia submitted an informal counter-resolution to the UN Security Council, stating that inspections should be intensified and extended to ensure that there was a real chance to the peaceful settlement of this crisis, and that the military option should only be a last resort.

March 1

Iraq began to destroy its Al Samoud missiles.

March 17

All diplomatic efforts ceased when President Bush delivered an ultimatum to Iraqi President, Saddam Hussein, to leave the country within 48 hours or else face an attack.

March 19

President Bush declared war on Iraq.

March 20

USA and British ground forces advanced into southern Iraq, entering the port city of Umm Al Qasr, near the major Iraqi city of Basra, while a second wave of air attacks hit Baghdad. Over the next several days, Iraqi militia (known as the Saddam Fedayeen) and holdout troops continued to resist Coalition forces, inflicting several casualties.

March 21

The major phase of the war began with heavy aerial attacks on Baghdad and other cities.

March 23

Coalition forces had seized H-2 and H-3, airfields in western Iraq, and controlled parts of Umm Al-Qasr, Basra and Nasiriyah. Armoured and mechanized forces had advanced to within 100 miles of Baghdad and forced a crossing of the Euphrates River at Nasiriyah, where Iraqi forces put up a stiff fight. In northern Iraq, the US launched an attack with 40 to 50 cruise missiles on forces of two Islamist parties opposed to the Pro-US Patriotic Union of Kurdistan (PUK); these two groups are Ansar Al Islam (Supporters of Islam), believed to be associated with Osama Bin Laden's Al Qaeda and Komala Islami Kurdistan (Islamic Society of Kurdistan).

Also on same day, US forces began airlifting troops into Kurdish-controlled northern Iraq in what appeared to be the opening move toward a second front against Iraqi forces.

Also on March 23, Iraqi forces ambushed the US Army's 507th Maintenance Company.

March 24

Troops marched within 60 miles of Baghdad. They encountered much stronger resistance from Iraqi soldiers and paramilitary fighters along the way, particularly in towns such as Nassiriya and Basra.

March 26

About 1000 paratroopers landed in Kurdish-controlled Iraq to open a northern front.

March 27

Fierce fighting erupted in the city of Samawah, where US forces were faced by up to 1500 Iraqi irregulars at a vital bridge over the Euphrates River. US forces eventually took control of the bridge and continued the advance to Baghdad. In northern Iraq, approximately, 1000 paratroopers of the US Army's 173rd Airborne Brigade parachuted onto an airfield in an effort to open a northern front against Iraqi forces. Within days, Kurdish Pishmarg troops of the PUK, along with US Special Forces Units, assaulted the stronghold of the Ansar Al Islam group along the Iranian border.

March 28

One missile successfully hit Kuwait City on March 28, inflicting damage on a shopping mall and causing minor wounds to two Kuwaitis.

March 29

US forces had advanced as far north as Karbala, where large battles with Iraqi forces took place. Major combat continued at Najaf, Nasiriyah, Basra and other locations as Iraqi guerrilla forces, many of whom belonged to the Saddam Fedayeen, proved to be formidable forces for the Coalition to overcome. Bombing raids on Baghdad and other Iraqi cities continued, as did Iraqi attempts to hit Kuwaiti-based targets with surface-to-surface missiles.

Also on same day, the first suicide bombing on Coalition forces occurred, killing four American troops at Najaf.

March 30

Six hundred British commandoes attacked near Basra, destroying Iraqi tanks and capturing nearly 300 prisoners.

April 2

US forces rescued Private First Class; Jessica Lynch, and recovered the bodies of several other members of the 507th Maintenance Company.

April 3

US forces reached Saddam International Airport on the outskirts of Baghdad.

April 5

US armoured forces entered Baghdad, conducting a large raid. Such incursions continued for several days. Iraqi civilians began widespread looting of the city.

April 7

British forces reached the centre of Basra and declared the city as being under Coalition control.

April 9

Baghdad fell to US troops.

US troops helped Iraqi crowds topple a large statue of Saddam Hussein. Coalition forces continued to extend their control over the city.

April 10

Kurdish fighters seized the northern city of Kirkuk from the Iraqi forces.

April 11

US forces and Kurdish troops entered Mosul in the north.

Kirkuk fell to Kurdish fighters.

April 13

US forces entered Saddam's hometown of Tikrit.

Marines rescued five US soldiers being captured by Iraqi troops on March 23 in Nasiriya and two pilots who had been shot down on March 24 near Karbala.

April 14

Major fighting in Iraq was declared over by the Pentagon, after US forces took control of Tikrit, Saddam Hussein's birthplace and the last city to exhibit strong Iraqi resistance. Saddam Hussein's whereabouts remained unknown.

April 15

Tikrit fell and the Coalition declared the war to be effectively over. Despite this declaration, violence continued, escalating into a low-grade guerrilla war.

General Jay Garner, appointed by the United States to run post-war Iraq until a new government was put in place, met with various Iraqi leaders to begin planning the new Iraqi federal government.

April 16

US forces captured Abu Abbas, a Palestinian terrorist living in Baghdad. Abbas is best-known as the leader of a group which hijacked the Italian cruise ship Achille Lauro in 1985. Abu Abbas later died in American captivity.

May 1

President Bush declared an end to major combat operation.

May 12

A new civil administrator took over in Iraq. Paul Bremer, a diplomat and former head of the counter-terrorism department at the US State Department, replaced Jay Garner, who was seen as ineffective in stemming the continuing lawlessness and violence taking place throughout Iraq.

May 22

The UN Security Council approved a resolution lifting the economic sanctions against Iraq and supporting the US-led administration in Iraq.

May 28

A defiant letter from Saddam Hussein to the Iraqi people indicated that US assassination attempts had failed. Resistance to US occupation from unidentified sources included sabotage of infrastructure and suicide bombings of US soldiers.

May 30

In separate speeches, US secretary of state, Colin Powell, and British Prime Minister, Tony Blair, denied that intelligence about Iraq's Weapons of Mass Destruction was distorted or exaggerated to justify an attack on Iraq. Both administrations faced mounting questions because no Weapons of Mass Destruction (WMD) had been found. Each had claimed that Iraq's WMD were an imminent threat to world security.

June 15

Operation Desert Scorpion launched, a military campaign meant to defeat organized Iraqi resistance against American troops. USA and British troops faced continued attacks; about one American soldier had been killed per day since the end of combat was declared.

July 7

Bush administration conceded that evidence as to Iraq was pursuing a nuclear weapons program by seeking to buy uranium from Africa, cited in January State of the Union address and elsewhere, was unsubstantiated and should not have been included in speech. Over summer Tony Blair faced even stronger criticism than his American counterpart concerning flawed intelligence.

July 13

Iraq's interim governing council, composed of 25 Iraqis appointed by American and British officials, was inaugurated. The council had power to name ministers and to help drawing up a new constitution for the country. The American administrator Paul Bremer, however, retained ultimate authority.

July 14

First meeting of US-appointed Iraqi interim council was held.

July 16

General John Abizaid, Commander of Allied Forces in Iraq who replaced retiring General Tommy Franks on July 7, called continued attacks on coalition troops a 'guerrilla-type campaign' and said soldiers who would replace current troops may be deployed for year-long tours.

July 17

US combat deaths in Iraq reached 147, the same number of soldiers who died from hostile fire in the first Gulf War; 32 of those deaths occurred after May 1, the officially declared date of end of combat.

July 22

Udai and Qusay Hussein; sons of Saddam, were killed by troops of the US 101st Airborne Division.

August

Increasing evidence showed that US and British governments 'improved' intelligence estimates to make a case that Iraq was still stockpiling Weapons of Mass Destruction (WMD).

August 9

US combat and noncombat casualties reached 255 at 100-day mark after declared end of combat on May 1; 43 British had died.

August 19

UN compound bombed by unknown Iraqi forces; killing at least 20.

August 22

Capture of Ali Majid (Chemical Ali) by US forces was announced. Ali was questioned about WMD programs but had not revealed any new information.

August 29

Explosion near Najaf Mosque killed over 90 including Shiite leader Ayatollah Mohammed Baghir Al-Hakim.

September 7

Continued violence and slow progress in Iraq led to President Bush's announcement that US$ 87 billion was needed to cover additional military and reconstruction costs.

October 2

According to an interim report by David Kay, the lead investigator searching for Weapons of Mass Destruction in Iraq, no WMDs had been found.

October 5

White House reorganized its reconstruction efforts in Iraq, placing National Security Adviser, Condoleezza Rice, in charge thereby diminishing the role of the Pentagon.

October 16

United Nations Security Council (UNSC) Resolution 1511 on Iraq, recognized the legitimacy of the American supported provisional Iraqi government and authorized UN aid to Iraq under US supervision, while at the same time calling for submission of a time-table for Iraqi self governance.

October 23-24

The Madrid Conference, an international donors' conference of 80 nations to raise funds for the reconstruction of Iraq, yielded US$13 billion in addition to the US$ 20 billion already pledged by the United States. This amount felled short of the overall target of raising US$ 56 billion, the figure the World Bank and the UN estimated that Iraq needs over the next four years.

October 27

Four coordinated suicide attacks in Baghdad killed 43 and wounded more than 200. Targets included the headquarters of the Red Crescent (Islamic Red Cross) and three police stations.

November 2

In the single deadliest strike since the Iraq war began, guerrillas shot down an American helicopter, killing 16 US soldiers and injuring 21 others.

Other attacks over the course of the month made it the bloodiest since the war began: at least 75 US soldiers died.

November 14

The Bush Administration reversed policy and in a deal with the Iraqi Governing Council, agreeed to transfer power to an interim government in early 2004.

December 9

A directive issued by Paul Wolfowitz, Deputy Secretary of Defence, barred France, Germany, Canada, Mexico, China and Russia from bidding on lucrative contracts for rebuilding Iraq, creating a diplomatic furore.

December 13

Saddam Hussein was captured alive by US forces.

2004:

January 15

Tens of thousands of Shiites held a peaceful demonstration in Basra in support of direct elections.

January 17

The number of US soldiers killed in Iraq since the start of the war reached 500. Of those, 346 soldiers died in combat and 154 died from accidents.

January 19

The United States asked the UN to intercede in the dispute over the elections process in Iraq. Shiite leader Ayatollah Al Sistani, at the centre of the debate, refused to meet with American officials. The UN weighed sending election experts to determine whether there is enough time to prepare for direct elections.

About 1,00,000 Shiites marched in Baghdad and other cities in support of Ayatollah Al Sistani's demand for direct elections. It was the largest protest since the occupation of Iraq.

February 1

About 109 Iraqis were killed by suicide bombings in Erbil.

February 2

Under pressure from both sides of the political aisle, President Bush called for an independent commission to study the country's intelligence failures.

February 10

About 54 Iraqis were killed in a car bombing while applying for jobs at a police station. The next day an attack killed about 47 outside an army recruiting centre.

February 12

UN envoy Lakhdar Brahimi, on a fact finding mission to Iraq to assess the feasibility of direct elections, met with Ayatollah Al Sistani.

February 19

UN Secretary General, Kofi Annan, announced the results of its report about Iraqi elections, concluding that "elections can not be held before the end of June, that the June 30 date for the handover of sovereignty must be respected, and that we need to find a mechanism to create the caretaker government and then prepare the elections sometime later in the future."

February 23

UN envoy, Brahimi, issued a report to the Security Council concluding that the earliest that credible, direct elections could be held in Iraq would be late 2004 or early 2005. He outlined several possible options for structuring an interim government that would rule the country after the June 30 hand over and until the results of elections in 2004 or 2005. He recommended that Iraqis themselves draw up a plan for the makeup of this provisional government.

March 1

Iraqi Interim Constitution agreed upon by interim government and approved by US.

March 2

Terror attacks-suicide bombings in Karbala and Baghdad killed 117 (US figures); 271 (Iraqi figures) Shiite worshippers during Ashura holy day rites.

March 8

The Iraqi Governing Council signed Interim Constitution, which included a bill of rights, a system of checks and balances, and a military subordinate to civilian rule. The signing was delayed by several days when Shiites objected that Kurds, a minority, were given too much power in the Interim Constitution.

March 17

At least 27 people were killed and 41 wounded in the car bombing of a hotel in Baghdad. The bombing came just two days before the anniversary of the first American attack on Baghdad that launched the war last year.

March 28

Coalition forces closed radical cleric, Mogtada Al Sadr's, rabidly anti-American newspaper; Al Hawaz.

March 31

Iraqi mob killed and mutilated four American civilian contract workers and then dragged them through the streets of Falluja, a city west of Baghdad that is part of the Sunni triangle.

April 4

US troops began assault on Falluja in response to March 31 assassinations of four US civilian contractors.

Coordinated attacks by Shiites were launched in the southern Iraqi cities of Kufa, Karbala, Najaf, Al Kut and Sadr City. The militias were led by radical cleric Mogtada Al Sadr.

April 9

An American contract worker, Thomas Hamill, was taken hostage. More than 20 foreigners kidnapped in Iraq.

April 11

USA ordered a ceasefire in Falluja to give political discussions a chance to break the cycle of violence. Two members of the Iraqi

Governing Council resigned in protest of American offensive in Falluja.

April 15

The Bush administration agreed to a UN proposal to replace the Iraqi Governing Council with a caretaker government when the US returns sovereignty to Iraqis on June 30.

April 17

The number of hostages taken by various Iraqi guerrillas reached about 40.

April 22

In a shift of policy, USA announced that some Iraqi Baath Party officials who had been forced out of their jobs after the fall of Saddam Hussein would be allowed to resume their positions. About 4,00,000 people lost their jobs, including teachers and members of the military, depleting Iraq of skilled and experienced workers to rebuild the country.

April 27

UN envoy, Lakhdar Brahimi, reported to the UN Security Council that by the end of May he would select a transitional government to run Iraq until elections were held in 2005. Proposed government would include a president, two Vice Presidents, a Prime Minister, and a consultative conference made up of about 1,500 Iraqis. The government would have limited control over Iraq and would not be authorized to enact news laws.

April 30

The appalling physical and sexual abuse and humiliation of Iraqi prisoners at Abu Ghraib prison near Baghdad came to light when photographs were released by the US media. The images sparked outrage around the world, especially in the Middle East. Abu Ghraib was a notorious prison and torture centre during the rule of Saddam Hussein. The Pentagon had been investigating these and other allegations of abuse since January. Criminal charges filed against seven US soldiers.

In an attempt to restore peace in Falluja, US Marines transferred security of the volatile city to a former Iraqi general.

May 8

Nicholas Berg, an American contractor, was beheaded by Iraqi militants, who claimed the grisly murder was in retaliation for the treatment of Iraqi prisoners.

May 17

A suicide bomber killed the Head of Iraq's Governing Council, Izzedin Salim, and six other people.

May 27

After seven weeks of fighting in Najaf, US forces and the militias loyal to Mogtada Al Sadr reached a truce.

May 28

Iyad Allawi was designated Prime Minister of the Iraqi Interim Government. A Shiite neurologist, Alawi had closed ties with the CIA, and many observers inside, and outside, Iraq said Alawi's selection was a sign of the US's continued attempt to assert control over the country.

June 1

Ghazi Al Yawer, a Sunni Muslim, was chosen president, a largely ceremonial post. The Governing Council decided to dissolve itself immediately rather than wait for the official handover of sovereignty on June 30 making way for a cabinet of 33 Iraqis including Sunnis, Shiites, Kurds and Christians. New government included former members of the governing council, former militants, professionals and opponents of Saddam Hussein.

June 8

UN Security Council Resolution 1546 on Iraq recognized the legitimacy of the Interim Iraqi Government and called on UN members to support it.

June 16

The 9/11 Commission (formally the National Commission on Terrorist Attacks) concluded in its report that there was no credible evidence that Iraq and Al Qaeda cooperated on attacks against the United States. The link between Al Qaeda and Iraq was used as one of the justifications for the war. President Bush disputed the report's conclusion the next day, insisting there was 'a relationship' between the two.

June 17

In a poll conducted by the Coalition Provisional Authority in May, 92 per cent of Iraqis saw the US as 'occupiers', 3 per cent saw them as 'peacekeepers' and only 2 per cent Iraqis viewed them as 'liberators'.

June 24

About one hundred people were killed in coordinated attacks throughout Iraq. Terror attacks were an almost daily occurrence as the date on which sovereignty was to be handed over to the Iraqis approached.

June 28

Iraqi Prime Minister, Iyad Allawi, took power for sovereign Iraq in a modest ceremony held two days before the deadline. US Administrator, Paul Bremer, left Iraq. NATO promised aid to Iraq in training security forces.

June 30

The Interim Government of Iraq took legal custody of Saddam Hussein and 11 other high-profile former Baath Party officials.

July 7

Prime Minister Allawi signed a law permitting him to impose martial law.

July 14

The British intelligence report on pre-Iraq War was released which echoed the American findings of the week before (though with a much milder tone) that pre-war intelligence exaggerated Saddam Hussein's threat. In particular, the British intelligence dossier asserting the widely suspect claim that Saddam Hussein could deploy weapons within 45 minutes was deemed highly misleading, and led to suspicions that it had been included because of its eye-catching character.

July 22

Australia released the Flood report, its assessment of pre-war intelligence on Iraq, and found the evidence supporting Iraq's possession of WMD 'thin, ambiguous and incomplete'. Like the earlier US and UK intelligence reports, it indicted the government of manipulating the intelligence.

A report on military prison abuse in Iraq identified 94 suspected or confirmed cases of abuse of prisoners, including the deaths of at least 20 prisoners. Prepared by Lieutenant General, Paul Mikolashek; the Army's Inspector General, the report maintained that abuse was not systemic. The report was one of 11 Pentagon investigations into prisoners abuse as a result of the Abu Ghraib scandal.

July 28

In the deadliest attack since Iraq's Interim Government took power, at least 68 were killed in a car bombing in Baqouba.

August 24

The Pentagon-sponsored Schlesinger report's investigation into the Abu Ghraib scandal, called the prisoners abuse acts of 'brutality and purposeless sadism', rejected the idea that the abuse was simply the work of a few aberrant soldiers, and asserted that there were fundamental failures throughout all levels of command, from the soldiers on the ground to Central Command and to the Pentagon.

August 27

A bloody, three-week battle in Najaf between the US forces and the militia of militant cleric Al Sadr ended in August when Shiite cleric, Grand Ayatollah Ali Al Sistani, negotiated a settlement.

September 7

The American death toll in Iraq reached 1,000; about 7,000 soldiers had been wounded. In August, attacks on American forces reached their highest level since the beginning of the war, an average of 87 per day.

September 15

The Bush administration requested that the Senate divert US$ 3.4 billion of the US$ 18.4 billion Iraqi aid package meant for reconstruction work to improving security measures. The worsening security situation, with pockets of Iraq essentially under the control of insurgents, threatened to disrupt national elections, scheduled for January. Republican and Democratic senators alike harshly criticized the request as a sign that the American campaign in Iraq had been poorly executed. Senators also denounced the slow progress in rebuilding Iraq; just 6 per cent (US$ 1 billion) of the reconstruction money approved by Congress last year had in fact been spent. Senator Richard Lugar, the Republican chair of the Senate Foreign Relations Committee, lamented that the slow pace of reconstruction spending meant that USA is failing to fully take advantage of one of its most potent tools to influence the direction of Iraq.

In a BBC interview, UN Secretary General, Kofi Annan, said the war against Iraq was illegal and violated the UN Charter. The US, UK and Australia vigorously rejected his conclusion.

October 1-3

US forces and Iraqi troops took control of Samarra, which had become a stronghold of the insurgency.

October 6

In the final report on the existence of Weapons of Mass Destruction in Iraq, Charles Duelfer, the leader of the Iraq Survey Group in 2004, concluded that there was no evidence that Iraq had undertaken weapons production program when the US began the war.

October 11

Rebel cleric, Mogtada Al Sadr's; Mahdi Army, began to surrender heavy weapons. Results deemed a mixed success.

October 14

Insurgents detonated two bombs in the Green Zone, home to Iraqi officials and the American Embassy.

October 24

Fifty new Iraqi soldiers were executed by insurgents loyal to Abu Musab Al Zarqawi.

October 6

The New York Times *reported that about 380 tons of powerful explosives disappeared from military installation called Al Qaqaa sometime after the US-led war began in March 2003. Before the US invasion, the explosives had been monitored and sealed by the UN's IAEA. The missing explosives could potentially be used to detonate a nuclear weapon.*

November

Coalition and Iraqi forces began attack on rebel forces in Fallujah, reputedly led by Abu-Musab Al Zarqawi, pegged by the US as a member of Al Qaeda.

Numerous civilians were killed in the attacks and Arab sources reported damage to mosques and hospitals; UN Secretary General, Kofi Annan, cautioned against the attacks, but Iraqi Prime Minister, Ayad Alawi, replied that the attack was necessary to restore order and allow for elections scheduled in January.

Alawi declared martial law after a series of attacks in various Iraqi cities.

December 19

Car bombers targeted Shiites and election workers in brazen attacks in Najaf and Karbala. More than 60 people were killed and 120 wounded.

December 21

Bomb exploded in US military tent at base in Mosul. At least 24 people died, including 19 American soldiers.

2005:

January 4

Ali Al Haidari, Governor of Baghdad Province, was assassinated by insurgents who were seeking to thwart elections scheduled for January 30.

January 7

US Lieutenant General, Thomas Metz acknowledged that large parts of nearly 25 percent of Iraq's provinces were not secure enough to hold elections. Baghdad was one of the four provinces cited. Violence continued on a daily basis throughout much of the country.

January 11

Iraqi Prime Minister, Ayad Allawi, admitted that some areas of Iraq were likely to be too dangerous to hold elections.

January 12

The White House announced that the search for Weapons of Mass Destruction in Iraq, one of the main justifications for the war, was officially over. No such weapons were found.

January 27

31 Marines died in a helicopter crash and 5 other US soldiers were killed by Iraqi insurgents elsewhere in the country making it the single deadliest day for American soldiers since the war began. The death toll of US soldiers reached 1,408.

January 30

Iraqis elected the Iraqi National Assembly. Shiites won a majority. Sunnis largely boycotted the vote.

February 22

The United Iraqi Alliance, the group of Shiite political parties that won the most votes in Iraq's January 30 election, selected

Ibrahim Al Jaafari to be the Prime Minister of Iraq. The 58-year-old doctor served as Iraq's Interim Vice President of Iraq after the fall of Saddam Hussein. Jaafari is a popular politician who is seen as acceptable to the Sunnis and Kurds as well as the dominant Shiites.

February 27

Syria handed over Sabawi Ibrahim Hassan, a half brother of Saddam Hussein, and other fugitives to the Iraqi government. Hassan is believed to have organized and financed the insurgency in Iraq.

February 28

In the deadliest attack ever by insurgents, suicide bomber blew up a car in Hilla, killing about 115 people who were seeking employment with the Iraqi police.

March 5

US soldiers shot at car carrying Giuliana Sgrena; an Italian journalist who had been held hostage by Iraqi insurgents and just released from captivity. Sgrena was wounded and an Italian intelligence agent was killed. Relations between Italy and the US grew strained.

March 16

Diverse group of 275 newly elected leaders to the Iraqi assembly convened for the first time in a largely ceremonial meeting. Shiites and Kurds, who fared best in January elections, had not yet appointed leaders. On March 29, the assembly met for the second time and failed again to agree upon the composition of the new Iraqi government.

March 31

Panel set up by President Bush called assessment on Iraq's weapons capabilities 'dead wrong' and found that intelligence agencies exaggerated evidence and relied on shaky sources in making the case for war in Iraq.

April 3

Iraqi Assembly named Hajim Al Hassani; a Sunni, as speaker, and Hussain Al Shahristani; a Shiite and Arif Taifour; a Kurd, as deputies. On April 6, Iraq Assembly selected Kurdish leader Jalal Talabani as President; Adel Abdul Mahdi; a Shiite politician, as Vice President, and Sheik Ghazi Al Yawar, the Sunni President of the Interim Government, as the second Vice President.

April 7

The Iraq Assembly named Shiite Ibrahim Al Jaafari as Prime Minister. Interim Prime Minister Ayad Allawi resigned.

May 1

The leaked, top-secret "Downing Street Memo"[2] of July 23, 2002, indicated that eight months before the Iraq war was launched, Blair and top British government officials acknowledged that the case [for war] was thin, but that Bush had made up his mind to take military action. The US wanted the war justified by the conjunction of terrorism and WMD. But the intelligence and facts were being fixed around the policy. Memo received enormous attention in the UK but not in the US.

June 3

Violence due to the insurgency continued relentlessly despite the installation of the new Shiite-led government on April 28. Since that date, more than 825 people, including Iraqi civilians and US forces, had been killed by insurgents.

June 23

General John Abizaid; Commander of US forces in the Middle East, stated that the Iraq insurgency had remained as strong as it had been six months earlier.

July 3

Ihab Al Sharif, who was to become Egypt's ambassador to Iraq, was kidnapped by gunmen in Baghdad. On July 7, the militant group Al Qaeda in Iraq said it has killed Sharif.

July 17

Suicide bomber detonated bomb under a fuel tanker in Musayyib killing at least 70 people and wounding more than 150. Four other suicide bombers hit Baghdad on the same day.

July 19

Two Sunnis involved in drafting the Iraqi constitution were shot in Baghdad.

July 20

Pentagon report assessing Iraqi security forces found that they were, at best, 'partially capable' of fighting the country's insurgency.

July 21

Algeria's top diplomat, Ali Billaroussi, and envoy, Azzedine Belakdi, were kidnapped by gunmen in Baghdad.

August 15

Iraq delayed the final drafting of the constitution, extending the deadline so that Sunni, Shiite and Kurdish delegates could reach a compromise on disputed issues, such as the distribution of oil revenues, issues of federalism, the rights of women and the role of Islam in government.

August 22

Iraqi leaders gave Iraqi National Assembly a partially complete constitution and promised to complete the document within matter of days.

August 27

Frustrated with demands of Sunni Arabs, Shiite and Kurdish leaders ended negotiations with Sunnis.

August 28

Iraqi National Assembly received the new constitution which was to be put to vote by Iraqi citizens on October 15. Sunni negotiators denounced the document.

September 10-11

USA and Iraqi troops launched successful offensive against insurgents in the northern city of Tal Afar.

October 2

Shiite and Kurdish leaders changed election rules. The rules said that constitution would fail if two-thirds of all registered voters, rather than two-thirds of those who vote, rejected it in three or more provinces. Changes, likely, ensured that constitution would pass in the national referendum on October 15. On October 5, facing pressure from the UN and US officials, the Iraqi National Assembly voted to reverse the rules changed.

October 11

Leaders involved in drafting constitution agreed to create a panel that could revise the constitution. In exchange, Sunni leaders said they would support the constitution in the upcoming referendum.

October 15

Millions of Iraqi voters went to the polls to vote on a constitution.

October 25

Electoral commission reported that constitution had passed, with 79 per cent of voters supporting it. But, it failed by more than a two-thirds majority in two Sunni-dominated provinces and by less than a two-thirds majority in the third, making the victory a narrow one. Turnout among Sunnis was high.

The number of deaths of US soldiers fighting in Iraq reached 2,000. The figure represented the number of fatalities since the war began in March 2003.

November 2

Iraqi Defence Ministry began recruiting former junior officers from Saddam Hussein's army to bolster army's forces and to wean fighters away from the insurgency.

November 7

Suicide bomber killed four US soldiers in Baghdad in the deadliest suicide attack since June.

November 10

Al Qaeda in Mesopotamia claimed responsibility for attack in a Baghdad cafe that killed about 30 people, including many police officers.

November 15

Prime Minister, Ibrahim Al Jaafari, announced a prompt inquiry into alleged torture of more than 170 prisoners, mostly; Sunnis by Shiite, police officers.

November 18

Two suicide bombers blew themselves up in two Shiite mosques in the Kurdish town of Khanaqin. About 70 people were killed.

November 21

For the first time, a group of Sunni, Shiite and Kurdish leaders signed a statement that demanded a specific time for the pullout of foreign troops.

November 30

President Bush unveiled his vision for victory in Iraq and rejected calls by Democrats and some Republicans for a timetable for withdrawal: "Pulling our troops out before they've achieved their purpose is not a plan for victory."[3]

December 2

Ten marines were killed and about a dozen wounded by a bomb attack in Falluja.

The Pentagon acknowledged that it had hired a US public relations agency, the Lincoln Group, to translate into Arabic, articles written by American soldiers. The agency then passed the stories on to advertising agencies that paid Iraqi news outlets to run them.

December 5

Witnesses in trial of former Iraqi president, Saddam Hussein, detailed horrifying examples of torture.

December 6

At least 36 people were killed and about 75 were wounded when two suicide bombers attacked the Baghdad Police Academy.

December 15

Iraq held parliamentary elections. As many as 11 million Iraqis turned out to select their first permanent Parliament since the overthrow of Saddam Hussein. More than 7,000 Parliamentary candidates from 300 parties were seeking to fill the 275 seats in Parliament. Violence was minimal.

December 19

Religious Shiites took an early lead in elections, according to preliminary figures released by election officials.

2006:

January 20

Preliminary election results were reported for the December 15, parliamentary elections. The Shiite United Iraqi Alliance, an alliance of Shiite religious parties, captured 128 of the 275 parliamentary seats. It did not succeed in winning the two-thirds majority needed to rule without coalition partners and sought to form a coalition over the next weeks.

January 23

Report by the Special Inspector General for Iraq Reconstruction found evidence of fraud that money for rebuilding was casually and insecurely stored, and contract work was improperly certified as complete.

February 15

A US Senate report on progress in Iraq indicated that despite the US spending $16 billion on reconstruction, every major area of Iraq's infrastructure was below pre-war levels. This included electricity, drinkable water, heating oil production, crude oil production and sewage service. The report also indicated that the number of insurgent attacks had increased; between March 2004 and December 2005, they had grown by more that 200 per cent.

February 22

The Shiite 'Golden Mosque' in Samarra destroyed in bomb attack.

March 7

The bodies of 24 men were found in five locations in Baghdad.

March 8

Gunmen kidnapped about 50 employees of a Sunni-owned security company in Baghdad. Witnesses said the gunmen were wearing police paramilitary uniforms.

March 12

Six car bombs exploded in Shiite section of Baghdad killing nearly 50 people and wounding 200.

March 15

Saddam Hussein testified for the first time in his lengthy trial. He was charged with ordering the killing of 148 villagers in Dujail in 1982.

March 16

The US military and Iraqi forces launched 'Operation Swarmer' near Samarra, a massive attack against insurgents. It was the largest air assault since the beginning of the war in 2003.

March 21

Over a two-week period, nearly 200 bodies were found in Baghdad. Most of the victims had been executed or tortured.

April 4

Iraqi court charged Saddam Hussein and six other defendants with genocide in attempting to eradicate Iraq's Kurdish population in 1988. More than 50,000 people were killed in the military campaign that destroyed about 2,000 villages.

April 5

Four months after elections, the appointment of Jaafari as Prime Minister was still not confirmed; Sunni Arab and Kurdish officials continued to reject him. Jaafari, a religious Shiite, was considered by many to be a divisive figure incapable of forming the government of national unity that was desperately needed for a country deeply enmeshed in deep sectarian violence. Iraqi and USA officials had urged him to step down to which he refused asserting that his appointment was reached by democratic means and that the Iraqi people would protest if they see the rules of democracy being trespassed.

April 7

Suicide bombings killed at least 50 people at a Baghdad mosque.

April 22

Nuri Al Maliki of the Shiite Dawa party was approved as Prime Minister ending four months of political stalemate.

April 29

The Los Angeles Times *reported that Parsons, the US company, awarded multibillion dollar contracts to rebuild Iraq's health and security infrastructure, would finish only 20 of 150 planned health clinics planned. It had spent US$ 60 million of* *the budgeted US$ 186 million for its own management and administration. On June 19, the Army Corps of Engineers announced it has cancelled a US$ 99.1 million contract with Parsons to build a prison. The company was more than two years behind schedule and was expected to go millions of dollars over budget.*

April 30

According to the April report of the Special Inspector General for Iraq Reconstruction (SIGIR), more than 75 per cent of oil and gas restoration projects were incomplete apart from 50 per cent of electrical and 40 per cent of water and sanitation projects. Yet, the most of the $20 billion Congress had allocated for reconstruction had been spent. Insurgent attacks had hindered reconstruction progress and security concerns had added to the costs. In addition, incompetence and fraud had characterized numerous projects. Stuart Bowen Jr., the Special Inspector General, was pursuing 72 investigations into corruption by firms involved in reconstruction.

May 10

President Jalal Talabani announced that more the 1,000 people were killed in Baghdad during April.

May 15

Saddam Hussein was charged with crimes against humanity. Ruling was part of his trial that focused on the execution of about 150 Shiites in Dujail in 1982.

May 20

A bomb killed 19 in Baghdad.

May 23

Bombs killed 20 in Baghdad.

June 2

A suicide bomber killed 33 in Basra.

June 4

Terrorists killed 21 in Baquba.

June 7

Abu Musab Al Zarqawi, the leader of Al Qaeda in Iraq and the most-wanted terrorist in the country, was killed when US warplanes dropped 500-lb. bombs on his safe house. Zarqawi was responsible for many of the most brutal and horrific attacks in Iraqi. His death was considered a major victory.

June 15

The Congressional Committee on Government Reform's Minority reported that despite US$ 50 billion in expenditures, oil and electricity production remained well below pre-war levels.

June 26

Bombing in Hilla killed 30.

July 1

Bombing kills 66 in a Baghdad market.

July 3

A former US soldier; Steven D. Green, was charged in a US federal court of raping and murdering an Iraqi girl as well as murdering her parents and young sister. Three other US soldiers were believed to have been involved in the murders in Mahmoudiya, which took place in March 2006.

July 10

A USA Government Accountability Office and independent investigative branch of Congress released a report maintaining that the Bush administration's Iraq strategy was inadequate and was poorly planned.

July 11

The US Army announced that it was discontinuing its multibillion-dollar deal with military contractor Halliburton which had provided service to the military in Iraq and elsewhere. Government audits had uncovered more the US $1 billion in questionable charges.

July 18

The UN announced that during June, an average of more than 100 civilians were killed in Iraq each day. During the first six months of the year, civilian deaths increased by 77 per cent reflecting the serious spike in sectarian violence in the country.

A suicide bomber in the Shiite city of Kufa killed 59.

July 25

The US announced it would move more US troops into Bagdad from other regions of Iraq in an attempt to bring security to the country's capital which had increasingly been subject to lawlessness, violence and sectarian strife.

July 27

The trial of Saddam Hussein, the former Iraqi president who faced charges of crimes against humanity, ended after nine months. He was accused of ordering the 1982 execution of 148 men and boys in a Shiite village.

August 3

General John Abizaid, the US military's top commander in Asia (CENTCOM), announced to a Senate panel that sectarian violence in Iraq had grown so strong that civil war was a distinct possibility.

August 10

A suicide bomber attempted to blow up the Shrine of Imam Ali in Najaf, killing 35 people and wounding more than 120.

August 15

According to Iraq's Health Ministry and the Baghdad morgue, a total of 3,438 civilians were killed in July, an increase of 9% over June.

August 30

General George Casey, the top US general in Iraq estimated that Iraqi security forces would need another 12 to 18 months before they could take over from American troops.

September 1

A Pentagon report found that since the new Iraqi government was established in May, civilian and security forces casualties had increased by 51%.

September 3

USA and Iraqi troops capture Hamid Juma Faris Jouri Al Saeedi; a senior leader of Al Qaeda in Iraq. He is believed to have overseen the bombing of the Shiite Askariya shrine in February that resulted in days of deadly sectarian violence.

September 23

A classified National Intelligence Estimate consensus view of all 16 US intelligence agencies signed off by Director of National Intelligence John D. Negroponte, was leaked to several newspapers. It concluded that the Iraq war has made the overall terrorism problem worse.

October 11

The Iraqi Parliament voted in favour of a law that would allow provinces to unite and form semi-independent regions. Sunnis in parliament, who opposed the move out of fear that Shiites and Kurds would control most of the country's oil, boycotted the vote.

October 17

Under pressure to control violence that had spiralled out of control, Prime Minister; Nuri Al Maliki fired two police generals. The security forces had been criticized for having been infiltrated by members of Shiite militias which had tortured and killed hundreds of civilians.

October 19

The US military acknowledged that its twelve-week-old campaign to establish security in Baghdad, which had been wracked by sectarian death squads and insurgents, was unsuccessful.

October 20

Shiite militias battled for control of the city of Amarra. The Mahdi Army; associated with Shiite cleric Mogtada Al Sadr, and the Badr Organization; armed wings for the Supreme Islamic Iraqi Council (SIIC) headed by Hadi Al Amiri destroyed police stations and brought the city to a standstill.

October 29

Report by the Special Inspector for Iraq Reconstruction said the US military had not appropriately tracked or maintained thousands of weapons that were sent to Iraq.

October 31

Following the demand of Iraqi Prime Minister Nuri Al Maliki, the US military removed checkpoints from Baghdad streets. The military had set up the checkpoints in an attempt to find a US soldier who had been kidnapped.

November 3

The New York Times revealed that a military authorization bill signed by President Bush in October included a provision that would abolish the Office of the Special Inspector General for Iraq Reconstruction on October 1, 2007.

November 6

Saddam Hussein was sentenced to death by hanging. He was found guilty of crimes against humanity for the execution of 148 Shiite men and boys from the town of Dujail.

November 22

Civilian deaths reached a record high in Iraq: some 3,700 Iraqi civilians died in October, the highest toll since the war began in

2003, according to the United Nations. Report also said that about 1,00,000 Iraqis fled each month to Jordan and Syria.

November 23

More than 200 people died when five car bombs and a mortar shell exploded in the Shiite-dominated Sadr City district of Baghdad. On November 24, Shiites retaliated against Sunnis, attacking mosques in Baghdad and Baquba. Dozens died in the attacks.

December 6

A bipartisan report by the Iraq Study Group was released. Led by former US Secretary of State, James Baker and former Democratic congressman, Lee Hamilton, it concluded that the situation in Iraq was grave and deteriorating and US forces seemed to be caught in a mission that had no foreseeable end. The report's 79 recommendations included reaching out diplomatically to Iran and Syria and having the US military intensify its efforts to train Iraqi troops.

December 18

A Pentagon report found that attacks on Americans and Iraqis averaged about 960 a week, the highest number since it began writing the reports in 2005.

December 21

Military prosecutors charged the Marines with the murder of 24 Iraqi civilians in Haditha in November 2005. Ten of the casualties were women and children. Four officers were also charged with dereliction of duty.

December 30

Saddam Hussein was hanged. On November 5, a court had sentenced Saddam to death for the killing of 148 Shiites in Dujail in 1982. On December 28, an Iraqi appellate court chief upheld the death sentence, and the execution was scheduled for two days later.

December 31

The American death toll in the Iraq war reached 3,000.

The UN reported that more than 34,000 Iraqis were killed from violence in 2006.

2007:

January 10

President Bush announced 20,000 additional US troops for sending to Iraq (Surge Strategy).

January 11

US troops stormed an Iranian diplomatic office in Erbil, Kurdish-controlled city and detained five people. Kurdish officials were outraged at the move.

January 16

The tally of death certificates and reports from morgues, hospitals and other institutions indicated more than 34,000 Iraqi civilians died in 2006.

January 28

250 were killed near Najaf as American and Iraqi troops fought with a Shiite militia. An American helicopter was shot down in the battle.

February 7

The US and Iraq began a new offensive in an attempt to increase security in Baghdad and quell the increasingly deadly attacks by insurgents and militias.

February 11

Officials showed weapons, including mortar shells, rocket-propelled grenades and explosively formed penetrators, which they said were used by Iraqi troops and manufactured in Iranian factories. They also claimed that Iranian government officials sanctioned the transfer of the weapons to Iraq.

February 17

US Senate's Democrats fell four votes short of forcing a debate on the troop build-up in Iraq. In the voting, 56–34, seven Republicans join Democrats in supporting the move.

February 21

British Prime Minister; Tony Blair, said as many as 1,600 of the 7,100 troops stationed in southern Iraq would leave in the next few months. "What all this means is not that Basra is how we want it to be, but it does mean that the next chapter in Basra's history can be written by Iraqis,"[4] Blair said.

February 26

The Iraqi cabinet passed a draft law on oil revenues that called on the government to distribute oil revenues to regions based on their populations and allowed regions to negotiate contracts with foreign companies to explore and develop oil fields.

In a policy shift, US officials said they would participate in high-level talks with Iran and Syria at an upcoming meeting about Iraq.

March 28

Seasoned diplomat Ryan Crocker replaced Zalmay Khalizad as US ambassador to Iraq.

April 12

Eight people, including two Iraqi legislators, died when a suicide bomber stroke inside the Parliament building which was located in Baghdad's fortified International Zone. An organization that included Al Qaeda in Mesopotamia claimed responsibility for the bold attack.

In another attack, the Sarafiya Bridge that spans the Tigris River was destroyed.

April 18

Five bombs targeting Shiite neighbourhoods killed about 200 people and ravaged the Iraqi capital in the worst violence in weeks. One bomb alone killed about 140 in Sadr City area.

April 30

Stuart Bowen Jr., head of the Office of the Special Inspector General for Iraq Reconstruction, faulted both the US and Iraq in his criticism of the poor construction and maintenance of several projects throughout Iraq. Problems included power generators that did not work, overflowing sewage systems and faulty electrical systems.

May 1

President Bush vetoed legislation from Congress funding the Iraq War but imposing deadlines for American withdrawal.

May 3

Muharib Abdul Latif Al Jubouri, a leader of Al Qaeda in Mesopotamia, died in a raid north of Baghdad. US officials said that Jubouri was involved in the kidnapping of American reporter, Jill Carroll.

May 12

Four soldiers died and three were captured in an attack near Mahmudiya, a mostly Sunni area. The Islamic State of Iraq, an insurgent group that includes Al Qaeda in Mesopotamia, said it was holding the soldiers.

May 15

President Bush selected Lieutenant General Douglas Lute to oversee war policy in Iraq and Afghanistan. Lute served as the top operations officer for the Joint Chiefs of Staff. Lute's nomination had to be confirmed by the Senate.

May 23

The body of one of the soldiers who was abducted on May 12, Private First Class, Joseph Anzack, was found in the Euphrates River.

May 25

Mogtada Al Sadr, leader of the Mahdi Army militia and an opponent of the US-led war in Iraq, re-emerged from hiding for the first time since January. In a speech, he called for a timetable for the withdrawal of US troops from Iraq.

May 31

With 127 deaths, May was the deadliest month for US troops since November 2004.

June 13

The revered Shiite Askariya mosque at Samarra was bombed for the second time in 16 months. Sunni militants connected to Al Qaeda were suspected in the attack.

June 16

US forces began a new offensive, targeting Al Qaeda in Mesopotamia in areas around Baghdad, where car bombings and other insurgent attacks had intensified.

June 24

Three Iraqi army officials, including Ali Hassan Al Majid, a cousin of Saddam Hussein who was known as 'Chemical Ali', were convicted and sentenced to death for carrying out the murder of about 50,000 Kurds in 1988, what was called the Anfal Campaign.

July 3

The Iraqi cabinet approved the hydrocarbon framework law, a component of a larger legislative package, which stated that the revenue from oil sales belongs to all Iraqis and outlined the function of the oil and gas council. Parliament needed to approve the legislation.

July 7

A truck filled with explosives destroyed dozens of homes and shops in Amerli; a Shiite village north of Baghdad. Hundreds were wounded in the attack.

August 1

The Iraqi Consensus Front, the largest Sunni faction in Prime Minister Nuri Al Maliki's cabinet, resigned, citing the Shiite-led government's failure to stem violence by militias, follow through with reforms and involve Sunnis in decisions on security.

August 14

Two pairs of truck bombs exploded about five miles apart in the remote north-western Iraqi towns of Qahtaniya and Jazeera. At least 500 members of the minority Yazidi community were reported killed and hundreds more were wounded making it the single deadliest insurgent attack of the war.

August 24

A review of progress in Iraq, called the National Intelligence Estimate, said the Iraqi government had failed to end sectarian violence even with the surge of American troops. The report also said, however, that a withdrawal of troops, a move supported by many Democrats would erode security gains achieved thus far.

August 26

In an attempt at national reconciliation, a group of Sunni, Shiite and Kurdish Iraqi leaders including Prime Minister Nuri Al Maliki, Vice President Tarqi al-Hashemi and President Jalal Talabani, announced that former Baathists; members of the party loyal to Saddam Hussein, could regain their government jobs that were lost in 2003's de-Baathification process.

August 28

More than 50 people were killed and hundreds were wounded when members of the Mahdi Army, the militia loyal to radical Shiite cleric Mogtada Al Sadr and the Badr Organization, a group of fighters that supports Prime Minister Nuri Al Maliki battle in the streets of Karbala during a pilgrimage celebrating the birth of Muhammad Al Mahdi. The following day, Mogtada Al Sadr announced that he had ordered the Mahdi Army to suspend its military operations for six months.

September 3

President Bush, Secretary of State; Condoleezza Rice and Defence Secretary; Robert Gates made a surprise visit to Iraq and visit Anbar Province, a Sunni stronghold. They met with Iraqi Prime Minister Nuri Al Maliki and other leaders. Bush stressed that progress in security and reconciliation had been made in Anbar and hinted that a troop withdrawal may start if such gains continue.

September 10

The US commander in Iraq, General David Petraeus reported to Congress on the war's progress.

September 13

In a nationally televised address, President Bush outlined a plan for withdrawing troops from Iraq. He said, by July 2008, troop levels would drop from the current high of 1,69,000 to 1,30,000. Calling the move a return on success, Bush said the progress from the surge of troops would be diminished if more troops returned from Iraq too quickly.

Abdul Sattar Buzaigh Al Rishawi, a leader of Sunni tribes in Anbar Province that had joined forces with the US to fight Sunni militants, such as Al Qaeda in Mesopotamia, died in a bombing. Such cooperation was credited with bringing relative peace and stability to Anbar Province.

September 16

Seventeen Iraqi civilians, including a couple and their infant, were killed when employees of American private security company "Blackwater"[5] which was escorting a diplomatic convoy, reportedly fired on a car that failed to stop at the request of a police officer. Iraqi Prime Minister Nuri Al Maliki threatened to evict Blackwater employees from Iraq.

October 8

British Prime Minister Gordon Brown announced that half of the country's 5,000 troops stationed in Basra would be removed by the end of 2008.

October 12

Lieutenant General Ricardo Sanchez, the former commander of US forces in Iraq, criticized the Bush administration for its catastrophically flawed, unrealistically optimistic war plan. Sanchez, who retired after being replaced amid the Abu Ghraib prison abuse scandal, said that "After more than four years of fighting, America continues its desperate struggle in Iraq without any concerted effort to devise a strategy that will achieve victory in that war-torn country or in the greater conflict against extremism."[6]

October 17

Turkey's Parliament voted, 507 to 19, to allow the deployment of troops into northern Iraq to deal with attacks on Turkey by Kurdish rebels in Iraq.

October 21

Kurdish militants in northern Iraq, members of the Kurdistan Workers Party, attacked and killed 12 Turkish soldiers about three miles inside Turkey.

November 6

Six American soldiers were killed in Iraq, bringing the total deaths in 2007 to 852, the highest annual total since the war began in 2003.

November 13

FBI investigators reported that 14 of the 17 shootings of Iraqis on September 16 by Blackwater guards were unjustified and the guards were reckless in their use of deadly force.

November 18

US military reported that for three consecutive weeks, the number of car bombs, roadside bombs, mines, rocket attacks and other violence had fallen to the lowest level since January 2006.

November 24

A brigade of 5,000 US troops started to leave Diyala Province, the first significant pullback of troops. Once the withdrawal was complete, there were to be 1,57,000 soldiers in Iraq, from earlier figures of 1,62,000.

December 16

With the help of the US military, Turkish fighter jets bombed areas in Dohuk Province in northern Iraq targeting the Kurdish militant group; the Kurdistan Workers' Party. At least one civilian was reported to be killed in the attack.

The British military transferred military control of Basra to the Iraqi government. It was the last region that was still under British control.

December 29

General David Petraeus reported that car bombs and suicide attacks had dropped by 60 per cent since June 2007. He also said that Al Qaeda in Mesopotamia remained the greatest threat to Iraq's security.

2008:

January 1

In the worst attack in Iraq in months, a suicide bomber killed 30 people at a home where mourners were offering their condolences to the family of a man killed in a car bomb.

February 1

At least 65 people died when two women suicide bombers attacked crowded pet markets in eastern Baghdad.

February 24

More than 50 people, who were headed to the shrine of Imam Hussein in Karbala to celebrate Arbaeen, were killed in a suicide attack at a rest stop.

March 19

President Bush claimed normalcy is returning to Iraq.

On the fifth anniversary of the US-led war in Iraq, President Bush insisted that the outcome of the war would be worth the sacrifice, yet he admited the cost of war had exceeded expectations in terms of money and loss of life. "Five years into this battle, there is an understandable debate over whether the war was worth fighting, whether the fight is worth winning, and whether we can win it,"[7] he said. "The answers were clear to me. Removing Saddam Hussein from power was the right decision, and this is a fight that America can and must win," he added.

March 25

About 30,000 Iraqi troops and police, with air support from the US and British military, attempted to oust Shiite militias, particularly the Mahdi Army led by radical cleric Mogtada Al Sadr, that controlled Basra and its lucrative ports in southern Iraq. Sadr declared a ceasefire in August 2007, but has allowed his forces to fight in self defence. Four days into the operation, the Mahdi Army maintained control over much of Basra. The assault, ordered by Iraqi Prime Minister Nuri Al Maliki, was criticized for being poorly planned and executed. Fighting spilt into the Sadr city section of Baghdad.

March 31

After negotiations with Iraqi officials, Mogtada Al Sadr ordered his militia to end military action in exchange for amnesty for his supporters, the release from prison of his followers who had not been convicted of crimes and the government's help in returning Sadrists to their homes. The compromise was seen as a defeat to Iraqi Prime Minister, Nuri Maliki, who was criticized for poorly organizing the campaign. In addition, more than 1,000 Iraqi soldiers and police officers either refused to participate in the operation or deserted their posts.

April 8

General David Petraeus delivered highly anticipated briefing to Congress. He was chosen as the next leader of US Central Command. General Raymond Odierno tapped to take charge in Iraq.

April 13

About 1,300 soldiers who either refused to fight or deserted the military's March operation in Basra to oust Shiite militias, were dismissed.

April 19

The Mahdi Army retreated from the last districts of Basra under its control. Iran endorsed the assault on the Mahdi Army, a group that it once supported.

April 24

After a boycott of almost a year, the largest Sunni block in Iraq's government, Tawafiq, announced it would return to the cabinet of Prime Minister Nuri Al Maliki. Tawafiq's leader, Adnan Al Dulaimi said by passing an amnesty law and launching an assault on Shiite militias, the government had met enough of its demands to end the boycott.

May 9

The US State Department renewed its contract with Blackwater Worldwide, the company whose guards killed 17 civilians in 2007, to provide security for US diplomats for another year. "We cannot operate without private security firms in Iraq,"[8] said Patrick Kennedy; a USA Undersecretary of State.

May 10

The government and leaders of the Mahdi Army agreed to end the fighting in the Sadr City section of Baghdad. As part of the deal, the government was to assume control over Sadr City and the rebels who didn't actively participate in the battles, which killed hundreds of people, were to avoid arrest. Iran helped to broker the truce. The ceasefire, however, failed to stem the violence in Sadr City.

May 20

Iraqi troops moved into Sadr City, meeting very little resistance from the Mahdi Army.

June 1

The US military announced that fatalities in Iraq in May dropped to 19, the lowest level since the war began in 2003.

June 7

Former Iraqi Prime Minister Ibrahim Al Jaafari was removed from the governing Dawa party for reaching out to a rival party.

June 17

At least 60 people were killed and about 75 were wounded when an explosive-laden minibus exploded at a bus terminal near a crowded market in a Shiite district of Baghdad. The blast caused an apartment building to burst into flames. The US military attributed the bombing to a Shiite militia leader, Haydar Mahdi Khadum Al Fawadi, saying he orchestrated the bombing to incite sectarian violence between Sunnis and Shiites.

June 19

The New York Times reported that Iraq's Oil Ministry had been negotiating no-bid contracts with Exxon Mobil, Shell, Total, BP and Chevron to service its oil fields. The announcement was greeted with scepticism as critics accused the Bush Administration of going to war in Iraq to profit from Iraq's oil fields.

June 30

In a 700-page study, called 'On Point II: Transition to the New Campaign', the US Army said that while it was capable of toppling Saddam Hussein, it was not equipped to rebuild Iraq into a functional country.

July 19

Parliament approved the nomination of six Sunni ministers to the cabinet. The ministers were all members of Tawafiq, a Sunni political party, who had boycotted Prime Minister Nuri Al Maliki's government for a year.

July 28

As Kurds in Kirkuk protested part of an election law that would dilute their control of the city, a female suicide bomber killed 17 people and wounded dozens. Kurds blamed Turkmen militants for the bombing, and in response began attacking Turkmen. About a dozen people died in the violence. In Baghdad, two female suicide bombers killed 32 Shiite pilgrims.

August 6

The Iraqi Parliament failed to pass the election law when negotiations collapsed over the issue of control in Kirkuk. Hopes that provincial elections would be held in 2008 were dashed. The elections were seen as vital to moving Iraqi's rival ethnic groups toward reconciliation. Kurds dominated the city, which also had a large population of Turkmens and Arabs, and had resisted any attempts to dilute their control through a power-sharing plan.

August 22

The United States said it would withdraw combat troops from Iraqi cities by June 2009 followed by the removal of all combat troops by the end of 2011.

September 1

The US transferred to the Iraqi military and police responsibility for maintaining security in Anbar Province,

General Raymond Odierno became commander in Iraq.

September 24

Iraqi Parliament passed a much-anticipated law that called for provincial elections to be held in early 2009. Elections had originally been scheduled for October 2008. Elections in the disputed city of Kirkuk, however, were postponed until reaching a separate agreement by a committee made up of representatives from each group involved.

October 1

The Iraqi government took command of 54,000 (mainly Sunni) fighters from the US, which had been paying the fighters for their support. The fighters, members of Awakening Councils, turned against Al Qaeda in Mesopotamia in 2007 and began siding with the US.

October 17

Iraq and the US completed a draft of a security agreement that called for all US troops to be withdrawn from Iraq by the end of 2011.

October 31

General David Petraeus became the head of Central Command and Oversee Military Operations in Iraq, Afghanistan, Pakistan, Syria, Iran and other countries.

November 16

After nearly a year of negotiations with the US, the Iraqi cabinet passed by a large margin a status of forces agreement that would govern the US presence in Iraq through 2011. The pact called for the withdrawal of all US combat troops by December 31, 2011, and the removal of US troops from Iraqi cities by the summer of 2009. In addition, the agreement gave Iraqi officials jurisdiction over serious crimes committed by off-duty Americans who were off base when the crimes occur.

November 27

Iraq's Parliament voted, 149 to 35, to approve the status of forces agreement.

December 4

The Presidential Council, made up of Iraq's President and two Vice Presidents, gave final approval to the status of forces agreement that would govern the US presence in Iraq through 2011.

December 14

"At a news conference in Baghdad, a reporter for Al Baghdadia; a Cairo-based satellite television network, hurls his shoes at former USA President, Bush, and calls him a 'dog'. The shoes narrowly miss Bush's head."[9]

2009:

January 1

United States handed over control of airspace and Green Zone to Iraq.

January 31

Iraq held local elections to create provincial councils. The elections were notable for their lack of violence and the noticeably diminished role the US played in their implementation. Voter turnout varied widely by area, with some regions reporting less than 50 per cent participation and others more than 75 per cent.

February 9

In the worst single loss to the American military in nine months, a suicide bomber killed four American soldiers in the northern Iraq city of Mosul. Three of the soldiers died at the scene while the other later died at a nearby hospital. Three Iraqis were also injured in the blast.

February 13

A female suicide bomber killed 35 Shiite pilgrims in Baghdad, the deadliest attack in a string of bombings. Most of the dead were women and children, who were walking in an annual procession to the holy city of Karbala to commemorate Arbaeen; which marks the end of the mourning period for Imam Hussein, grandson of the Prophet Muhammad, according to The New York Times.

February 27

In front of a crowd of Marines in Camp Lejeune; North Carolina State of USA, President Obama announced his intention to withdraw most American troops out of Iraq by August 31, 2010. As many as 50,000 troops will remain there for smaller missions and to train Iraqi soldiers. Camp Lejeune is the largest marine camp on the East Coast.

March 8

A suicide bomber killed 28 people and injured 57 when his motorcycle, laden with explosives, blew up near a Police Academy in Baghdad. Five of the dead were police officers.

March 10

33 people were killed by a suicide bomber in Baghdad, aimed at a group of Iraqi army officers while 46 others were injured.

April 10

A suicide bomb in Mosul, Iraq killed five US soldiers and 2 Iraqis, the deadliest attack against the American military in Iraq in

13 months. The bombing took place at the police headquarters of the city. At least 70 people in the area were wounded.

April 23

At least 80 people were killed in three separate suicide bombings in Baghdad. This was the largest death-toll due to attacks since February 2008. One of the bombings was reportedly set off by a female, who was standing among a group of women and children receiving food aid.

April 24

60 people were killed in two attacks set off outside the holiest Shiite site in Baghdad, the shrine of Imam Musa Al Kadhim. At least 140 people were killed and another 240 wounded in Iraq in the past two days.

May 11

An American soldier being treated at a counselling centre in Baghdad killed five fellow servicemen. The shooter; Sergeant John M. Russell, was serving his third tour in Iraq, and had been ordered to undergo psychological counselling and relinquish his gun. The shooting occurred at Camp Liberty; a large American military base.

June 30

As a signal of the United States' diminishing role in Iraq, and in compliance with the status of forces agreement between the US and Iraq, US troops completed their withdrawal from Iraqi cities, including Baghdad, and transferred the responsibility of securing the cities to Iraqi troops. Iraqi Prime Minister, Nuri Al Maliki, named June 30th as 'National Sovereignty Day' and declared a public holiday.

August 19

Two massive bomb attacks killed at least 95 and wounded over 600 in Baghdad. Though violence had been escalating in recent weeks, this was the worst attack in the region since the US military ceded control of the security of the country back to its government, on 30th of June.

References

1. "*Consensus emerges that Iraq elections cannot be held before 30 June – Annan*", United Nations News Centre, February 19th , 2004
2. It is the note of a secret meeting of senior British Labor government, defense and intelligence figures discussing the build-up to the war, which included direct reference to classified United States policy of the time.
3. "*Bush Gives Plan for Iraq Victory and Withdrawal*" , New York Times, December 1st, 2005
4. "*Blair announces Iraq troops cut*", BBC News, February 21st, 2007
5. Blackwater is a private military company which has a wide array of business divisions, subsidiaries, and spin-off corporations but the organization as a whole has courted much controversy.
6. "*Ex-Commander says Iraq Effort is a Nightmare*", New York Times, October 13, 2007
7. "*Five years later, Bush says Iraq war must go on*", CNN News Agency, March 19th, 2008
8. New York Times, May 9th, 2008
9. New York Times, December 15th, 2008

Bibliography

1. Books

1. "*Directory of Persian Gulf Region and Countries*", Abrar Moaser, Iran, 2005 (In Persian)
2. Abed Ibrahim and Hellyer Peter, "*United Arab Emirates: A new Perspective*", Trident Press Ltd, London, 2001
3. Abrahamian Ervand, "*History of Modern Iran*", Cambridge University Press, New York, 2008
4. Alnasrawi Abbas, "*Iraq: Economic Sanctions and Consequences, 1990–2000*", Carfax Publishing Ltd., London, 2001
5. Amirahmadi Hooshang and Entessar Nader, eds. "*Iran and the Arab World*", St. Martin's Press, New York, 1993
6. Anderson Ewan W. and Bayne Fisher William, "*The Middle East: Geography and Geopolitics*", Rutledge, USA, 2000
7. Ansari Ali M., "*Confronting Iran: The Failure of American Foreign Policy and Next Great Crisis in the Middle East*", Basic Books, USA, 2006
8. Asadian Amir, "*US Policy in Persian Gulf*", Strategic Studies' Research Centre, Tehran, 2001 (In Persian)
9. *Brassey Defence Yearbook*
10. Bush George and Scowcroft Brent, "*A World Transformed*", Knopf, New York, 1998
11. Casey Michael S., "*The History of Kuwait*", Greenwood Publishing Group, USA, 2007
12. CIA World Fact Book, 2005
13. CIA World Fact Book, 2007
14. CIA World Fact Book, 2009
15. Coddy Eric and Wirtz James J. and Larsen Jeffery A., "*Weapons of Mass Destruction: An Encyclopaedia of Worldwide Policy, Technology and History*", ABC-CLIO, USA, 2004
16. Cordesman Anthony H., "*Saudi Arabia Enters the Twenty-first Century*", Greenwood Publishing Group, USA, 2003

17. Ebrahimi-far Tahereh, "*the Patterns of Confidence Building Measures in The Persian Gulf*", The Institute for Political and International Studies, Iran, 2006 (In Persian)

18. Elahi Homayoun, *The Persian Gulf and Its Problems*; 8th edition, Ghoomes, Tehran, 2005 (In Persian)

19. Ferdosipour Mojtaba (Collector), "*Collection of Monographs of Fourteenth Persian Gulf's International Conference in 2004, Persian Gulf; Regional Transitions after Iraq's Occupation*", Iran Foreign Ministry's Publication Centre, Tehran, 2004 (In Persian)

20. Fisk Robert, "*The Great War for Civilization*", Vintage, UK, 2007

21. Freedman Lawrence, Karsh Efraim, "*The Gulf Conflict: Diplomacy and War in the New World Order 1990-1991*", Princeton, USA, 1993

22. Frum, David, "*How We Got Here: The '70s*", Basic Books, New York, 2000

23. Gray Colin S. and Sloan Geoffrey, "*Geopolitics, Geography and Strategy*", Routledge, USA, 1999

24. Hafeznia Mohammad Reza, "*Persian Gulf and Strategic Role of Strait of Hormuz*", 4th edition, Samt, Tehran, 2005 (In Persian)

25. Hafeznia Mohammad Reza, "*Principles and Concepts of Geopolitics*", Popli Publications, Iran, 2006 (In Persian)

26. Haji Yusefi Amir Mohammad, "*Iran's Foreign Policy Based on Regional Transitions: 1991-2001*", Iran's Foreign Office's International and Political Studies Office, Tehran, 2005 (In Persian)

27. Hajjar Sami, "*US Military Presence in the Gulf: Challenges and Prospects*", Strategic Studies Institute, USA, 2002

28. Halbouty Michel Thomas, "*Giant Oil and Gas Fields of the Decade; 1990-1999*", AAPG, USA, 2003

29. Hodge Carol C. and Nolan Cathal J., "*US presidents and foreign policy: From 1789 to the Present*", Abc-Clio Inc., USA, 2006

30. Hoff Joan, "*A Faustian Foreign Policy from Woodrow to George W. Bush*", Cambridge University Press, USA, 2008

31. Ikenberry John and Moon Chung-in, "*The United States and Northeast Asia: Debates, Issues and New Order*", Rowman and Littlefield Publishers, USA, 2008

32. Katzman Kenneth, "*Searching for Stable Peace in the Persian Gulf*", US Army War College, USA, 1998

33. Kechichian Joseph A., "*Oman and the World; The Emergence of An Independent Foreign Policy*", RAND, USA, 1995

34. Kolko, Gabriel, "*The Age of War; Things Go Wrong*", Lynne Rienner Inc, USA, 2007

35. Laqueur Walter, "*Confrontation, the Middle East War and World Politics*", Harper Collins, USA, 1974

36. Little Douglas, "*American Orientalism: The United States and The Middle East since 1945*", University of North Carolina Press, USA, 2002

37. Litwak Robert, *"Regime Change: US Strategy Through the Prison of 9/11*", Woodrow Wilson Publishers, USA, 2007

38. Loveman Brian, "*Strategy for Empire: US Regional Security policy in the Post Cold War Era*", Rowman and Littlefield, USA, 2004

39. Mahajan, V.D. "*International Relations since 1900*", S. Chand and Company Ltd., New Delhi, 1989

40. Mojtahedzade Piroz, "*The Islands of Tunb & Abu Musa; An Iranian Argument in Search of Peace and Cooperation in the Persian Gulf,* ", Institute of Political and International Studies, Tehran, 2007 (In Persian)

41. Moller Bjorn, "*Oil and Water: Cooperative Security in the Persian Gulf*", Mac Milan, USA, 2001

42. Niblock Tim, "*Saudi Arabia; Power, Legitimacy and Survival*", Routledge, USA, 2006

43. Pauly Robert J., *"US foreign policy and the Persian Gulf* ", Ashgate, London, 2005

44. Pelletiere Stephen, "*Land-power and Dual Containment: Rethinking America's Policy in the Gulf*", Strategic Studies Institute/ United States Army War College, USA, 1999

45. Potter Lawrence, "*Iran, Iraq, and the legacies of war*", MacMillan, USA, 2004

46. Rajaee, Farhang, "*The Iran–Iraq War: The Politics of Aggression*", University Press of Florida, USA, 2001

47. Reich Bernard and Major Gotowicki Stephen H., "*The United States and the Persian Gulf in the Bush Administration*", *Royal United Services Institute and Brassey's Defence Yearbook*, London, 1991

48. Shaw Martin, "*The New Western Way of War*" , Polity Press, UK, 2005

49. Smolansky Oles M., "*The USSR and Iraq*", Duke University Press, USA, 1991

50. Sokolsky Richard D., "*The United States and the Persian Gulf: Reshaping Security Strategy for the Post-Containment Era*", University Press of the Pacific, USA, 2004

51. Sokolsky Richard D., "*Persian Gulf Security: Improving Allied Military Contributions*", RAND, USA, 2000

52. Statesman's Year Book, 2008
53. Tabarsa Naghi, "*The Sovereignty Over Abu Musa, Lesser and Greater Tunbs Islands in the Iranian Foreign Policy*", The Centre for Documents and Diplomatic History, Tehran, 2008 (In Persian)
54. Thomas Keaney, Cohen Eliot. A, "*Gulf War Air Power Survey*", United States Department of Air Force, 1993
55. Till, Geoffrey, "*Maritime Strategy and the Nuclear Age*", McMillan, London,1984
56. Yaphe Judith, "*The Middle East in 2015: The Impact of Regional Trends on US Strategy Planning*", University Press of the Pacific, USA, 2002

2. Articles

1. "*Enterprise in UAE Project,*" Platt's Oilgram News, volume 74, number 132, July 10th , 1996
2. "*Getting amputees back on their feet*", *Washington Post,* October 25, 2005
3. "*Iraqi Air Force Equipment — Introduction*", Global Security
4. "*More than 10,00,000 Iraqis murdered*", Opinion Research Business, September 2007
5. "*President's Address to the Nation*", USA Office of the Press Secretary, *January 10*, 2007
6. "*The Unfinished War: A Decade Since Desert Storm*", CNN In-Depth Specials, January 15, 2001
7. "*Army Chief Says British Troops Should Be Pulled Out of Iraq.*" The Independent, UK, October 13, 2006
8. "*Bahrain: Iran a Potential Threat,*" United Press International, May 15, 1999
9. "*Bahrain-Iran Eye Good Relations*", Arab News Agency, February 4, 2009
10. "*Big rise in Iraq deaths in April*", BBC News Agency, May 1, 2009
11. "*Blair announces Iraq troops cut*", BBC News, February 21, 2007
12. "*Bush gave Saddam Hussein and his sons 48 hours to leave Iraq*", Global Policy Forum, March 18, 2003
13. "*Bush Gives Plan for Iraq Victory and Withdrawal*", New York Times, December 1, 2005
14. "*Bush to Endorse Petraeus Plan*", Washington post, September 12, 2007
15. "*Canal to Bypass Strait of Hormuz*", Dow Jones, September 8, 2008
16. "*Cheney to Meet Oman's Sultan for Talks on Iran,*" Voice of America, March 19, 2009
17. "*Clinton sees consensus forming on Iran steps*", Reuters, January 28, 2010

18. "*Consensus emerges that Iraq elections cannot be held before 30 June; Annan*", United Nations News Centre, February 19, 2004
19. "*Crude price pegged at $39.6 a barrel under next year's budget*", IRNA, December 5, 2008 (In Persian)
20. "*Despair not an Option in Iraq War*", CNN, October 17, 2006
21. "*Exxon Aims For Big Role In Iraq's Oil Sector*", Reuters News Agency, March 9, 2009
22. "*Five years later, Bush says Iraq war must go on*", CNN News Agency, March 19, 2008
23. "*Foreign exchange Reserves Reach $80 billion*", Iran Daily, December 4, 2008 (In Persian)
24. "*Global Economic Crisis: A Catalyst for Change in Saudi Arabia?*", The Brookings Institution, May 3, 2009
25. "*Impact of Crisis on UAE Economy is Mild*", Gulf News Agency, November 7, 2008
26. "*Iran warns of closure of Hormuz Strait if threatened*", China View, July 5, 2008
27. "*Iran, Oman Discuss Military Cooperation,*" Middle East News line, August 27, 2008
28. "*Iran, Oman Prepare Security Pact*", Middle East Newsline, May 20, 2009
29. "*Iran-Bahrain relations*", BBC News, *BBC Persian*, April 5, 2009 (In Persian)
30. "*Kuwait Oil Field, World's 2nd Largest Needs IOC; International Oil Companies*", Dow Jones Newswires, September 22, 2009
31. "*Kuwait Supports Peaceful Nuclear Program*", Iran Daily, October 5, 2005 (In Persian)
32. "*Kuwait, Saudi Arabia to discuss joint oil projects in border areas*", Kuwait Times, January 5, 2004
33. "*Kuwaiti economy set to contract*", Middle East Business Intelligence, March 30, 2009
34. "*Kuwaiti Emir Congratulates Ahmadinejad On Re-election*", IRNA, June 14, 2009 (In Persian)
35. "*More congratulations for Ahmadinejad on election win*", Iranian Press TV, June 15, 2009 (In Persian)
36. "*Muscat to Musandam by Sea*", BBC News Agency, July 30, 2008
37. "*Obama Visits Saudi King Before Speech*", CBS News, June 3, 2009
38. "*Obama: Policy on Iran to be different*", United Press International Journal, February 9, 2009

39. "*Oil Squeeze*", Time Magazine, February 5, 1979

40. "*Oman Dismisses US Concerns on Iran Nuclear Issue*", Fars News Agency, December 28, 2008 (In Persian)

41. "*Omani Plants Likely To Process Gas for Iran*", Thai Press Reports, September 5, 2008

42. "*Petraeus says strike on Iran could spark nationalism*", Reuters, February 3, 2010

43. "*Politics-USA/Middle East, Strategic Consensus*", Inter Press Service News Agency, October 4, 2006

44. "*Rare Shiite protests in eastern Saudi Arabia*", DAWN, A Leading Daily English Newspaper of Pakistan, February 25, 2009

45. "*Reagan's mixed White House legacy*", BBC News, June 6, 2004

46. "*Recession in UAE cannot Be Ruled Out*", Arabian News Agency, May 6, 2009

47. "*Saudi vows to keep oil flowing*", CNN, *May* 31, *2004*

48. "*Tension in Iran-Bahrain Relations after Kayhan Editor Claims Bahrain Is Inseparable Part of Iran*", The Middle East Media Research Institute, August 3rd, 2007

49. "*The World; British Miners Settle for Less*", New York Times, January 24, 1982

50. "*UAE-Iran relations strong, says top envoy*", Gulf News, July 17, 2008

51. "*US Democrats in dry dock over ports*", Asia Times, Mar 15, 2006

52. "*US sells weapons to Taiwan, angering China*", Washington Post, January 30, 2010

53. "*US Senate Backs New Sanctions Against Iran*", BBC News Agency, January 29, 2010

54. "*US Speeding Up Missile Defences in Persian Gulf*", New York Times, January 31, 2010

55. "*US Steps Up Arms Sales to Persian Gulf Allies*", Washington Post, January 30, 2010

56. "*US Warns Iran of Defense Umbrella Over Gulf States*", Irish Times Agency, July 23, 2009

57. "*Why Iraq Was a Mistake*", Times, April 9, 2006

58. Aghai Diba Bahman, "*Closing the Strait of Hormuz*", Persian Journal, November 10, 2006 (In Persian)

59. Al Issawi Tarek, "*Saudi King Abdullah invites Iran's Rafsanjani to Saudi Arabia*", Bloomberg, May 15, 2008

60. Al Rumaihi Mohammad, "*The Gulf Monarchies, Testing Time,*" Middle East Quarterly, December 1996

61. Ali Khan, Ghazanfar, "*GCC warns Iran against making hostile remarks*", *Arab News*, February 23, 2009

62. Bayne Fisher William, "*The Cambridge History of Iran*", Cambridge University Press, Volume 4, 1975

63. Beehner, Lionel "*Shiite Muslims in the Mideast*", Council on Foreign Relations, USA, June 16, 2006

64. Blanford Nicholas, "*Kuwait hopes for answers on its Gulf War POWs*", Christian Science Monitor, 2001

65. Borer Douglas A., "*Inverse Engagement: Lessons from US-Iraq Relations, 1982–1990*", US Army Professional Writing Collection; US Army, 2003

66. Byman Daniel L., "*Saudi Arabia's Own Iraq Nightmare*", Saban Centre for Middle East Policy (Brooking Institute), February, 8, 2007

67. Caldwell Dan, "*Flashpoints in the Gulf: Abu Musa and the Tunb Islands*", Middle East Policy, Volume 4, Number 3, March 1, 1996

68. Coman Julian, "*Egyptian Suicide Bomber Blamed for Attack in Qatar*", The Independent, March 21, 2005

69. Conetta Carl, "*Wages of War*", Project on Defence Alternative; Appendix 2, October 20, 2003

70. Dagher Sam, "*Basra Oil Fuels Fight to Control Iraq's Economic Might*", Christian Science Monitor, September 19, 2007

71. Dwyer, Paula, "*Pointing a Finger at Reagan*", Business Week, June 23, 1997

72. Ertan Fikret, "*Strait of Hormuz: The place to watch*", Turkish Today's Zaman Magazine, July 6, 2008

73. Ewell M. Webster, Brito Dagobert, and Noer John, "*An Alternative Pipeline Strategy in the Persian Gulf*", The Baker Institute, April 1997

74. *Ex-Commander Says Iraq Effort is a Nightmare*", New York Times, October 13, 2007

75. Fassihi Farnaz , "*In Iran, grim reminders of Saddam's arsenal*", New Jersey Star-Ledger, October 27, 2002

76. Feller Ben, "*Obama sets firm withdrawal timetable for Iraq*", The Detroit News, February 27, 2009

77. Garvin Jr. C.C., "*The Oil Glut in Perspective*", Annual American Petroleum Institute Issue; Oil and Gas Journal, November 9, 1981

78. Gause III Gregory F., "*The Illogic of Dual Containment*", Foreign Affairs Journal, March/April 1994

79. Gyorgy, Andrew, "*The Geopolitics of War: Total War and Geostrategy*", The Journal of Politics, Volume 5, November 1943

80. Halliday Fred, "*Arabs and Persians Beyond the Geopolitics of The Gulf*", Le Monde Journal, No 22, July-December 1996

81. Hershay D. Robert, "*Worrying* Anew *Over Oil Imports*", The New York Times, December 30, 1989

82. Higgins Alexander G., "*U.N.: 100,000 Iraq refugees flee monthly*", *Boston Globe*, November 3, 2006

83. Hough Harold, "*Iranian Intentions-The Strait of Hormuz or Beyond?*", Jane's Intelligence Review, Volume 7, Number 10, October 1, 1995

84. Ibrahim Youssef, "*Iran is Said to Expel Arabs from Gulf Island*", The New York Times, April 16, 1992

85. Isenberg David, "*A game of chicken in the Persian Gulf*", Asia Times, *January* 10, *2008*

86. Klare Michael , "*Will Iraq be a Global Gas Pump?*", Huffington Post, August 27, 2009

87. Klare Michael, "*The Geopolitics of Natural Gas*", The National Magazine, January 30, 2006

88. Laos Nicolas K., "*International Security in the Post-Cold War Era*", Journal of International Affairs, December 1999- February 2000, Volume IV, Number 4

89. Larijani, *Omani Ambassador Call for Regional Cooperation*", Iranian Student News Agency, January 27, 2009 (In Persian)

90. Liu Henry C. K.; Independent Critical Analysis and Commentary, "*The Burden of Being Superpower: part 5*", Asia Times Online, August 14, 2004

91. Major Randy B. Bell, "*Expansion of American Persian Gulf Policy By Three Presidents*", Global Security, 1990

92. Miles Donna, "*Saudi Arabia Pledges to Support Iraq, Promote Regional Stability*", American Forces Press Service, August 1, 2007

93. Murphy Caryle, "*Iran Claims Sovereignty over Small, Oil- Producing Gulf Island*", The Washington Post, September 25, 1992

94. Nasr Vali, "*When the Shiites rise*", Foreign Affairs, Volume 85, Number 4, New York, July-August 2006

95. Parker Christopher, Moore Pete W., "*The War Economy of Iraq*", Middle East Report Online

96. Parsons, Tim, "*Updated Iraq Study Affirms Earlier Mortality Estimates*", *The JHU Gazette*, October 16, 2006

97. Pope Charles, "*Cheney changed his view on Iraq*", Seattle Post-Intelligencer, September 29, 2004

98. Rasheed Ahmed, "*Saddam admits Iran's gas attacks*", The Australian, December 19, 2006

99. Shelly Alexander and Gould Deane, "*Factors in the Settlement of the Dispute Over Abu Musa and the Tombs*", M.A. Thesis, The American University, 1979

100. Shuster Mike, "*Export of Iran's Revolution Spawns Violence*", National Public Radio, USA, February 14, 2007

101. Smith Robert, "*New Laws Urged to Deter Racism*", Gulf Daily News, Jan. 26, 2005

102. Smith William D., "*Price Quadruples for Iranian Crude Oil at Auction*", the New York Times, December 12, 1973

103. Susman Tina, "*Poll: Civilian Death Toll in Iraq, may Top 1 Million*", Los Angles Times, September 14, 2007

104. Sutton, John and Kemp Geoffrey, "*Arms to Developing Countries 1945-1965*", The Institute for Strategic Studies, London, 1996

3. Official Documents and Governmental Reports

1. Annual Report of American Petroleum Institute
2. *British Petroleums* Statistical Review of World Energy, June 2008
3. CIA's final report/ Conflict in Iraq
4. Congressional Research Service's Report to USA Congress, November 25, 2008
5. Council on Foreign Relations, USA
6. EIA; USA Energy Information Administration Reports of 2006, 2007 and 2008
7. EIA; USA Energy Information Administration/ Short Term Energy Outlook
8. EIA; USA Energy Information Administration; Country Analysis Briefs
9. EIA; USA Energy Information Administration; Regions' Analysis Briefs
10. Facts About the Three Occupied UAE Islands, Issued by United Nation's International Office/UAE
11. Former US President Bush's nationally televised address in September 2003
12. Former USA President Reagan Address to the Nation on the Iran Arms and Contra Aid Controversy in 1986
13. Former USA President Reagan Address to the Nation on the Iran Arms and Contra Aid Controversy in 1987
14. Testimony of General Petraeus; The commander of USA forces in Iraq, to Congress
15. Institute for the Analysis of Global Security; Report on Kuwait, 2004
16. Institute for the Analysis of Gulf Security; Report on Oman, 2003
17. Iran's Foreign Office's International and Political Studies Office (In Persian)
18. James Baker Institute; an institute for public policy of the Rice University in Texas, USA

19. Kurdistan Regional Government Official Website
20. Kuwait's Ministry of Oil
21. Memorandum of August 24, 1928 on Persian Gulf's Disputed Territories, India Office Library and Record, File No. L/P@ S/18/B 397,pp. 4512-4528
22. Official Documents System of the United Nations
23. OPEC Annual Report 2007
24. OPEC Annual Statistical Bulletin 2007
25. OPEC Annual Statistical Bulletin 2008
26. Pentagon's Report on Iraq War Casualties, page 5, December 2006
27. Piroz Mojtahedzade's letter to Mr. Javier Solana; Former High Representative of the European Union For Common Foreign and Security Policies, June 10, 2004
28. President George W. Bush's Address to the Nation in 2007
29. President Obama's Inaugural Address in January 2009
30. Report of Ministry of Information/ Sultanate of Oman, 2002-2003
31. The Australian government official website
32. The Contras, Cocaine and Covert Operations: Documentation of official USA knowledge of drug trafficking and the Contras; The National Security Archive/George Washington University/ Iran-Contra Affair
33. The United Nations Convention on the Law of the Sea
34. *Transcript of Powell;* US Secretary of State in 2003, *UN Presentation*
35. Transcript of Blix; Head of the UN Monitoring in 2003, UN presentation
36. UAE Official Website
37. UK *Royal United Services Institute*
38. United Nations News Centre
39. United States Department of Air Force Surveys
40. United States Department of Justice Report on Iran Contra Affair
41. United States General Accounting Office (GAO)
42. University of Texas/ Libraries
43. US Army Professional Writing Collection; US Army
44. US Army War College
45. US Department of State/ Background Note/Saudi Arabia, January 2009
46. US Department of State/ Human Rights and Labour/ Report on Iran
47. USA Department of Defence' Study on Iraq War in March 2008
48. USA Department of Defense, Report to Congress, June 2009
49. USA Military Academy

50. USA Office of the Press Secretary
51. White House Official Site

4. Organizations

1. Bloomberg Institute
2. Brookings Institute
3. Defence Alternative Institute
4. Global Policy Forum
5. Global Security Institute
6. Greenwich Meantime
7. Iran Center for Documents of The Imposed War
8. Iran Foreign Ministry's Publication Centre
9. NASA; National Aeronautics and Space Administration
10. PBS Organization
11. Reagan Presidential Foundation
12. Saban Centre for Middle East Policy
13. Strauss Centre for International Security and Law, the University of Texas
14. The Institute for Strategic Studies, London
15. The Middle East Media Research Institute

5. Encyclopaedia

1. Britannica
2. Encyclopaedia of American Foreign Policy
3. Military History Encyclopaedia
4. MSN Encarta
5. Wikipedia

6. Newspapers and Magazines

1. Akhbar Al-Khaleej (Bahrain)
2. Al-Arabia
3. Arab News
4. Asia Times
5. *Boston Globe*
6. Business Week
7. Cambridge University Press
8. China Daily News

9. China View
10. Christian Science Monitor
11. DAWN, A Leading Daily English Newspaper of Pakistan
12. Dow Jones Newswires
13. Foreign Affairs Journal
14. Foreign Policy
15. Guardian News
16. Gulf Daily News, the Voice of Bahrain
17. Huffington Post
18. Independent
19. Iran Daily (In Persian)
20. Iran's Jam-e Jam newspaper (In Persian)
21. Jane's Intelligence Review
22. Journal of Politics
23. Journal of International Affairs
24. Khaleej times
25. Kuwait Times
26. Le Monde Journal
27. *Los Angeles Times*
28. Mashaal; National Iranian Oil Company's Employees' Gazette, June 1st, 2008, volume 396 (In Persian)
29. Mashaal; National Iranian Oil Company's Employees' Gazette, June 1st, 2008, volume 397 (In Persian)
30. MERIA, Middle East Review of International Affairs, Journal
31. Middle East Business Intelligence
32. Middle East News line
33. Middle East Policy
34. Middle East Quarterly
35. Middle East Report Online
36. MuseLetter Energy Bulletin
37. Nation Magazine
38. New Jersey Star-Ledger
39. Oil and Gas Journal
40. Opinion Research Business
41. Pars Times (In Persian)

42. Persian Journal (In Persian)
43. Platt's Oilgram News
44. Thai Press Reports
45. *The JHU Gazette*
46. The New York Times
47. The Washington Independent Journal
48. The Washington Post
49. Time Magazine
50. Turkish Today's Zaman Magazine
51. United Press International
52. United Press International Journal
53. WAM; Emirates News Agency

7. News Agencies

1. American Forces Press Service
2. Arab News Agency
3. Arab News Agency
4. Associated Press News Agency
5. BBC News Agency
6. BBC News Agency/ Persian
7. CBS News
8. CNN News Agency
9. Fars News Agency
10. France Press News Agency
11. Inter Press Service News Agency
12. International Herald News
13. Iran Daily
14. Iranian Press TV
15. Iranian Student News Agency
16. Irish Times Agency
17. IRNA; Islamic Republic News Agency
18. PBS Channel
19. Reuters News Agency
20. USA National Public Radio
21. Voice of America

8. Internet

1. Greg Croft Inc.
2. Jan Krogh's Geosite
3. Lonely Planet Site
4. Msnbc.msn.com
5. oilempire.us
6. Sajed; Imposed War Official Website
7. Suite 101
8. unimaps.com
9. Website of Total Oil Company
10. World Atlas
11. Worldpoliticswatch.com
12. ww.iht.com; International Herald News website
13. *www.alarabiya.net*
14. *www.ameinfo.com*
15. *www.angelfire.com*
16. *www.arabicnews.com*
17. *www.armedforcesjournal.com*
18. *www.austrade.gov*
19. *www.austrade.gov.au*
20. *www.brookings.edu*
21. *www.country-studies.com*
22. *www.dawn.com*
23. *www.defenselink.mil*
24. *www.eia.gov*
25. *www.emirates-islands.org.ae*
26. *www.encylopeadia.com*
27. *www.eoearth.org*
28. *www.geocities.com*
29. *www.globalsecurity.org*
30. www.GulfSecurityReport.com
31. *www.historyofwar.org*
32. *www.iranian.ws*
33. *www.iraqbodycount.org*
34. *www.krg.org*

35. *www.NationMaster.com*
36. *www.Paleopolis.com*
37. *www.presstv.com*
38. *www.srilankadot.com*
39. *www.timesonline.co.uk*
40. *www.un.org*
41. *www.whitehouse.gov*
42. *www.xe.com*

Index

Allawi, Iyad, 46
Anglo-Persian Oil Company (APOC), 129
Arabian strategic Islands, 208
  Bubiyan Island, 209, 210
  Hawar Archipe lago, 210, 211
  Musandam Peninsula, 208, 209

Baath Party, 46
Bahrain Centre for Human Rights (BCHR), 28, 29
Bahrain, 170
  Gas resources, 171, 172
  Oil resources, 170, 171
Barham Salih, 152
Brzezinski, Zbigniew, 8, 9

Casualties of War, 312, 334
  Coalition casualties, 334
  Combat casualties, 312, 313
  Civilian casualties, 313
  Iraqi casualties, 335, 336
  Iraqi refugees, 336
Cheney, Richard, 267
Churchill, Winston, 119
Clinton, Hillary, 110, 344, 391
Cohen, Saul B., 7
Cold War era, 11
Conclusion and recommendations, 381-401
Criticism of war, 337, 338

Drag Reduction Agents (DRA), 194

Economy, 20, 21
EIA (Energy Information Administration), 13
  Short Term Energy Outlook, 1
Enhanced Oil Recovery (EDR), 142
Ethnic groups, 19
Events of 1990, 303, 304
Events of 1991, 304
  January 1991, 304-308
  February 1991, 308-311
  March 1991, 311
Events of 2001, 319, 320
Events of 2002, 320, 321
Events of 2003, 321
  April 2003, fall of Baghdad, 323-326
  March 2003, beginning of the Operation Iraqi Freedom, 321-323
Events of 2004, 326, 327
Events of 2005, 327, 328
Events of 2006, 328, 329
  Iraq study group, 329, 330
Events of 2007, 330-332
Events of 2008, 332, 333, 334
Events of 2009, 334
Events of Eight years of War of Attrition (1980-1988), 282-290
  Attacking nuclear reactors, 295
  Casualties of War, 297
  Superpowers and Gulf States' involvement in War, 297, 299
  Tanker War, 290, 291, 292
  Using chemical weapons by Iraq, 293-295
  War of cities, 295, 296

Evolution of regional order of the Persian Gulf region, 230-275

Frederick L Schuman, 117
Free Trade Agreement (FTA), 31

Geopolitics of Bahrain, 22-32
- Economy, 30-32
- Ethnic groups, 28, 29
- History, 22-24
- Military power, 29, 30
- Natural resources, 32
- Population, 26
- Religion, 26-28
- Territory, 24-26

Geopolitics of Iran, 33
- Economy, 42, 43
- Ethnic groups, 39-41
- History, 33-35
- Military power, 41, 42
- Natural resources, 43, 44
- Population, 38
- Religion, 38, 39
- Territory, 35-38

Geopolitics of Iraq, 44
- Economy, 55-58
- Ethnic group, 52, 53
- History, 44-47
- Military power, 53-55
- Multi-National Force–Iraq (MNF-I), 55
- Natural resources, 58, 59
- Neutral zone, 49, 50
- Population, 50, 51
- Religion, 51, 52
- Territory, 47-49

Geopolitics of Kuwait, 60
- Economy, 67, 68
- Ethnic groups, 65, 66
- History, 60, 61
- Military power, 66, 67
- Natural resources, 68, 69
- Population, 63
- Religion, 64, 65
- Territory, 61-63

Geopolitics of Oman, 69
- Economy, 80, 81
- Ethnic groups, 78, 79
- History, 69-72
- Madha, 75-77
- Military power, 79, 80
- Musandam, 74, 75
- Natural resources, 81
- Population, 77
- Religion, 77, 78
- Territory, 72-74

Geopolitics of Qatar, 81
- Economy, 88, 89
- Ethnic groups, 85-87
- History, 81-83
- Military power, 87, 88
- Natural resources, 89, 90
- Population, 85
- Religion, 85
- Territory, 83-85

Geopolitics of Saudi Arabia, 90
- Economy, 100, 101
- Ethnic group, 97, 98
- History, 90-93
- Military power, 98-100
- Natural resources, 102
- Population, 95
- Religion, 95-97
- Territory, 93-95

Geopolitics of the Persian Gulf region, 16-113
Geopolitics of the regional states, 22
Geopolitics of United Arab Emirates, 102
- Economy, 110-112
- Ethnic groups, 108
- History, 102, 103
- Military power, 108-110
- Natural Resources, 112, 113
- Population, 106, 107
- Religion, 107, 108
- Territory, 103-106

Geopolitics, 3, 4, 12
  definition, 16
Geostrategic importance of the Persian Gulf, 117-172
Geostrategy, 4-9, 13
  definition, 117, 118
Gholam-Hossein Nozari, 145
Gorbachev, Mikhail, 345
Gulf of Aden, 17
Gulf States, Arabs and Persians, conflict between, 19
Gulf War, 11
  in 1990, 10
  in 1991, 19

Hajj pilgrims, 99, 100
Hasan Firouzabadi (Maj. Gen.), 192
Hassan Hakimian, 101
Haushofer, Karl, 117
Historical evolution, 11
History, 17

Iran, 10, 141
  Gas resources, 146-149
  Oil resources, 141-146
Iran, sanctions imposed by the western countries on, 390-394
Iran's nuclear program, 387-390
Iran-GCC States (except Saudi Arabia), 255, 258, 259
  Iran-Bahrain, 255
  Iran-Kuwait, 255, 256
  Iran-Oman, 256, 257
  Iran-Qatar, 257
  Iran-United Arab Emirates, 257
  Iraq-Saudi Arabia, 257, 258
  Saudi-Arabia-rest of the GCC States, 259
Iran-GCC States (except Saudi Arabia), 264
  Iran-Bahrain, 264-266
  Iran-Kuwait, 266, 267
  Iran-Oman, 267, 268
  Iran-Qatar, 268, 269
  Iran-United Arab Emirates, 269
  Iraq-Saudi Arabia, 270
  Iraq-GCC States, 270, 271
  Saudi Arabia-rest of the GCC States, 271, 272
Iranian strategic islands
  Abu Musa Island, 206, 208
  Greater Tunb, 204
  Hengam Island, 203
  Hormuz Island, 200, 201
  Larak Island, 201
  Lesser Tunb, 206
  Qeshm Island, 202, 203
  Tunb Islands, 204
Iran-Iraq War (1980-1988), 279
  Border disputes, 281
  Ethnic Schism, Arab versus Persian, 280, 281
  Introduction, 279
  Political differences, 281, 282
  Religious schism, Sunni versus Shiite, 280
Iran-Iraq War 1980-1988, 10, 18
Iran-USA as two major powers of the region, 382-387
Iraq War (2003 onwards), 10, 11, 313-316
Iraq, 149
  Gas resources, 154
  Oil resources, 149
Islamic Republic News Agency, 145
  Revolution, 13
Islamic Revolutionary Guards Corps (IRGC), 41

Kevin J. Cosgriff, 192
King Fahd Causeway, 25
Kissinger, Henry, 8
Kjellen, Rudolf, 16
Kurdistan Regional Government, 58, 59
Kuwait, 155
  Gas resources, 158
  Divided zone, 157
  Oil resources, 155

Laden, Osama bin, 66
Lincoln, Abraham, 192
Liquefied natural gas (LNG), 21

Macedonian King Alexander, 17
Mackinder, Halford, 5
Mahan, Alfred, 5, 176
Mahmud Ahmadinejad, 145
Median Line, 21
Military power, 20
Mohammad Reza Hafeznia, 119
Mohammad Reza Pahlavi, 123
Mottaki, Manouchehr, 266
Mustafa Alani, 195

Napoleon Bonaparte, 177
National Oil Company (NIOC), 142
Natural resources, 21, 22
Nouri Al Maliki, 398

Oil and Gas Journal, 1
 resources, importance of, 118-121
Oil crisis (1973), 122, 123
 (1979), 123, 124
 (2000s), 125
 definition of, 121, 122
 since 1973, 121-125
Oil Glut (1980s), 124, 125
Oil price shock (1990), 124, 125
Oman, 167
 Gas resources, 169, 170
 Oil resources, 167-169
Organization for Economic Cooperation and Development (OECD), 131
Organization of Petroleum Exporting Countries (OPEC), 136, 137, 138
Other Emirates gas resources, 163, 164
Other Emirates oil resources, 161
 Abu Dhabi gas resources, 162
 Dubai gas resources, 162
 Gas resources, 161
 Sharjah gas resources, 163
Ottoman Turks, 45
Oxford Business Group (DBG), 101

Parthian Empire, 17
People's Democratic Republic of Yemen (PDRY), 70, 71
Perestroika, 345
Perry, William, 344
Persian Gulf countries (Bahrain, Iran, Iraq, Kuwait, Qatar, Saudi Arabia and the United Arab Emirates), 1
Persian Gulf gas resources, 133, 134
Persian Gulf region in Cold War era, 235-238
Persian Gulf region in post-cold war era, 259, 260
 Regional order, 260
Persian Gulf region in post-Iraq war era, 273-275
Persian Gulf region, 2
 role of USA, 343-377
Persian Gulf Region's Oil and gas resources, 126-129
 Exports to Europe, 132
 Exports to Japan, 132
 Exports to USA, 132
 Oil, discovery of, 129-131
Persian Gulf War (1990-1991), 299-302
Persian Gulf's disputed Islands, 211-214
 Iran's claims and UAE's counter claims, 225, 226
 Iran's position, 214-216
 Reasons of Iran's interest in Abu Musa, 216, 217
 Reasons of UAE's interest in Abu Musa, 225
 UAE's position, 221-224
 UAE's claims and Iran's counter claims, 217-220
Persian Gulf's islands, 199
 introduction, 199, 200
Population, 19

Post-1991 War, 316-318
Post-1979 era, 11
Post-cold war era, 12
Present problems, 12
President Barak Obama (Democrat), 2009 onwards, 370, 371
  Policy on Iran, 372-376
  Policy on Iraq, 371, 372
  Policy on GCC States, 376, 377
President George W. Bush (Republican) 1989-1993, 356-360
President George W. Bush (Republican), 2001-2009, 364-365
  Counter Proliferation Policy, before Sept. 11, 2001, 365, 366
  Policy on Iran, 367, 368
  Policy on GCC States, 369, 370
  Policy on Iraq, 366, 367
  War on Terror Policy, after Sept. 11, 2001, 366
President Gerald Ford (Republican) 1974-1977, 349
President James Earl Carter (Democrat) 1977-1981, 350, 351
President Richard Nixon (Republican) 1969-1974, 347, 348
  Twin Pillars Policy, 348, 349
President Ronald Reagan (Republican) 1981-1989, 351
  Iran-Contra Affair, 354-356
  Strategic consensus policy, 352-354
President William Jefferson Clinton (Democrat) 1993-2001, 360, 361
  Dual containment policy, 361-364

Qatar, 164
  Gas resources, 166, 167
  Oil resources, 164

Rafsanjani, Ali Akbar, 345, 346
Recommendations, 400, 401
Red Sea, 97, 196, 197, 198
Regional Order of Persian Gulf region in Cold War era, 243, 244
  Pax Americana, 246, 247
  Pax Britannica, 244
  Pax Saudi-Iranica, 245, 246
Regional order, 9, 13, 14
Regional order, definition of, 232
  Anarchical, 233
  Balance of power, 234
  Consortium, 233
  Hegemonic, 233
  Hierarchical, 233
  Liberals and constructivists, 234
  Realists, 233
  Theoretical perspective on, 232, 233
Regional order, essential, 394-400
Regional Pacts in Cold War era, 247
  CENTO, 247-249
  Gulf Cooperation Council (GCC), 249-252
Regional States' oil and gas resources, 134
Regional States' relation in post-cold war era, 261
  Iran-Iraq, 263, 264
  Iran-Saudi Arabia, 261-263
Regional States' relations in Cold War era, 252
  Iran-Iraq, 254-255
  Iran-Saudi Arabia, 252-254
Rogers, William, 130
Roosevelt, 344

Saddam Hussein, 54, 92, 125
Saifur Rahman, 111
Sassanid Empire, 17
Saudi Arabia, 134
  Oil resources, 134-141
Sheikh Zayed, 105
Sokolsky, 346
Spykman, Nicholas, 6
Strait of Hormuz and Persian Gulf Islands, geostrategic importance of, 176-226
Strait of Hormuz, 10, 13, 18, 176

Geographical specifications, 179-181
Introduction, 176-179
Strait of Hormuz, events in since 1980, 190
Collision between USS Newport News and Japanese Tanker Mogamigawa, 191
Collision between USS Hartford and USS New Orleans in 2009, 192, 193
Downing of Iran Air Airbus 655, 191
Iran threatened to close in 1984, 190
Iran threatened to close in 1997, 191
Iran threatened in close in 2008, 191, 192
Praying Mantis, 190
US-Iranian Naval dispute in 2008, 191
Strait of Hormuz, geostrategic role of, 184
Events which threaten the strait's oil transit, 187, 188
Impacts of the closures, 185-187
Posible events, 188-190
Strait of Hormuz, law of the sea, 181
Traffic separation scheme, 182-184
Strait of Hormuz, substsitute routes, 193
Advantages of the oil pipeline networks, 196
Disadvantages of the oil pipelines networks, 196-198
Existing pipelines, 193, 194
Pipelines, 193
Planning pipelines, 195
Substituting canal, 198, 199
Strategic Petroleum Reserves (SPR), 126
Sunni and Shiite, 19
Superpowers and the region, 238
President Carter Era (1977-1981), 239, 240
President Nixon Era (1969-1974), 239
President Reagan Era (1981-1989), 240
Soviet Union, 240-243
Twin Pillar Policy, 239
United State of America, 238

Territory, 18, 19
Trade route between the Middle East and South Asia, 1
Treaty of Jeddah, 94

UAE offset Group, 113
UN Security Council Resolution, 55
United Arab Emirates, 159
Abu Dhabi Oil resources, 160
Dubai oil resources, 161
Oil resources, 159
Sharjah oil resources, 161
United Nation High Commissioner for Refugees (UNHCR), 52
United Nations' sanctions against Iraq, 318, 319
United States of America, 10
USA, 2
policy on Persian Gulf region, 347
role of, 14, 15

Wars of the Persian Gulf region post 1979, 278-338
Wars of the region since 1979, 10-11, 14
Wilson, Harold, 343
World Fact Book, 28, 35, 55, 57
World Trade Organization (WTO), 42

Yousuf Bin Alawi, 268